The Saving Lie

The Saving Lie

Harold Bloom
and Deconstruction

Agata Bielik-Robson

NORTHWESTERN UNIVERSITY PRESS
EVANSTON, ILLINOIS

Northwestern University Press
www.nupress.northwestern.edu

Printed in the United States of America

10 9 8 7 6 5 4 3 2 1

Library of Congress Cataloging-in-Publication Data

Bielik-Robson, Agata.
    The saving lie : Harold Bloom and deconstruction / Agata Bielik-Robson.
      p. cm.
    Includes bibliographical references and index.
    ISBN-13: 978-0-8101-2728-9 (pbk. : alk. paper)
    ISBN-10: 0-8101-2728-8 (pbk. : alk. paper)
    1. Bloom, Harold. 2. Criticism—United States—History—20th century.
    3. Literature—History and criticism—Theory, etc. 4. Deconstruction.
    5. Romanticism. 6. Jews—Intellectual life. I. Title.
    PS78.B53 2011
    809.1—dc22

                               2011000490

CONTENTS

Acknowledgments

First of all, I would like to express my gratitude to the Kościuszko Foundation. My stay at Yale, where the majority of this book was written, was made possible through their financial assistance.

I would also like to thank Harold and Jeanne Bloom for the kindness, encouragement, and hospitality they showed during my stay in New Haven. The commentaries that Harold Bloom was willing to provide on his own works proved extremely valuable, and the enormous patience that he showed in listening to my ideas, especially when he disagreed, meant a great deal to me.

I am also grateful to those who helped in the preparation of the final version of the manuscript and smoothed out my English: Alissa Vales, Benjamin Paloff, and Christopher Cain Elliott. Many thanks also go to my reviewers, David Mikics and Marc Redfield, whose comments greatly improved my argumentation. Finally, I would like to thank my editors, Jennifer Banks and Henry Carrigan Jr., without whom this book would never have appeared in print.

Abbreviations of
Harold Bloom's Works

A   *Agon: Towards a Theory of Revisionism* (Oxford: Oxford University Press, 1982)

AC   "The Future of Literary Criticism as Art," in *The Art of the Critic: Literary Theory and Criticism from the Greeks to the Present*, vol. 11 (New York: Chelsea House Publishers, 1990)

AI   *The Anxiety of Influence: A Theory of Poetry*, with a new preface on Shakespeare (New Haven: Yale University Press, 1997)

AR   *The American Religion: The Emergence of the Post-Christian Nation* (New York: Simon and Schuster, 1992)

BJ   *The Book of J* (New York: Harper, 1990)

BV   *The Breaking of the Vessels: The Wellek Library Lectures at the University of California*, ed. F. Lentricchia (Chicago: University of Chicago Press, 1982)

DC   *Deconstruction and Criticism*, ed. Harold Bloom (New York: Continuum, 1979)

"F"   "Freud: Frontier Concepts, Jewishness, and Interpretation," in *Trauma: Explorations in Memory*, ed. Cathy Caruth (Baltimore: Johns Hopkins University Press, 1995)

FA   *Fallen Angels* (New Haven: Yale University Press, 2007)

H   *Hamlet: Poem Unlimited* (Edinburgh: Canongate Books, 2003)

"I"   Olivier Revault d'Allonnes, introduction to *Musical Variations on Jewish Thought* (New York: George Braziller, 1984)

JY   *Jesus and Yahweh: The Names Divine* (New York: Riverhead Books, 2005)

KC   *Kabbalah and Criticism* (New York: Continuum, 1975)

LF   "Freud's Concepts of Defense and the Poetic Will," in *The Literary Freud: Mechanisms of Defense and the Poetic Will*, ed. Joseph H. Smith (New Haven: Yale University Press, 1980)

MM   *A Map of Misreading* (Oxford: Oxford University Press, 1975)

OM   *Omens of Millennium: The Gnosis of Angels, Dreams, and Resurrection* (New York: Riverhead Books, 1996)

PI   *Poetics of Influence: New and Selected Criticism*, ed. John Hollander (New Haven: Henry R. Schwab, 1988)

PR   *Poetry and Repression: Revisionism from Blake to Stevens* (New Haven: Yale University Press, 1976)

RST   *Ruin the Sacred Truths! Poetry and Belief from the Bible to the Present*
        (Cambridge, Mass.: Harvard University Press, 1989)
RT   *The Ringers in the Tower: Studies in the Romantic Tradition* (Chicago:
        University of Chicago Press, 1971)
S   *Shakespeare: The Invention of the Human* (New York: Riverhead Books,
        1998)
SLC   *The Strong Light of the Canonical: Kafka, Freud and Scholem as Revisionists
        of Jewish Culture and Thought* (New York: City College Papers, 1987)
SM   *Shelley's Mythmaking* (New Haven: Yale University Press, 1959)
VC   *The Visionary Company: A Reading of English Romantic Poetry* (Garden
        City, N.Y.: Doubleday, 1961)
WC   *The Western Canon: The Books and School of the Ages* (New York: Harcourt
        Brace, 1994)
WS   *Wallace Stevens: The Poems of Our Climate* (Ithaca, N.Y.: Cornell
        University Press, 1977)
WSW   *Where Shall Wisdom Be Found* (New York: Riverhead Books, 2004)
Y   *Yeats* (New York: Oxford University Press, 1970)

The Saving Lie

Introduction

Life as an Argument: Harold Bloom's Antithetical Vitalism

A fresh poem written now, a fresh critical essay written now, a fresh story or novel, competes against a vast overpopulation. That, I think, is what criticism must address itself to. But that is not the class-struggle: it is a question of how we individuate.
—Harold Bloom, in an interview with Imre Salusinszky

One needs to think about Kierkegaard's declaration that he had fought for becoming an 'individual' in the strictest meaning of the word, but that he had failed—yet, despite all this, he had an idea that his funeral inscription should simply read: "this individual."
—Martin Buber, *The Eclipse of God*

If there is a slogan which captures the force of Bloom's theoretical efforts, from his earliest works on romanticism, through his engagement with deconstruction, to his latest inquiries into the aesthetics of genius, it ought to be drawn from the marginal notes of Blake: "To Generalize is to be an Idiot. To Particularize is the Alone Distinction of Merit. General Knowledges are those Knowledges that Idiots possess" (Johnson and Grant 1979, 440).

However, trying to give justice to a *living singularity* is not exactly a topic for theory: in order to avoid "general knowledges" it must simultaneously "resist theory," and this resistance can succeed only to a certain point. This is precisely why Harold Bloom is such a paradoxical theorist, and, a fortiori, why the project to write about his peculiar antisystematic mode of thinking must always conceed the possibility of failure. However, it is a risk worth taking, for the position, which will eventually emerge from our—hopefully—strong misreading of Bloom's work, appears as not only original but also urgently lacking in the panorama of contemporary ideas. Bloom's stance—as I propose to call it here, *antithetical vitalism*—goes completely against the grain of deconstructive, reductive, and deathbound tendencies that dominated the scene of the twentieth-century thought. Yet, despite the philosophical angle, very strongly present in this book, I will not attempt to make Bloom an heir of Heidegger, or a revisionist of the deconstructivist tradition. On the contrary, my aim will be to stage an intensely polemical juxtaposition thanks to which Bloom could emerge as a strong thinker with a new discursive, not just poetico-critical, voice of his own.

The Saving Lie is a consciously belated book. Yet, written almost forty years after the clash between Bloom and deconstruction had taken place, it does not limit itself to a reenactment of the past debate. I chose the word "clash" quite deliberately, for, despite all appearances, there was, in fact, *no* debate; Bloom's "High Argument" from the '70s, first stated in *The Anxiety of Influence*, and then elaborated in the three remaining works of his famous tetralogy (*A Map of Misreading*, *Kabbalah and Criticism*, *Poetry and Repression*), was almost entirely neglected by his deconstructionist opponents. The reason for writing this book, therefore, came from a feeling of a missed chance or a "missed encounter" which, I thought, needed to be restaged in an almost Benjaminian gesture of reading the recent history of the humanities against the grain in order to recover its lost, or simply wasted, chances.[1]

The other reason for writing *The Saving Lie* was more personal, but not without theoretical bearings. When reading Bloom, I was always struck by an intriguing affinity between him and myself, both the descendents of East European Jewry, a refreshingly "agonistic" ingredient that I wanted to decipher in order to understand better my own instinctive discontent with contemporary philosophy, and embolden my so far deeply repressed desire for a strong "counter-narrative."[2] Obviously, I am not the first to notice Bloom's obsessive Jewishness that singles him out from the group he mockingly labeled "Heidegger and his French flock"; there were others before me who have already focused on this theme: Geoffrey Hartman, Cynthia Ozick, Susan Handelman, Jean-Pierre Mileur, Norman Finkelstein, and Moshe Idel.[3] Yet, my own approach is somewhat different; I try to argue throughout this book that Bloom's agonistic engagement with the Western tradition of philosophical *logos* (word), culminating in his dispute with deconstruction, actually managed to produce a strong "counter-narrative" of *davhar* (meaning "word" in Hebrew), a truly new theoretical position deriving "out of the sources of Judaism," which I decided to call "antithetical vitalism."

Having almost nothing in common with the philosophical type of vitalism, originating in Nietzsche and then developed by German *Lebensphilosophie* (philosophy of life), this "Hebrew vitalism," as Bloom calls it himself in *The Book of J*, is manifest most of all in the ubiquitous blessing of more life, *l'chaim*, and offers a peculiar vision of life in constant quarrel with itself: *life against life*. Thus, while the whole philosophical formation "from Jonia to Jena"[4] derives the power of negativity from the confrontation of life with, in Hegel's words, "death, the absolute master," which appears as the main agent of dynamics and change, the Jewish tradition avoids the idolization of death and locates the primary source of negativity in the vital agon between two manifestations of life: on the one hand, the natural life, which is reconciled with the cyclic and seasonal rhythm of nature—and, on the other, the non-natural, intensified life, which wants to break out of the "oceanic" cycle of becoming and perishing and establish its own dominion on a "dry, open land." Therefore, the gist of this antithetical vitalism lies in a crucial passage—a *passover*, or an *exodus*—from *mere life* to *more life*; it consists in founding a new way of being that will defy the apparent necessity of natural laws. In this vision, death is just one of these laws, perhaps the most severe—but it is inadvertently portrayed as an offense, and never as an "absolute master," which first provokes rebellion but in the end always teaches the "wisdom" of submission and reconciliation with the natural order of things. As Bloom's work on the tradition of modern poetry asserts, the poet is a particularly strong bearer of this vitalistic strain; he is driven by the most intense "fear of death," while, at the same time, he is also least prone to give in to any dubious lessons taught by death, which, for him, is not so much an "absolute master" as rather a bully, a notoriously offensive tyrant, unworthy of any glorification. The poetic creation, therefore, is "a noble lie against our own origin, a lie against mortality" (*BV*, 13). As Norman Finkelstein comments in *The Ritual of New Creation:* "When the narcissistic self is wounded by the inescapable knowledge of its impending mortality, the result in strong writers is the 'lie against time' that is the text" (1992, 28).

Jewish "folly" cannot recognize reconciliatory Greek "wisdom," which is precisely why Bloom, fully partaking in the Jewish agonistic tradition, can never accept the lesson of sublimation that appears to him as the true kiss of death, the first and most decisive act of thanatic resignation, curtailing the "magnificent infinity" of our drives. This is also why he refuses to take any Heideggerian lessons of death, for he does not need death to produce *Angst*. Anxiety of influence, which constitutes the major force of Bloom's poetic agon, is the anxiety caused by a desire for a fuller, more intense, "blessed life" which makes the poetic ephebe fear the domination of any deadening power, including tradition, that demands his immediate surrender. We can thus read Bloom's poetic agon, as it has been done before, in narrower terms of his revisionary theory of creative originality, but we can also interpret it in the broader context of what he himself calls "religious criticism," or a "frontier speculation" on the most vital issues of life and death.[5]

Meanders of Life

> Meaning wanders, like human tribulation, or like error, from text to
> text, and within a text, from figure to figure.
> —Harold Bloom, *Kabbalah and Criticism*

Bloom's vitalism constitutes a rare life-affirming tendency in contemporary thought, almost entirely overshadowed by the death-accepting gesture of Heideggerian *Gelassenheit* (releasement) and the Lacanian elevation of Thanatos as the sole drive of the human psyche. By reintroducing his own version of agonistic dualism, in which he tries to defend Freud's original insight into the irreducibility of the conflict between Eros and Thanatos, Bloom challenges the rule of the thanatic monism that deprived the notion of life of any conceptual force. In Bloom's theory of poetic agon, life once again becomes an *argument*: it regains the power to engage in a struggle with the principle of death, and though it can never ultimately win, it can nonetheless sustain a "glorious defeat." In this book, I would like to propose my own reading of Bloom's poetic agon, which will remove it, at least partially, from the usual background of literary criticism and insert it in a new wider context; I would like to offer an interpretation both Freudian and Jewish, reflecting Bloom's lifelong quest after Freud's elusive "Jewishness," which he felt to be as idiosyncratic and "far-fetched" as his own. Peter de Bolla, David Fite, and Graham Allen—to name just a few—have written excellent studies on Harold Bloom, offering insightful analysis of his critical theory, but they seem to have avoided the broader scope of Bloom's speculation, which reaches far beyond the academic problems of modern poetics.[6] By contrast, in my book I would like to take absolutely prima facie Bloom's thesis, borrowed by him directly from Wallace Stevens, according to which a "theory of poetry" is at the same time a "theory of life."[7] This mysterious equation seems to me the very gist of Bloom's unique way of thinking: a constant substitution of (mis)reading for living, and *vice versa*.

For Bloom, Freud is the master of a specific mode of thought, called by him "speculation," which is strongly opposed to philosophy: "Freud's peculiar strength," he writes in the essay "Freud: Frontier Concepts, Jewishness, and Interpretation," "was to say what could not be said, or at least to attempt to say it, thus refusing to be silent in the face of the unsayable" (F, 113). Thus, if philosophy, in its Greek love for order, certainty, and epistemological clarity, follows the Wittgensteinian rule of "keeping silent in the face of the unsayable," speculation, quite to the contrary, refuses to be silent when confronted with the most mysterious, yet at the same time most personal and painful, vital issues of life and death. "Frontier speculation marks both the Hebrew prophets and the Greek sages, whether pre-Socratics or later Neoplatonists" ("F," 114), says Bloom, immediately adding that it has nothing to do with philosophical mode of thinking. As Bloom himself frequently admits, for a long time he harbored thoughts of writing a book on Freud, especially on his concept of transference, but failed to do so and, in the end, abandoned the whole project. Nonetheless, one can argue that everything he has written or is still writing amounts to the stubborn and obsessive revision of Freud—most of all *Beyond the Pleasure Principle*.

For the scheme of the agon—as presented in *The Anxiety of Influence* and *A Map of Misreading*—is, in a way, nothing else but a kabbalistically systematized trajectory that life takes in order to evade and then, eventually, meet its *own* death. The canvas of this story is unfolded by Freud in *Beyond the Pleasure Principle*, whose hero, singular life, confronted with a threat of death, begins to "meander" in hope of finding a way "to die in its own fashion," or preparing for itself a "death of its own." Each of the six ratios in Bloom's account of poetic struggles with anteriority represents a specific defensive "meander," or evasion, which singular life, emblematized by a poet-ephebe, assumes against the threat of poetic death (i.e., the traumatizing influence of tradition, summed up in the figure of a precursor). *Clinamen, tessera, kenosis, daemonization, askesis,* and finally *apophrades* mark the dialectical points in a labyrinth of misreading in which the ephebe both recognizes the necessity of dying and rebels against the finality of this verdict, or, in terms of Bloom's theory of poetic revision, both recognizes the necessity of participation in literary tradition and rebels against joining it without leaving a trace of one's own.

Thus, if the Freudian strategy of denial, *Verneinung*, was given a temporal dimension, it would probably look the way it does in Bloom's six-staged story of the agon. *Yes, but not yet*—this belated acceptance, where belatedness makes all the difference, aims at changing the nature of the verdict; death will come any way, tradition will engulf any individual talent, who cannot just start *ex nihilo*—but the "wrestler," whose paradigmatic figure in Bloom's thought is always Jacob, will be rewarded with the "blessing of more life," which, paradoxically only on the first glance, amounts to the blessing of my own death. To die a death of one's own, which also means to win one's own, truly proper name, or the Kierkegaardian "funeral inscription," appears here as the highest vital achievement—and this shift from Freudian pessimism to a moderate optimism is the most characteristic feature of Bloom's revision of Freud. On the surface, it may seem that this transformation is a very small achievement, indeed, hardly indicative of "a power of the mind over the universe of death" (*KC*, 47) and, as such, cannot constitute a challenge to the philosophical primacy of Thanatos. Yet, the chief purpose of this book will be to convince the reader that this seemingly slight change of tone and emphasis is, in fact, a difference that makes a difference; this is precisely how life can once again become an argument and assert itself against the overwhelming power of the death-drive.

The reason why Bloom's revisionary scheme equates, after Wallace Stevens, "the theory of poetry" with "the theory of life," lies in his highly ingenious troping of the notions of life and death—indeed, as daring and original as Freud's figuration of the death-drive as a repetition compulsion and the life drive as a power of breaking forth toward new psychic organizations. Obviously, Freud himself stands in the long line of the speculative tradition which metaphorized life and death, taking them out of their naturalistic literality; in *Beyond the Pleasure Principle*, he choses Empedocles as the precursor, with his eternal agon of Love and Strife. Yet Bloom's precursorial lineage is somewhat different: it starts with Jacob's struggle with the Angel of Death, which ends with the latter bestowing on the Hebrew hero the blessing of *more life*, and continues with further troping of death as the dark mythic land of *mizraim*-Egypt, symbolizing the bondage to nature and its repetitive cycle of becoming and perishing. Bloom thereby redefines Freud's Eros as the force of Exodus, the power of getting out: "the defense of life as a drive towards agonistic achievement, an agon directed not only against death but against the achievements of anteriority, of others, and even of one's earlier self" (*A*, 97). Thus, in yet another imaginative twist, Bloom tropes death into everything that bears a trace of mere citation, literal repetition and "deadening reduction" which drowns a new subject in an

endless sea of influence, thus annihilating his "newness." "*Literal meaning equals anteriority quals an earlier state of things equals death equals literal
meaning.* Only one escape is possible from such a formula, and it is a
simpler formula: *Eros equals figurative meaning*" (*A*, 107; my emphasis).
Defenses of life are thus essentially the same as defenses of a poem: they
both use the same power of figuration that defends against the return of
deadening literality. This is precisely why for Bloom, the best ground to
test the efficiency of these defenses has always been modern poetry, most
of all the romantic lineage of both British and American poets, which,
in Bloom's own projective definition of romanticism, begins with John
Milton and ends, so far, with John Ashbery.

We shall see how this Freudian-Jewish-Romantic-American troping
of life and death encounters a parallel process in European philosophy:
from Hegel, via Heidegger and Lacan, to the masters of deconstruction, according to Bloom's own description: "the Continental dialectics
that have surged from Hegel through Heidegger on to the contemporary Deconstruction of Jacques Derrida and Paul de Man" (*A*, 335).
Following Bloom's argument, I will argue that the Hegelian privilege
given to "death, the absolute master" indeed culminates in deconstruction where it produces yet another, particularly vicious thanatic trope:
the trope of Truth, conceived now as general distrust in linguistic figurations that tend to be regarded as mere "fictions." In an agonistic thrust
against deconstructionist thought, Bloom, convinced that we can only
"perish of this truth,"[8] comes up with yet another variant of his "defense
of life"—this time, *a willing error:*

> a trope is a *willing error*—he says in *A Map of Misreading*—a turn from
> literal meaning in which a word or phrase is used in an improper
> sense, wandering from its rightful place ... Put another way, a trope
> resembles those errors about life that Nietzsche says are necessary
> for life. De Man, expounding Nietzsche's theory of rhetoric, speaks
> of all causal fictions as being cumulative errors, because all causal fic-
> tions are reversible. Influence, for de Man as for Nietzsche, is such
> a causal fiction, but I myself see influence as a trope-of-tropes, an
> apotropaic or warding-off sixfold trope that surmounts its own errors
> eventually by recognizing itself as the figure of a figure. (*MM*, 93)

This fragment can become a guiding light for our interpretation here,
for it allows us to inscribe the whole discussion into the idiom of *Beyond
the Pleasure Principle*—not just Bloom's scheme of the agon but also the

most fundamental adversary argument of deconstructive thought. While deconstruction (most of all in the de Manian version) acts according to the thanatic principle of reversing to the earlier, basic state of things—all figurative fictions can be undone and turned back to the truth of non-referentiality—Bloom's vitalism invests in the *errors of Eros* (later on we shall call it *Erros*) that enforce themselves in their antithetical stance and thus are able to defend themselves *as errors* (i.e., become immune to the demystifying efforts of deconstruction). While simple errors, unaware of their erring nature, usually perish under the suspicious eye of a demystifier—those *willing errors* are stronger because they can recognize themselves as a power of figuration, which opposes the inertial force of literality; they surmount their merely fictitious character by justifying their "wandering-warding off," apotropaic distortion as a defense of life that escapes the ultimate *verdict*, the truth of death. "Does that make it less of an *untruth*?"—asks Bloom in his "Gnostic" interpretation of Wallace Stevens. "Surely not, but the truth is mortal, would make us perish immediately, and so *we need the lie of life, and the life of lying*" (*A*, 250; my emphasis).

This focus on defenses produces a notion of vitalism which is very far away from a triumphant, infinite life of German *Lebensphilosophie*: from Nietzsche, through Dilthey, to Simmel. It is a *post-Freudian vitalism of finite existence* ("The future is death and death only" [*A*, 332]), which nonetheless creates an inner counter-current against the verdict of death Bloom calls a *lie against time*—a little, seemingly insignificant eddy, whose underlying fantasy is an intimation of individual immortality, best embodied by poets. The willing error, opposing the deadening *truth*, is thus also supported by a powerful *fantasy*, which defensively veils its traumatic core. This is precisely why the figurations of poetic Eros can never start from nothing and spring into pure creativity. Creation, unable to begin *ex nihilo*, must always take a defensive form of revision, that is, work through the trauma of influence, which—taken in its literal truth—is too shattering; when confronted in the form of "the unmediated vision," as Geoffrey Hartman called it, it deprives the ephebe of any chance of individuating emancipation. The vitalistic mind, therefore, is full of anxiety that constantly accompanies its restless defensive activity of negation and evasion, its permanent, stubbornly mendacious "perversity" and "extravagance" (*A*, 250) that flies from the paralyzing directness of truth: "Indeed, the mind is never-resting because it knows its status as fiction, and in knowing that, it knows *delight, as untruth and as poetry*" (ibid.). It enjoys and thrives on what Wallace Stevens calls the perverse "accent of deviation in the living thing that is its life preserved."

This self-delight in poetical un-truth, this narcissistic investment in oneself as a willing error, conscious lie, and self-constituted fiction is the true manifestation of the poetic Eros. And here, as in *The Song of Songs*, "love is as strong as death": not simply "life," but life augmented, self-confirmed, self-willed, and self-posited against its mighty opponent—the kind of life the Hebrew tradition calls "love" and which stands for "life" both in Freud and in Bloom. Many critics complained about the categorial incompatibility of the opposition Eros-Thanatos in Freud as juxtaposed with the neat pre-Socratic symmetry of Love and Strife, from which it supposedly derives. Freud used to conceal his Jewish sources, but it is clear that his famous antithesis comes not so much from Empedocles as from the Hebrew tradition of *The Song of Songs* which introduces a notion of life intensified and blessed, and as such already sublimated and metaphorized by Eros. This tropological maneuver serves also to demonstrate that life, indeed, *is* a constant Exodus executed by the power of figuration, or a marching forward, Nietzschean "army of metaphors," and thus manifests itself only in its own figures, while death is basically what it is: dull and immobilizing in its barren truthfulness.[9]

In the Gnostic Maze of Confusion

> I myself agree with the Gnostics, who said that we fell when we, and the angels, and the cosmos, were all created simultaneously. On the Gnostic account, which became also the Kabbalistic and Sufi stories, there never were unfallen angels or unfallen men and women or an unfallen world.
> —Harold Bloom, *Fallen Angels*

Bloom's commentators, even those most sympathetic to his theoretical enterprise, are usually puzzled by the esoteric names he had given to the revisionary ratios that define the ephebe's position against his precursor. As Jean-Pierre Mileur put it in *Literary Revisionism and the Burden of Modernity*, "They apparently do not understand why anyone would want to write in such a way—inviting accusations of self-contradiction, esotericism, irresponsibility, etc.—and not in some other, more reassuring manner" (1985, 15). Indeed, why assemble together all these queer-sounding terms deriving from very disparate traditions? The obvious answer is that, by creating such an assembly, Bloom imitates the manner of ancient Gnostics whose natural element was an eclectic melting pot of Hellenized sacred cults and religions. For Bloom, who often draws analogies between the milieu of Alexandrian Gnostics and the late modern Western academia, this manneristic mixture is an equally natural idiom. Put together, *clinamen*, *tessera*, *kenosis*, *daemonization*, *askesis*, and *apophrades* form an intriguing, idiosyncratic whole that overshadows the terminological inventiveness of even the most notorious, restlessly eclectic Egyptian speculators who, without any sense of inhibition, blithely combined elements of Jewish, Christian, Pythagorean, and Syrian cults.[10]

Thus, *clinamen*, which in Bloom's revisionary system signals the first defensive "meander" of the ephebe, swerving away from a direct identification with the precursor, is the Latin translation of the Epicurean *parenklisis* (deviation), coined by Lucretius in *De rerum natura* (*The Nature of Things*), and subsequently given a new, more literary spin by Coleridge in his *Aids to Reflection*; it belongs to a marginalized, now almost completely discarded philosophical heterodoxy of Greek atomists (strangely enough, the only thinker next to Coleridge who paid a serious attention to the notion of *clinamen* was Karl Marx in his magisterial dissertation on Democritus). *Tessera*, the next revisionist maneuver that Bloom calls "antithetical completion," comes from the secret Pythagorean rituals whose participants were given broken parts of one talisman and thus, by putting their parts together, could recognize each other as members of the same sect; the choice of this name symbolizes a secret tie of partnership between the precursor and his ephebe. *Kenosis*, the third of the ratios, is the Paulian term for the humbling of Christ, who abandoned his divine status to become a man, and as such plays a crucial role in the mystical writings of Byzantine Christianity: this stage can be called sobering, for it prepares the ephebe for a more mature, less infatuated confrontation with his past master. *Daemonization*, the fourth defense, is Bloom's own term, coined in direct reference to W. B. Yeats, who passed among the members of the hermetic order of the Golden Dawn as "brother Demon" (his full secret nickname was *Demon Est Deus Inversus*); this stage of demonic inversion marks the moment in which the ephebe's defenses against the precuror become truly bold and aggressive. *Askesis*, the fifth position, draws on the medieval practices of self-sacrifice and self-mutilation and emphasizes their antinomian lesson of a "gain through loss"; in this stage, the ephebe learns that "less is more," that is, that he has to give up on a large part of his poetic self, still dependent on the precursor's influence, in order to individuate more thoroughly. And, *apophrades*, whose name comes from the "unlucky days," the ancient Athenian ritual of commemorating the dead, is the sixth and most intricate defensive maneuver, in which the ephebe finally accepts the influence of the precursor and allows for the identification, but only when it is enacted on his own terms.

On top of that, every ratio represents one rhetorical figure, each of which corresponds to one of the Freudian defensive mechanisms: *clinamen* is irony and reaction formation; *tessera* is synecdoche and reversal; *kenosis* is metonymy and undoing; *daemonization* is hyperbole and repression; *askesis* is metaphor and sublimation; and *apophrades* is metalepsis and introjection. The link between tropes and defenses is delivered here by the Nietzschean psychology of rhetoric, which perceives figures of speech as evasions against the deadening power of literality, or a "moving army of metaphors," serving the strategic goals of the "cunning of life." And in *A Map of Misreading*, which presents a full chart of the revisionary ratios (*MM*, 84), there will also appear concepts derived from Isaac Luria, Bloom's favorite kabbalist: contraction and restitution, or, in his rendering: limitation and representation, attributed alternately to all six stages. "In their rather self-conscious eclecticism—comments Mileur—the very names of the ratios comprise a heterodoxy, and each strives to assert an identity between a poetic relationship or situation, a Freudian defense, a rhetorical figure or trope, and a concept drawn from religious or philosophical heterodoxy" (1985, 7).

But, again—why would Bloom want to concoct such a modern Gnostic convolution, such a recondite, as Norman Finkelstein called it, "ritual of new creation"? Is it because literature, and poetry in particular, is "religious" for him in a different way than defined by any accessible normative orthodoxy? And different to such an extent that it cannot even be approached by any thesis on secularization and the modern transmission of religious motifs that has been formulated so far within the Western literary theory, from Matthew Arnold to M. H. Abrams, and from Karl Löwith to Northrop Frye? In Bloom's opinion, the religious core of the literary tradition is indeed deeply *heterodoxical* and as such calls for a radically different approach that would state at once its difference from normative religions. It comes closest to what he himself calls a "frontier speculation," dealing in a necessarily oblique way with the "unsayable" questions of life and death, and while it tends to be avoided by dogmatic orthodoxies of any sort, it combines the hermetic wisdom of "Greek sages" and the messianic folly of "Hebrew prophets." Yet, despite his own declarations of keeping the symmetry between these two traditions, it will soon become clear in this book that it is rather the latter to which Bloom is truly faithful.

This rift between the two hermetic traditions comes to the fore in the very structure of the agon. At first glance, this syncretic compilation of various heterodoxies—religious, mythological, philosophical—offers a modern Gnostic, as opposed to an ancient Gnostic, version of the myth of eternal return based on the figure of a cycle, which, according to Walter Benjamin, constitutes the very essence of mythological thought.[11] It would seem as if, in the final stage of *apophrades*, "the wheel has come a full circle" (*AI*, 16) and the ephebe finally embraces the inevitable: the burden of tradition that no longer causes anxiety; the postponed identification with the precursor who no longer looms as a threatening numinous shadow of the past; and the "just" verdict of death which sentences his singularity to obliteration. Yet, this mythic appearance is nothing but deceptive. As Bloom often emphasizes, defending his revisionary system against the interpretive inertia of his commentators, who automatically fall into the trap of mythological thinking, *apophrades* is *not* a solution; it is not a *grand finale* of restitution and reconciliation, but the last available defense, or the last manifestation of the anxiety of influence. Therefore, instead of procuring the reassuring "full circle," or the Eliotesque wisdom of *in my beginning is my end*, *apophrades* does precisely the opposite: it augments anxiety by leaving the ephebe, who has already exhausted the last line of defense, alone and helpless—and with no clear sense of poetic success. For, if this success is to be measured, truly radically, against the only real originality of Adam, who in his paradisiac innocence named things for the first time, the agon can never achieve it. The last revisionary ratio does not conclude anything; it does not *reverse* time, it only arranges the most brazen *lie against time*. It does not restore the lost chance of absolute originality, it merely teaches the ephebe that he could have tricked his precursor only because the precursor himself was a "liar" and had no access to the true origins of poetic creativity. "Poems cannot restitute, and yet they can make the gestures of restitution. They cannot reverse time, and yet they can lie against time" (*KC*, 85). Hence, instead of closing the circle, *apophrades* opens an infinite space of "falling into time," which is the very opposite of the agoraphobic, vacuum-fearing mythology: a Gnostic dimension of Fall, Exile, and Wandering Meaning. Thus, regardless of Bloom's own penchant for "Greek sages" (which he seems to be sharing with his most immediate precursor, Freud), here we enter a dark domain about which they had no idea; a domain that belongs uniquely to Gnostically minded Jewish "speculators," most of all the kabbalists.

And it is hard to walk there without any props; whoever has read Bloom in his most intensely Jewish-Gnostic registers knows that he is in a bad need of some thoroughly updated "guide for the perplexed." In my book I cannot promise to offer one, but I can at least appease the reader's sense of perplexity by trying to explain the reasons why this Jewish-Gnostic component cannot help but be so confusing. Confusion is the hidden name of the "middle world," the world-in-exile, spun between the redemptive hope and the ultimate fall. Confusion is the mode in which the inhabitants of this "middle world" live; however hard they try to understand their condition, in the end they only manage to produce more puzzlement: their "meaning wanders, like human tribulation, or like error" (*KC*, 82). In one of his most dense, abstruse—and, so to say, paradigmatically confusing—texts, "Freud: Frontier Concepts, Jewishness, and Interpretation," Bloom gives a portrait of such a confused soul in terms that we might call today *psychotheological*.[12] Here, Freud's vision of psychic life, stuck in the "middle world," cut off from its origins (both the maternal Abyss, and the paternal traumatizing Word), wandering restlessly from one *nachträglich* (belated) interpretation to another, exposed to all the "injustice of the outwardness," interferes with the kabbalistic image of the exiled Shekinah, the homeless, home-seeking spirit, fallen in time and lost in the "universe of death":

> The psychical representative of the drive, not in the individual consciousness, but in human history, allegorically or ironically considered, is the image of a wandering exile, propelled onward in time by all the vicissitudes of injustice and outwardness, all the bodily oppressiveness that is inflicted upon the representatives of interpretation itself, as they make their way along the frontiers between mind and body, known and unknown, past and future. (*F*, 127)

"The psychical representative of the drive," which is an amphibolic creature—neither pure instinct, nor pure spirit—is a psychoanalytic analogue of the kabbalistic Shekhinah, who, once a part of Godhead, now separated from its fountain of light, wanders in the darkness of the created world and, in the midst of the injustice and fall, seeks her own way to redemption. What at first may appear as a strange equivocation on Bloom's part—a wandering of meaning from "the psychical representatives of the drive" to "the representatives of interpretation," suggesting their vague affinity or even identity—is, in fact, a true master move which comprises Bloom's revision of the Freudian theory of the drives. What it says in its condensed manner is that we can never know libido in its pure form, for all that is accessible to us is the middle sphere of *interpretation*. We do not know the prelapsarian state in which, in Blake's beautiful formulation from *Marriage of Heaven and Hell*, "energy is eternal delight," pure, simple, and direct—all we know is "contamination of drive and defense" (ibid.), the state of Fall and Exile that at once constitutes our psychic "middle world." We no longer know the original pleroma of the "magnificence of our drives" (ibid.), where pure energy that needs no justification equals pure bliss and thus constitutes, in Adorno's words, "the utopia of blind somatic pleasure, which, satisfying the ultimate intention, is intentionless" (2006, 61). All we know is the condition of conflict, where drives—exiled from their energetic pleroma, displaced, dispersed, and confused—hit us with all their bare force that appears now as an enigmatic demand, as an injustice and offense of "outwardness." Once, in their utopian form, they were "intentionless" and self-satisfied in their blind facticity—here and now, however, in the psyche's "middle-world," they emerge as offensive, alien, and puzzling, raising a dramatic question: *Che Voi?* What do they want? Too powerful for the psychic vessel to contain them, the drives tear it apart, so the psyche, in order to prevent "the breaking of the vessel," filters them through her own defenses; to her, in her actual "middle" state, *energy is eternal sorrow*. Hence, drives mix with defenses and pass into "wandering meanings"; they lose their purely "force-like" status and slowly, as well as painfully, turn into "representatives of interpretation," the function of which is to produce meaning. As we shall see later on, this psychotheological portrait interferes also with the image of a traumatized, wounded life, which meanders on its crooked path to death in *Beyond the Pleasure Principle*, the essay that became a canvas for Bloom's theory of the poetic agon.

In his very early writings, Gershom Scholem speculates on this condition of pain as the true bedrock of meaning; he sees the origin of human language in "lamentation," the Hebrew *kina*.[13] Similarly, Bloom makes *moaning* the very beginning of *meaning* (*DC*, 1). Or, to put it in Freudian terms, meaning appears here as a product of a working-through which defends against trauma.[14] The sole hope of the psychic "middle world" lies, therefore, in *interpretation*, a constant "production of meaning," which, unable to reverse the whole process and return to the original energetic pleroma, aims instead at eliminating all force and all suffering caused by the sadomasochistic games of fallen powers (configurated as the six ratios in Bloom's theory of the poetic agon), in order to turn the psychic "middle world" into a playground of free figuration. In other words, interpretation aims at putting end to itself; its ultimate goal hovers between the restorative vision of the fullness of a pure, blissfully meaningless and intentionless energy and the proleptic projection of a state in which language, finally liberated from the need to produce meaning, will emerge as an equally powerful *presence:* the self-performative presence of *davhar*, whose redemptive potential is already anticipated (but *only* anticipated) in every strong poetry. Norman Finkelstein, particularly sensitive to this crypto-messianic element in Bloom's thought, comments:

> A sage is one who knows, but more importantly, a sage is also one who remembers. Although he would probably deny it, Bloom longs for the impossible act of *tikkun* [redemptive return] that would restore the entire textual cosmos, an act of criticism above and beyond the mere gestures toward *tikkun* he finds in individual texts. We may say then that Bloom *remembers forward*, and that is what we must expect from our sages as we wander toward what appears to be a post-literate world. Scholem speaks of the messianic idea in Judaism as constantly moving between the restorative and the utopian. I celebrate and mourn the work of Harold Bloom, which is caught forever in that heart-breaking dialectic. (1992, 48)

"Heart-breaking" is just another, more compassionate, term for "confusing": caught forever in his restorative-utopian dialectic, Bloom emerges as a true neokabbalistic sage of the "middle world," perhaps not completely devoid of messianic hopes, yet, at the same time, knowing firmly that—to use the famous phrase of Franz Kafka from his conversation with Max Brod once again—"they are not for us." And it is precisely this dark knowledge that places him miles apart from Jacques Derrida, who, in phases Bloom would undoubtedly dub as "angelic," foresees the end of the interpretive struggles of the psyche in a happy finale of liberated text-play. Unlike Derrida, who may be accused in the Hegelian manner of procuring the messianic fulfillment in one, purely declarative decision, "swift as a pistol shot," Bloom is too deeply aware of the predicament of the Fall where battle never ends. The gist of the poetic agon, he says, is

nothing but a battle[15]—which means that the redemptive peace of liberated figuration, where interpretation will no longer serve as a defense
against the offensive presence of force (most of all: death and the anxiety
it causes), not only is nowhere near in sight, but also defies our imagination. We cannot think but in terms of perpetual "contamination," which
is unable to tell "the representatives of the drive" from "the representatives of interpretation," and *vice versa*. The liberated and joyful *jeu du
texte* (play of text) is simply "not for us."

If, therefore, Bloom *is* a religious thinker, he belongs to this notorious group, which, in Scholem's famous words, situates itself on the
brink "between religion and nihilism"; just like Kafka, to whom Scholem
originally refers, Bloom is so thoroughly immersed in the reality of the
Fall that he can offer us no clear way out, pointing unambiguously in
the redemptive direction.[16] In one of his latest books, *Jesus and Yahweh*,
Bloom mentions Nahman of Bratslav, the hassidic sage and writer who
deeply influenced Kafka; with dark fascination he describes his metaphor of the fallen world as a universal swamp in which every attempt to
get out only exacerbates our situation, and every effort to save ourselves
only makes us drown deeper.[17] Where all moves are "contaminated,"
there can be no uncompromised saving gestures; according to this antinomian logic, the most noble actions can only aggravate the fallen *status
quo*, whereas the spark may hide in the most dubious corners of the crea-
turely world.

And what can be darker, less noble, and prone to idealization than
a *lie*, this truly Nietzschean "murky workshop" of the psychic "middle world"? Just like Sabbathai Zevi chose "redemption through sin"
as his antinomian method of salvation, Harold Bloom, propelled by the
same "nihilistic" impulse, chooses the *lie*, the lowest, seemingly most
unreedemable psychic vice, as the instrument of his wrestling Gnosis.
"'Influence,' substituting for 'tradition'—says Bloom in *Kabbalah and
Criticism*—shows us that we are nurtured by distortion, and not by apos-
tolic succession" (103). Hence the title of this book—*the saving lie*. Where
no light of revelation pervades the Gnostic space of *kenoma* (emptiness),
vacated and abandoned by God; where all visible lights are luciferic,
and all true sparks lie dormant in the darkness of a "starless night"—the
only chance (perhaps, hope would be too strong a word) might consist
only in the stubborn denial of the state we are in; a determined, "willing
error" against the literality of sheer, mechanically clashing forces, which,
when taken fully in their truth, spell nothing but death. A strangely
conscious, chosen lie, determined to break through the ranks of the

oppressive hopeless truth; an attitude that, in opposition to a naive illusion, is thoroughly disenchanted, yet not disappointed. How can this
complex state of mind be achieved and maintained? In this book I will
try to prove that studying Bloom may provide a key to answering this
question.

But, as we have said, contamination of the "middle world" also means
confusion: every Gnostically minded thinker, operating on the front
lines between religion and nihilism, is bound to be confused and even
expose his confusion as an inescapable syndrome of the fix we are in.
Bloom is a thinker who abounds in contradictions, who piles them one
upon another almost deliberately, in order to stay faithful to his Gnostic
recognition of the Fall. He does not pretend to know what redemption
is about; he offers us no halachic instructions (where "halacha" precisely
means "learning how to walk"). To the contrary, his maps are labyrinths,
his solutions are inescapably precarious, and his style, constantly oscillating between sublime enthusiasm and dark irony, often meanders into
comic self-parody. Yet, of all the confusions, great and small, that popu-
late Bloom's creation, there is a truly serious one which will become one
of the leading themes of this book: a certain mix-up between two, truly
irreconcilable perspectives—*the mythic* and *the messianic*; a certain hesitation as to the ultimate meaning of the poetic agon, whose outcome may
be seen either as "the eternal return of the same" (and not just due to an
interpretive bias that tends to perceive Bloom's agon in terms of a self-
enclosed circle), or a redemptive progress; either as a hopeless cycle of
sadomasochistic submission and domination, or as, at least a momentary,
exodus, a breaking out of the fallen, mechanical repetition. "Bloom is no
deconstructionist"—says Norman Finkelstein—"but the wandering of his
revisionary system comes as close to a deconstruction of Jewish tradition
as one might have while still appropriating its salient features" (1992,
44).[18] Constantly alternating between nihilistic disenchantment and messianic promise, between sparks lost and regained, Bloom can appear as
either extremely reductive, speaking in the deidealizing idiom of power
so cynical that it dwarfs in comparison any post-Foucauldian discourse of
suspicion—or, to the contrary, suddenly hopeful and optimistic (though
always moderately). In his first "nihilistic" mode, he cannot grant the
poet any other victory as becoming a "haunting presence" for the next
generation, a "burden of influence" for the poets to come, which only
perpetuates the fatal cycle of domination and submission: "And what is
power? *Potentia*, the pathos of more life, or to speak reductively, the language of possession" (*BV*, 3). Yet, in his second, nonreductive, and more

difficult mode, which I hope to decipher and develop here, he offers the chance of a way out, an exodus from the magical circle of sheer power and possession, or, in other words: the lesson of *the Jewish metamorphose of exile into achievement* ("I," 6.)

"The anxious Bloom never engages or is reconciled with the hopeful Bloom," writes Jean-Pierre Mileur (1985, 72), and there is more than a grain of truth in this diagnosis, but, from my point of view, it sounds a little too final, not appreciative enough of the dialectical depths of which the Jewish tradition—and Bloom as its representative—seems capable. In this book, I will thus offer a highly dialectical reading of Bloom's thought, which—although always endangered by "a serious split" (ibid.)—nonetheless breaks through, at least occasionally, into a new position that is neither simply Gnostic nor simply Orthodox, but a "mixed mode" of both. I will argue that in his theory of antithetical vitalism, Bloom proposes a moderately hopeful vision of human life, which, instead of lamenting its lost origins in the Gnostic, precreational Abyss, "limps forward" and makes a nolens volens constructive use of its condition of fallenness. Putting things bluntly: it tries to make exile a home, however uncanny and inhospitable. In his latest study on *Fallen Angels* Bloom says:

> I myself agree with the Gnostics, who said that we fell when we, and the angels, and the cosmos, were all created simultaneously. On the Gnostic account, which became also the Kabbalistic and Sufi stories, there never were unfallen angels or unfallen men and women or an unfallen world. To come into separate being was to have fallen away from what the orthodox called the original Abyss but the Gnostics called the Foremother and Forefather. The angel Adam was a fallen angel as soon as he could be distinguished from God. As a latter-day Gnostic *I cheerfully affirm that we are all fallen angels.* (*FA*, 29; my emphasis)

And then, while talking about Jacob, Bloom's favorite figure who epitomizes the very idea of a mixed blessing that goes with the Jewish notion of "more life," Bloom says:

> Jacob portrayed by the Yahvist or J writer is a wily trickster, a survivor generally more distinguished for cunning than for courage. Indeed, his astonishing and desperate courage in ambushing the angel of death is so persuasive only because he does not truly change when he

> receives the angelic blessing. *A kind of fallen angel when he is Jacob, he remains a fallen angel when he becomes Israel.* (*FA*, 52–53; my emphasis)

The blessing of more life, therefore, goes to a fallen angel whose fallenness means nothing more nor less than the status of a "survivor": a
separate being, "overwhelmed by awareness of one's mortality" (*FA*, 63),
yet not overwhelmed passively, as Heidegger would say: *gelassen* (quietly),
but agonistically and antithetically. The blessing *affirms* the separation
and a proleptic, however lame, "limping forward"—and not the reverse
move toward the original Abyss. It expects from us to make a *different use of death:* not to submit to it too quickly in an idealizing gesture
that elevates death as the sublime, absolute master (which, according
to Bloom, determines the default mode of philosophical thinking), but
to resist it, postpone its necessary arrival and thus turn it into a life-
enhancing trauma that constantly propels new survivals, new "crossings,"
new exoduses. "And yet, that is the painful glory, or glorious pain, of our
existence as fallen angels. Call it *yeziat*, 'get thee out,' Abraham from
Ur, Moses from Egypt, or Jacob *into* Israel, Yahweh's Promised Land"
(*FA*, 71).

Can exile metamorphose into exodus? Is there a hope—also for us, the
inhabitants of the confused middle-world? These are the questions that
constantly occupy Bloom in his lifelong project to revive the archaic
sparks of the earliest "Hebrew vitalism" that continue to appear in the
life-affirming agon of poetic ephebes against death, which they fear most
intensely and anxiously of all people. The psychic middle-world of a
poet, this emblematic human being, stripped down to its most essential interest in survival, becomes an arena of a constant struggle between
overwhelming forces of outwardness and the elusive spark of inwardness
which comes to the fore only rarely, if ever, and only due to hard-won
victories. We can thus read Bloom's poetic agon in the narrower terms
of his revisionary theory of creative originality, but we can also interpret it in the broader "religious" context of his most far-fetched "frontier
speculation" on the ultimate battle between life and death. It will be my
aim in this book to demonstrate that this latter strong (mis)reading is
not only more rewarding and productive, but also explains the significance Bloom attached to his generally misunderstood and ignored agon
with deconstruction, which he identified—as we shall see not without
good reasons—with the last, but particularly aggressive, reincarnation of
the thanatic syndrome that has been plaguing philosophy from its very
beginning.

A Jew, an American, a Romantic, and a Gnostic: A Party of One

> The accent of deviation in the living thing
> That is its life preserved, the effort to be born
> Surviving to be born, the event of life.
> —Wallace Stevens, *The Poems of Our Climate*

> As Parmigianino did it, the right hand
> Bigger than the head, thrust at the viewer
> And swerving easily away, as though to protect
> What it advertises
> —John Ashbery, *Self-Portrait in a Convex Mirror*

In *The Breaking of the Vessels*, Bloom paints his own variant of the self-portrait in a convex mirror, showing himself as a lonely and isolated figure with all currently available discourses of humanities pushed into the shadowy background. Just like Parmigianino, the early manner-ist Italian painter described by John Ashbery, he tries to make a defiant gesture with his right hand, flying unproportionally large in the eyes of the viewer. At the same time, however, he seems to remain imprisoned in "its hollow," stuck in the small room of contemporary theory.[19] He thus simultaneously makes a gesture of escape and anxiously sees himself immobilized by the claustrophobic rituals of modern academia:

> The interpreter here is a Jewish Gnostic, an academic, but a party or
> sect of one, equally unhappy both with older and with newer modes
> of interpretation, equally convinced that say Abrams and Jacques
> Derrida alike do not aid him in reading poems as poems. (*BV*, 3)

And although the idiosyncratic, singling out identification with Jewish Gnosticism, forming a neokabbalist "party of one," looms large in this picture, it doesn't mean that the rest is simply unimportant: what Bloom tries to distance himself from, as well as what he seeks to evade and negate, is of equal significance. Bloom's originality, despite his frequently misleading self-commentaries, does not derive from a happy Emersonian self-reliance but from a constant rebellion against everything that manages to establish itself, even momentarily, as an orthodoxy; the Stevensian "accent of deviation" is to him a necessary maneuver, thanks to which he seeks to stick out from any immobilizing "hollow." Old and new modes of interpretation, therefore, represented both by Abrams and

Derrida, also find their more or less indirect way into Bloom's system, whose main formal characteristic is, as we have already noticed, a complex syncretism of many, philosophical and religious, heterodoxies, or— simply put—"deviations." In the first part of the introduction, I focused mostly on Bloom's self-professed Jewish Gnosticism; now, however, it is time to evoke his other significant influences, those appropriated and those rejected—and see how they interact within Bloom's system with the Jewish-Gnostic strain of his thinking.

Always more interested in Living Particulars than in the generalizing "grayness" of theory, Bloom could never stay for long in any of the "schools" offered by the academic establishment. His progress was never straight, but as bent and crooked as the revisionary way of the poets he wrote about. He was never fully at home within the sterile formalities of the New Criticism which overshadowed his early education—yet, although he always aimed, like his colleague Geoffrey H. Hartman, to get "beyond formalism," he never gave up a speculation on the structure of a poetic form as such. Though part of the Yale critical ferment, he never became a proper deconstructionist—at the same time, however, he would never ally himself with traditional hermeneuts and humanists, like Gadamer or Ricoeur. For quite a long time he remained under the spell of Northrop Frye's system of symbolic archetypes, but rebelled against it by creating his own version of "deidealized" Gnostic quasi mythology—at the same time, however, his rebellion would never go so far as to side with French demystifiers operating with a thoroughly disenchanted notion of myth, like Roland Barthes or Michel Foucault. He scorned the Angelic School of T. S. Eliot and C. S. Lewis—but this scorn never turned him toward the strategies of suspicion widely used by the cultural left.[20]

It would be thus wholly acceptable to perceive Bloom as the heir of the specifically American, romantic-pragmatic Emersonian extraction with its characteristic "evasion of philosophy,"[21] or, in fact, any thought that tends to discipline its followers into well-defined "schools"—and leave him there, in his splendid isolation of the self-reliant party of one. But, although that would probably be an option most to Bloom's liking, we are not going to choose it here. We want to see how Bloom *wrestles* with the "hollow" of the philosophical tradition of universalizing claims and general concepts and employs his American "evasions" and "deviations" to deal with the puzzles posed by the last representatives of this tradition he himself gathers under the dismissive heading of "Heidegger and his French flock." As a thinker, he seems to be intriguingly stuck in between the full evasion and full embrace of philosophy. He cannot either completely ignore it, the way the American pragmatist tradition has been doing for ages—from Emerson's decree of shedding bad European influences, most of all the issues of Cartesian and Kantian epistemology, to Rorty's famous "primacy of democracy over philosophy"—or engage himself with total seriousness with the philosophical problematics of the writing subject, which so strongly preoccupies the Deconstructive Company. The concern of this book would be, partially, to resolve this "stuckness" and show how "evasiveness" can become a powerful instrument *within* philosophical discussion—not so much an "evasion *of* philosophy," but an "evasion *in* philosophy," a position highly original, and so far untested by either American or European thinkers.

Bloom's thinking, especially from the period of his most passionate polemic with European deconstruction, leads us to such hybridical novelty which, simultaneously, echoes the oldest tradition of speculative "evasiveness" (i.e., the tradition of Jewish resistance to Greek philosophical thought). Bloom is a Jew, an American, and a Gnostic—and this triple characterization forms, as I will argue, a quite convincing and integral theoretical identity, which combines the oldest Hebrew component with the newest American one in a constant, Gnostically intense struggle with what Bloom perceives as the most barren consequences of European Hellenism (once again, "Heidegger and his French flock"). As I have already indicated, in Bloom's speculatively "evasive" approach, philosophy has always been and is bound to remain a "meditation on death" (i.e., a skeptical science of impossibility rather than possibility), while his "theory of poetry" strives to give us a "meditation on life," a vitalistic plea for a "possibility of possibilities" that opens the infinite perspective of the Jewish blessing of more life, *l'chaim*.[22] In his quarrel with philosophy's teaching of a "good death," Bloom rallies what remains of the scattered vitalistic sources—Hebrew theology, Romantic desire for immortality, Pragmatic disregard for the deadening philosophical skepticism—and makes of this concoction his own defense of life, being at the same time, as the motto to *The Anxiety of Influence* reveals, a defense of poetry.

Now, if we extrapolate Bloom's idea of influence as the "trope-of-tropes" from the poetic agon itself to the *theory* of the poetic agon, we will see that it is governed by exactly the same figure of conscious evasion that, during subsequent stages of defense, eventually matures into a full-blown challenge. In Bloom's theoretical writings, the initial, purely defensive figure of the "evasion of philosophy," typical for

American pragmatism, gradually grows into a far more complex trope of confrontation between two modes of thinking: the traditional, deathbound Continental philosophy, with its epistemological focus on Truth—and a new, lifebound, epistemologically evasive, Jewish-Gnostic-Romantic-American thought with its new approach toward literary fiction as an exemplary "vital error." The uniquely Bloomian combination of Jewishness, Gnosticism, romanticism, and Americanness allows him to take the maneuver of evasion to the highest state of art, where it becomes, by one stroke of speculative imagination, "an antithetical flight away from art and nature alike, towards the solipstistic grandeur that is a new Gnosis" (*A*, 332).

This flight has produced its own version of negativity which Bloom advertently calls the "American Negative" or the "Jewish Negative," and which differs radically from its Hegelian, Continental counterpart: "It must not yield either to the school of Deconstruction or to the perpetual British school of Common Sense" (*A*, 335). Unlike the positive, commonsensical method, therefore, it must employ a suspicious hermeneutics in the interpretation of literary artifacts, yet, at the same time, employ it for different reasons than the discovery of "truth, which must destroy apparent facts and must deconstruct texts" (ibid.). The negative suspicion here is directed toward the machinery of lies that constitutes every written text, yet not for the sake of exposing their primordial, fictionless truth—but for the sake of unveiling the ruses of life that defends itself against the nullity of death, the inertial force of reduction and limitation which, as John Ashbery put it, tries to make every soul "fit its hollow perfectly." Writes Bloom, alluding to the American lineage of poets from Whitman to Ashbery,

> An American Orphic wandering in the Emersonian legacy, can afford to surrender the soul in much the same temper as the ancient Gnostics did. The soul can be given up to the Demiurge, whether of art or nature, because a spark or *pneuma* is more vital than the *psyche*, and fits no hollow whatsoever." (*A*, 334–35)[23]

In this peculiar American-Jewish-Gnostic amalgam, the only—yet crucial—difference between the American and the Jewish modes of negativity registers on the emotional plane: while the Emersonian romantic transcendentalism seems complacently certain as to the existence of this untouchable spark—Jewish Gnosticism is less self-assured and declares the necessity of a constant agon with the demiurgic world of oppressive "hollows."[24] Yet, in both variants, this Negative differs from its Hegelian "philosophical" version, for it takes the side of life and life's own style of "cunning"—while "the Philosophical Negative" works under the auspices of the "cunning of reason" whose truth serves as a deconstructive measure of all things.

Thus, gradually but inevitably, Bloom's scattered criticism of philosophy as the science of lethal truths, unable to give an account of what it means to be a singular living self in possession of the unique pneumatic spark, begins to gravitate toward—and this is one of my main theses—the most important agon in his intellectual biography: the war he wages against deconstruction. If we just glimpse at the portrait of Bloom as a young man, writing on his romantic visionary company, from the dissertation on Shelley to the magnum opus on Yeats, we can see how—similarly to Browning's Childe Roland, Bloom's favorite "antithetical quester"—he, "after a lifetime training for the sight," finally comes "upon the place" where he can inaugurate a true agon. Would this be an outrageous exaggeration to say that such "sight" was finally offered by deconstruction, which, almost in the manner of the Black Tower, emerged suddenly in the middle of the Yale campus and demanded to be fought against? As we shall see, for Childe Harold, romanticism all amounts to the "antithetical quest," engaging itself constantly in a confrontational *via negativa*. Thus, being a true contemporary romantic, he met deconstruction in exactly the same way in which his ancestors were encountering nature—as "the great other" which, in Wordsworth's phrasing, "cannot be put by." Cycles, closures, circular rhythms, recurring structures, obliteration of singularity and subjectivity, obsession with Truth at the expense of fantasy, negativity and imagination—all this presented a challenge from which a die-hard romantic could not back down. He had to test himself in confrontation with this antihumanist, subjectless thought, which sprang as if from Being itself and spoke with the ominous voice of the nature of things. This voice had to be counteracted once again by a human, all-too-human cry; or, to evoke once again his kabbalistic pun, by a "moaning" ascending toward "meaning" in the senseless "universe of death." He just had to prove his antithetical strength against the anonymous, lethal murmur of the science of "what is." For what Bloom primarily deplored and abhorred in deconstruction was never the demise of the epistemological subject of truth and certainty (as we have already said, he has always been "evading" this subject in a typically American-pragmatist manner, to the endless astonishment of his Yale colleague, Paul de Man), but, in Yeats's phrasing, the obliteration of "the antithetical" in favor of "the primary": the disappearance of the singular living self which, defeated by the Truth, can no longer confirm its existence through the will to contrariness.[25]

Also, it will be one of the purposes of this book to demonstrate that Bloom's agon with deconstruction is, in some very important aspect, a continuation of his earlier quarrel with the line of the critics, most of all T. S. Eliot and C. S. Lewis, whom he dubbed with the name of the "Angelic School." Calling de Man and Derrida "the angels of death," Bloom took the critique of "deconstructive angelism," formulated by his former teacher, M. H. Abrams, to its speculative extremes. In the deconstructionist "abandonement to language," he found a note analogous to Eliot's insistence on the sacrifice of the individual idiom for the sake of literary institution. Blanchot's dying-in-language, Derrida's self-offering for the freeplay of signifiers, or de Man's sacrificial mode of reading—all may thus be said to belong to the traditional, essentially premodern model of initiation, so close to Eliot's Anglo-Catholic heart but fully contested by the modern, Gnostically minded Bloom. Built around the notion of symbolic death, this model of initiation compels the self to give up on its singularity and "fit its hollow perfectly" (i.e., join a super-individual whole without remainder)—whereas Bloom fosters a modern understanding of tradition as "distortion" and "betrayal," feeding on the "accents of deviation" of new initiates who invigorate their inheritance by rebelling against its demand for submission.

The book will concentrate, therefore, on Bloom's time of war.[26] It will make only isolated excursions into the later two decades, which I propose to call the period of dissociation (from around 1982 to the present), distinctly marked by the end of Bloom's romanticism, which he has, I think, finally considered a "failed quest." The Gnostic spark, however, has not evaporated. It now resides in what Bloom calls "religious criticism," expounded in such splendid works as *Ruin the Sacred Truths!*, *The Strong Light of the Canonical*, *The Book of J*, or, most recently, *Jesus and Yahweh* and *Fallen Angels*—where the restless fire of negativity still burns on. In this later phase, the antithetical explicitly becomes "the Jewish Negative"—while Bloom's literary theory gravitates toward a "primary," less confrontational type of conservatism, which, continuing the Victorian tradition of Arnold and Pater, focuses mostly on defending aesthetic sensibility against reductionist generalizations of what he dubs scornfully the School of Resentment.[27] But it can be said that even in his third life phase Bloom behaves like a typical romantic, who eventually tires of antithetical quests (especially if they were never properly noticed or recognized by his antagonists) and, as Friedrich Schlegel or William Wordsworth before him, falls back on the solid grounds of tradition. Yet, the strange and intriguing amalgam of "A Jew, an American, a Romantic, and a Gnostic," spawned in the alchemic furnaces of his early formation, gradually undergoes a process of dissociation; the elements emerge now as separate. A Jew in Bloom writes his brilliant commentaries on the nonnormative Judaism of our times; an American in Bloom writes *American Religion;* a postromantic aesthete in Bloom produces "appreciative," Pateresque essays like *Western Canon, Shakespeare, How to Read and Why,* or *Genius;* while a Gnostic in Bloom writes half a novel and half an esoteric treatise, *The Flight to Lucifer,* and an equally strange work of cultural criticism, *Omens of the Millennium: The Gnosis of Angels, Dreams, and Resurrection.*

Although I am not going to analyze in detail Bloom's more accessible, "postacademic" writings, which made him one of the most recognizable American public intellectuals, my book can still be read as an indirect answer to the question: why did such an esoteric and notoriously difficult writer undergo a change so radical to become one of the most popular, exoteric thinkers of our times? As I have already suggested, the answer belongs partly to the sphere that Walter Benjamin used to call a "history of neglect": had Bloom's High Argument against deconstruction been noticed and discussed, perhaps the shift, marking his deep disappointment with American academia, would not have occurred. In *The Ritual of New Creation,* Norman Finkelstein, drawing upon the dual role a Jewish intellectual can assume in the world of modern humanities, suggests that he can either become a "defiantly recondite theorizer," or, if this first option somehow fails, he can go public and begin to aspire to a function of "an elder statesmen if not cultural *nabi*" (1992, 18). Bloom can therefore be seen as having evolved from a position resembling Jacques Derrida's to the one once occupied by Lionel Trilling—yet with a different, more aggressive spin put on both these figures. Unlike Derrida, Bloom made Judaism, however unorthodox, a central constituent in his most esoteric work, not just contending himself with passing allusions to a vague "Jewish *différance*" (ibid., 22)—and unlike Trilling, who was rather timid with his "back door Judaism" (ibid.), Bloom, as a public intellectual, consciously tries to style himself as "the Yiddisher Dr. Johnson" (ibid., 18). And it is precisely this "aggressively Jewish self-identification" that translates into Bloom's "fiercely oppositional stance" (ibid., 22), which, in both his roles, harbors the seed of a strong counter-narrative. In his esoteric incarnation, it tells—but also hermetically protects—the secrets of poetic transference, which transfer the model of sacred interpretation into the domain of literary inheritance, thus blurring the dividing line between the sacred and the profane, between the religious and the secular. While in his exoteric mode it guards the cogency of the Western canon and, in a gesture reminiscent of Talmudic commentators, "builds a hedge about" the chosen texts that, in this manner, become exempt from the weak and reductive misreadings of the contemporary School of Resentment, or—to evoke another of Bloom's epithets—"social science of literature." On this account, there would be no contradiction between these two modes of Jewish *sagesse* (wisdom): in both cases, the emphasis points to the necessity of deep reading, whether in the form of a complex theory of poetic misprision, capable of producing new powerful texts, or in the form of general instruction of "how to read and why" in the postliterary era. "Fallen angels, as Shakespeare and Milton emphasize, should never stop reading" (*FA*, 65), says Bloom in his most recent book, *Fallen Angels*, which epigramatically sums up all his sides or aspects: his Gnostic Jewishness, obsessed with the notions of Fall and Cosmic Catastrophe; his lifelong interest in British Romanticism and its two most powerful precursorial figures; and his later, public crusade for maintaining standards of reading.

Harold Bloom is indeed "a party of one," a truly strong poet of his own mode of religious-literary criticism who, in a typically Emersonian manner, "makes his own circumstances" and "sheds influences" by incorporating them into his idiosyncratic theory. The appropriated elements come from such disparate traditions—Judaism, Gnosis, romanticism, American pragmatism, but also, especially recently, Victorian Aestheticism—that it is easier to see them separate than together, forming a dialectical, difficult whole in a constant quarrel with itself. Yet, this is precisely the image of "life-in-antithesis," which constitutes Bloom's highest speculative achievement. It will be my purpose, therefore, to bring all these "Blooms" together and, despite their own tendencies toward dissociation, let them speak *unisono:* in one, an almost harmonious voice that will clearly utter the principles of a new speculative position—Bloom's antithetical vitalism. In the first part, "The Antithetical Quester," I will present Bloom's theoretical development, focusing mostly on his romantic period, which prepares him for the confrontation with deconstruction; in the second chapter of this part, I will also try to explain the reasons why this theoretically ambitious agon went seriously wrong and dissolved into a series of misunderstandings in the reception of Bloom's High Argument. In the second part, "Agon with the Deadly

Angels," I will engage in close encounters between Bloom and his two main deconstructive adversaries, Paul de Man and Jacques Derrida, and show the fundamental differences in their respective approaches to the vital issues of life and death that play crucial roles in Bloom's speculative "counter-narrative." And in the third, final part, "Wrestling Harold," I will offer my own reading of the six ratios of the poetic agon where I will attempt to demonstrate how life, gathering all its most cunning defenses and dispersed "arrows of desire," once again becomes a powerful argument—a "presence not to be put by" any contemporary theory.

Part I

The Antithetical
Quester

Chapter 1

Life in Agon: From Romanticism to Deconstruction and Beyond

Take man and his struggle of contraries out of nature, and you are
left with the barren, with the same dull round all over again, the
merely cyclic movement, if such it can be termed, of negations.
  —Harold Bloom, "Dialectics of *The Marriage of Heaven and Hell*"
  (*RT*, 62)

Although Bloom considers himself to be a heir of the romantic tradition, his own understanding of this "visionary company," which has
haunted his imagination for years, is, in fact, highly *re*visionary. It runs
completely against the popular cliché according to which romanticism
was an attempt to recreate a mythical reconciliation with nature in the
unwelcoming circumstances of modern disenchantment. Thus, if Bloom
allies himself with the Romantic struggle against "the universe of death,"
it is not in favor of a naturalistic notion of life with its Schillerian pagan
overtones, but in favor of his own idea of life as thriving on Blakean contraries; a life that transcends natural limitations and multiplies its vitality
by engaging in an idiosyncratic "antithetical quest."

FROM CONCERN TO ANTITHESIS

Then was the serpent templeform'd, image of infinite
Shut up in finite revolutions, and man became an Angel,
Heaven a mighty circle turning, God a tyrant crown'd.
  —William Blake, *Europe*

The romantic phase in Bloom's progress starts in 1959 with the publication of his dissertation, *Shelley's Mythmaking*. It goes through collections of essays on early and late romantics written in the '60s, culminates in *The Anxiety of Influence* and *Yeats*, and then begins to wane, producing in 1976 yet another volume of separate texts, *Figures of Capable Imagination*. On the other hand, to call Bloom's interest in romanticism a "phase" is somewhat misleading, for, as I will argue in this book, Bloom never abandoned his romantic self: his agon with deconstruction, which, starting with *The Anxiety*, lasted more than a decade (*Agon* being the last book in this series), is densely suffused with romantic tropes and motives. The romantic "phase," therefore, can be seen as a preparatory stage in which Bloom first repeats the lessons he took from his early masters—M. H. Abrams and Northrop Frye—and then gradually sheds their influence by seeking more antithetical solutions. Thus, if the book on Shelley concerns itself mostly with *mythopoiesis* (mythmaking) as a poetic way of finding, however transient, the moment of reconciliation with the world of nature, his later work will show more and more signs of discontent with the very notion of myth. His anti-Fryean reading of Blake, whom he will portray as a poet of tireless strife, scoffing any reconciliation with the fallen world, as well as his severe criticism of Yeats's penchant for mythological thinking, shutting his *Vision* in "finite revolutions," betray a tendency that will eventually become dominant. Instead of looking for mythopoiesis in romantic poets, Bloom will detect in their writings a partly Gnostic, and partly messianic anxiety, which then will become a principal attribute of his favorite hero, *the antithetical man*.

Shelley's Mythmaking, although drawing its explicit inspiration from Martin Buber's *I and Thou*, is still a very Fryean book. Poetry is understood here as a myth made in a different way, but the introduction of Buber's mystical encounter between mind and a part of the world, momentarily elevated to dialogic heights, as the canvas of poetic mythopoesis, immediately creates a tension the book cannot yet resolve. Says Bloom, "I do claim that a certain group of Shelley's poems manifest precisely the mythopoeia that I have defined above," that is, in Buberian terms. "Their myth, quite simply, *is* myth: the process of its making, and the inevitability of its defeat" (*SM*, 8).

This "inevitability of defeat," very strongly emphasized by Bloom throughout the whole book, results from two clashing tendencies. One, faithful to Frye and his teaching of symbolic archetypes, looks for the universal, the confirmation of one and the same Idea that governs the *whole* of the world of nature—the other, borrowed from Buber, seeks instantaneous, singularized moments of recognition in which *fragments* of nature appear to the poetic eye as individual and subjectified. The one aspires to the "possibility of a Thou as a kind of universal mind in nature" (*SM*, 23–24), which would be able to ground *logos*, also poetic one—the other derives from nondiscursive, rapturous encounters with particulars which, when recollected poetically, sink into abstraction of language and thus unavoidably lose their original power. Later on, Bloom will drop Buber altogether, recognizing that his speechless mysticism of enchanted moments is a kiss of death for poetry, hopelessly codemned only to "recollect" and live up to the lost instant of existential intensity.[1] At the same time, however, he will retain Buber's intuition of the mystical that underlies the mythopoetic effort as always connected with strictly singular epiphany, against Frye's archetypal understanding of the mythical as the ever-recurring figure of meaning which reconfirms and reinforces itself in various poetic disguises. Or rather, he will enhance the opposition between myth and epiphany, which, in Frye's account, resembles more mutual completion than a tension.[2]

Thus, although it was Frye who, according to Bloom's own late testimony, introduced him into his favorite idiom of "religious criticism," Bloom's whole subsequent work on British Romanticism is a clear swerve away from Frye, gravitating toward his former teacher, M. H. Abrams, who, especially in *Natural Supernaturalism*, played down the archetypal, mythological aspect of the romantic religiosity and emphasized the opposite moment of the messianic: dispersed, subdued, and half-naturalized—but nonetheless still teeming with restless negativity, forever unable to find a reconciliation with the fallen world.[3] *Shelley's Mythmaking* is still at the crossroads: it seems to be lured by Frye's ideal of *fulfillment*, as the poetic recognition of the world in its perfect harmony with itself, and simultaneously disturbed by the reality of *inevitable defeat* that meets all poetic efforts of such mythological reconciliation. He still seems to be caught between what Frye himself called the two types of symbolism: the cyclic and the dialectical, the pagan sacrum of repetition and recreation versus the religious holiness of the history of salvation.[4]

It is only later that Bloom will truly learn to appreciate this "inevitable defeat" as a mark of the vitalizing irreconciliation between the singular and the whole of being to which it belongs. He will recognize that every fulfillment is linked to the "idiocy of generalization," while every effort to particularize (i.e., to give justice to singularity as sticking out from the "system of what is") must end in failure. Yet, he will also elevate this failure, as the only form of resistance to mythic closures, to the status of a proud "glorious defeat." But even in *Shelley's Mythmaking*, the poets—Shelley, Coleridge, and Wordsworth, whom Bloom juxta- poses in the crucial chapter on Mont Blanc as the obligatory theme of their major poetic epiphanies—are anything but naive. To their modern eyes nature appears almost hopelessly disenchanted; they realize that the glory does not reside *in* the flower anymore, and the rocky Alpian sum- mit remains essentially indifferent to their raptures. Colerdige's "Hymn Before Sunrise" fails miserably, falling straight into the abyss of what Ruskin would later call "pathetic fallacy": the poem cannot even dis- guise the bare mechanism of emotional pojections, unable to touch and transform its object, which in the end seems even more cold, distant, and inscrutable. Wordsworth's Mont Blanc fragment from *The Prelude* too easily allows itself a comfort of natural religion, automatically assum- ing "the mind's reciprocal dealings with nature" (*SM*, 20), even when the true inspiration is lacking. Only Shelley's "Mont Blanc" seems to come close to an unforced, instantaneous encounter with the Thou of the mountain, whose intensity comes and goes, leaving the poet's mind alternately in the state of wonder and doubt. All three, however, can- not help but constantly ask questions: "What is the relation between the I, the individual mind of a man, and the phenomena that surround him in the physical universe? To what extent is the mind independent on phenomena of this kind—does it actively construct them, or does it simply passively record them? Put another way, does it confront them in relationship as Thou's, or does it merely experience them as It's?" (*SM*, 23–24). To rescue natural things from their "it-ness" becomes the pri- mary directive of romantic poetry, which already very consciously reacts to modern *Entzauberung der Welt* (disenchantment of the world)—but this is also a cause of its "inevitable defeat." The disoriented, half- naturalized messianic spark tries to fight and save nature on nature's own grounds—and loses, unavoidably. Being a part of nature, but also against nature; forcing nature toward Vision, yet from within herself, press- ing her to become something else, better than she *is* now—this tangled, paradoxical predicament soon becomes for Bloom the secret token of recognition of all romantic poets, and a position with which Bloom—as we shall yet see—will also strongly identify, fully partaking of its heavy burdens.

A *naturalized negativity*, springing forth without the help of God, or any other transcendent Spirit—this paradoxical idea, which emerges in Bloom's thought as a revision of Abram's naturalized supranaturalism, develops gradually into a major theme of his later queries into the nature of romantic condition, passing via *Blake's Apocalypse* and culminating in *Yeats*, from whom Bloom takes one of his most beloved figures: "the antithetical man." Already the first pages of the book, written as early as 1962, mark the decisive departure from Northrop Frye: "Critics of a Platonizing kind . . . refuse to see poetic influence as anxiety because they believe in different versions of what Frye calls the Myth of Concern: 'we belong to something before we are anything, nor does growing in being diminish the link of belonging'" (*Y*, 5).

"Critics of a Platonizing kind," following Greek philosophical tradition of belonging—to Being, world, nature, cultural heritage—tend to neglect poetic anxiety as an unjustified, merely psychological factor obscuring the benevolence of influence which, in the end, only shows us our right place in the great chain of being.[5] "Myth," says Frye in *Fearful Symmetry*, "is the language of concern: it is cosmology in movement" (1969, ii). Yet, the spirit of negativity Bloom had discovered very early as the demon of the "inevitable defeat" in the process of poetic mythmaking scorns any "right place" within a harmony where it is supposed to fit in. Thus, while influence is for Bloom the signal of *belonging*, forcing the ephebe to take the "right place," anxiety becomes a mark of *displacement*, a negative defense of one's own singularity which refuses to participate in cosmological orderings.

In his latest book, *Jesus and Yahweh: The Names Divine*, Bloom once again makes reference to Frye, where a new tone sets in, suggesting that the difference between him and his teacher is also the one between a Jew and a Christian: "In old age I appreciate the irony that my criticism is to his as the New Testament is to the Tanakh, which is spiritually the paradoxical reverse of our spiritual preferences" (47).[6] The thought that a radically different "spiritual preference" lies at the core of their difference is definitely worth considering. There is an obvious disparity between Frye's and Bloom's treatments of poets' mythopoetic efforts. For Frye, the poet's greatness lies in his supraindividual part that connects him with the Myth of Concern; the clearer the archetypes, which speak the universal language of human longing and desire, the greater the poetic genius who thus manages to strike the eschatological chord, dormant in all of us. "One essential principle of archetypal criticism," says Frye, "is that the individual and the universal forms of an image are identical" (1972, 432). For Bloom, on the other hand, the greatness of a poet lies in his attempt to privatize the language of desire, to break the "great code" of archetypes and open them to individual revisions.

This divergence is, indeed, as deep and final as the rift between the two theologies that lie behind Frye's and Bloom's writings: Christian and Judaic. In a nutshell, it all boils down to the difference between revelation complete and incomplete. From the Christian point of view, represented by Frye, the list of all archetypes that refer to "sacred history" is concluded: the coming of Jesus as the God incarnate supplies the image of redemption which only needs to be reenacted and recreated in the process of universal salvation. From the Jewish point of view, however, this list can never be finished and, so to say, "rounded," for it misses the crucial element: the image of Messiah. From the Christian perspective, the saving pattern had already been set, thus closing—at least, if not in reality, then in the imaginative world of vision—the cyclic myth of creation, fall,

and redemption. A Christian *knows what to do:* he has to imitate Christ, and it is of secondary significance whether he perceives his task in dull, catechism-like terms or in the highly idiosyncratic way of a William Blake for whom Jesus forms the insurpassable model of the highest Vision.[7] Yet from the Jewish perspective, the saving pattern remains beclouded by "mystery"—precisely this mystery Blake saw as an obstacle in seeing and then following the perfect example of Jesus—which leaves the sacred history permanently open and does not allow it to close into a cycle. A Jew (and a Jew of a Gnostic strain in particular) does not know exactly what to do to bring about the process of redemption; the pharisaic minimalism of sticking to the prescriptions of halachic morality shows more disorientation in this respect than true knowledge. Messiah is a mystery, an empty signifier which ruins the cyclic order of the myth of salvation.[8] The list of archetypes is not finished, which also means that to Jewish imagination, there can be no archetypes in the strict sense of the word. There is nothing to imitate or repeat; everything is in the state of revision and commentary. Moved back on the plane of literary history, this difference means that while the "Christian" critic will tend to perceive the succession of writers in terms of their more or less successful adherence to the already set archetypal patterns, the "Jewish" critic will see it truly as a *history*, that is, as a time-immersed process of an ongoing revisionistic commentary. The "Christian" critic will follow the blueprint of timeless *imitatio*, while the "Jewish" critic will see the diachronic development of midrash.

Frye is obviously *not* a mythic thinker in the strict sense of the word, for myth knows nothing of redemption, it is wholly based on circular rhythms of nature which know—and need—only regeneration. Frye is not an Eliade of literary criticism; if anything, he is, as Bloom himself suggests, a literary incarnation of Saint Paul. The difference between him and Bloom is thus subtler, but it still looms large. For what is impossible from the Jewish point of view—what is, so to say, an "abomination for the Jews" in Frye's reading of the "sacred history"—is the very phrase: "myth of redemption."[9] This is the contamination no Jewish thinking can allow, that is, the suggestion of an intelligible cycle of archetypes which governs the whole *Heilsgeschichte* (history of redemption): from creation, through fall, to the final apocalypse. Such *mythicization* of the motif of redemption does not yet spell a full return to the mythic world of natural rhythms, but—even if anti-naturalistic in its explicit message—it comes dangerously close to imitate nature's Great Wheel, precisely in its closed, circular form. This is how Frye reads Blake's interpretation of Ezechiel's Vision: "wheels within wheels" siginify the cyclic myth of redemption which has the power to reverse the grinding wheels of fallen nature; and if the Great Wheel of Fire, which turns in the direction opposite to natural cycle, cannot achieve it, it can be done by "the mechanism of poetry" (1969, 359). But can one wheel reverse the degrading work of another? The "Jewish" critic would beg to differ—and this is why in Bloom we do not meet a one praise of any kind of cyclicity; his "mental fight" strives toward infinite diachronics and open dialectics that break all archetypal closures.

The mental space of *imitatio Christi* (imitation of Christ), in which Frye's "religious criticism" devolves, knows no negativity either. In Frye's interpretation of Blake, Christ forms a paradigm of absolute positivity and fulfillment, "eternal joy and freedom" (1969, 401), while negativity becomes the distinctive attribute of Satan: "Satan, Blake says, is a 'Reactor'; he never acts, he only reacts; he never sees, he always has to be shown" (ibid., 401). The pattern of *imitatio Christi* we can find in Blake (as well as, not so surprisingly, in Nietzsche who, after all, saw himself as a crucified Dionisos, the archetypal "hanged Orc" in Blakean idiom) is thus based on total rejection of negativity, which is perceived only as "reactionary," that is, weak, secondary, and as such undeserving to exist (or, as in Nietzsche, undeserving to be rewarded by the treat of eternal return).[10] But the rejection of negativity implies impossibility of dialectics: the clear-cut opposition between Jesus's life, which is freedom and joy, and death, which "represents full integrity of nature and reason" (ibid., 400), the cloven fiction of painful necessities, prevents any form of dialectical negotiation. The pattern of imitation, therefore, favors radical solution of "escape from time and pain." Just as in Emerson, to imitate Christ means to be a full-fledged visionary who "sheds all influences." Whereas the Jewish mode of engaging with the Cherub of tradition, as well as with the "unseen world of mystery" of the transcendent God, is based on negativity which "reacts" to the never sufficient, always dissatisfying positivity of the already given. In the same way the negativity in Bloom's speculation, far from being simply "reactionary," constitutes the major form of evasive negotiation with "covering" totalities: there is nothing more openly negative as *lying*, and it is lying—and not a clearcut solution of radical escape—that is the only weapon of the poets who form Bloom's visionary company. Their bows of burning gold never shoot straight arrows of desire, and their spears are not so obviously phallic; there is, in fact, quite a substantial share of what Blake used to call disdainfully "female will" in their cunning.

In the time, when Bloom is already falling away from Frye (still in the early '60s), he becomes intensely fascinated with the Blakean double figure of Tharmas—the Covering Cherub: the unified, harmonious body of *being-nature-tradition* in which all the "critics of a Platonizing kind" swim like fish in a water and in which less aquatic, and more antithetical creatures, craving for a "wide, open land," cannot live. What for the former constitutes wholeness and perfection of an uninterrupted flow of being and thinking (the deceptive beauty of Tharmas), for the latter spells the highest danger (claustrophobic limitation by the Covering Cherub). Bloom writes in *Yeats:*

> Before the Fall (which for Blake is before the Creation, the two events being one), the Covering Cherub was the pastoral figure Blake named Tharmas, a unifying process making for undivided consciousness—the innocence, pre-reflective, of a state without subjects and objects, yet in no danger of solipsism, for it lacked also a consciousness of self. Tharmas is a poet's (or any man's) power of realization, even as the Covering Cherub is the power that blocks realization. (6)

Perhaps turning against Tharmas and falling is also one and the same thing—but this, too, marks creation of a new poet, living from this moment on in a "hell of his own." Being "antithetical" means precisely to be able to *turn* in such way (or, as Bloom will call it later, to *swerve*): first, to be in the state of belonging, and then, to fall away from its fake and oppressive pleroma. In Yeats, the antithetical is synonymous with the subjective (i.e., with "that which creates"), and as such strictly opposed to the objective or the primary which is the principle of servitude and belonging.[11] It means to be "anti-natural," which is more than just "non-natural": while the latter mode of existence may come from outside nature ("non-natural" meaning also supranatural, i.e., transcendent to natural condition), the former one participates in nature but only in order to turn against her. "Antithetical" in the rendering of Yeats and Bloom is thus a paraphrase of Abrams's *natural supernatural* as *natural anti-natural.* Says Bloom:

> *Antithetical* for Yeats does not mean "contrasting" or "opposite" but "anti-natural" (not "unnatural"); and certainly in this sense would have been accepted by Wordsworth as a descriptive adjective for his Solitary. In *Alastor,* the Poet's quest is again clearly set against the context of nature, for nothing natural can ever fulfill him. But in Browning and in Yeats the quester finds nature not so much an antagonist as an irrelevance . . . Shelley, in *Alastor,* is a poet of controlled phantasmagoria; in *Childe Roland to the Dark Tower Came* and *Byzantium* the phantasmagoria takes control. (*Y,* 21)

Yet, this irrelevance can only last to a certain point and then soon reveals itself as a flippant, hubristic disguise of a far deeper anxiety which never goes away: a poet can escape nature in her "mere natural appearances" (*Y,* 21), but he cannot escape her *essence*—the static system of repetition, cycle, and homeostatic balance. This triad constitutes the greatest fear of an antithetical spirit, which wants the very opposite: singularity, open space, and movement. Yet, *A Vision,* an esoteric treatise of Yeats to which Bloom devotes the whole second part of his book, is precisely such *system* which, in the end, buries all hopes of the antithetical principle. "The Great Wheel," comprising all twenty-eight stages of life, revolves in a circle which moves due to the alternate change of phases: from "primary" to "antithetical" and back to "primary." The antithetical becomes coupled with its opposite—"the primary" as a principle of belonging and affirmation—and thus imprisoned within a systematic balance. Yeats's esoteric "wisdom," feeding on "spiritual balances" (which can be compared to Jung's overwhelming tendency to replace Christian trinity with a "more balanced" quadrangle including Mary—or, not so far in this context, Heidegger's quite analogous invention of his quasi-pagan fourfold, *das Geviert*), spells the end of his visionary poetry. "The antithetical" loses its anarchic negativity by being given a balanced counterpart. The mythic "Great Wheel" steals the negative energy which now fuels the eternal return of the same: "For him," says Bloom, "there is only the cyclic renewal of quest, and the renewed necessity for heroic defeat" (*Y,* 230). When static balance replaces dialectics, there is no longer any movement or development: "*Antithetical* and *primary* are becoming wholly separate from one another, and soon self and soul will hold no dialogues. In this condition the imagination dies" (*Y,* 259).

The second part of the book on Yeats, which was written in the same time as the first drafts of *The Anxiety of Influence,* brings the culmination of Bloom's reflections on the nature of romantic subjectivity: the agon between esoteric Yeats and his precursor, apocalyptic Blake, won by the latter; the refinement of the notion of the antithetical man, taken from Yeats but rescued from his rigidly systematic symbolism of *A Vision;* and maturation of his own theory of literary criticism, finally beyond Frye. A true romantic in Bloom's vision is a man of a highly condensed antithetical energy which feeds on the primary (belonging, affirmation, influence) in a tense dialectical way, never falling under its domination (as in the case of Frye, who in the end subordinates all dialectics under the primary principle of the Unity of Being)—but also never letting itself go free into a separate Condition of Fire (as in the case of Yeats, who severs all the connections with the primary soul and chooses the inhuman). Referring to Yeats's strong misreading of Blake's poem "The Mental Traveller," he says firmly, stating clearly his own spiritual preference: "Blake, unlike Yeats, took no joy in the Wheel" (*Y,* 74):

> Man flees to the willful mental darkness in which he is terrified by Tygers of his own negative creation, but to Yeats these forests are the symbols he seeks, for they become his "image of infinite/shut up in finite revolutions," the system of *A Vision. What Blake presents as disaster Yeats accepts as revelation* ... Blake implies the dialectical necessity of choice; this is the Fall, but Imagination can reverse the Fall. Yeats makes explicit a cyclic necessity, which he implies the imagination must accept. (*Y,* 261; my emphasis)[12]

Yet, despite all this strong Blakean criticism of Yeats's "finite revolutions," we can detect in Bloom's approach to Yeats's esoteric Gnosticism a certain vacillation as to which model of the Negative (as well as the Antithetical) he should choose himself, a theme that will somehow bother him continually through many decades: whether it be the heroic, death-driven, inhuman, radically Gnostic Negative that "disdains all that man is," a cold perfection of "life-in-death," forming the Phase 15 where Yeatsian Gnosis culimates in a supranatural vision—or more ambivalent, humanist, and less contemptuous Negation which has no need of a superhuman; a warm imperfection of *more life!,* which, after Shelley's

[handwritten annotation in top margin]

famous punning from *Adonais*, may be "stained," yet is so full of "colors." As Bloom writes in "Yeats, Gnosticism, and the Sacred Void," a later text from the volume *Poetry and Repression:*

> A Gnostic Sublime ... necessarily emphasizes the process of Negation, since both the Gnostic true God and the Gnostic pneuma or true, antithetical self are utterly alien to all natural or even cosmic imagery. Hence, the powerfully negative aura of the Gnostic Sublime in Yeats's *Byzantium*, where the superhuman is haled equivocally as "death-in-life" and "life-in-death," respectively Phases 15 and 1 of *A Vision*, both of them phases where human incarnation is negated and so made impossible. (*PR*, 225)

Negation, then, is necessary, but which one? For Shelley, who in this essay replaces Blake as Yeats's adversary, life is a many-colored dome staining the white light of eternity; its impurity engenders colors that can flourish only in the condition of the fall. The Shelleyan Negative is ambiguous, not so eager to evacuate itself from the colorful realm of life, while the Yeatsian Negative is simple and nondialectical in its unequivocal move *beyond* life: "Whereas Shelley's 'stains' is a paradox, meaning both 'defiles' and 'colors,' Yeats's 'distains' or 'disdains' [*all that man is*] has only negative meaning" (*PR*, 226). As we shall yet see—especially in part 2 of this book—the choice of the Negative is not just a secondary issue; philosophically speaking, it is the most crucial choice a thinker can make.

The next step in coining Bloom's own version of the antithetical is "The Internalization of Quest Romance." The first two opening essays of *The Ringers in the Tower*, "First and Last Romantics" and "The Internalization of Quest Romance," are written in 1968 as a passionate defense of romantic rationality.[13] In a vein similar to Frye, who scolded "bulky mules of hysteria," Bloom attacks first of all the late romantic plunge into irrationalism, and second, the typically '68 alliance of "the last Romantics" with Freudians. "Blake and Coleridge do not set intellect and passion against one another, any more than they arrive at the Freudian simplicity of the endless conflict between Eros and Thanatos" (*RT*, 15), says Bloom, convinced that British Romanticism has its specific features that cannot be obliterated in the synthesis with its European— German, especially—counterpart. Freud is portrayed here as an antagonist for whom romanticism boils down to "illusory therapy": illusory because it's unable to come to terms with reality principle.

From the Freudian, strictly naturalistic perspective, romantics lead a dreamy life under the rule of pleasure principle—and the last romantics, bullied into this corner by Freud's seemingly scientific naturalism, submit to his dismissive verdict. For Freud, *any* attempt to challenge reality principle is and inevitably must be an indication of an escapist, infantile, and pleasure-seeking attitude. Bloom, however, wants to distinguish between two models of impeaching the dictate of reality: one based on illusory evasion, the other based on conscious "mental fight." And while he admits that there are plenty of cases of the former within the so-called romantic body of texts, High Romanticism, especially in its British variant, works mostly according to the latter. The essay is not just an agon with Freud; one can clearly see that it is also an early attempt "to wrestle with Sigmund" in order to wring his theory into a shape that would be more suitable for analyzing literary, most of all romantic, tradition. Creative shifts in Freudianism, which will form the skeleton of *The Anxiety of Influence*, are here already at hand. What is now presented still as an irremediable rift between romanticism and psychoanalysis—a complex development of the imaginative desire versus dualistic simplicity of the Freudian categories of inner conflict—will eventually mature into a more dialectical image of both "Romanticism Psychoanalyzed" and "Romanticized Psychoanalysis."

Unlike Freud, for whom desire is a finite amount of energy that submits to the laws of psychic entropy, High British Romantics—and Blake is here the most important point of reference—believe that human desire is infinite: "Psychologically," says Bloom, "they stem from the child's vision of a more titanic universe" (*RT*, 15). They refuse to think about desire in the form of a self-devouring serpent: the Ourobouros "image of infinite, shut up in finite revolutions," evoked by Blake in *Europe*. Desire's infinity cannot be "shut up" in the finite circle of the ever-recurring inner conflict; conflict has to give way to quest, a dialectical progress that can be diverted but never stopped by any obstacle it encounters. The internalization of the motif of quest romance by High Romantics serves exactly this purpose: before it meant a movement "from nature to redeemed nature," now however, it is a movement "from nature to imagination's freedom" (*RT*, 16). As internalized, withdrawn from the arena of nature and society, "the quest is to widen consciousness as well as intensify it, but the quest is shadowed by a spirit that tends to narrow consciousness to an acute preoccupation with self" (ibid.). Solitude, solipsistic askesis, alienation, thanatic stillness, and the Blakean State of Satan indicate a point of necessary contraction, where desire withdraws from the endless cycle of dissatisfaction to contemplate a more cunning plan of development. This contraction is a move both "downward and inward" (*RT*, 21), but its solid bottom is not, as Frye would still have it, "a ground of identity between man and nature." "The directional part of this statement is true," Bloom writes, "but the stated goal I think is not" (ibid.). Nature is now left far behind; if romantics indeed were seeking nothing but such ground of identity between the self and natural reality, they would eventually have to give in to Freudian naturalism. Their falling away, downward and inward, deliberately misses safe natural bottoms— and continues, while looking for a different, non-naturalistic definition of desire. Writes Bloom:

> Implicit in all the Romantics and very explicit in Blake, is a difficult distinction between two modes of energy, organic and creative (Orc and Los in Blake, Prometheus bound and unbound in Shelley, Hyperion and Apollo in Keats, the Child and the Man, though with subtle misgivings, in Wordsworth). For convenience, the first mode can be called Prometheus and the second "the Real Man, the Imagination" [Blake's phrase, in a triumphant letter written when he expected death]. (*RT*, 21–22)

Promethean phase is easy to grasp: it marks the heroic struggle of a daring, individual self against all sorts of institutional orthodoxies and their mechanically self-understood claim to power. It is a phase of political, social, and literary revolution in which natural libido appears as an ally against the death-stricken rigidity of repression. "The Real Man, the Imagination," says Bloom, "emerges after terrible crises in the major stage of the Romantic quest, which is typified by a relative disengagement from revolutionary activism, and a standing-aside from polemic and satire, so as to re-center the arena of search within the self and its ambiguities" (*RT*, 22). These terrible crises the romantic self undergoes in its Promethean stage are closely connected to its inner ambiguities. The self discovers that, while struggling against all tyrannies, it is tinged with tyrannical element itself; that in order to fulfill its liberating task it has to purge itself first from everything that is, in Shelley's words, "the unwilling dross that checks the Spirit's flight." The romantic self withdraws from the cycle of hope and disappointment to the point of zero calm and indifference to liberate itself from the horrible necessity of that very cycle. Like Shelley in *Prometheus Unbound*, "Through his renunciation, he moves to overturn the tyranny of time itself" (*RT*, 28), the tyranny which sets pattern to every cyclical repetition. Or, like Blake, he outgrows the recurring antagonistic embrace of Orc and Urizen in order to find creative energy of Los, unhindered by the barren clash of the opposites: Eros and Thanatos, pleasure and reality, id and superego, anarchy and institution. This is the stage which Bloom himself translates into psychoanalytic idiom in *Yeats:* "The questing libido and the censorious superego cease to be at the center of the struggle; the ego, at strife with itself, and allied with a *new version of the id*, becomes crucial" (229; my emphasis).

No wonder that at this stage natural libido ceases to be a friend: but what is this "new version of the id" and how is it formed? "In the Real Man, Imagination, stage," says Bloom, "nature is the immediate though not the ultimate antagonist. The final enemy to be overcome is a *recalcitrance in the self* . . . The best single name for the antagonist is Keats' Identity, but the most traditional is the Selfhood, which is of Blake's coinage" (*RT*, 22; my emphasis). In this new antithetical stage, Prometheus turns inward: instead of "forming men to his image,"[14] he begins to form himself to no image available—and encounters a resistance within himself.[15]

This form of desire, which seeks its infinity in escaping the natural cycle of inner conflict (to stick to Freudian terms), is not simple or direct: it undergoes an askesis and moves beyond erotic love that bounds ego with an object through an "elective affinity," and thus "resists enchantment in the name of a higher mode than the sympathetic imagination" (*RT*, 23). To put it in Blake's idiom: the desire moves from Beulah, which corresponds to the stage of primary family romance and its chosen objects, to Eden, the realm of apocalyptic romance, in which "the objects of love altogether lose their object dimension" (*RT*, 24). The Edenic creation solves the seemingly insoluble ambiguities of the natural state of love whose object forms an uneasy composite of external canvas and subjective projection, and as such always spells the bitter end of every cathexis, which sooner or later withdraws the subjective element, while looking for a fitter target of amorous affinity. In the state of Eden, the self loves what it creates, full stop; it is a stage of a fully unleashed, self-asserted imagination, where the play of election, projection, and subsequent withdrawal is no longer necessary: "A liberated creativity transforms its creation into the beloved" (*RT*, 31), or "it must make all things new, and then marry what it has made" (*RT*, 35). The romantic, post-Promethean askesis, therefore, is not simply renunciatory: here life pauses and, in its state of momentary contraction, imitates death, but it is clearly a case of *reculer pour le mieux sauter* (a retreat for a better jump). Just like Falstaff, it pretends to have died—in order to survive, stronger and immune to disappointment. "The love that transcends the Selfhood," writes Bloom, "has its analogues in the renunciatory love of many traditions, including some within Christianity, but the creative Eros of the Romantics is not renunciatory though it is self-transcendent" (*RT*, 24). Rather, it is "a fusion between the libido and the active or imaginative element in the ego; or simply, *desire wholly taken up by imagination*" (*RT*, 24; my emphasis).

Thus, the force which creates the new version of desire is not exactly, despite some "analogues," *askesis*—rather, it is *antithesis*. The difference is subtle but essential. Askesis kills desire—antithesis transforms it. Askesis is set against life as such and aims to imitate death—antithesis negates life in its natural repetitive form of desire and disappointment, but does not give up on the idea of life augmented and intensified, going beyond the eternal return of the same. Askesis is thanatic—antithesis is erotic, although this is a nonnaive Eros which already knows frustration, sacrifice, and death. Askesis sucks the whole of id into superego, which then swells of perverse morbid jouissance—antithesis liberates id of its imprisonement within the Great Wheel of nature and fuses its energy with ego's craving for freedom and imagination. Askesis is anti-naturalist, with God or Nothingness in the background—antithesis is equally anti-naturalist, but simultaneously also vitalist, for it has no other authority than life, conceived, as in Blake, as both energy and joy.

This juxtaposition brings us to the last issue with which Bloom grapples in his romantic "phase": the issue of vitalism. Bloom seems certain that his position is clearly vitalist—in *The Anxiety of Influence* the ephebe will have only one argument against the whole authority of dead precursors, the argument of his own life—but he is still searching for a proper label. In *Yeats* he dismisses naturalistic vitalism as self-canceling and incoherent: "Its vitalism [of Yeats's *Vision*]," he says, "like all modern vitalisms since Rousseau's, is a protest against reductiveness, against the homogenizing of experience, but its dialectics are themselves reductive, and tend to diminish man" (211). Also, in "Dialectic of *The Marrriage of Heaven and Hell*," he is still in doubt about whether he should rescue the word "vitalism" from its biologistic degradation:

> Blake . . . will not tolerate the vision of recurrence, as Nietzsche and Yeats do. The altogether human escapes cycle, evades irony, cannot be categorized discursively. But Blake is unlike Lawrence, even

> where they touch. The Angel teaches light without heat, the vitalist—
> or Devil—heat without light; Blake wants both, hence the marriage
> of contraries ... Blake's dialectical stance, with its apotheosis of the
> physical and its rejection of the merely natural, is most frequently
> misunderstood at just this point. (*RT,* 59, 61; my emphasis)

Bloom is exceptionally modest here. Blake's "apotheosis of the physical
and its rejection of the merely natural" has, in fact, always been misunderstood because the position that derives from it belongs uniquely
to Bloom and constitutes his highest claim to originality as a theorist:
Bloom's speculation on "poetic desire" (or "poetic will") forms a truly
new proposition, opening territories so far uncharted by philosophy.
The gate to this new land leads through a subtle neither-nor: "*Against
the supernaturalist,* Blake asserts the reality of the body as being all of the
soul that the five senses can perceive. *Against the naturalist,* he asserts the
unreality of the merely given body as against the imaginative body, rising through an increase in sensual fulfillment into a realization of its
unfallen potential" (*RT,* 61; my emphasis).

   Therefore, despite Bloom's misgivings about the word "vitalism,"
expressed in his reference to D. H. Lawrence, an earthly bearer of heat
without light, we shall nonetheless clarify this stance and call it after
all an *anti-naturalist vitalism,* or *antithetical vitalism* (Bloom calls it even
occasionally an *apocalyptic vitalism*[16]), which maintains that all energy
comes from the body, yet it is not bound by its natural point of origin. This energy of infinite and unstoppable desire is precisely what
will later on in this book appear as *Erros,* the eternal wanderer—instead
of the simple Eros that remains limited by the natural cycle of life and
death.

American Freud

> Freud showed us that poetry is indigenous to the very constitution
> of the mind; he saw the mind as being, in the greater part of its
> tendency, exactly a poetry-making faculty.
>   —Lionel Trilling, *Beyond Culture*

> Freud thought all men unconsciously wished to beget themselves, to
> be their own fathers in place of their phallic fathers, and so "rescue"
> their mothers from erotic degradation. It may not be true of all

men, but it seems to be definitive of poets *as poets.* The poet, if he
could, would be his own precursor, and so rescue the Muse from her
degradation.
                    —Harold Bloom, *Yeats*

"The Internalization of Quest Romance" presents Freud as a theorist inimical, or at best indifferent, to the idea of poetry. At the same
time, however, Freud's idiom, strangely amalgamated with Blake's,
provides the language in which Bloom discusses the intricacies of the
post-Promethean, antithetical phase of poetic desire. The essay seems
paradigmatic as to Freud's presence in Bloom's writings: officially exor-
cized, unofficially used and abused, that is, misread and twisted in a
typically agonistic relationship with a mighty precursor.

"Internalization" offers Bloom's first attempt to psychoanalyze the
romantic self, an attempt that probably would not be possible without
the prior *romanticization of psychoanalysis:* a lesson he learned from Philip
Rieff and Lionel Trilling, two American readers of Freud who saw that,
in the former's words, "the notion of man's being natively artistic is central to Freud" (quoted in *Y,* 215). "The relationship is reciprocal," says
Trilling in "Freud and Literature," an essay written in 1940, "and the
effect of Freud upon literature has been no greater that the effect of literature upon Freud" (1957, 32). The appreciation of the "archaic mind,"
living within human psyche—although alien to Freud himself, whose
rhetoric was rather the one of enlightenmental sobriety—remains the
most characteristic feature of this particularly American reception of
psychoanalysis: stretching from Lionel Trilling and Philip Rieff up to
Jonathan Lear.

In "Freud and Literature" Trilling first accepts Freud's diagnosis—"as
for the artist, he is virtually in the same category with neurotic" (1957,
40)—but then dismisses, and in the end practically reverses his harsh
judgment. We already know Freud's opinion: artists, like neurotics, cannot cope with reality principle and escape into pleasurable realms of
illusion. "Reality is a honorific word, and it means what is *there,*" Trilling
comments, adding, "illusion is a pejorative word, and it means a response
to what is *not there*" (ibid., 41). For Freud, therefore, there are just two
ways of dealing with external reality. One way, which painfully adapts
to reality principle, is practical, reasonable, and enlightened. The other
one, which Trilling calls characteristically "antithetical" (ibid., 41), is
fictional, based on escapist illusion, and on the whole countereffective.
Instead of this simplistic dualism, Trilling proposes a more dialectical

solution, which amounts to an at least partial rehabilitation of art as a
higher and more successful kind of neurosis. The antithetical strategy
allows to lift the heavy burden of reality principle and thus make room
for negotiations: "The illusions of art," he says, "are made to serve the
purpose of *closer and truer relation with reality*" (ibid., 43; my emphasis).
Thus, in the end, regardless of his own views on art,

> Freud's psychology is the one which makes poetry indigenous to the
> very constitution of the mind. Indeed, the mind, as Freud sees it, is in
> the greater part of its tendency exactly a poetry-making organ ... In
> the eighteenth century Vico spoke of the metaphorical, imagistic lan-
> guage of the early stages of culture; it was left to Freud to discover
> how, in a scientific age, we still feel and think in figurative formations,
> and to create, what psychoanalysis is, *a science of tropes*, of metaphor
> and its variants, synecdoche and metonymy. (ibid., 50; my emphasis)

The idea of psychoanalysis as *a science of tropes*, making Vico a direct precursor of Freud, is a clear source of Bloom's later understanding of trope
as primarily a *defense mechanism*—precisely a defense against the tyranny
of reality principle with its reductive imperative to stick always to "what
is there." The Bloomian concept of the trope as a figure of will, which
clings to the antithetical and develops it into a complex strategy, transcending far beyond the escapist pleasures of illusion, has its roots in
Trilling's defense of poetry as the language of human mind that cannot—and must not—accept reality as it presents itself in its immediate
there is. Bloom admits this influence in his essay "Freud and the Sublime:
The Catastrophe Theory of Creativity," which begins with his musings
on Jacques Lacan as being "wiser in his cultural vision of Freud" than in
his "distrust in American pragmatism" and "his polemic against ego psychology" (*A*, 91). Bloom points even to a certain affinity between Lacan
and Trilling when it comes to regarding psychoanalysis as a post-Vichian
"science of tropes": "That psychoanalysis is a science of tropes is now
an accepted commonplace in France, and even in America, but we do
well to remember how prophetic Trilling was, since the *Discours de Rome*
[*The Rome Lecture*] of Jacques Lacan dates from 1953" (*A*, 93), while
Trilling's essay *Freud and Literature* was first published in 1940. And then
he confirms the Trillingian association of the antithetical with the poetic
strategy: "Negation is of *no* therapeutic value for the individual—he
says—but it *can* liberate him into the linguistic freedoms of poetry and
thought" (*A*, 109).

The antithetical investment in liberating abilities of fiction, which, in his strong misreading of Freud, Trilling discovers as the crucial insight of psychoanalysis, will later on, in *Beyond Culture*, take the form of "the adversary intention," allowing an individual to step virtually out of the system of norms and conventions that form his social reality principle (1965, xii). In Trilling's account, the adversary intention is highly paradoxical: since culture pervades our whole psychic being, and there is no single instance within our psyche which could be isolated as free from this influence, the adversary intention seems, literally, based on nothing:

> In its reference to the larger meaning the phrase "beyond culture" can be said to make no sense, for if all the implications of the word's definition are insisted on, it is not possible to conceive of a person standing beyond his culture. His culture has brought him into being in every respect *except the physical*, has given him his categories and habits of thought, his range of feeling, his idiom and tones of speech. No aberration can effect a real separation: even the forms that madness takes ... are controlled by the culture in which it occurs. No personal superiority can place one beyond these influences: the unique gifts of genius are understood to be conditioned by the cultural conditions in which they developed; only in that time and place could they have appeared. (ibid., iii–iv; my emphasis)

Although following partly the Emersonian, typically American tradition of "shedding all influences" for the sake of one's uniqueness, Trilling is much less naive than Emerson—and Bloom, who likes to locate himself in that lineage too, will also partake in Trilling's relative sobriety. Culture brings us into being in every respect *except the physical*, and the whole concept of self-creation *ex nihilo* is a sheer impossibility. This is a wrong kind of fiction which refuses *any* negotiation with reality principle, whereas the right fiction—Wallace Stevens would say, the supreme one—springs from *wisdom that accepts limitation without prematurely setting limits* (*Y*, 215).[17]

I have emphasized the phrase *except the physical* for a reason. In "Freud: Within and Beyond Culture," an essay written three decades later than "Freud and Literature," Trilling once again takes up the issue of a possible rooting of the idea of the antithetical—the adversary in human psyche—and comes up with a solution which is now openly vitalistic. In his discussion of Eros and Thanatos in *Beyond the Pleasure Principle*, Trilling suggests that Freud's death-drive is nothing but a poetic name for the "existence out of nature," the Yeatsian "artifice of eternity" (1965, 85). And as much as "death" takes us out of nature, "life" takes us out of culture. Life, conceived in the most reductive manner as precisely *the physical*, which remains excepted from cultural intervention, is precisely this other ground that can be used by the adversary intention as its point of departure. Thanatos is a residue of inorganic being, which allows, at least for a moment, a nirvanic, Schopenhauerian evasion of the business of nature. Eros, on the other hand, is a residue of bare life, which allows a vantage point against what Hegel used to call "the *terrible* principle of culture" (ibid., 93), "terrible" because of its overwhelming tendency to capture the whole of human being:

> Now Freud may be right or he may be wrong in the place he gives to biology in human fate, but I think we must stop to consider whether this emphasis on biology, correct or incorrect, is not so far from being a reactionary idea that it is actually a liberating idea. It proposes to us that culture is not all-powerful. It suggests that this residue of human quality, elemental as it may be, serves to bring culture itself under criticism and keeps it from being absolute. (ibid., 98)

Thanks to this ingenious maneuver, Trilling reverses the tragic Freudian diagnosis from *Civilization and Its Discontents*, and turns it, in the typically American romantic-pragmatic vein, from a constraining predicament into a liberating opportunity: the inner-psychic conflict between culture and biology, which constitutes the main source of suffering for Freud, in Trilling's account not only does not sound reductive but works in favor of human sense of freedom that uses biology to escape from the suf-focating totality of culture. One could even say that—considering the premature and indefinite character of human drives, which are even more "bare" than animal instincts—it is precisely this "derailed" biology which constitutes human sense of freedom. Trilling writes, "It is a resis-tance to and a modification of the cultural omnipotence. We reflect that somewhere in the child, somewhere in the adult, there is a hard, irreduc-ible, stubborn core of biological urgency, and biological necessity, and biological *reason*, that culture cannot reach and that reserves the right, which sooner or later it will exercise, to judge the culture and resist and revise it" (ibid., 99).

The idea of the "opposing self,"[18] finding its ground of adversarial, antithetical attitude toward culture in the biological "residue" of life (however perverse and derailed), this truly modern idea of being both "within and beyond culture" will soon play a crucial part in Bloom's theory of agon where, as I have already suggested, the ephebe has *nothing* in his possession to wrestle with "the terrible principle of culture" but his own bare life. In their omnipotent complacency the precursors say to the ephebe: you are *nothing* but us, so how can you fight us? And in his resistance to the omnipotence of culture, the ephebe dares to answer: but you are dead, while I am alive. The idea of life, my own natural being here and now, emerges here as a force strong enough to oppose the claustrophobic splendors of tradition. The always remaining, residual part of the *id*, resisting absorption into culture-influenced *ib-id*, remains stubbornly alive: it refuses to be fossilized by dead letters of ancestral "citation."

Trilling's and Rieff's vindication of the poetic-magical mind, which refuses to adapt smoothly to reality principle, whether natural or cultural, is one obvious source of Bloom's natively American psychoanalytic inspiration. But there is also another, much braver in the development of the "magical" theme, represented mostly by Norman O. Brown and, partly, though much less intensely, by Herbert Marcuse. Bloom, himself fascinated by shamanism and its reincarnation in modern poets, seems to have taken a lot from Brown's *Life Against Death:* not only the eponymous struggle against the "universe of death," but also Brown's critique of sublimation, coupled with his emphasis on the "grandiose narcissistic fantasy of self-begetting," which will later become the central, almost obsessive motif of his own theory of poetic revision. Yet, this is not a straightforward loan: Bloom allows himself to be inspired by Brown's prophetic, deeply romanticized, Schillerian psychoanalysis, but only to a certain point. While taking on Brown's diagnosis of the neurotic ego, anxiously caught between life and death, he does not share his regressive-utopian vision of a great psychic healing that would return us to the protective embrace of the "Oedipal Mother," the all-encompassing matrix of belonging which stills the uhappy, neurotic movement of individuation.[19] And while participating in Brown's misgivings about the value of sublimation, which in orthodox Freudianism functions mainly as an adaptive device, he also rejects Brown's critique of repression. In *The Anxiety of Influence* Bloom will discard sublimation, yet at the same time, he will be in favor of strong repression, far exceeding the one Herbert Marcuse calls in *Eros and Civilization* a "surplus repression"—a combination, which at the moment may seem mysterious but will find its explanation in the second part of this book.

It is instructive to juxtapose Bloom's variant of antithetical vitalism (with its "new version of id" that I decided to call *Erros*) and this simple, nondialectical praise of Life and Eros that dominates in Brown's inspired thinking. Bloom's is the vitalism-with-negativity, life hardening itself in a constant adversary struggle with everything that influences it in a manner of limitation—while Brown's is the vitalism of "post-negation." The "Dionisian ego" of Brown's vision, deeply indebted to Nietzsche's ideal of *Ja-Sagen* (Yeah-Saying), "does not negate any more" (1977, 175); free of negation, sublimation, fantasy, and lie, it can immerse itself in the "instinctual reality" that no longer needs *Realitätsprinzip* (reality principle), this scarecrow for unruly drives. It lives the life as it is—and not the life it only dreams about:

> Sublimation—says Brown about the Apollinian construction of the Western self, which always wants more than life can offer—is the search for lost life; it presupposes and perpetuates the loss of life and cannot be the mode in which life itself is lived. Sublimation is the mode of an organism which must discover life rather than live, must know rather than be. (ibid., 171)

Negation is nothing but an instrument of askesis which invests in a fantasy of "more than life," but ends up in a melancholy nostalgia after life irretrievably lost. Moreover, "sublimation perpetuates the negative, narcissistic, and regressive solution of the infantile ego to the problem of disposing of life and death" (ibid., 168), and as such it is a main defensive mechanism of "the ego not strong enough to die, and therefore not strong enough to live": the ego "sealed with the sign of negation" (ibid., 160). Such ego can only bear life in a diluted form—and "this dilution of life is desexualization" (ibid., 161). "Sublimations as desexualizations," continues Brown, "are not really *deflections* (changes of aim) of bodily Eros, but *negations*" (ibid., 161); they presuppose ascetic renunciation rather than a polymorphously perverse continuation of Eros.

Bloom's *clinamen*—the first phase, with which the vicissitudes of the poetic drive begin—is obviously a *deflection*, as against negation in the form of *renunciation*, which simply kills the drive or, as Nietzsche would have it, makes it irreparably "ill." Yet, it is also, simultaneously, a *negation*—although conducted not in the ascetic but in the antithetical way, that is, for the sake of the development of id, rather than for the good of superego. This is a crucial difference which does not permit Bloom to participate in Brown's and Marcuse's naturalism that looks for a "healthy animal" in humans ("their proper perfection as an animal species" [ibid., 73]). Although a vitalist, Bloom is *not* a naturalist; even stronger, he is an *anti-naturalist vitalist* who wants to transgress the limitations which nature imposes on our image of life. Thus, when he talks about deflection of the drive rather than renunciation, he sides with "life against death"—yet also he sides with the deflection as an inner-psychic catastrophe that could not occur "spontaneously" but only due to the trauma and the issuing repression.

This curious "third" position locates Bloom in psychoanalytical typology somewhere in between the Lacanians, with their death-driven, ultimately ascetic notion of trauma—and the "Californians," with their utopian vision of a nontraumatized, natural life. His is the concept of the trauma which is life-enhancing rather than lethal; the trauma that does not produce a spectral after-life of ascetic sublimation, but leads to the vitalizing deflection of drives and their further questing vicissitudes. In Bloom's conception, life is anxious (i.e., fearful of death), and does not seek any reconciliation with dying—either by askesis, or by incorporation. "Presumably any poet wishes to end *as a poet*, if at all, only in his own fashion," says Bloom. "Perhaps we can say that a man, even as a man, is capable of wishing to die, but by definition no poet, *as poet*, can wish to die, for that negates poethood" (*MM*, 91). Thus of all vitalisms offered since Nietzsche, Bloom's position seems the only one that is truly and properly vitalistic, precisely because of its *stubborn refusal to accept death in any way:* if he is to choose between death and more anxiety, he will always go for the latter.[20] "Anxiety is a response to experiences of separateness, individuality and death," writes Brown (1977, 115), and Bloom would endorse this sentence immediately. While, in their imperative to acknowledge, or even enjoy, death in order to reduce anxiety—whether by means of submission to lethal trauma that Lacan calls "destitution," or by means of redefining death as an intrinsically pleasurable "Nirvana principle"—the French and the Californian Freuds shake hands in agreement.

Contrary to this capitulation before death, Bloom's version of psychoanalysis will take anxiety and neurosis to the highest state of art: in its antithetical stage, the poetic self turns inward and engages in its own great Oedipal project of *conquering* death and lying against time by becoming a father of oneself. It does, therefore, everything that both the Lacanians and the Brownians expose and condemn as a syndrome of the narcissistic ego "not strong enough to die"; everything that is strictly *not* recommended for the so-called psychic health. "Psychic health, Freud discovered, depends on abandoning the fantasy that one can be one's own child," says Jonathan Lear in *Love and Its Place in Nature* (1998, 3), and it is precisely this piece of therapeutic advice that the poetic ego so blithely disregards. It will either beget itself—or, literally, it will die. "The Oedipal project . . . is the quest to conquer death by becoming father of oneself" (Brown 1977, 120).

For Brown, this narcissistic Oedipal project constitutes "the sexual organization . . . constructed by the ego in its flight from death" (ibid., 113), and should be abolished with the formation of the ego ready to accept its mortality.[21] The aim of the Oedipal project is to transpose absolute dependence of the child on its significant others, together with the alienating effects of this early seduction, into a situation that is exactly opposite: a position of active omnipotence, marked by "the rebellion against passivity." "Hence it seeks to transform passivity into activity with the Oedipal project of having a child by the mother; that is to say, by becoming father of oneself" (ibid., 118). Or, as Freud puts it in his *New Introductory Lectures in Psychoanalysis:* "All the instincts, the loving, the grateful, the sensual, the defiant, the self-assertive and inde-pendent—all are gratified in the wish to be the *father of himself*" (1933, 154; my emphasis). This is precisely the highest state of satisfaction "the poet in a poet," the least healthy of all animals, can achieve.

We shall find a similar appreciation of the archaic poetic mind, doing its magic tricks, in Kenneth Burke, a literary theorist and critic, who also deeply influenced Bloom's thinking. Burke espouses a pragmatic attitude toward the magical power of words which, he believes, sustains efforts of all poets. As he says in *The Philosophy of Literary Form:*

> The magical decree is implicit in all language for the mere act of naming an object or situation decrees that it is to be singled out as such-and-such rather as something-other. Hence, I think that an attempt to *eliminate* magic, in this sense, would involve us in the elim-ination of vocabulary itself as a way of sizing up reality . . . If magic says *let there be such and such*, religion says, *please do such and such*. The decree of magic, the petition of prayer. (1957, 5; my emphasis)

Bloom would definitely agree that poets participate more in defiance of magic than in humbleness of prayer. Freud's archaic mind, discovered by Trilling, Rieff, and then Bloom to be in full operation in "poets as poets," lives in the magical realm of an omnipotent word and is very reluctant to give in to reality principle. In Burke's terminology, it works according to the "rhetoric of dream" (1957, 6; alongside the rhetorics of prayer and chart). "The choice here is not a choice between magic and no magic, but a choice between magics that vary in their degree of approximation to the truth" (ibid., 7). The poem "is doing something for a poet" (ibid., 20), it is his "symbolic action" in "settling with the world, on paper, symbolically" (ibid., 17). The poem is an agon—"works embody an agon" (ibid., 70)—of a poet with the situation he is thrown in, it is an "enactment" of the problematics, its "dancing out" in a rhetoric of symptomatic expression. Every poem, therefore, reveals vital stakes, ago-nistic strivings: "Critical and imaginative works are answers to questions posed by the situation in which they arose. They are not merely answers, they are *strategic* answers, *stylized* answers" (ibid., 3). Fully accepting this portrait of a poet, who settles his scores with the world using magical powers of naming, Bloom would introduce only one small change. What matters, he will later say, is not so much what the poet does for himself in his poem, but what he does for himself *as a poet*. It is not his biograph-ical person that enters the magical agon, but "the poet in a poet," who has his own very specific "problematics" to enact: namely, the struggle for originality, undertaken in the name of his grandiose Oedipal project of self-begetting. All magical tricks he will use in his "strategic answer," which constitutes the process of revision as "lying against time," will come from the strictly poetic, and not existential, concern.

Yet the clue leading to this correction is already present in Burke him-self. According to him, modern poetry is particularly preoccupied with the problematics of self-renaming: an inner transformation aiming at the poetic construction of a new self. This constructive part, however, can often be overshadowed by the destructive act of "slaying the old self":

> And we detect, under various guises, the abandonment of an old self, in symbolic suicide, parricide, or prolicide. Psychologists, particularly Otto Rank, have characterized this manifestation of art as the result of a "death wish." But I should contend that this interpretation is not "dialectical" enough. Look closer at poetic examples of the "death wish," and you will see that the symbolic slaying of an old self is com-plemented by the emergence of a new self ... *I should want to treat even suicide in real life as but the act of rebirth reduced to its simplest and most restricted form* (its least complex idiom of expression) ... and in much contemporary art, introducing into the act of poetic construc-tion itself an aesthetic of disintegration unmatched by an aesthetic of integration, we come close, even in the poem, to a "pure" suicide. Rather, we come *closer* than in most art of the past; but there is still an appreciable margin of difference, inherent in the act of composition

itself. Implicit in poetic organization *per se* there is the assertion of an identity. (ibid., 33–34; my emphasis)

It is, therefore, not a "death wish" but the wish for "reidentification" (ibid., 36) which constitutes the strongest desire of modern poets and writers who, often in most drastic images of sloughing off, killings and murders, would want to "obliterate their whole past lineage" (ibid., 36)— and thus arrive to a perfectly incestuous situation of being able to beget themselves and then narcissistically commune only with themselves, free of the cumbersome, embarassing identity not of their own choice. In their faithfulness to most archaic, narcissistic fantasies, poets refuse a common technique of consolation Burke calls "socialization of losses" (ibid., 43), which simultaneously equals the refusal to sublimate, if sublimation is to be understood as a strategy of substituting what had been primarily lost by its ersatz.

Bloom fully endorses Burke's vitalistic optimism, which even in the minimal idiom of an almost "pure suicide" sees traces of the poet's magical strategy to give himself a new name and a new life. Death is never what it seems in a poet's antithetical self-transformations; it is always a pretense, a subterfuge, yet another ruse of life. As we shall see in part 2, fully devoted to the agon between vitalists and thanatists, deconstruction, working under auspices of Death, would love to literalize poetic activity as coming as close to "pure suicide" as possible, while Bloom's "aesthetic of integration" (or, as he calls it himself in *A Map of Misreading*, "representation") would insist on the Burkean reversal. It is not "suicide" which lies at the bottom of poetry, understood as poet's sacrifice to language, but, quite to the contrary, it is poetic wish to rename himself which motivates even the simplest idiom of "suicide in real life." Let us recall this quote from *A Map of Misreading* once again, this time in full extension:

> Presumably any poet wishes to end *as a poet*, if at all, only in his own fashion. Perhaps we can say that a man, even as a man, is capable of wishing to die, but by definition no poet, *as poet*, can wish to die, for that negates poethood. If death ultimately represents the earlier state of things, then it also represents the earlier state of meaning, or pure anteriority; that is to say, repetition of the literal, or literal meaning. Death is therefore a kind of literal meaning, or from the standpoint of poetry, literal meaning is a kind of death. *Defenses can be said to trope against death, rather in the same sense that tropes can be said to defend*

against literal meaning, which is the antithetical formula for which we have been questing. (*MM*, 91; my emphasis)

We can see now how this particular brand of American Freudianism influenced Bloom's interpretation of the romantics. For it may very well be that its uniqueness lies precisely in Bloom's clinging to the most original, archaic, and magical fantasies of the poetic psyche, coupled with a complete disregard for the most cherished dogma of the romantic tradition, especially in its German version: the Goethean "late wisdom" of *Bildung* (education-edification). Nothing is more alien to Bloom's intuitions than this apology of maturation that gives up feverish high hopes of "early childhood" (*Entsagung*) and seeks reconciliation (*Versöhnung*) with the world as it is and its reality principle, however cruel it may be. Bloom's absolute obsession with origins aims at a total revindication of all claims issued by "early childhood," even if it goes back to the period of infancy with its fantasy of self-begetting and omnipotence—and emphatically opposes itself to any wisdom of resigned sublimation, which constitutes the very gist of Bildung.[22]

This obsession with origins, however, has far deeper roots than just belief in magical powers of the archaic mind. In Bloom's "religious criticism," the obsession of origins plays the role of a theological cornerstone. It may be called simply Gnostic—in a sense that everything which happens *later* is nothing but a constant fall from irrevocably lost grace of fullness—but, before every Gnosis, it is Jewish. Robert Alter, in *Necessary Angels*, writes about an analogous rejection of the Bildung motif among the group of German-Jewish thinkers who, at the brink of war, targeted it as the most characteristic feature of German culture, and began to perceive it as increasingly alien to their Jewish identity:

> This whole turning back toward origins was the fundamental expression of the rebellion against the German bourgeois patrimony ... The controlling cultural concept of that legacy ... is the idea of *Bildung*—moral-aesthetic education by gradual steps in response to the demands of social discipline always oriented toward the future, toward the achieved self that the educated person has the potential to become. In April 1937, at a moment when the bourgeois ideal of *Bildung* and the concomitant notion of German-Jewish symbiosis lay in ruins, Martin Buber delivered a lecture at the Frankfurt Lehrhaus titled "Bildung und Weltanschauung" ["Education and Worldview"]. Buber, himself a longtime champion of symbiosis, now voiced

reservations about the fixation on the future implicit in *Bildung* and wondered whether the point of departure might not be as important as the point of arrival. Benjamin and Scholem had already been pre-occupied with point of departure two decades earlier. The intellectual line both pursued . . . followed the immanent structure of Jewish tradition. *Everything originates in the incandescence of revelation, which is then sustained through time in the myriad mirrorings and refractions of exegesis. The whole system is imaginatively focused on the great moment of its origination, however bold and surprising the "spontaneity" of later interpreters.* (1991, 99–100; my emphasis)

Translated into Bloomian idiom, this passage would sound: *Everything originates in the incandescence of election, which is then sustained through time in the myriad mirrorings and refractions of revision. The whole system is imaginatively focused on the great moment of its origination, however bold and surprising the "spontaneity" of belated revisionists.* The obsession of origins privileges the moment when the unconscious of the ephebe was seized by the poetic idiom of a great precursor, who himself stands closer to the source, and the strategy of lying against time has only one purpose: to locate oneself in the precursorial lineage in the position that is *earlier* than the position of the poetic father, thus, in the end, even closer to the vital origin. Originality is, therefore, literally: *being close to origins.* It is to be able to draw, as Scholem has put it, on its "eternal fruitfulness" (1995, 287), which can engender an infinite number of interpretations; its reception can never be passive.

On the other hand, the sense of belatedness, which lies at the heart of the anxiety of influence, denies the poet his originality, for it locates him too far away from the origins in the real sequence of time. In his poetic commentary on Benjamin's *One-Way Street*, Scholem wrote: "And where God once stood now stands: Melancholy" (1989, 81). In exactly the same way, the Bloomian belated poet must suffer *melancholia.* In his case, too, melancholy spells the lost presence of origins—a sense of belatedness that can never, as it is the case with Bildung, come to anything better than what already had been. His melancholy cannot be cured by a Hegelian late wisdom of Minerva's eagle (which, as Hegel himself admitted, constitutes a philosophical version of the Goethean Bildung). Coming late holds no promise of accumulated maturity. Based on the forbidding scheme of Jewish revelation, it means only one thing: falling, further and further away, from the "eternal fruitfulness" of the source. Writes Bloom, bitterly renouncing Whitman's fantasy:

> But the ephebe cannot be Adam early in the morning. There have
> been too many Adams, and they have named everything. *The bur-*
> *den of unnaming* prompts the true wars fought under the banner of
> poetic influence, wars waged by the perversity of the spirit against the
> wealth accumulated by the spirit, the wealth of tradition. (*Y*, 4)

The clash between American optimistic vitalism, which joyfully
asserts self-reliant powers of human mind able to break through every
limitation, and Jewish cultural pessimism, which sees every generation falling away from the vital origin and plunging into melancholy
world of mere citations—forms an absolutely crucial "crossing" in
Bloom's theory. It forces him to coin his new version of vitalism in a
highly dialectical and nonnaive way, in a full awareness of the challenge that meets every new "poet as a poet." For even if the poet
discovers in himself the freshness of his Adamic-archaic mind, he has
to employ it in a struggle with all those Adams before him, who already
named—or rather, "over-named," to use Benjamin's expression[23]—
everything. He will need something more than just the power of his
unsubdued Oedipal project. He will also need a "perversity of spirit,"
able to wage cunning wars against the wealth of tradition. This is how
a poetic child, an ephebe, becomes a warrior. So, if *Bildung* is the synonym of maturation in German romantics, in Bloom's world it can be
only one, precisely reverse, attitude—*perversity*. Instead of growing into
old age of consent with everything that parented him, the poet matures
into a slayer ready to kill—"magically" and symbolically—all his
fathers.

This complex dialectical situation calls for a solution that needs to
draw not only on the American, but also Jewish Freud; not only the
post-Vichian discoverer of the archaic mind, but also the author of
"Mourning and Melancholia," with its teaching on losses, traumas, and
repression. The key to this dialectic lies in the concept of *defense* and the
essentially *defensive war* the ephebe has to wage against the overwhelming powers of the enemy. As Bloom says:

> "Creativity" is thus always the mode of repetition *and* of memory
> and also of what Nietzsche called the will's revenge against time and
> against time's statement of "It was." *What links repetition and revenge*
> *is the psychic operation that Freud named "defense,"* and that he identi-
> fied first with repression but later with a whole range of figuration,
> including identification. (*A*, 98; my emphasis)[24]

The Next Step: Romantic Consciousness Psychoanalyzed

> There are no longer any archetypes to displace; we have been
> ejected from the imperial palace whence we came, and any attempt
> to find a substitute for it will not be a benign displacement but only
> another culpable trespass . . . For us, creative emulation of literary
> tradition leads to images of inversion, incest, sado-masochistic
> parody.
> —Harold Bloom, *A Map of Misreading*

We have already seen that for Bloom romantic consciousness is everything *but* the autonomous, unique, inner I, the source of sovereign
Vision, which has become the shibboleth of popular romanticism. Or,
on the other hand, it *is* the naive romantic consciousness—yet with this
one crucial difference that it has undergone a "creatively destructive"
process of psychoanalysis. Instead of being what it is: the truly sovereign self, it is now a *mensonge romantique*, "the romantic lie" whose role
consists in *repressing* the uneasy truth of belatedness and the anxiety of
influence threatening the autonomous position of the I. The declaration of the self's intangible autonomy serves here as merely a rhetorical
mask, or a psychoanalytic *Verneinung* (denegation), this most complex
of tropes where truth manifests itself *only* in the disguise of negation.
The romantic consciousness is thus as double, dynamic, and torn internally as the Freudian psyche: it is a composite of false self-knowledge,
which declares full autonomy and thus renounces all dependencies, and
a deeply repressed truth of being a helpless, dependent object of influences. The source of resistance against this truth, as well as its only
surface recognition, is anxiety, and specifically: *the anxiety of influence.*

Bloom may not be the first author to conduct a psychoanalysis of
romantic consciousness, but certainly he is the first critic who in *The
Anxiety of Influence*, which appeared in 1973, saw a perverse unity in the
romantic soul. His theoretical approach is thus simultaneously close to
and remote from René Girard's *Mensonge romantique et verité romanesque*
(the title has been translated as *Deceit, Desire, and the Novel*, but literally means *Romantic Lie and Novelistic Truth*), a book published in 1961
which attempted a partly structuralist and partly deconstructive analysis of romanticism. This deconstruction avant la lettre was noticed and
taken over in the Gauss lectures from 1967 by Paul de Man, who cred-
ited Girard for revealing the crucial romantic aporia of autonomy and
dependence.[25] Bloom could have known this theme while he was writing

The Anxiety of Influence in 1971, yet he claims that he never read Girard
(up to the moment, apparently, when Girard, a few years later, during
a private meeting, somewhat bitterly accused Bloom of plagiarizing his
ideas). The similarity might, indeed, seem striking at the first glance, yet
any further look into Bloom's and Girard's development of the initial
idea of *the romantic lie* would suffice to show that their ultimate positions are very different: Girard acts as a structuralist defender of truth,
while Bloom, already showing his Nietzschean penchant for emphasizing the mendacity of literature, takes the romantic lie at its face value
and puts it in the center of his theory of poetic revision. Yet, there are
also convergences which, in projective hindsight, allow one to see how
the Girardian protodeconstructive, critical notion of mensonge romantique can be transformed by Bloom into his leading affirmative motif to
which he will give a new, richer, more complex spin coming from the
dynamics of Freudian psychoanalysis.

Girard's line is, indeed, very true to the structuralist enterprise, especially to its never-questioned *idolatry of truth.* He accuses the romantics
of creating a fiction of an autonomous self whose sole function consists in concealing the truth of their real dependence on others. To this
"romantic lie" he opposes a "literary truth," *la verité romanesque,* which
is more honest in displaying the condition of the modern individual
whose desire, far from flowing spontaneously from the depth of the
transcendental I, is always, as Lacan says, *le désir de l'autre* (the desire
of the other). The solitary romantic desire, the grandness of Will and
Spontaneity, is thus a deceit covering the truth of the *désir triangulaire* (a
triangular desire): a peculiar *ménage à trois* in which the individual always
chooses to want what is already wanted by somebody else. Modern man,
says Girard, is never original in his wishes: he always copies the desires
of significant others who are his "mediators."

Girard begins his analysis of the triangular desire from the reading
of *Don Quixote* which concentrates on the figure of a mediator standing between the subject and the object of desire: the role model of the
proper chivalric existence, the knight Amadis. Usually desire is portrayed
as a straight line connecting the subject and the object, yet, says Girard:

> The straight line is present in the desire of Don Quixote but it is
> not essential. The mediator is there, above that line, radiating toward
> both the subject and the object. The spatial metaphor which expresses
> this triple relationship is obviously the triangle. The object changes
> with every adventure, but the triangle remains. The barber's basin or

Master Peter's puppets replace the windmills; but Amadis is always present. (1965, 2)

Girard detects traces of this "desire according to the Other" (ibid., 5) in the most paradigmatic modern writers of the French tradition: Flaubert, Stendhal, and Proust. His argument runs according to the standard secularization thesis which perceives modernity as the period of the gradual decline of the divine aura. In consequence, the modern choice of mediators becomes more and more "down to earth": from the sublime *imitatio Christi*, via the magical mimesis of the legendary, chivalrous hero, to the Sartrian "hell of others," where mediation becomes a matter of the Flaubertian-Proustian snobbery. Divine love and admiration slowly turn into a more ambivalent mixture of envy and competition in which the mediator is present most of all as a rival: "A *vaniteux* [the vain one]," writes Girard, "will desire any object so long as he is convinced that it is already desired by another person whom he admires. The mediator here is a *rival*, brought into existence as a rival by vanity, and that same vanity demands his defeat" (ibid., 7). Thus, the external mediation, that was characteristic of the premodern triangular desire, is being replaced by the mediation which is strictly internal and immanent; as a result, the whole process of imitation turns into a violent agon. The subject of desire becomes a typical Schelerian "man of resentment," filled with conflicting emotions of love and hate, admiration and rivalry. So, while in the external mediation there is hardly any place for competition with a higher being, whose superior position is ontologically secured, the internal mediation lets loose the hell of ambivalence, already inscribed into the demonic triangle of desire. Eventually, this ambivalence becomes too unbearable to stay on the surface of consciousness: it has to be repressed, concealed, turned into the Nietzschean "murky shop" of resentment which seeks its deception in the form of lies. One of these lies is the romantic deceit in which the individual renounces all his dependence on the other as a mediator. This defensive lie is subsequently unearthed by "the literary truth" whose *romanesque* (novelistic) complex psychology thrives on the demystification of the *romantique* deception.

In a way, Bloom takes over and maintains the Girardian scheme, but simultaneously introduces a significant correction which was already suggested by de Man: he transforms Girard's static, structuralist model of blunt oppositions into a dialectical mechanism where truth and lie coexist within one dynamic structure. This move, he claims, enables him to create a more comprehensive view of romanticism as a universal modern paradigm, no longer limited to just a few poets, suffering from particularly strong narcissistic wounds. In Bloom's account it is not only Goethe or Shelley who are truly romantic; it is also Nietzsche with his demystifying project of genealogy; Flaubert with his keen analysis of bovarism; and Emerson with his seemingly contradictory, simultaneous praise of transcendental freedom and man's dependence on "the beautiful necessity" of fate.

Only as spun between these two poles does romantic consciousness appear in its splendidly nonharmonious fullness. The romantic idea of a reconciliation, which found its poetic form in Goethe's *Entsagung* (renunciation) and its most systematic expression in Hegel's dialectical *Versöhnung*, is, in fact, constantly propelled by the desire to appease the conflict which, from the very beginning, haunts the romantic consciousness. Therefore, romantic consciousness is more a syndrome of the underlying problem than a solution—and precisely as such, as a syndrome, it maintains its validity until today. The malaise of influence discovered by the romantics, the first modern individualists, says Bloom, has not yet been cured: our current defensive techniques in which we try to repudiate the necessity of dependence are just as vehement as they were two hundred years ago.

In his contribution to the volume *Deconstruction and Criticism*, "The Breaking of Form," Bloom draws explicitly on Girard's *Le bouc émissaire* (*The Scapegoat*) to demonstrate that, first of all, there *is* such a phenomenon as anxiety of influence; second, it is universal, and, as Girard shows in his book, its traces can be found in all world mythologies; and third, the anxiety of influence becomes particularly acute in modern times, precisely because of the emphasis modernity puts on the notion of separate, monadic, independent individuals. Bloom's argument, therefore, combines a universalistic, anthropological approach with a typically modern feel for historical change. Modernity brings two such dramatic changes. First of all, it promotes Cartesian individualism which is ontologically hostile to any idea of influence. Second, it unleashes a process of secularization and disenchantment which deprives influence of its former transcendental aura and turns it into a shameful malaise: a pathological predicament of the Particular which cannot fully assert its single status, for it is always endangered by omnipresent reduction. The modern universe, therefore, is the one in which "the identity of everything with everything is bought at the cost that nothing can at the same time be identical to itself" (Horkheimer and Adorno 2002, 8). Influence, says Bloom aphoristically, thus becomes *influenza:* a state of disease which cannot be cured, but for that very reason has to be concealed from the public or even private eye; an irremediable pathology that becomes more and more *verdrängt*, "pushed down" into the dark regions of the unconscious.[26] And this is why, from this time on, "creative emulation of literary tradition" also begins to take on morbid forms and inevitably "leads to images of inversion, incest, and sado-masochistic parody" (*MM*, 31).

But by introducing the notion of Freudian *repression*, Bloom wants to achieve yet something more. Now, instead of the Nietzschean aporia of modern man, hopelessly stuck between the two vectors of memory and oblivion, the burden of the past and a forced forgetfulness, we get one concept which comprises these two opposites: *repression* is both remembering and forgetting, and functions very much along the lines of Nietzschean *aktive Vergessenheit* (active forgetfulness). Thus, for the static aporia, which first appeared in Nietzsche, then in Girard, only to resurface finally in de Man's famous essay "Literary History and Literary Modernity,"[27] Bloom ingeniously substitutes the dynamic, psychoanalytic concept of repression, *die Verdrängung*, which promises a possible way out of the sterility of the structuralist impasse. And this is also the moment when his enigmatic formula of "a poet in a poet" begins to make full sense: by substituting the dynamic repression for the static aporia, which since Nietzsche up to de Man determined the condition of modern creativity, Bloom engages in a highly original project we may call *psychoanalysis of the writing subject*. Not the usual psychoanalysis of the subject *as person*, suffering from all kinds of existential afflictions—but the unique psychoanalysis of the subject *as poet* whose only pain comes from his "condition of belatedness" and the resultant complex dialectic of remembering and forgetting.

This ingenious Freudian maneuver, allowing Bloom to move beyond the structuralist aporia, is precisely the one which immediately sets him apart from the main credo of deconstruction. For if there is one general characteristic of the deconstructive reason, it is definitely a privilege given to aporia over any kind of dialectics, a theoretical inclination toward all sorts of "blockages" coupled with a mistrust toward all story and movement. What for Girard and de Man constitutes the aporia of modern subject—the clash between influence and spontaneity, mimesis and creativity, autonomy and subjection—and thus a starting point of its further deconstruction, for Bloom is just an initial contradiction engendering the whole future narrative of repression and, at least, partial recovery of the repressed content. His Freudian reading of the romantic consciousness—combining both, the American "optimist" and the Jewish "pessimist" Freud—permits him to *pass beyond the aporia* without "naïveté," that is, without any simple return to the transcendental dogma of self-possessed subjectivity.

Notes Toward a Supreme Fiction of the Self: A Romantic Fantasy

> The imagination is not an evasion of the Oedipus complex but a rejection of it. From a certain perspective, that rejection is purely illusory, a fiction. To reject the Oedipus complex is not, after all, to dispel it. *But the fiction is a necessary and saving one;* it founds the self and secures the possibility—the chance for a self-conviction—of originality. And so Wordsworth can turn to his "conscious soul" and say, "I recognize thy glory."
> —Thomas Weiskel, *The Romantic Sublime*

> The essential paradox of fantasy consists in the temporal short circuit when a subject as a gaze precedes himself and becomes a witness of his own begetting.
> —Slavoj Žižek, *Looking Awry*

If you ask any historian of ideas about the difference between romanticism and transcendentalism, he is likely to be in trouble. He would probably answer that the ideatic content of romanticism is nothing but a poetic variation on the transcendental, philosophically more elaborated theme of the self-constituting, autonomous I. This, however, is nothing but a reductive cliché since, in fact, romanticism and transcendentalism offer two completely different approaches toward the problem of subjectivity—and Harold Bloom was the first thinker who, already equipped with psychoanalytical apparatus, was able to spot this difference and explain it theoretically. The gist of this difference lies in their varying treatment of the notion of *fantasy* or, in Wallace Stevens's formulation I used for the title of this section: "supreme fiction." Transcendental philosophy, which still lingers in the background of the Girardian and de Manian analysis of romantic thought, remains firmly within the paradigm of truth as the never-questioned absolute value—whereas romantics begin to dissent from this *verocentric* tradition and experiment with what we have been defending here from the very beginning as an autonomous value of *imagination, fantasy, fiction,* or even simply a *lie.* As the epigraph from Thomas Weiskel's seminal *Romantic Sublime* suggests, the romantic fiction is not simply *false:* it is also "necessary and saving," and this is how it defends its autonomy against the tyranny of truth (in this case, the oppressive reality of Oedipus complex, a synonym of an absolute dependence of the psyche which simultaneously wishes to be sovereign).

According to Weiskel's suggestion, romantics come out not as prototranscendentalists, but quite the contrary, as the first bold revisionists of the long, verocentric heritage of the West, and their curious "antiphilosophy" a first system of defense against the all too self-evident authority of *logos.* The romantic revision, a school of thought started with M. H. Abrams, and then continuing with the works of Geoffrey Hartman, Thomas Weiskel, and most of all Harold Bloom, shifts this seemingly marginal discovery of the romantics into their main asset; *the praise of error,* which culminates in Bloom's antithetical criticism, derives strongly from the typically romantic, Keatsian "negative capability," bracketing the self-evidence of all sorts of "truths." Yet, by moving romanticism away from matters of truth, its revisionists claim to move it simultaneously away from philosophy, apparently tyrannized by the primacy of truth and *logos* beyond possible redemption.[28]

Romanticism is linked with transcendentalism only by a common point of departure: *the pain resulting from the awareness of influence.* In his *Encyclopedia of Philosophical Sciences in Outline,* Hegel describes this state as a "disease" which is characteristic of *die fühlende Seele,* "the sensuous soul," constituting the prereflexive state of consciousness: "the sensuous soul" already has a *Selbstgefühl* (i.e., an embryonic sense of itself), but it is still contaminated by its entanglement with the world of direct influences, it isn't yet properly "pure." And this is precisely the point where the romantics and the transcendentalists diverge *philosophically:* the former accept the condition of *die fühlende Seele* as the only possible predicament of subjectivity—the latter treat it merely as a transient, incipiently pathological stage in the development of a full-fledged "pure consciousness," whose negative power is strong enough to sublate the reality of all influence. The most significant divergence begins with the romantic uneasiness with the typically transcendental maneuver of invalidating the reality of the external world which constitutes the source of the painful influence; though the romantics agree that "the sensuous soul" finds itself in the state of Fichtean *Leiden* (i.e., simultaneously suffering and disease—*pathein* being the source of pathology), they are ready to withstand the impact of the empirical world and stay within its limitations.[29]

The parallel difference emerges in their respective treatment of the question of subjectivity. Whereas transcendentalism approaches consciousness as the primary and indubitable *reality*, the most solid foundation and thus the paradigmatically strong being, romanticism imagines the inner core of subjectivity, the Novalisian *Ichheit* (I-ness), in the form of a *fantasy*, "something" whose ontological status is, at least temporarily, put in brackets. Yet, it does not indicate the weakness of romanticism; it does not mean that romanticism merely "fantasizes" instead of discovering, as transcendental deduction or intellectual intuition does, unimpeachable facts. Quite the contrary: by insisting on the fantastical notion of the self, romanticism seems to come closer to its reality than any idealist, Kantian or Fichtean, mode of reasoning. It comes to the paradoxical essence of subjectivity almost as close as Freud, who defined "psychical reality" as a realm of being founded uniquely on fantasies.[30]

Just as psychoanalysis helps Bloom to understand the role of narcissistic fantasy in the writings of High Romantics, the romantic insistence on its constitutive power shapes Bloom's understanding of Freud; the influence is mutual. For, unlike most of Freud's followers who try to demetaphorize his language in desperate pursuit of scientific clarity (most notably, Lacan), Bloom does precisely the opposite: not only does he take all Freudian metaphors for granted—repression, psychical reality, protective shield, and so forth—but reads Freud as a "strong poet," that is, as an inventor of a new, wholly metaphorical discourse which, for him, is the only language fit to describe the postromantic form of subjective life. So, instead of finding clarifying conceptual replacements for few central metaphors in Freud's theoretical language, Bloom interprets Freud's insights into the nature of human sexuality in the manner characteristic for ancient Alexandrian Gnostics with whom he feels very much at home: namely, as brave spiritual figures referring to the most secret fantasies of the human soul. Begetting one's own father (a metaphor created by Valentinus and then, almost two thousand years later mysteriously repeated by Kierkegaard), having intercourse with one's own mother, probably in order to make her pregnant with oneself (a fantastical desire, most often quoted by Freud)—all these images are to be interpreted as contents of a truly primary fantasy of autonomy.

In Bloom's strong, phantasm-oriented misreading of Freud, fantasy is not just a blunder clashing with the rules of reality principle; not just a feeble phantom, which dissolves in confrontation with harsh truths, but a formula of an alternative being which arises and persists in adversary attitude toward the *Realitätsprinzip* as such. If it weren't for this original conflict with reality principle, the "psychical reality" could never constitute itself in its, however precarious, sovereignty. Thus, what prima facie may seem a weak and purely defensive phantasm, standing no chance toward the overwhelming power of the real world, becomes, in fact, a paradoxical place of origin of a subjective being, a site of *ontological provocation*. For if it weren't for the adversary boldness of fantasies against the real, the psychic being could never achieve even the lowest degree of autonomy, and thus could never constitute itself as a subject.

The essence of these paradigmatic phantasms consists in their defiance of the logic of reality principle in wanting the impossible. In Bloom's succinct formulation, "they lie against time," which is the most intransigent, the least reversible of all laws of reality, here, however, reversed; fantasies of sovereignty derive their force from a strong anticipation of an expected effect and thus undo the order of causal determination; in their strangely reversed temporality the result precedes the cause (this is precisely why Bloom's favorite master trope is metalepsis, a rhetorical figure which subverts the temporal sequence of causation). These earliest narcissistic fantasies are the best instance of what Lacan has called not so kindly "the Kleinian magic": they sport an image of the self as mature and independent from the very beginning, thus denying all primal dependencies. The absolute dependence of a young psyche engenders an overwhelming anxiety of influence, as well as an envy of autonomy and fullness that seems to be in possession of the Other; in consequence, these two initial emotions trigger a formative process which is both mimetic and competitive, or, as Bloom puts it, a dialectical process of an identification with a swerve, a *clinamen*.[31] What is most significant here is that these fantasies defy reality *as reality* and refuse all compromises: as such, by swerving away from the pressure of its tyrannizing truths, they build the core of the counterreality in what will eventually indeed *become* a relatively autonomous, subjective life.[32]

Long before Kant's and Fichte's concept of *Selbstsetzen*, or self-constitution, was formulated, Milton's Satan from *Paradise Lost* held the famous speech in which all the seeds of the future transcendental creed were already present:

> Who saw . . .
> When this creation was? remember'st thou
> Thy making, while the Maker gave thee being?

> We know no time when we were not as now;
> Know none before us, self-begot, self-rais'd
> By our own quick'ning power

This fragment can serve as a motto to everything Harold Bloom has ever written; as he himself frequently admits, its rhetoric was the source of the most powerful influence he ever experienced as a critic of poetry. No wonder, for this is an epitome of Bloom's favorite hero, a "strong poet" whose own creative "quickening power" comes not from a rejection of the burden of tradition but, quite to the contrary, is a late result of a revisionist process of working through the inheritance. The strong poet is an embodiment of the romantic fantasy: at once accepting and fighting influence; at once admitting and denying the anxiety of influx; at once afraid and boldly defiant of it. A strong poet, therefore, mediates between two rigid stances: between a deadly loyal defense of the canon which protects the tradition's continuity by seeing to its faithful imitation—and, on the other hand, post-Nietzschean prophets of the new who want to find sources of unlimited creativity in breaking with, as Nietzsche called it in "On the Uses and Disadvantages of History for Life," "heavy burden of history." From the point of view of these well-defined cultural roles which divide our contemporary spectrum, the strong poet is as paradoxical as the fantasy he incarnates: he is both the victim and the beneficiary of the influence, both deeply influenced and agonistically free to become an individual.[33]

Bloom's choice of the romantic hero has a deep theoretical significance which often—and probably, quite deliberately, for Bloom dislikes philosophy—eludes him. In promoting the romantic fantasy of an "impossible" subjectivity, he pioneers a highly original line of defense against the deconstructive "death of the subject," whose main advantage is that it doesn't fall back on the well-trodden blind alley of the transcendental tradition. The satanic addition of *grand narcissistic hubris* is absolutely essential here. It is to answer the question, which constitutes Bloom's fundamental and ever-recurring problem: How is it possible for the subject to defend itself against heteronomous influences if there is *yet* no independent, autonomous self? How is this reversal, this *lying against time* possible? How does it work that the self can make such an enormous effort of appropriation of alien contents in a situation where it has hardly anything of its own? Freud's ego, caught neurotically in the fight between two energetic giants, id and superego, has hardly any energy itself: its role is to withstand and compromise. Bloom's I, which constitutes a more militant variant of the Freudian ego, is from the very start agonistic: it doesn't grow in the safe inner temple of transcendental consciousness but in a highly unfriendly environment it cannot oppose without a totally unreal, fantastical notion of itself as something grand, in Satan's words, already self-raised and self-begotten. Here, the eternal cause of antinomies within transcendental philosophy, which could not conceptually grasp the *idea* of *Selbstsetzen* without falling into a vicious circle, appears in a wholly different light. The antinomy is solved, but not on the conceptual level: the *idea* of self-constitution begins to make sense only as an effective *fantasy* of self-constitution, as an expression of a powerful *will to selfhood*, which is an antithetical offshoot of initial aggressivity and frustration with the situation of total dependence. The narcissistic anticipation of the self as a strong subject, the antirealistic *self-image* full of romantic hubris and pathos, functions in the manner of a self-fulfilling prophecy. In Schiller's words, from his poem "Die Philosophen" ("The Philosophers"): *Du kannst, denn Du sollst* (You can, so you should) (1906, 208).[34]

Despite his penchant for reckless battle cries, Bloom is, in fact, very far from just being indignant with deconstruction: quite to the contrary, in its antisubjectivist tendency, he perceives an infallible logic. Seen from his romantic perspective, deconstruction simply deconstructs the transcendental faith as merely an *illusion*, that is, something infinitely less significant than *fantasy*. As such, it remains within the either/or of the reality principle it itself does not attempt to deconstruct; it accepts, in deep accordance with the logocentric tradition it otherwise promises to weaken, the rigid alternative of influence and autonomy. As Simon Critchley, describing the contemporary antisubjectivist climate, puts it in his essay on every future concept of postdeconstructive subjectivity:

> Regionalized, marginalized, and rendered secondary, one might say that, within this *doxa, the subject is subject*, recalling a widespread meaning of the word in political philosophy . . . Rather than the subject being the autonomous, independent human agent—whether the monarch of nature, the possessive individual, or the bourgeois citizen endowed with certain inalienable rights—the subject is displaced into a heteronomous relation of serfdom and dependency. *Subjectivity is constructed by structures that exceed the individual agent.* (1996, 26; my emphasis)

The moment the predicament of influence becomes so strong that it cannot be negated by, as Kierkegaard had called it, the transcendental magic of *eins, zwei, drei, kokolorum* (1992, 192), the "empirical knowledge" (or what Girard calls "literary truth") comes back with the vengeance, claiming a full *subjection* of the subject, and forcing it to a nonnegotiable "heteronomous relation of serfdom and dependency." Transcendental illusion, once usurping itself a status of an objective truth of the self, becomes replaced by another candidate for knowledge, still within the same dominion of *logos*.[35]

Could it be, then, that Bloom, after his romantic precursors, is a more thorough deconstructor than all those who brought about the demise of the logocentric subject, yet fully in harmony with the logocentric logic? Ironic as it may sound, it is nonetheless quite true. By under-mining the dominion of "that bully, *logos*," he could begin to defend the notion of the subject, yet on the wholly new, nonlogocentric grounds of the romantic tradition, which saw the origin of the subjective life in the fantastical defiance against everything real. Thus, just like the decon-structors, Bloom believes that the subject *is* an impossible figure, but draws from this *fact* a radically different conclusion. Here, the fantas-tical desire of the impossible, taken fully consciously at its face value, becomes the defining feature of that particular saving error: the supreme fiction of the self.

Chapter 2

Literary Lie and Philosophical Truth: Tarrying with the Deconstruction

> The spirit of negation has been so active, so confident and so intolerant that the commonplaces about the romantic provoke us to wonder if our salvation, if the way out, is not the romantic. All the great things have been denied and we live in an intricacy of new and local mythologies, political, economic, poetic, which are asserted with an ever-enlarging incoherence.
> —Wallace Stevens, *The Necessary Angel*

In *Violence and the Sacred* Girard talks about rituals that go wrong: instead of appeasing the mimetic violence that every now and then seizes community and turns it into a de-differentiated mob, it merely enhances aggression and unleashes forces of destruction beyond reach and control of any ritualistic containment. Perhaps, it is a little far-fetched analogy—but something similar seems to have happened to Bloom's polemic with deconstruction. It certainly turned into an agon that went seriously wrong.

In the beginning, both sides seemed to get along reasonably well: Bloom even contributed to *Deconstruction and Criticism*, the anthology he coedited with Geoffrey Hartman, though in the latter's preface we read that "Bloom and Hartman are barely deconstructionists. They even write against it on occasion" (*DC*, ix). Most books written about deconstruction in America—by Culler, Norris, Lentricchia, Felperin, Donoghue, Riddel, Bruss, and many, many others—make room for Bloom's "ferocious alphabet" and the kabbalistic extravaganza of his "antithetical criticism," but only as an eccentric periphery, a strange, barely traceable detour from the deconstructive center, which is always solidly occupied by Derrida and de Man. Years after the first publication of *The Anxiety of Influence*, in his 1997 preface to the book's new edition, Bloom complains about "how weakly misread *The Anxiety of Influence* has been, and continues to be" (*AI*, xxiii), and he is certainly right. Bloom's reception in the late 1970s and early 1980s (when he received the greatest attention in print) has not proved particularly fruitful or interesting. In practically all cases there emerges a dominant, predictable pattern: first, Bloom garners half-hearted praise for joining deconstruction, which is interested in the rhetorical dimension of literary language; second, he is scolded for not being radical enough and for falling back into the psychological scheme of an Oedipal rivalry between the ephebe and his precursor; and finally, he is ambivalently dismissed as a more or less traditional humanist who simply cannot do without the hypothesis of the subject. His "psychologism" and "subjectivism" are the two centrifugal tendencies that push Bloom away from what appears to be the deconstructionist center: a subject-free zone of pure textual analysis.[1]

Both parties have changed since then. Deconstruction has undergone a typically revolutionary transformation. Beginning with quite radical demands in the '60s, it split in the mid-'70s into an ideologically mobilized, academic mass movement, on the one hand, and a critical avant-garde, on the other, which in the '80s grew more and more revisionist. Everything written by the older Derrida, dating from the mid-'80s, is deconstruction in revision, critically reexamining the radicalism of its earlier claims. Whereas in the '60s, in his famous essay "The Ends of Man," Derrida was opting for a "sublation of humanism" and a total subversion of "anthropological primacy," of which the classical notion of the subject was the most definitive example, later he began to revise this claim by stating it in a far more attenuated form. Now and again he would repeat that his critique of subjectivity, based on the idea of total self-presence, was not meant to ban the concept of subjectivity altogether, but merely to "de-center" it and render it less obvious and transparent than was widely assumed in the post-Cartesian tradition. It remains questionable whether he, or any other High Deconstructionist, gave us a new notion of subjectivity that we could use in place of the old one. What counts, however, is that Derrida, who had once accused Heidegger of not having been radical enough in the demolition of the Western subject, was not essentially opposed to such a project toward the end of his life.

But as with any other revolutionary movement, what really causes trouble is not the critical, self-revisionist vanguard, but "party masses," those who tend to *believe* and therefore use highly skeptical, deconstructive devices as a set of dogmas. Therefore, when Bloom attacks "deconstruction," he very rarely opposes the high-deconstructive giants (he writes on Derrida and de Man with much admiration and respect), but rather almost always what he calls "the adepts of the School of Resentment," "the critics who value theory over the literature itself" (*S*, 9). It should thus be made clear at the very outset: Bloom's feud with deconstruction mostly amounts to his war against the School of Resentment, and vice versa.[2] And while we can suspect that he has many critical things to say about Derrida and de Man, they do not add up to anything like an "assault." Quite the contrary, his position on high-deconstructive matters is subtle and nuanced. More than that, if we juxtapose what he says about deconstruction in his theoretical books from the '70s with the self-doubts into which deconstruction finally matures in the '80s and '90s, Bloom and Derrida will suddenly appear to have a lot in common. The principal aim of this book is to examine this common, yet uncharted, space and to demonstrate how Bloom's alternative, vitalistic, and postromantic notion of subjectivity was and remains the missing link that late deconstruction has been seeking to complete its revision.[3]

In the '70s, Bloom's proposition had no chance of breaking through deconstruction's revolutionary ranks. In the following decade, however, when the deconstructive mandarins began to "slacken" and open to dialogue, Bloom "hardened" considerably: his involvement in the battle around "the Western canon" reinforced his antiresentment position, which made him appear openly "anti-deconstructive" and not very well disposed toward dialogue. But all this is at least in part a misunderstanding that resulted from bad timing. When Derrida had already begun contemplating a return to the notion of narcissism as essential to his posttraditional subjectivity, Bloom, who had developed a beautifully complex theory of the narcissistic self, was still scourged—this time by the angry party masses—for his putative "psychological fallacy." Thus, we merely have to synchronize their arguments without paying too much attention to the emotions that surrounded them.[4]

Two Charges

> In the beginning was the troper.
> —Harold Bloom, *Wallace Stevens: The Poems of Our Climate*

This may not be a book about a feud, but it is also not about a total reconciliation. There are obvious points on which Bloom and High Deconstruction would never agree. First of all, Bloom would never accept any theory or philosophy that values itself over literature, or that fosters any pretension to a "philosophical truth" placed above a "literary lie." Bloom often professed his dislike of philosophy, contemptuously calling it a "stuffed bird,"[5] a dead thought fit only for the contemplation of death, such that it seems almost perverse to attempt to convert him, as I do here, into a philosopher or, at least, into a thinker who engaged in one of the most crucial philosophical debates of our time. Bloom is a speculator, a literary critic, a wisdom writer—but certainly not someone who would easily identify himself with philosophical discipline.[6] And yet the history of philosophy is full of dissenters who escaped from the harshness of "philosophical truths" into the phantasmagorical realm of "literary lies": Kierkegaard's pseudonymous masquerades and Nietzsche's choice of rhetoric are but two examples of dissents that paved the way for Bloom and his followers.[7] Furthermore, we could even say that Bloom's emphatic "non-philosophy" belongs to those antitheories which were outlined and projected by Adorno in *Negative Dialectics*, and whose distinctive feature is a conscious fear of the oppressiveness of conceptuality, counteracted by an equally conscious indulgence of rhetorical freedom.

In its own way, deconstruction also followed Adorno, who defined negative dialectics as a "logic of disintegration": "of a disintegration of the prepared and objectified form of the concepts which the cognitive subject faces, primarily and directly" (2003, 145).[8] But deconstruction followed this course without relying on "the strength of the subject," which resides in its singular name, but instead by concentrating on the internal logic of textuality, revealing the *weakness of the concept* which, when approached in a "technically correct way" (de Man 1986, 19), should be able to deconstruct itself without appeal to any external, agonistic agent. There is no place here for the Adornean reverse proportion between the weakening of the system and the strengthening of singular subjectivity. But it is precisely this proportion—or, in Bloom's words, *the ratio*—that governs Bloom's agonistic strategy: when Language, belonging to the mighty Other, becomes weak, the individual subject grows in power. And when Language is powerful, the subject dwindles. Here it is never Language, or Text, that deconstructs itself, but the Who, the singular, subjective name that resists its power. And resistance to this power is the *only* aspect of subjectivity that interests Bloom.

So, once again: Is Harold Bloom a deconstructionist? Or is this question still worth asking? For a while, Bloom became pigeonholed as one of "The Yale Critics," a rather helpless description that never really acquired a flesh of its own. The treatment he got from his younger Yale apprentices, who produced a volume of criticism under this title, was noticeably secondary to their main theoretical interest, which focused more closely on Paul de Man and his French inspirations, Blanchot and Derrida. He was therefore never confronted in a thorough intellectual debate, but simply circumvented. Although the authors—Godzich, Martin, and Arac—agreed that Bloom's theory is deconstructive in so far as it follows "Nietzsche's deconstruction of the self" (Arac 1983, xi), they remained uneasy with its lapse into "psychological naturalism" and the conception of poetry as "the self's direct struggle with life" (ibid., xxxii). Consequently, their unease with Bloom's "psychological fallacy," a reproach sufficient to discourage a pedigree deconstructionist, prevailed, and his Nietzschean argument was left unexamined.[9] The verdict provided by Frank Lentricchia in his preface to Bloom's *The Breaking of the Vessels*, that it is "self-deluded" to align Bloom with the deconstruction movement (xii), has hovered from the very beginning as an inevitable conclusion to a discussion that had never really begun. Later on, John Hollander offered a witty comment to this uneasy misidentification: "Indeed, associating Bloom with a 'deconstructionist school,' or even mentioning him and Paul de Man in the same taxonomic breath, would be as touchingly naive as some genially garrulous Anglican clergyman, circa 1635, comfily squatting in the middle of his *via media*, referring to 'You know, Calvin and Loyola and that crowd'" (*PI*, xii).

But is Bloom really so far from "that crowd"? Or is this rather a case of mutual misunderstanding, first on the part of self-proclaimed deconstructionists who condemned him to psychological fallacy, and then on the part of his advocates, who defended his allegedly old-school humanist approach? For reducing Bloom's theory of poetry in *The Anxiety of Influence* to a description of "the self's direct struggle with life" is as "touchingly naive" as pushing him, against his demonstrated intentions, in the direction of Angelic Schools, with their good-natured, trusting interpretations of the humanist literary tradition. Both approaches seem equally wrong. There is nothing "direct" in Bloom's complex Nietzschean-Freudian rhetoric, which is entirely based on the indirectness of figuration. Nor is there any "self" to speak of, at least if we define it phenomenologically as a form of self-presence; the only access Bloom's poetic self has to itself is mediated by the series of evasions and

differences it creates in defense against becoming *like* the self of the precursor. And there is not even a hint of positivity here, merely a play of
purely negative deferrals and differences that in fact very much resemble
Derrida's own nonconcept of *différance*.

Two fundamental misunderstandings need to be clarified at this
point: first, the fatal issue of "psychological fallacy"; and second, a good
deal of bad faith in the deconstructionists' mistreatment of Bloom's
proposition of the subject. These two misconceptions are closely inter-
related, and they have done equal harm to Bloom's reception among
contemporary theorists. The fatal issue of psychological fallacy—combining the Husserlian verdict on all naive, phenomenologically untested
approaches to subjectivity and the Ruskinian critique of pathos and its
expressive projections—has a special standing among the advocates of
deconstruction, for rather obscure reasons. It is somehow generally
agreed that "after Heidegger" we no longer speak about the subject, and
whatever subjective residue had been left in existentialism has long since
been exhausted by the poststructuralist intervention. The subject, therefore, is an uneasy topic that tends to be evaded by the dogma of pure
textuality.

And the dogma of pure textuality is itself a strange development
that does not find complete confirmation in the original findings of the
Founding Fathers. Derrida, for that matter, always claimed that his aim
was not to liquidate the subject, but merely to decenter it and situate it
within the textual realm, which means, among other things, that he was
willing to abandon the philosophical notion of the subject as a secure,
self-present outsider, with its untouchable "view from nowhere," and
head toward less secure and self-evident manifestations of subjectivity.[10]
Yet his singular ontology—for despite many assertions on the contrary,
this surely *is* ontology—does not allow him to talk about the very act
of the subject's *situating* itself within the text: we are merely left with
the traces of such activity that immediately erases its extratextual origin.
Thus, even if there is a *desire to mean* that produces texts—and this is how
Derrida interprets his native French *vouloir-dire* (meaning)—it is intrac-
table in all but its concrete textual results, the written black marks on
white paper. His famous thesis, *"il n'y a pas de hors-texte,"*[11] should therefore be read in the Kantian critical sense that the outside-of-the-text
is strictly unthinkable—and, even more critically, that there is no transcendental deduction that might give us the operative illusion of being
somehow able to think it. This highly complex, semitranscendental thesis, however, was easily transformed into the dogma of self-enclosed

textuality, which, in America especially, helped to reinforce the waning formalist approach of the New Critique and build a new version
of an even more sterile, more dead-end formalism that was eventually
embraced by de Man and some of his pupils.[12]

This evolution is far from obvious, since de Man himself started out
as a follower of Husserl, who famously criticized the psychologist fallacy
and was convinced that the subject should be thought only phenomenologically, as a pure source of transcendental constitution. De Man's
essays on Georges Poulet (the last Cartesian in the world of literary theory) and on the "sublimation of the self"—which is initially tinged with
concrete, existential, and affective impurity, but eventually purges itself
into a subject constituting a text[13]—clearly testify to de Man's idealist
bias, a bias that, when frustrated, easily turned into an equally purified
formalism. For de Man, the Derridean *il n'y a pas de hors-texte* must have
sounded like redemption from the failed quest for the sublimated subject of writing: the permission not to take the subject into theoretical
account, not to need it as a viable hypothesis, was more than welcome as
a pretext for abandoning the belated crusade for a pure cogito in literary texts.

Derrida's and de Man's "interests of theory" were thus completely
divergent from the very start, and only an external imperative to maintain
the cohesion of the "School" against the slings and arrows of outraged
defenders of tradition could be responsible for silencing this divergence.
Derrida, let us repeat, was primarily interested in bringing down the
philosophical subject, thereby finishing the job of Heidegger, as well
as of Adorno (oddly enough, he tried to reconcile them): for Derrida,
shifting the subject into the text meant depriving it of its inexplicably
self-asserted "nowhereness," but also forcing the subject to live—"to
live on"[14]—not outside, but within its own textual manifestation. But de
Man's primary interest rested in the continuation of a certain type of
theory, which since Kant and Hegel has been described as *streng, echt*,
and *rein*, meaning most of all "pure": free of contingent, empirical impurities, elegantly formal, transparent, and a priori. Unlike Heidegger,
Adorno, or Derrida, de Man was never essentially hostile to the philosophical *concept* of the subject, nor was he, as follows from the former,
ever really attentive to any other understanding of subjectivity.[15] He nevertheless dropped this concept the moment a better theory presented
itself as a new candidate for formalist purity. And there exist at least a
few significant documents that clearly reveal to what extent Derrida and
de Man never really understood one another.[16]

This is also to say that the so-called charge of "psychological fallacy," so often leveled by deconstructionists, is based on an equivocation, that is, that it means different things dependent on the position they assume toward "textuality." From the formal purist perspective, this reproach refers to anything outside the text that would claim its authority over the text, be it conscious intention or unconscious desire. This, however, is a serious distortion of the primary deconstructive project: to claim that *there is nothing outside the text* means also *not to leave anything outside the text.* Such a limited and limiting understanding of the "text," which implicitly preserves the dualism of the subject (intention or desire) and the object (as de Man used to say, after Hegel, "these marks on this sheet of paper" [de Man 1986, 42]), is unjustifiable in light of this project. This dualism may be underplayed, turned deeply implicit or merely negative, but it nevertheless is a fully operative category in the de Manian "mere reading": the rhetorical reader knows precisely what to "cut off" from his interpretation of the text, for he knows that the reference simply doesn't make it into the world of writing.

Derrida's position, on the other hand, suggests a radically different, and much more promising, development. Just like André Gide in *The Counterfeiters*, who wanted "to put everything into the novel," Derrida wants to put everything into the text. His approach to the text, therefore, closely resembles—or even revises in its own secular way—one of the most celebrated Jewish sayings on the reading of Torah from *Pirke Aboth* (*Wisdom of the Fathers*): "Turn it, and turn it, for everything is in it."[17] Derrida issues an analogous imperative: he wants us to turn and turn (i.e., trope and trope) the body of text, for *everything* is in it, that is, the whole reality made both present-absent in the universal mode of writing. Whereas de Man, mirroring Derrida's directive precisely, replies: however you turn it, no further trope will ever reverse the error of figuration which always and inevitably leads away from the truth of any possible reference, and to *nothing.* "One more 'turn' or trope added to a series of earlier reversals will not stop the turn toward error" (1979a, 113).

Thus, if we were to stick to Derrida's "talmudic" metaphysics, it would become clear that textuality is not something left over from the old, unresolved Hegelian schism between subjective and objective spirit (as it is in de Man's case), but it is *everything that exists:* textuality becomes the ultimate ontological mode of existence. In this second sense, the charge of "psychological fallacy" has a different, more difficult meaning: it does not refer to anything subjective that would soil the purity of an isolated text, but merely to such a notion of subjectivity that implies an ontologically privileged, external, self-enclosed, and nontextual status. It can be a Cartesian monad and its numerous philosophical avatars—but it can also be an ordinary, folk-psychology self of introspection, deeply convinced of its own infallibility in knowing what it wants, feels, thinks, and says *an sich und für sich* (in and for itself). Any model of subjectivity that seals itself hermetically in perfect self-presence, an ontological realm of its own; any model of subjectivity that refuses contamination with the Fichtean *nicht-Ich* (not-I) or claims Hegelian control over the process of its objectification—falls within this sort of fallacy. But the same is not necessarily true of models of subjectivity that inscribe it in the text, situate it within the realm of textuality, and take its contamination for granted. Thus, if there *is* such subjectivity, able to pass *the test of inscription*—and I will demonstrate how the Bloomian subject is precisely a case in point—it should be more than welcome in Derridean deconstruction.

The second charge brought against Bloom deals with the specific interpretation of his putative "psychological fallacy." Even sympathetic commentators get it wrong when they stubbornly perceive Bloom's poetic agon with regard to the Oedipal struggle between father-precursor and son-ephebe, although the critic who was most responsible for coining this *trivium* can hardly be called sympathetic. In his review of *The Anxiety of Influence*, Paul de Man practically dissects Bloom into two independent parts: the theoretical and the irrelevant. The first closely resembles de Man's own intertextual pursuits, if stated in an inadequate idiom, whereas the second boils down to an obsolete recapitulation of the Freudian Oedipal triangle, regarded by de Man as a "step backward" on the map of contemporary literary theory. De Man writes:

> We can forget about the temporal scheme and about the pathos of the oedipal son; underneath, the book deals with the difficulty or, rather, the impossibility of reading and by inference, with the indeterminacy of the literary meaning. *If we are willing to set aside the trappings of psychology*, Bloom's essay has much to say on the encounter between latecomer and precursor as a displaced version of the paradigmatic encounter between reader and text. (1971, 273; my emphasis)

"We can forget" about "the trappings of psychology," de Man suggests, and everything in Bloom will turn out just fine; *oubliez Freud* (forget Freud), and the scheme of Bloomian misprision will be but another version of the de Manian allegory of reading, endlessly dispatching the missed encounter between reader and text. This simple dissection, neatly cutting Bloom in two—the obsolete Oedipal ritual on the one hand, and advanced textual analysis on the other—proved so persuasive that it has rarely been questioned as a paradigm of Bloom's reception among his contemporary, deconstructionist commentators. In this sense, no one has attempted to approach Bloom's proposition as an integral whole. De Man's unfairness toward Bloom—very much like his unfairness to Kierkegaard's conceptual struggles to save the embodied, concrete self—hides some unavowed anxieties on de Man's part and, without a doubt, did the most harm in establishing this authoritative pattern of interpretation. After de Man, a legion of critics would reiterate with less and less understanding how *The Anxiety of Influence* would have been a great tool in textual analysis if only it had not fallen into the trap of old, bad, predictable psychoanalysis.[18]

But how accurate is this identification of an Oedipal conflict in Bloom? The psychoanalytical context in which Bloom's narrative is set is not at all as literal as it might seem to de Man. Bloom's intricate revision of Freud is a separate topic, which we will try to analyze later, but it certainly moves in the opposite direction from the received trend of literalizing Freud's metaphors: Bloom revises Freud in a way that transforms the misguided, self-professed scientist into a "strong poet," that is, a deliverer of powerful tropes. Whatever seems literal or scholarly in Freud, Bloom turns back into a poetic metaphor, and the whole of psychoanalysis into a kind of *gray mythology*, instead of a thoroughly bleached, "white" philosophy, a language still half-conscious of its rhetorical power. For Bloom, therefore, the Oedipal struggle is merely a figure for a more fundamental, agonistic attitude that can hardly be grasped in its literal state: a troped, indirect expression of the most elemental fantasy-wish "to become distinct," to be singular beyond the leveling context of endless repetition, and not to be conflated with anybody else, not to be a copy or replica.

Contemporary thinkers, including both literary critics and philosophers, tend to regard this fantasy of originality as yet another obsolete landmark of the romantic heritage, yet another "idol" of modern humanism, intrinsically coupled with the cult of the philosophical subject.[19] This, however, is again very confusing, for such "romantic" distinctness not only has nothing to do with philosophical subjectivity but emerges in full opposition to the stifling generality of its concept. For the romantics—and let us not forget that Bloom is definitely, if belatedly, one of them—the once integral Cartesian unity of cogito and sum breaks into a stark antithesis:

Ich denke (I think) of Kant, Fichte, and Hegel seems to be a far too general characteristic of human consciousness to give account of its uniquely individual *Ich bin* (I am).[20] The struggle for distinctness, therefore, is fought by the romantics under the aegis of *Ich bin:* the subject asserting its positive, concrete existence instead of a negative, general movement of thinking. And through *Lebensphilosophie* this eventually spawns not only Heidegger's *Dasein* but also, perhaps more importantly, the Freudian concept of the unconscious life, the subject of *being* which cannot be exhausted in thinking alone. Thus, even if this romantic *Ich bin* is underplayed in Freud in favor of the normative, enlightened, and reassuring self-consciousness of the ego, his more romantically minded followers had no trouble finding its sparkling trace therein: D. W. Winnicott, the greatest romantic of Kleinian psychoanalysis, and for whom Bloom feels a distinct affinity, reinterprets Freud's imperative *wo Es war, soll Ich werden* (where id was, the ego should emerge) in favor not of the ego, but of "I am," the *Ich* of the Schellingian *Ich bin*. The Freudian ego merely wants *to be and to be accepted* in its attempt to survive in the unwelcoming world of universal *Unbehagen* (discomfort), while the romantic, Winnicottian-Bloomian "I" wants *to be and to be distinct*, to be recognized as a separate entity that seizes its own chance of being in a unique way. The difference here, therefore, is between *acceptance* and *recognition;* between mere consolation and triumph over the reductive world of nature; between existence as subsumption into the great chain of being and existence as solitary quest and adventure; between sublimation and agon.

Unlike the romantic self, therefore, Freud's ego still partakes of the philosophical concept of subjectivity. Its imperative of sublimation, linking itself to the great chain of being for the sake of being accepted, repeats the paradigmatic Hegelian gesture of shedding "lazy existence" and becoming one with the universal, pure, and negative moment of the spirit, the first act of *Ich denke*. Philosophical subjectivity offers a particular existence the chance to become one with the universal aspect of being, whether in a way that is triumphant and Hegelian or Freudian and sadly resigned. The romantic subject, on the other hand, *blocks* the passage of sublimation: it does not wish to identify with the general, but to remain at the level of its own existence, however "lazy" or "unruly," and assert its singularity in the face of all inconveniences.

Hence in Bloom the Oedipal struggle is nothing but a *parable* telling the story of the romantic spark Ich bin, which refuses to be included in the great chain of being and fights for its own unique understanding of the fact of existence. For the romantic self, *I-here-now* is a golden occasion, not just a grammatical occasionality, which must share the sorry fate of every Hegelian *das Diese* (this). In telling its story of individuation, the self—very much like the Lévi-Straussian *bricoleur*, the maker of mythologies—takes whatever it has at hand to express its predicament, which cannot be narrated in a fully conscious, self-detached, conceptual way; the semimythological form mirrors the self's deep immersion in the process it simultaneously attempts to tell.[21] And the elements of "family romance" are just the first, most available bricks in this bricolage. Thus the precursor/father represents the power of *what already exists:* he, strong and distinct, poses a mimetic threat to any newcomer anxious about his own possibility of "I am." The muse/mother represents the power of *becoming*, of finding within the static monolith of being still more loose energy toward creative potentiality. And the ephebe/son is a *new name*, a paradoxical being mostly "made of" universal stuff but also, through the very act of naming, pushed in the direction of individuation. His will to distinctness is, in its initial state, nothing but a *fantasy:* a nonreality, even a wish agonistically opposed to all reality, a *great original lie against everything that already exists.* As Adorno says in *Negative Dialectics,* such individuality "cannot be deduced from thought," for it defies—lies against—every logic. Yet if such individuality succeeds, it nevertheless *becomes what it is,* thus also becoming a scandal and an error that no ontology can possibly accommodate.[22]

And the stage of this agon is not the poet's psyche, not the inner sanctuary of his deep self, but the *text:* the domain of the necessary *contamination*, where everything singular has to pass the test of inscription and confront the universal, where everything new has to wrestle with the already extant. The "family romance," which delivers a canvas for the story of poetic becoming, is thus merely a handy metaphor for intertextual relations, though not reducible to the de Manian idiom, and not a literal story of, as Freud used to call them, the "dependent relationships of the ego." In analyzing poems, Bloom is never primarily interested in the biographical details of poets' lives: if he discovers, for instance, a fear of Shelley in Yeats, it is not because Yeats was known to be obsessed with Shelley. Bloom reads the anxiety of influence *from the poem* because a poem itself is nothing but this "anxiety achieved": a compromise symptom that, as we know from *Beyond the Pleasure Principle*, mediates between the ego's certainty of its own autonomy and the traumatic, unconscious knowledge of being totally dependent on the precursor. Anxiety, therefore, cheats both the unconsciousness (by deferring the reexperience of the trauma), as well as consciousness, by smuggling some element of the "fear of contamination" into the ego's illusory sense of independence. Anxiety itself is both a huge, double lie (just another name for the compromise defense) and, at the same time, the true domain of poetry, or even of creativity, potentiality, and distinction. "The anxiety may or may not be internalized by the later writer, depending upon temperament and circumstances," Bloom writes in *The Anxiety of Influence*, "yet that hardly matters: the strong poem is the achieved anxiety. 'Influence' is a metaphor, one that implicates a matrix of relationships—imagistic, temporal, spiritual, psychological—all of them ultimately defensive in their nature" (*AI*, xxiii). This is, as we have already suggested in our analysis of Bloom's "revision" of Girard, a *psychoanalysis of the writing subject*.

It is, therefore, absolutely crucial to remember that *this* late and revised romantic subject is not some fantastic entity, accessible through immediate self-experience, but a "contaminated" subject, simultaneous and synonymous with its anxiety, "achieved" only in the world of texts. The most daring invention of Bloom's vision of rhetoric is his suggestion that textuality is not so much the subject's doom, but, on the contrary, its *asylum:* a welcome *escape* for the traumatized poetic psyche that flees from the unbearable insistence of the precursory voice. This shift is very aptly described by Geoffrey Hartman's "Words and Wounds," in which he places himself in proximity with Bloom, saying about a poem:

> Words have been found that close the path to the original words. This absolute closure is what we respond to, this appearance of definitive detachment and substitution. The words themselves block the way. There is no going back, no stumbling through ghostly or psychoanalytic vaults: *the "dread Voice" exists as a poem or not at all.* (1981, 157; my emphasis)

The voice that "wounds through the ear" (ibid.), leaving its "original words," is *displaced*—that is, troped: repeated, substituted, attenuated, differentiated, and deferred—and this displacement, just like the displacement of trauma executed by phobic syndromes, is the only function of a poem that, when the poem fulfills it, becomes an "achieved anxiety." Hartman makes fully explicit the idea (very much present in Bloom's concept of poetic revision) that this "displacement"—a word as crucial for Bloom as "return" was for Freud and "dissemination" for Derrida— can only take place in the realm of the text, which brackets reference, thus "closing the path" to the original trauma and producing "an appearance of definitive detachment and substitution." Here, the same textual predicament that in both Derrida and de Man seems catastrophic for a subjectivity conceived as a self-enclosed presence becomes a saving context for the self, now conceived as a *traumatized subject*, a subject that seeks to displace itself from its painful origins.[23]

Bloom has often expressed his irritation over the literal, naively psychological interpretation of his Oedipal parable. In the late preface to *The Anxiety of Influence*—written in 1997 and devoted mostly to what seemed missing in the book's first edition, the figure of William Shakespeare, the great *deus absconditus* (hidden God) of the modern world—Bloom lashes out at the thoughtless abuse of "the Oedipal complex," used to explain the intricacies of such infinitely rich Shakespearean personages as Hamlet. It is the other way round, he says, for although Freud was an exceptionally strong poet, he still cannot compare to the divine "inventor of the human" who comprises Freud, merely his later revisionist:

> I never meant by "the anxiety of influence" a Freudian Oedipal rivalry, despite a rhetorical flourish or two in this book. A Shakespearean reading of Freud, which I favor over a Freudian reading of Shakespeare or anyone else, reveals that Freud suffered from a Hamlet complex (the true name of the Oedipus complex) or an anxiety of influence in regard to Shakespeare. (xxii)

The Oedipal complex, therefore, makes sense through Hamlet, or rather—and this is how this passage should be read—the Oedipal parable in Bloom's work makes sense only through Hamlet, who, as a figure, overrules the rhetorical authority of the Freudian invention. And indeed, what Bloom refers to as "Hamlet's complex" is, in the end, a better, deeper version of the poetic family romance he has in mind. Hamlet's "spirit of revenge" can hardly be reducible to the desire for his mother, perversely transformed into vengeance. Instead, it is a fear of losing his name, even though he, as a young prince, was from the very beginning expected to be only a copy or replica of his father, whose name he bears. The son's spirit of revenge does not derive from an erotic rivalry with the father, but from a conviction that the prince, as an avenger, can restore the power of the wronged name and appropriate it for himself, and thus become the one and only, truly memorable Hamlet. He is "wounded through the ear" (Hartman 1981, 157), and the only way that he can begin to heal this wound is to turn himself into a poet, his life into a "poem unlimited," and everybody else into personages in his poem, speaking his own "words, words, words."[24] It is precisely this shift in agonistic attitude that makes Hamlet a paradigm of the modern individual, whose main concern is not so much the erotic will-to-power as the autonomy of his or her singular "I am," looking for a realm of its own in displacement from the imperative of imitation.

Bloom's reading of Hamlet as tropologically superior to Oedipus is curiously mediated by François Lyotard's first *clinamen* from the standard Freudian interpretation of the Danish Prince in his "Jewish Oedipus": in Lyotard's "Judaic" rendering Hamlet becomes so un-Greek that in the end he hardly resembles the Sophoclean Oedipus at all. Asks Lyotard:

> What's in Hamlet that's not in Oedipus? There is non-fulfillment . . .
> In Hebraic ethics, representation is forbidden, the eye closes, the ear
> opens in order to hear the father's spoken word. The image figure is
> rejected because of its fulfillment of desire and delusion; its function
> of truth is denied. (1977, 402)

The "non-fulfillment" Lyotard talks about refers to the impossibility of identification: of taking on father's image, becoming one with it, taking his place, assuming his power. As Susan Handelman, commenting on this fragment, rightly notices, "In Jewish thought, *the difference between the father and son is irrevocable.* There is no fulfillment of the word in an ontological return to the sameness of son and father, as there is for Christianity" (1982, 35; my emphasis), or as it is, although negatively and in failure, for Greek tragedy. The irreversibility of the difference between the father and son means that the stake of the game is no longer identification but, on the contrary, further and more distinct differentiation. The stake, therefore, is the Hebrew, time-engendering, historical, agonistic difference and not the time-collapsing, mythical, returning substitution; it is the separation from the Father and not an attempt to become one with him. Unlike Oedipus, therefore, who willy-nilly substitutes his father, Hamlet does not want to be Hamlet-the-Father—and this is precisely what makes him a figure of a strong poet desperately longing for his precursor's power but, at the same, trying to evade identification with him.

This reading of Hamlet as Shakespeare's "Judaic contribution" (Lyotard 1977, 406), which sets the Danish Prince cultural poles apart from Greek Oedipus, is confirmed by Bloom's recent work on Hamlet—*Hamlet: Poem Unlimited*—in which he deliberately describes the Prince's narcissistic affliction in terms he earlier used to depict the deepest malaise of the Jewish soul which feels, alternately, "nothing and everything in itself" (see *H*, 10, and *RST*, 148). This pulsation, which is also the most elementary dynamics of a strong poet's revisionary development, is once again typical of what we call here *a dialectics of the name*. It is the fantasy of the proper name—*I am, here and now, and my name is Hamlet*—which, alternately, creates an illusion of omnipotent power and reveals an inner emptiness that only calls for a concrete, truly singular "filling."

THE BLACK SUN OF SUFFERING

> But one cannot deny a word-wound, the thread of such a threat.
> —Geoffrey Hartman, *Saving the Text*

> Where does it come from, this black sun? From which galaxy do these invisible and heavy rays emerge, which tie me to the ground, to bed, to silence, to resignation?
> —Julia Kristeva, *The Black Sun: Depression and Melancholia*

We have begun to relieve Bloom of most of the charges brought against him by High Deconstruction. Instead of perceiving him as a victim of "psychological fallacy," "personalist heresy," traditional Freudianism, and an old-fashioned, subject-oriented humanism, we have found in his writings a promising sequel to the aborted deconstructive quest for subjectivity, which seemed to be lost beyond reach in the abysses of the textual world. Some deconstructionists, however, most notably de Man, have also raised the question of Bloom's "naturalism" or "vitalism," concentrating on "the self's direct struggle with life."

This charge is more difficult to dismiss, because it is first necessary to explain why it is a *charge* in the first place. There is nothing wrong with being a *vitalist*, which, for the sake of clarification—and we have already discussed this issue in the previous chapter—should not be conflated too easily with "naturalism" and its all too "direct struggles."[25] Bloom definitely belongs to the noble line of vitalistic and simultaneously non-naturalistic thinkers—from Spinoza to Freud—whose origins may even be as ancient and remote as what Bloom calls "early Hebrew vitalism," the most precious doctrinal core of "the book of J," this oldest and most powerful document of Hebrew literature. For Bloom, as for Spinoza, "wisdom is meditation on life and not on death," and life forms "presence not to be put by"—even if, from a purely conceptual point of view, life is trauma, error, and scandal that should best be "put by" a theory.[26]

Life is trauma, error, and scandal because, from the logical perspective long favored by philosophy, it is a paradox, a sheer contradiction in terms. Life, Hegel asserts, is contradictory in itself, for it produces individual beings who cannot account for their individuality: we exist separately, but actually we are nothing more than examples of a species. Our essence being general, we nonetheless emerge in a misleading disguise of particularity. It is therefore death that is the truth of every life, every natural being, for death returns nature's false particulars to generality. Hegel tells us, "In death natural life is victorious and cancels its own individual modification" (1976, 203). The "sensuous soul" (*die fühlende Seele*), which asserts the concrete "I am" and obstructs the passage to the universal "I think," also partakes of the "error" of life that inevitably makes it "unhappy." As Adorno puts it, *pace* Hegel, in an effort to defend its "erroneous" status, "the individual consciousness is almost always the unhappy one, and with good reason. In his aversion to it, Hegel refuses to face the very fact he underscores where it suits him: how much universality is inherent in that individuality" (2003, 45). Therefore, what we have already called the paradox of the name appears to be primarily a general paradox of life, of which the "sensuous soul" becomes acutely aware. The sensuous soul is made of universality, but it "feels"—Hegel calls it first of all *die fühlende Seele*—unique and singular. Along these lines, Hegel writes in the *Encyclopedia of Philosophical Sciences in Outline*:

> The sensuous totality is as individuality essentially that which differentiates itself in itself and wakes up in itself to be a judgment, according to which it has particular affections and defines itself as subject toward these determinations. The subject as such constitutes them in itself as its own affections. The subject is immersed in particularity of its affections, yet, at the same time, through the ideal aspect of their particularity, it builds itself into a subjective whole. In this way it becomes a *Selbstgefühl*, a self-affection—but always a particular one ... [It is, therefore,] still prone to pathology, which consists in its stubbornly sticking to the particularity of its own self-affection, which it cannot (or, will not) work through and raise to the level of ideality.[27]

Hegel's recipe for getting out of the pathology of the sensuous soul is to move on, to leave behind *die faule Existenz* (lazy existence), with its unresolved, unhappy paradoxes, and become one with the universal negativity of *der Geist der stets verneint*, "the thinking spirit." *Pathe, pathos,* and *pathology*—"sensing, suffering, and affliction"—form the biggest "evil," the evil of laziness and passivity, not far removed from Kant's famous *selbstverschuldigte Unmündigkeit:* the self-inflicted immaturity of a soul that *refuses* to raise itself to the higher level. Only when the soul discovers the "absolute negativity of the spirit," which, by imitating death, can even liberate itself of its own existence (Dasein) (i.e., when the soul is able to subsume its *Ich bin* in *Ich denke,* and dissolve the former in the latter), does it begin to intimate true freedom: "This being-for-itself of a free universality," Hegel writes, "is a higher awakening of the soul into the I of abstract universality . . . which excludes from itself the natural totality of its determinations and from this time on refers to it as an object, a part of the external world."[28]

But it is the vitalist who refuses to move on and "stubbornly sticks"—*beharren bleibt*—to his or her "unhappy" particularity. It is therefore no accident that the greatest vitalists have always paid special attention to the fact of *suffering*—pathe, pathos, and pathology at once—in which they would look for their Archimedean point and Ariadne's thread. Furthermore, if the truth of life is death, then sticking to life means meandering away from the truth, that is, deliberately seeking an error, *lying.* Summoning Wilde, who praised art for being "lying for its own sake," and Nietzsche, who similarly defined art as a defense against the siege of obnoxious facts, Bloom explicitly glorifies error and lie as a means of warding off death in the Nietzschean fragment of his recent *Where Shall Wisdom Be Found?:*

> We possess art lest we should perish of the truth. If a single apothegm could sum up Nietzsche on the aesthetic, it would be that. *Poetry tells lies, but the truth, being the reality principle, reduces to death, our death. To love truth would be to love death.* This hardly seems to me, as it does to Gilles Deleuze, a tragic conception of art. The world is rich in meaning because it is *rich in error, and strong in suffering,* when seen from an aesthetic perspective. Sanctifying a lie, and deceiving with good conscience, is the necessary labor of art, because error about life is necessary for life, since the truth about life merely hastens death. The will to deceive is not a tragic will, and indeed is the only source for an imaginative drive that can counter the ascetic drive against life. (*WSW,* 216; my emphasis)

This kind of vitalism, therefore, not only is *not* naturalism, but is strongly opposed to it: human life, it says, thrives only in an environment that is openly antithetical to nature and its "mess of facts."[29] Once again, contradictions and paradoxes abound—not to be abolished, however, but to be upheld, maintained, and endured. Human life makes room for itself by pushing against its own natural predicament; being a part of nature, it simultaneously exits nature, although merely into an imaginary realm of "beautiful lying," and this antithetical defiance is and must be the source of constant, unquenchable suffering wherein this living aporia becomes its own flesh. Bloom may therefore be an "aesthete," but, just as in Wilde, his aestheticism is but a luminous layer covering the dull pain of stubborn antithesis, in which man, as part of nature, refuses to be reduced to natural truths and seeks a saving *displacement* from their oppressiveness. And it is precisely the insistence on the pathos of this peculiar human pathology that makes Bloom suspicious of deconstruction as a mode of criticism that places itself on the opposite—playful but cold—pole of contemporary aestheticism. He states this firmly in *The Breaking of the Vessels:*

> Any mode of criticism, be it domestic or imported, that would defraud us of this true context of suffering must at last be dismissed with a kind of genial contempt. Perhaps there are texts without authors, articulated by blanks upon blanks, but the strong poet has the radical originality that restores our perspective to *the agonistic image of the human which suffers,* the human which thinks, the human which writes, the human which means, albeit all too humanly, in that agon the strong poet must wage, against otherness, against the self, against the presentness of the present, against anteriority, in some sense against the future. (82; my emphasis)[30]

Everything follows from *the agonistic image of the human who suffers:* it is both a foundation and a lead, the Archimedean point and Ariadne's thread. In the modern philosophical tradition from Descartes through Georges Poulet, it was cogito that served as the thread, preventing us from getting lost in a labyrinth of texts and clarifying their moments of undecidability: the thread "unrolls from the threshold of the labyrinth," says Poulet (1972, 48), and is kept by a subject placed safely outside the textual maze. Bloom, after Blake, Nietzsche, and Freud, changes the weave and texture of this thread into something thicker and less subtle: once woven of conscious intention, it is now densely mixed with the unconscious symptoms of psychic pain; it becomes—as in Hartman's shrewd punning—a *thread-threat.* Weaker subjects, indeed, may disperse in the realm of textual contamination, but strong poets "have radical originality that restores our perspective to the agonistic image of the human which suffers": they allow us to resee the painful duel between what is singular and what is universal within them, which, in fact, amounts to almost everything: otherness, self, present, anteriority, future. Strong poets risk their originality by propping it, very much in the vein of Freudian *anaclisis* (propping), against the energy of suffering that is most common and banal, but they manage to make the twist that pertains only to the greatest literature, the twist that transforms, directly and almost imperceptibly, *moaning into meaning*, sheer pain into verbal icon, human loss into poetic treasure.[31] Where there is singular pain, there is singular meaning as well, and the negation is also true: where there is no pain, there is no meaning either. Yet this grim, Nietzschean "poetics of pain" (*WSW*, 213), which says "that authentic meaning is painful, and that the pain itself is the meaning" (ibid., 210), is not at all tragic. It implies not a hopeless denial, which eventually has to come to terms with its hubristic impossibility, but a stubbornly vitalist, if somehow desperate, endorsement of life, which is so "strong in suffering" and, accordingly, so "rich in error," too.

Bloom proposes to "dismiss with genial contempt" any thought that would do the same to "the human which suffers" and, in a spirit of either playfulness or formalist purity, disregard the heavy load of psychic pain. This charge is perfectly accurate in the case of the de Manian "knights of chastity," whose practice of reading consists mostly in castigating all traces of "moaning" from the sterility of "meaning," but it is perhaps not completely fair to Derrida. Derrida is not a chaste knight of reading; as we have already asserted, he is entirely in favor of "putting everything into the text." But despite all his fervently "ethical" assertions on the contrary, we often can't help but come to the conclusion that anything as serious as pain or suffering would merely slow down the swiftness of his masterly play.[32] And, it is either play—or drama.[33] Pain, after all, is obsessive, obsessions are self-centered, and any center, even as provisory as that made of pain, inevitably becomes "a point of gravitation," *le point de capiton*, which captures the signifiers and keeps them forever in chains. It is pain which guards the poet's obsession of origins, not allowing him to escape into a freeplay of signifiers. Though unable to constitute itself as the sound metaphysical center of a structure of signification—the way the Platonist idea or the Cartesian, self-present cogito was able to—it nevertheless *functions* as a center, which hinders freeplay and the dissemination of signs. Pain, suffering, and trauma are not presences in any form that deconstruction was designed to detect and dismantle, yet they function as center and origin, an invisible black hole that nevertheless curves the space around itself and does not allow signifiers to disperse. The black sun of suffering is thus a vitalist alternative to the Platonist bright sun of vision, an alternative never properly examined by the deconstructionists, who, indeed, merely dismiss it with—not so genial— contempt. For them, suffering appears as an even less likely candidate than cogito, because it combines the worst sins of the two worst falla- cies: the psychological and the pathetic. This not only brings back the subject as a centering device but also enslaves the text to its inexhaustible expressive needs, keeping it tight on the leash of suffering.

This obsessive theme of suffering from which everything else follows made Bloom vulnerable also to other, this time ethical, charges. Some critics, for instance Frank Lentricchia in *After the New Criticism*, found it objectionable as an expression of inadmissible selfishness on the part of strong poets and their embattled spokesman. All they care about, says Lentricchia, is their own originality and distinctness, which makes them a bunch of "onanistic" egomaniacs on the verge of absurd, self-destructive solipsism. In the earlier period of his career, Lentricchia continues, espe- cially in *Shelley's Mythmaking* and *Visionary Company*, Bloom tended to be concerned with the redemptive aspect of romantic poetry: with the Vision which transforms a cold universe of death into a meaningful rela- tionship of the Buberian I and Thou. Later on, however, he turned away from Vision toward Revision, and, by plunging into troubled waters of poetic "family romance," he lost interest in the poet's stance toward the world, now uniquely concentrating on the poet's stance toward himself as mediated by his precursor. He thus shifted his view of a romantic poet as a quasi-messianic healer of reality to a view of a romantic poet as an ironic and almost solipsistic self, engaging in an endless, self-reflexive quest for originality. Lentricchia writes:

> We are left by Bloom with alternative theses about romantic tradi-
> tion: either it is held together by a faith in a saving, transformative
> humanism . . . —or it is unified by a commonly held, tough-minded
> dualism that we have trouble seeing in earlier romantics because
> (here comes the recent Bloom) later romantic poets like Stevens, and
> modernist critics like Brooks, willfully misread them as noumenally
> naive believers in the healing powers of imagination." (1980, 325)

Lentricchia—as well as few other critics, including Fite and Bruss—per- ceive this shift as a dramatic change, but I don't really find it radical at all. In fact, early and late Bloom form a dialectical unity which has to be read as one dynamic whole. The visionary and healing aspect of poetry has always been and to this day remains a crucial issue for Bloom; at one point, however, he discovered that "his full commitment to the mythopoeic imagination" (ibid., 323) could not be maintained without some previous "curing" of the ground. For, if the ground of Vision is indeed the Buberian transformation of experience into I and Thou, then it cannot occur if the I on which the Vision relies is not *truly* an I. How can a self, which is no longer sure of its selfhood, conduct such transformation? How can it carry the burden of transforming Vision? Lentricchia says: "The uncentered self can hardly be the anchor of anything but continuing drama and conflict" (ibid., 325), and he is absolutely right. *Unless* a poet truly becomes a separate I-*eye* of his own Vision, as long as he is mostly an *ear*, plagued by the Voices of other poets, no poetic salvation, no redemptive "scene of nomination" can take place. Some centering must precede the act of Vision, and this is precisely what the whole process of Re-Vision is for.[34]

A VITALIST DECONSTRUCTION?

> And when that day dawns, or sunset reddens, how joyous we shall
> all be! Facts will be regarded as discreditable, Truth will be found
> mourning over her fetters, and Romance, with her temper of
> wonder, will return to the land. The very aspect of the world will
> change to our startled eyes . . . But before this comes to pass we must
> cultivate the lost art of Lying.
> —Oscar Wilde, *The Decay of Lying*

But is it possible to be a *vitalist deconstructionist*? The phrase is not as absurd as it might seem. Such a qualification would make Bloom a deconstructionist of a different, older persuasion than the denomination followed by Derrida and de Man, who, if only for this reason, would be eager to marginalize Bloom's impact. Bloom's faithfulness to the first project of deconstruction as outlined by Nietzsche and subsequently by Freud, but already fully operative in the European romantic antithetical tradition, makes him strangely tangential to the heirs of Heidegger and his linguistic French commentators. Mentioning him in the same taxonomic breath as de Man and Derrida is hence as obvious and, at the same time, as impossible as arranging Judaism and Christianity as closely related to one another, though, from a more distant perspective, they remain variants of the same revelation. For the "Derrideans," Nietzsche and Freud are two original sources that need to be corrected by the arrival of Heidegger. For Bloom, who has often disparaged the Schwarzwaldian sage, this arrival is simply an unlawful revision that breaks the continuity of the project and replaces it with a linguistic paraphrase or, simply, a parody.

What is the difference between these two deconstructive denominations? We could say that *the primary deconstruction of the philosophical subject* in Nietzsche and Freud was conducted in the name of life, which they both defined as an erotic army of metaphors rallying against the literal return of the same—whereas Heidegger's deconstruction of the subject took place under the guiding auspices of death as the ultimate truth of Being. The Nietzschean-Freudian deconstructive prototype served to free the power of life as an error, a deviation of becoming from the truth of being, or a detour of Eros from the truth of death—while the Heideggerian intervention, very much in the Hegelian vein, deconstructed the error of life simply *as error* and thus returned it to the truth of Being, where it originated. Nietzsche and Freud were obsessed by the theme of suffering, which they saw as the only truly irreducible feature of the singular living human self—whereas Heidegger and his followers attempted to deconstruct suffering, at least the excess of it, by redefining it as a mere illusion of alienated, modern subjectivity. Risking some inevitable simplification, we could thus venture the hypothesis that the first deconstruction saw itself as a guardian of *life as error*, while the second understood itself as a myrmidon of *death as truth*.[35]

It is precisely the imperative to guard life, even—or rather, especially—when it is nothing but error, that underlies Bloom's lifelong, obstinate obsession with the idea that the subject, which stands behind the strongest literature, is the self equipped with extraordinary powers of lying. Its primal fantasies of autonomy, a strong investment in the *imago du nom propre* (image of the proper name), a wish for distinctness, the evasion of all hasty "solutions" to the paradoxes of its singular-general existence, and most of all a will to be *displaced* from the "place of truth," which is synonymous with death—all of these are based on the *art of lying*, lying as necessary existential cunning and skill.

This claim is interesting enough on its own, but it becomes truly fascinating when properly confronted with the traditional philosophical approach to subjectivity, which has always privileged the contrary subjective powers of gaining truth through knowledge. This privilege, however, has long been withdrawn. Modern philosophy, which had once erected a monument to subjectivity as a solid warrant of truth, pulled it down when the subject failed to deliver the anticipated epistemological revenues, thus leaving us suddenly with no *discursive sense of our selves.* Some may try to convince us, in a misguided belief that the harms done to subjectivity by philosophical theory can be undone only on the pragmatic principle of "least said, soonest mended," that we do not need a discursive sense of ourselves. Some would claim, paraphrasing Laplace, that they do not need such hypotheses, and they can do without any notion of subjectivity. But both these ways of silencing the subject are equally deadly for the subject, which is, above all else, a discursive entity; the subject renews itself only in a constant effort of self-interpretation, and its only cure is the *talking cure.* This book, therefore, attempts to *speak* about subjectivity *in der dürftigen Zeit.* For if the veracious subject, based on truth and self-knowledge, is no longer viable, perhaps the mendacious one—which not only suffers, but also actively *wants* error—will fare better?

The Lying Self

> After all, what is a fine lie? Simply that which is its own evidence.
> —Oscar Wilde, *The Decay of Lying*

> Only man can maintain an error in the world, by making it last in the form of a fictitious discourse.
> —Alexandre Kojève, *Introduction to the Reading of Hegel*

The moment we mention the cheating, lying, sneaking subject of literature, we leave the planet of philosophical trueness; to paraphrase the title of Bloom's Gnostic novel, now we take a risky "flight to Lucifer." We move into more daring speculatively areas that are partly beyond truth and falsehood.

Bloom's extrapolation of the literary lie in the domain of subjectivity, traditionally occupied by veracity in all its possible variations, is capable of radically changing the rhetorical register in which we discuss the fateful problem of the subject. It would be too easy to place him on the side of Homer and against Plato in the ongoing debate between literature and philosophy (although, as his latest work, *Where Shall Wisdom Be Found?*, attests, Bloom wouldn't mind such partisanship). It would be too easy, for his discovery of the *lying self* goes beyond this ancient opposition and creates perspectives from which philosophy, bound for so long to truth and truth alone, could finally begin to benefit. Deconstruction preferred literature to philosophy, but, paradoxically, by reason of literature's higher *philosophical* consciousness of the self, which knows that it inescapably loses its truth in the labyrinth of language. Bloom, on the other hand, privileges literature to any other kind of discourse by reason of its higher consciousness of the lie, which results in what he calls a "willing error," and which is his name for rhetorical figuration. In literature, the self knows that it is lying, and this knowledge not only does not stop it from lying but, quite the contrary, augments its will to do so. And the literary self, as we shall yet see, is the subject a fortiori: it consciously elevates the cunning of deceit to the highest state of art.

The subject's "strength," therefore, rests in its defiance to, evasion from, and lying against the whole of everything that exists—for the very reason that it *already* exists. Groucho Marx famously said, "Whatever it is, I'm against it," a quip often repeated by Bloom himself, who would lend it a philosophical twist by emphasizing the "is." Whatever it *is*, I have to lie against its existence, because the moment it springs into existence it already constitutes the burden and horror of the Nietzschean "it was." Whatever it is, I have to take my revenge on it for the sake of something new and singular for which there is no room in this overdetermined, Koheletian universe. In such a world, there is no *honest* way of creating anything new, for all honest methods have already been exhausted by God and his fatal *he war*, Joyce's German-English linguistic stroke of genius from *Finnegans Wake*, which tersely sums up what is at stake here: an agon with the warring God, who jealously created everything that was, is, and will be. "Is there any thing whereof it may be said, See, this is new? It hath been already of old time, which was before us," preaches the book of Kohelet. The self, therefore, does not have a ready-made, spontaneous Vision, a brand-new image of its inner truth that it wants to offer to the world; in fact, it exists only as an *error*, the Hegelian "pathology" of *die fühlende Seele* which *is* part of that repetitive world, but, at the same time, *feels*, without any ontological backup, that it is nonetheless particular and unique. The new and the singular can thus appear under the sun only *through lie*.

This wisdom—Adorno and Horkheimer call it "arid wisdom"[36]—is, in fact, skeptical, dark, and far less prone to idealize the creative-foundational powers of subjectivity than is classical philosophy. Still, it has the obvious advantage that, while it does not overestimate the subject, it has no reason to abandon it, despite its disappointments. The subject does not have a Vision of its own and no inner truth to offer, but it nonetheless *wants* to create a new image with which it could identify. To use the Buberian vocabulary, which was once very close to Bloom's heart (and despite his protestations, is still present in his writings as an idealistic, visionary, regulative idea of the process of revision): as it is, helpless and paradoxical, the subject has no power to turn "it" into a meaningful and dialogic "Thou," but this is precisely why the subject *must* become an "I." Not just for itself, but for the power of Vision, the power of—after Wallace Stevens's *Necessary Angel*—"seeing the Earth again," or *reseeing* it so it can show a different, more epiphanic and redemptive aspect than the bleak Koheletian universe of repetition and reduction. Thus, *pace* most of Bloom's critics we have just mentioned, it has to be stated clearly and emphatically that Vision and Revision are practically the same process: poet's becoming one and singular coincides perfectly with the awakening of his powers to "see [the world] again" as equally singular and fresh.[37]

At the beginning, however, the poet has nothing to back up the hubris of his individuation. The *truth* of his actual situation speaks utterly against him, turning his fantasy of visionary autonomy into, as de Man used to call it, a "fiction" (1979a, 201). And it *is* a fiction, but not one to be easily dismissed by truth-seeking philosophers. Having no Vision of one's own, no inner truth to tell, no ready salvation for the fallen, repetitive world at hand, no background for his individualistic hubris—the subject can nonetheless resort to *lying*, which will *displace it from truth*, and thus it enters a different ontological sphere, "rich in error," built wholly on a negative gesture of defiance (which, as Oscar Wilde nicely put it, "shows nature *its place*"). *Ich hab' mein' Sache auf Nichts gestellt* (I have put my cause on nothing), Max Stirner, the only truly consequent solipsist, famously remarked, and the inevitable touch of solipsism, with its *nichtig*, evasive and deceitful foundation, appears in the formation of every subjectivity. But the best the subject can do is to *forget* that it is based on nothing, reject the need for a foundation, and then go on as a *fine lie*, which—Wilde again—is able to sustain itself as its own evidence.

THE SCANDAL OF THE NAME

> And our name shall be forgotten in time, and no man shall have our
> works in remembrance, and our life shall pass away as a trace of a

cloud, and shall be dispersed as a mist, that is driven away with the
beams of the sun, and overcome with the heat thereof.
    —Wisdom of Solomon, 2:4

The oldest fear, that of losing one's name, is being fulfilled.
    —Horkheimer and Adorno, *Dialectic of Enlightenment*

And this is precisely where the ontology of the name comes in, the
ontology so often invoked by Adorno, who hoped to bring down with it
the dominion of concepts; by Benjamin, who believed that names have
meanings undetectable in the fallen languages of man; and by Derrida,
who would gladly submit all signs to the grinding mills of deconstruction, *sauf le nom*. The name is also the greatest, though implicit, hero of
Bloom's tetralogy, which deals with the strong poet's struggle to achieve
and preserve his name—not just his *life*, but his *name*—not *mere life*, but
the singular, remarkable *more life* whose name will never perish "in the
time without boundaries."

The scene of nomination is a curious paradox in itself that contemporary thought only just begins to approach. We are not given names
because we are being born new and full of ourselves—a truly self-reliant
philosophical subjectivity, left to its inner vision and presence, that never
needed a name and existed anonymously for ages—but because we
are lacking in the singularity that we are only instructed, through the
act of naming, to deliver. We are, in fact, asked to deliver both singularity and similarity, rupture and continuity, difference and repetition.
Hence, name-giving is a double bind that must be disobeyed in order to
be obeyed. The name signifies the claim to differ without any positive,
meaningful explanation for this difference. The name just stands there,
opaque and inexplicable in its distinction, strangely defiant, hubristic.
The name claims to belong to something that does not give away its right
to possess it, to be the proper name's proprietor. We can only assume that
it has the right to stand there and denote a unique being, whose uniqueness remains unknown to us. And the subject bearing the name is in an
even worse situation: he also remains unaware of the uniqueness that has
been imposed on him, as if from the outside, by the act of naming. *Le nom
oblige* (the name obliges) ... the obligation to be distinct and separate,
singular and new, despite the fact that there is nothing new under the
sun, is inscribed into the name as such. The subject of the name *suffers*.

Benjamin called man a "name-giver."[38] But isn't he first a "name-
bearer," so overburdened by the obligation that the name carries with

itself, projecting this unhappiness on everything that exists? To have a
name means to summon a force of negativity without any safeguard or
backup, that is, to be forced *to lie* against the whole of everything "which
was before," against all the images that fill our senses, all positive meanings given to things. To say, after Kafka, that "what is laid upon us is to
accomplish the negative; the positive has been already given,"[39] means
to express the heavy load of the name, which can only realize itself in a
pure, absolutely unfounded negativity.

So far we have dwelled on only one dimension of the paradox of the
name: the Lacanian-Hartmanian clash between the fantasy of the *nom
propre* (proper name) and the image of *le corps morcelé* (disarticulated body),
or the Hegelian universality of life processes that not only do not account
for this fantasy but testify against it. This aporia, however, has a deeper
layer that goes back to what Bloom calls the Scene of Instruction, the act
of giving the name, of nomination, annunciation, initiation, and vocation.
Its fundamental paradox consists in the fact that the name comes from
the outside: the imperative to become unique, to gather one's being made
of heterogeneous stuff into something distinct and singular, is not born
out of inner autonomy but via violent imposition, a traumatizing revelation. Harold Bloom believes that the moment in which a poet, instructed
by an older poet, acquires his poetic name, is both a catastrophe and creation, or, as he calls it in *A Map of Misreading*, a *creation by catastrophe*.

This scene—as Bloom himself often asserts—has its prototype in
God's instruction of Adam. Adam is made in God's image, which is to say
that to be God's *zelem* (image) means simultaneously to be like and unlike
God, to be a copy or replica that knows that the difference between itself
and the original is both irrevocable and elusive. God's image is imprinted
on Adam, yet Adam cannot be just like God: *sicut Dii* (you shall be like
gods) is the logic of Satan, who pretends to ignore the complex dialectic of zelem. Instruction, through which the name is given, is always a
double act as well as, to use Derrida's favorite expression, a double bind.
It overtly says: be like me, take my image, my vision—yet its clandestine
message is precisely the opposite: you are not me, so even in the most
faithful repetition you are bound to betray me.[40]

Derrida, who speculated a great deal in his later period about the
predicament of the name, found this scene of nomination-instruction
absolutely outrageous and unbearable. In *Sauf le nom*, he says:

> To give a name, is that still to give? Is that to give some thing? ...
> One can have doubts about it from the moment when the name

not only is nothing ... but also *risks to bind, to enslave or to engage the other*, to link the called, to call him/her to respond even before any decision or any deliberation, even before any freedom. *An assigned passion, a prescribed alliance as much as promise*. And still, if the name never belongs originally and rigorously to s/he who receives it, it also no longer belongs from the very first moment to s/he who gives it. (1995a, 84; my emphasis)

It is precisely this paradox of the name that, for Bloom, paralyzes even the most dialectical logic and, for this very reason, starts its own game of lying, escaping, evading, circumventing, deferring, and displacing the ambivalent message of the Scene of Instruction. "*Be me but not me* is the paradox of the precursor's implicit charge to the ephebe. Less intensely, his poem says to its descendant poem: *Be like me but unlike me*. If there were no ways of subverting this double bind, every ephebe would develop into a poetic version of a schizophrenic ... the double bind must be disobeyed to be obeyed" (*AI*, 70). And if Bloom ever insisted on the primacy of the Scene of Instruction over the Derridean Scene of Writing, it was *only* because of this postponing movement, which helps explain why we need *écriture* (writing); why, in escaping the voice, we choose to write. In the chapter of *A Map of Misreading* devoted to "The Primal Scene of Instruction," Bloom writes:

> Writing, as Derrida tropes it, both keeps us from the void and, more aggressively (as against voicing), gives us a *saving difference*, by preventing that coincidence of speaker with subject that would *entrap us in a presence so total as to stop the mind*. (*MM*, 43; my emphasis)

It seems, therefore, that the difference between Derrida and Bloom would not be so stark twenty years later, in 1993, the year in which Derrida's three essays on the name appeared, but a grain of discord would still remain. "What makes us write," Derrida notes in *Glas*, "is also what scatters the semes, disperses *signacoupure* and *signacouture* ... The bell tolls always for the idiom or the signature" (1981b, 192b). For Derrida, the way out of the aporia of the name, which distinguishes and simultaneously enslaves the recipient, is the maneuver of *dispossession*: once the name makes its way into the text, where it can be traced as a signature, it is no longer owned by either party. Writing, this miraculous *menstruum universale* (universal solvent), frees everything and dissolves all claims to ownership. The subject is *saved* when it frees itself from itself: it saves the name (sauf le nom: save the name) when it excepts itself from the own-ership of the name (sauf le nom: except the name). Hence, in Derrida, the moment the subject plunges into the realm of writing it immediately disappears as a narcissistic entity, obsessed with its *Meinigkeit* (mineness), thus liberating itself from the unbearable predicament of the name. In Hartman's apt comment, "Derrida views language as a School of Virtue chastening the eternally narcissistic ego" (1981, 110). In Bloom, on the contrary, the subject escapes into the realm of writing, away from the presence of voice, in order to save itself, save the name, and survive. The former sees the text as a domain thankfully free from the insoluble "paradoxes of narcissism" (Derrida 1995a, 12); the latter, on the other hand, perceives the text as the arena in which these paradoxes can only begin to untangle themselves in a process of differing and deferring, very closely resembling "Derrida's coinage, *différance*" (*MM*, 43). The unendurable presence of voice in the Scene of Instruction freezes the paradox of the name, which cannot move either closer to or away from the origin of voice: it is stuck between the two irreconcilable demands the instructing voice imposes (*annunciation* and *denunciation:* be like me, be unlike me). It is thus only in writing, which offers an infinite possibil-ity of displacement in "errors of figuration," that this aporia of identity and difference can be, if not resolved, then at least dealt with, worked-through: *durcharbeitet*.

This brings us once again to the discussion on Girard, which ended by comparison between the latter's stopping at the structuralist aporia and Bloom's dialectical use of psychoanalysis designed to pass beyond the impasse. Also Bloom's own version of the deconstructionist aporia differs from that of both Derrida and de Man. If, in the case of the latter, aporia is a question of the undecidability of meaning due to the loss of subjective control over language, in Bloom it has from the very beginning a distinc-tively Freudian flavor. Aporia is an "achieved anxiety," a symptom of the compulsion to repeat, which reveals two opposite "expressive needs": on the one hand, to return to the place of trauma and, on the other, to sever all genetic ties to the traumatic Scene of Instruction. When it leads to nothing but a futile clash of opposites, aporia is, poetically speaking, fail-ure. But as aporia becomes a *crossing*, a dynamic compromise formation, neither return, nor dissemination, but *displacement*, a new, integral figure emerges that, when truly "achieved," transgresses the initial contradic-tion and erases the path leading back to trauma.[41]

The name is pushed along the road of difference without wanting or expecting it: this is truly a *kata-strephein*, a "sudden turn." Its only task is to find a meaning for its difference, to fulfill the *imago du nom propre*, to pour a secret content into its empty shell.[42] The Scene of Instruction is a traumatic puzzle which simultaneously imprints the ephebe's unconscious with the precursory voice and demands of him to become worthy of his name (i.e., singular and unique). The precursor, therefore, nests itself in the ephebe's id and disowns it. "Freud, unlike Nietzsche and Derrida," says Bloom, "knows that precursors become absorbed into the id and not into the superego" (*MM*, 50). And somewhere else: "If fixation becomes the inscription in the unconscious of the privileged idea of a Sublime poet, or strong precursor, then the drive towards poetic expression originates in an agonistic repression, where the agon or contest is set against the pattern of the precursor's initial fixation upon an anterior figure" (*A*, 109).[43]

The id, therefore, becomes a "citation"—an *ibid.*[44] But not completely; there is still in the *it* the remainder of life that can never be fully subsumed by the power of citation. In all this flooding (Bloom's favorite metaphor of instruction), there remains one dry spot, designated by the name, which does not allow this inundation by the Other to become totally overwhelming, disowning, and alienating. This is precisely what makes Bloom's Scene of Instruction so different from Lacan and then Laplanche's theory of seduction; its inner ambiguity—*be like me, be unlike me;* between citation and nomination; between replica and proper name—leaves room for a defensive maneuver that cannot occur in a psyche totally and passively given over to the Other. This "dry spot" is precisely the part of id which Bloom wants to turn into a "new version of id," mingling with the ego: condoning the latter's repression of the "ib-id" and, already as *Erros*, prepared to *err;* that is, to displace itself into new realms of figurative individuation. To continue Santner's punning: while the id seized by the precursor may be called *ib-id*, thus the remainder of id coming into complicity with ego may be called *id-iom*. Where the ibid was, I shall become: where there was only precursory citation, my own idiom shall emerge.

And if all "honest" ways to do so are closed, the only way out is to enter the path of deceit. The "saving difference" that lies in writing is at the same time *the saving lie:* when philosophical truth cannot save the living self, only a "willing error" can do so.

Part II

Agon with the Deadly Angels

Chapter 3

Life and Death in Deconstruction: From Hegel to de Man

Tell all the Truth but tell it slant—
Success in Circuit lies
Too bright for our infirm Delight
The Truth's superb surprise
As Lightening to the Children eased
With explanation kind
The Truth must dazzle gradually
Or every man be blind—
        —Emily Dickinson, "Tell all the Truth but tell it slant"

Who could want to be . . . a memorial volume with a blurred inscription?
        —Søren Kierkegaard, *Repetition*

It is as if I were made of stone, as if I were my own tombstone, there is no loophole for doubt or for faith, for love or repugnance, for courage or anxiety, in particular or in general, only a vague hope lives on, but no better than the inscriptions on the tombstones.
        —Franz Kafka, *The Diaries*

Literary theorists often agree that Harold Bloom is somehow too idio-syncratic to be approached in what they may call a proper theoretical way. Being so contrary, almost to the point of a spitefulness that pushes him to write *in spite* of every possible received opinion, he puts him-self in the uncomfortable position of someone who actively hinders his own interpretation. His kabbalistically complex trope of poetic influence seems to be so closely linked to his own private idiom that it hardly survives as a *scheme*. It would almost seem that, by implicating his position in an endless, quasi-midrashic self-commentary, Bloom does not wish to be repeated or, at least, makes repetition extremely difficult. There is something in his idiom that resists repetition and defies all attempts to elaborate a "Bloomian theory," in which his own original inscription would have to be blurred in order to give way to abstract schemes.

Unlike de Man, who gave rise to a powerful school of deconstruction, Bloom's own effort to dismiss deconstruction never managed to bloom into a proper antideconstructive theory. The theoretical interest in Bloom waxed and waned in the '70s, trying and failing to repeat fruitfully what has been said in his famous tetralogy, and since then (i.e., from the beginning of the '80s), there has appeared no single serious attempt to continue Bloom's speculation.[1] This is why I do not propose here to repeat what from the very beginning was doomed to failure. I do not want to isolate a scheme based on Bloom's vision of influence; I intend to follow a different path of repetition. I wish to examine what made this failure inevitable, namely: Harold Bloom's most vitalistic ingredient, his famed *contrariety*.

Self-Sacrifice and Its Rewards

> This impossible position is precisely the figure, the trope, metaphor as a violent—and not as a dark—light, a deadly Apollo.
> —Paul de Man, "Shelley Disfigured"

> But what contributes most of all to this Apollonian image of the destroyer is the realization of how immensely the world is simplified when tested for its worthiness of destruction . . . No vision inspires the destructive character. He has few needs, and the least of them is to know what will replace what has been destroyed.
> —Walter Benjamin, "The Destructive Character"

It is easy to understand why de Man's writings could deliver a secure canvas for his pupils' philosophical elaboration, but it is a much more difficult task to understand Bloom's relative defeat. This difference, however, boils down to one seminal opposition: whereas de Man's theory is founded on the gesture of *renunciation*, the ascetic sacrifice of one's individual self, which acknowledges its own erasure in the moment of naming, Bloom's speculation relies on *defiance*, an equally archetypal, lingering gesture of refusal to offer one's own self for the benefit of abstraction. Whereas de Man's attitude is a complex contemporary version of the ascetic imperative that preaches truth as the highest value, however negatively or implicitly, Bloom's position is a revision of the Nietzschean antithetical ideal, which praises the value of resistance and, most of all, *a resistance to the temptation of truth*. And it is obviously easier to follow the pattern than to follow the resistance against the pattern; it is easier to be in the company of masters than in the impossible company of rebellious hysterics.

For Nietzsche, who at the beginning of *Beyond Good and Evil* famously stipulates, "Suppose truth to be a woman ... ," truth is feminine precisely because it poses the threat of seduction; like a woman, truth is a *Versuchung* (temptation) that "must, and cannot be, resisted" (Harpham 1987, 219). This paradoxical tension of the Nietzschean *Versuchung*, to which we must surrender, if only eventually and reluctantly, pervades the whole of Bloom's written corpus and sets it in a strong, though subtle, opposition to those more "ascetic" critics who, like de Man, have chosen truth more unequivocally in order to liberate themselves from *the anxiety of seduction*.

In the *Concluding Unscientific Postscript to "Philosophical Fragments*," Søren Kierkegaard reveals the gist of this opposition by drawing a clear demarcation line between the "objective knowledge" that demands instantaneous self-renunciation and what he termed a "singular truth," characterizing concrete, embodied subjectivity: "the sensuous soul" stubbornly sticking to her process of life despite all obstacles and contradictions. Says Kierkegaard, obviously against Hegel and his idealist approach:

> That the knowing spirit is an existing spirit, and that every human being is such a spirit existing for himself, I cannot repeat often enough, because the fantastical disregard of this has been the cause of much confusion. May no one misunderstand me. I am indeed a poor existing spirit like all other human beings, but if in a legitimate and honest way I could be assisted in becoming something extraordinary, the pure I-I, I would always be willing to give thanks for the gift and the good deed. If, however, it can occur only in the way mentioned earlier, by saying *eins, zwei, drei, kokolorum* or by tying a ribbon around the little finger and throwing it away in some remote place when the moon is full—then I would rather remain what I am, a poor

existing individual human being ... The way of objective reflection
turns the subjective individual into something accidental and thereby
turns existence into an indifferent, vanishing something. *The way to
the objective truth goes away from the subject.* (1992, 92; my emphasis)

Paul de Man, whose deconstructive theory proved a lasting, lifelong target for Bloom's stubborn antitheoretical resistance, is for Bloom as Hegel
was for Kierkegaard. Wrestling with de Man had been as important for
Bloom as his revisionistic effort to dispel the influence of Lacan, or perhaps even more so: it would be difficult to imagine a more contrasted pair
of thinkers, yet *A Map of Misreading,* the second book of Bloom's tetralogy, was nonetheless dedicated to his distinguished Yale colleague. The
same thought as in Kierkegaard, who refused self-sacrifice for the benefit of theory, but with the opposite valorization, appears in de Man's
early text from 1953, "Montaigne et la transcendence" ("Montaigne and
Transcendence"): "Without this *sacrifice,*" says de Man, meaning the necessary renunciation of one's individual self, "there can be no truly objective
knowledge" (1953, 1015), and it will not be an exaggeration to say that
the whole of his career, devoted to perfecting abstract schemes of future
deconstructive strategies, has fully confirmed this early existential choice.[2]
    Whereas Bloom's choice was radically different from the very begin-
ning. He sides with Kierkegaard, who challenged the motif of "necessary
self-renunciation" and attempted to make true the very reverse of the
objective knowledge, that is, the principle according to which *the way to
the subjective truth goes away from the object.* And Bloom, following Freud,
makes this challenge even more dramatic. The subjective truth not only
has to "go away." It has to *run* away, *evade* the objective influence, *outwit*
its natural advantage, *swerve* from truth into error, and find its dark path
"in the wilderness" of *misprision,* past the reach of objective knowledge.
The stake of all those risky procedures is the very opposite of thinking
which "turns existence into an indifferent, vanishing something": it is
"the subjective way" of reflection that creates a rhetoric whose tropes
are deliberately "life-enhancing." This is why Bloom's perception of the
major theoretical difficulty will also differ from de Man's. Whereas de
Man locates *temptation* on the side of subjectivity's "lethargic" belief in
its own powers of self-expression and *renunciation* on the side of rhetorical askesis, which is wise enough to abandon all hopes of authenticity,
conceived by de Man as a grave epistemological error—Bloom sees *temptation* along Kierkegaardian lines, as an easy way out from the paradoxes
of concrete subjectivity, and *renunciation* as a painful process which resists

the lures of objective knowledge and stays within the dubious realm of "errors" and "lies." Far from being "lethargic" and complacent about his "subjective way," Bloom becomes militantly theoretical—although his theory is, philosophically speaking, a *paradox* which constantly revises its own impossibility as—to use Wallace Stevens's phrase, forming a motto to *The Anxiety of Influence*—a "theory of life."[3]

This does not mean, however, that he comes closer to the truth, or that he can demonstrate the falsity of the de Manian practice of "mere reading." As de Man himself asserts without any conceit, a properly conducted rhetorical reading of a text is always right, and there can be no error in deconstructing errors committed by the blind desire of writing.[4] Bloom does not try to approach de Man on his own ground by contesting the very idea of this ground; he rather follows Wittgenstein, who gave up fighting skepticism within its own premises and moved the whole discussion to a wider plane of language as *Lebensform* (form of life). Like the author of *On Certainty*, which ironically denounces certainty as the main objective of philosophical reasoning, Bloom wants to move beyond the aporias of traditional epistemology. He prefers to talk about truth as his adversary (as well as the adversary of all strong poets) and falsity as a saving lie—and all this in an emphatically "extra-epistemological sense."

De Man, on the contrary, remains faithful to epistemology. His choice of "self-renunciation" remains within the spell of the Hegelian concept of language as, first of all, annihilating its reference, with this only difference that, unlike in Hegel, it never gives anything instead. For if the idealist tradition rewards renunciation of one's living self with the magical discovery of "pure consciousness," in de Man this sacrifice merely reveals "the primacy of fiction" (1979a, 201), an essential intangibility of life looming behind the pseudonym of the singular self. And "I" truly is a *pseudo-name*, for it names nothing: its pseudo-reality has to be undone either by proceeding to a higher level of selfhood, the transcendental *reine Ichheit* (pure I-ness), or by unmasking its essential nothingness. The romantic self, therefore, as reconstructed by de Man, differs from the idealist self in only one respect: instead of rising to a higher reality, it paradoxically asserts itself by demonstrating its own impossibility. "The Self as the relentless undoer of selfhood" (ibid., 173) rises above the fictitiousness of its own life, but does not enter any new realm of ideal existence. There is no "subjective way," but, in knowing this, the romantic self becomes as superior to its former existential naïveté as is the Fichtean-Hegelian "pure consciousness" toward the earlier stages of *die fühlende Seele*. It is superior, for it reaches "the higher truth of the untruth"; it begins to know its status of a mere fiction. The self-sacrifice is necessary, even if the "objective knowledge" it brings amounts to a purely "negative insight."

As Rodolphe Gasché explains in his book on de Man's philosophy, *The Wild Card of Reading:* "For de Man deconstruction amounts to negative cognition . . . it is an invitation to endlessly and in an infinite process debunk the totalizations of knowledge, *its own included*" (1998, 27; my emphasis). It is thus constantly engaged in the tautological, circular, Ourobouros-like motion of undermining its own master position, which nonetheless always poses itself as a possibility. And all this motion "takes place, indeed, in the name of the 'higher' truth of *the untruth*, the lie that metaphor was in the first place" (ibid., 56). Gasché shyly puts the adjective "higher" in ironic inverted commas, but it is, I think, a needless caution; the master position of truth, even as negative as de Man's, is an inevitable reward within the logic of self-renunciation.

Bloom's constant reproach to de Man goes exactly along this line: de Man's position, despite all his deconstructive persuasion as to the uncontrollable nature of language, generates nonetheless a typically epistemological, *operative* illusion of meta-discourse whose function is to *get hold of language:* arrest its chaotic movement of eternal parabasis and take it under control. Says Bloom in *The Anxiety of Influence:*

> Any stance that anyone takes up towards a metaphorical work will itself be metaphorical. My useful (for me) decades-long critical quarrel with Paul de Man, a radiant intelligence, finally centered upon just the contention stated in the previous sentence. He insisted that an epistemological stance in regard to a literary work was the only *way out of the tropological labyrinth*, while I replied that such a stance was no more or less a trope than any other. Irony, in its prime sense an allegory, saying one thing while suggesting another, is the epistemological tropes of tropes, and for de Man constituted the condition of literary language itself, producing that "permanent parabasis of meaning" studied by deconstructors. (xix–xx; my emphasis)[5]

Yet, it would be unfair to attribute to de Man a naïveté as to a possible metarhetorical position which would allow a "way out" of the tropological labyrinth of errors. In fact, this is precisely his argument against Nietzsche, who, according to his reading of *On Truth and Lie in Extra-Moral Sense*, did not manage to resist the lure of mastery—he was not "ascetic" enough—and turned his higher rhetorical consciousness into yet another instrument of subjective control. It would seem that de Man knew very well what he could be reproached for and thus attempted to exorcize the threat by wrestling with the thinkers from whom it most likely comes, that is, Nietzsche and his pragmatist-vitalist followers. On the other hand, it can also be said that de Man's constant caution as to the possibility of reestablishing the vantage point of mastery and control merely confirms such a possibility as a danger already incipient in his "unerring" method of reading, and that his unceasing effort of self-deconstruction asserts that such a position has indeed been *constructed* and therefore constantly needs undoing. His theory, therefore, has to be incessantly reminded that it cannot constitute itself as a theory and therefore it should abrogate its "totalizing" ambitions. This "disruptive *Selbst-Setzen* [self-constitution]," to use Gasché's phrase, results in the curious oscillation of de Man's position, which shimmers ambiguously between absolute humility and absolute superiority.[6]

In trying to secure his ambiguous upper hand, de Man criticizes Nietzsche's dealings with rhetoric as too overt in his intentions to take control over language. As he says in *Allegories of Reading:*

> For this deconstruction [i.e., Nietzschean] seems to end in reassertion of the active performative function of language and it rehabilitates persuasion as the final outcome of the deconstruction of figural speech. This would allow for the reassuring conviction that it is legitimate to do just about anything with words, as long as we know that a rigorous mind, fully aware of the misleading power of tropes, pulls the strings. (1979a, 131)

Yet, his own insistence on correcting the errors of writing too often produces an image of such a "rigorous mind" whose knowledge of rhetorical tricks allows him to pull the strings of the buffo theater of language. This rigor may be now purely negative and revel in the tautological truth of the un-truth, but it does not change radically the stance of mastery, which is taken here with an even more assured self-certainty. He explicitly states that

> all rhetorical structures . . . are based on substitutive reversals, and it seems unlikely that one more such reversal over and above the ones that have already taken place would suffice to restore things to their proper order. *One more "turn" or trope added to a series of earlier reversals will not stop the turn towards error.* (ibid., 113; my emphasis)

But his own reversals frequently remind one of the ultimacy of Platonic inversions which claim to undo the shadowy reflections of the linguistic mise en abyme and head straight for the final truth. The more often he emphasizes that no vantage point is possible, the more pregnant becomes the self-defeating effect of negative mastery which practically puts an end to the abyssal self-mirroring of tropes. This truth may not be a vulgar truth of an academic skepticism, which bluntly contradicts itself by saying that there is no truth, but still it *is* a kind of ultimate truth which reaches the farthest ends of "the negative insight." The master position, with its metalanguage taken out of the labyrinth of tropes, reemerges, again and again, with a mechanical obstinacy of a Russian Doll. The more you push it down, the quicker it springs back. In the case of de Man, the "ascetic" logic of self-sacrifice and mastery is particularly perspicuous because the latter builds itself on the former directly, as its immediate reverse.[7]

It is precisely this logic—the system of seemingly necessary sacrifices and subsequent compensations that lead to the emergence of all sorts of "higher" master positions, hovering over the clatter of life—that Bloom will fiercely fight against.

THE SPLENDID HYSTERIC AND HIS MASTERS

> Man in his human, i.e., speaking existence, is nothing but *death*, only self-consciously deferred.
> —Alexandre Kojève, *Introduction to the Reading of Hegel*

> I have tackled the function of speech in analysis from its least rewarding angle, that of empty speech, where the subject seems to be talking in vain . . . If we now turn to the other extreme of the psychoanalytic experience . . . we shall find that . . . to *obsessional intrasubjectivity* is to be opposed *hysterical intersubjectivity* . . . The realization of full speech begins here.
> —Lacan, *Écrits*

The Nietzschean anxiety of *Versuchung* and his mistrust in the master discourse of truth situates Bloom very close to the position of the Lacanian hysteric, who is also characterized by his (or rather her) resistance to the seduction of authority, a resistance that is all the stronger the fewer reasons there are for resistance. To resist truth means to defy the most irresistible of all authorities and, clearly, for no reason at all, because all reasons, by definition, have to belong to the authority of truth.

Moreover, potraying Bloom as a stubborn hysteric is a move deliberately aimed at confusing the feminist critique, which inadvertently perceives Bloom as elitist, masculinist, or racist, and "the strong poet" as the very summation of dead white maleness. Putting Bloom's hero as well as Bloom himself in the shoes of the Lacanian hysteric gravely complicates the gender issue, for the position of the hysteric is traditionally the one of the woman who rebels against the patriarchal domination of the master. In my account, therefore, the strong poet and his or her theorist begin as "women" faced with the overwhelming splendor of their precursory patriarchs. And even if they end by achieving some sort of mastery, it is never the self-assured position of the Lacanian master who identifies with the power over discourse.

Thus, there is nothing pejorative in calling Harold Bloom hysterical. If there is one obvious characteristic of the hyperbolic, sublime, rhetorically overcharged style in which all his books are written, it is certainly *splendid hysteria*. Lacan, whom Bloom studied carefully, assigned a special role to the language of the hysteric, which he opposed to the language of the master. In fact, the hysterical language, compared to the roundness of the master's discourse, is only paralinguistic: it hovers on the edges of discourse in order to make itself heard by the master in, as Wallace Stevens would have it, a set of "intricate evasions." At the same time, however, the hysteric is someone who, by rebelling against seduction and absolute dependence, simultaneously *asserts* the fact that he or she had been seduced and made totally dependent on the other. A hysterical, paradoxical tension marks the passage from the bad faith of a falsely isolated ego, which fashions itself as autonomous, to a budding, reluctant awareness of this truth. It is here, in hysteria, that "the obsessive *intrasubjectivity*," the empty shell of a self-deluded inwardness, gives way to "hysterical *intersubjectivity*," in which the absolute dependence on the other makes itself known for the first time and begins to take shape in the intimations of "full speech."

For Lacan, however, the only value of the hysteric is that his or her hyperbolic resistance to the scene of seduction, despite its being "made up of lies" and full of militant, hectic deception, leads to "the birth of truth in speech" (1989, 47) to the revelation of an inescapable, absolutely primary, intersubjective influence. One needs only to break down the hysterical paradox of the *resistance to truth* to reveal its precious kernel, *the truth itself.* From the perspective of therapeutic progress, a hysteric is thus better than an obsessive neurotic, for she does not delude herself about her autonomy, even though she would fight for it with hopeless anger, spite, and despair. This anger, spite, and despair, however, are the last contradictions that need to be solved before the analysis reaches ultimate truth. But from the point of view of a hysteric, they are the last bastions of resistance to, as Derrida called it in his critique of Lacan, "the lure of truth," the hysteric's last exertion against truth's dead, masterly, matter-of-fact authority.[8]

The hysteric, as Lacan asserts in his *Ethics of Psychoanalysis,* is a person who "wants to come alive in her own sphere" (1992, 255). This phrasing has its obvious negation, which says that the hysteric does not want to *die* in the sphere that is not her own, but that belongs to the Other, the sphere of the anonymous *ça parle,* "it speaks." What motivates the hysteric is not the master's (and, most notably, the psychoanalyst's) question of truth and error, but the vital question of life and death; not the question of *logic,* but the fateful question of *ethics,* which comes from a different dimension, that of the singular being confronted with his or her particular suffering. The hysteric wants to be alive, she does not want to die, and the stage on which this emphatic wish comes to the fore to clash with reality is language, the everyday, the most common situation of speech: the grinding "Satanic mills" of words that derive their validity from the neutralized *ça parle.*[9]

The evidence of language as a "well-oiled machine" (Lacan 1992, 255) of anonymous generality is one of these blinding—castrating, in the psychoanalytical idiom—truths that constitute the very essence of the Law, the human law that, in its sternness, imitates the most intransigent law of nature, the law of death. The death-drive that organizes the rhythm of natural existence is also responsible for taming the anarchy of human desire; "everyone must die" translates here into the ordering principle according to which *everyone must die in language.* The *ça parle* becomes the dominion of Thanatos, which offers a passage from *lex naturalis* (natural law) to a new, unnatural form of law, still propped against the old law. Thus, just as sexual pleasure leans on the self-perpetuating functions of life, the first and strongest inhibition, which initiates psyche into the realm of law and order, leans on death. The hysterical resistance to the necessity of dying-in-language therefore amounts to defying the most fundamental truth, which forms the very center of the human universe: the person who says "I" does not want to die by saying it, but desires to come alive in her own sphere, which, ideally, would be the sphere of her own private language. She wants to speak, but not in the masterly terms of *ça parle*; she wants to speak her own idiosyncratic idiom, of which she, and not the Other, would be the proper subject. For the hysteric, therefore, the act of saying "I" is never a straightforward giving in to the necessity of law: "From its beginning," Lacan says, "the 'I' as thrust forward in an antagonistic movement, the 'I' as defense, the 'I' as primarily and above all an 'I' that refuses and denounces rather than announces, the 'I' in the isolated experience of its sudden emergence— which is also perhaps to be considered as its original decline—this 'I' is articulated here" (ibid., 56). Bloom comments that, in this manner, "subjectivity combines its own abdication and the birth of the symbol" (*AI*, 81), but does so unwillingly, resentfully, spitefully.

Since Nietzsche, the main issue of the subject has concentrated not on the Cartesian ownership of certainty, but on the relation to language: "*Who* is speaking?" is the right question here, also for the Lacanian hysteric. The antagonistic motion of refusing to be absorbed by the neutral *ça parle* hovers in the air for the short moment of its articulation, and then, once the meaning of the spoken word "I" reveals itself, vanishes. The initial cry passes into linguistic utterance, the shadow of original defiance passes into an ordered *logos*, and the sudden emergence of the singular self passes naturally into its decline. The Lacanian hysteric is stuck in a barren repetition that offers no hope of breaking through the enemy line of the linguistic killing machine. Just like the primitive form of life in Freud's *Beyond the Pleasure Principle*, the hysteric's "I" springs to life in order to disappear almost simultaneously with the act of its emergence.

This analogy is not just a rhetorical embellishment. As we will see, it is essential to understand how a hysterical resistance to the Law can ultimately prevail and constitute more complex forms of *survival-in*-language, indeed as complex as those Freudian organisms that had managed to emancipate themselves temporarily from the law of death and survive for a period long enough to establish a new way of being, something called "life proper." This Lacanian—or rather, already Bloomian—revision of the Nietzschean question, *who is speaking?* shifts the whole problematic from the traditional domain of mastery into the domain of survival. The issue now is not the subject who masters the language it speaks, but the subject who manages to survive in language long enough to establish a new idiom—or, in other words, to die in language, *but* to die in its own fashion. Wishing to live, yet at the same time facing imminent death, the hysterical "I" can only count on a miracle for survival, that is, on living long enough to postpone the moment of its inevitable decline.

Survival is a peculiar category, absolutely central to Freudian speculation. By surviving, life accepts the final sentence of death, yet in delaying this sentence it manages to find its own place. Survival gets beyond the simple dualism of life and death, for it admits the priority of the economy of death in which life becomes no more than a temporal deviation, a postponement of the ultimate verdict. In their interpretations of *Beyond the Pleasure Principle*, both Derrida and Bloom agree that human life is human only insofar as it is pervaded by death, that it is a "life death—death life" in which Eros and Thanatos, desire and danger, are so closely intertwined that the very process of living becomes indistinguishable from the postponement of dying. The human life, painfully finite, plagued from early on by the fear of death, impregnated by the seed of death, merely "survives," merely "lives on," by sending itself—or, as Derrida would have it, by *posting itself*—to its final destination along a circuitous route that delays, as long as possible, the moment of delivery.

The whole point of survival, therefore, consists in turning the moment of delay into something less futile and more positive, less destructive and more enabling, not just a waiting for death, which *returns* with the force of an ultimate, irresistible truth that was known and merely denied from the outset. The speculation based on the concept of survival wants to take the notion of defiance in face of the obvious truth to its logical limits; it wants to reward the resistance of the evident and inevitable. This is precisely what Freud, and his later ephebes, Bloom and Derrida, try to achieve. Derrida casts himself against the oppression and "the lure" of truth by taking the liberty of dissemination, thanks to which all truths become suspended (*relevé*), and nothing simply dies or lives anymore, especially in language. In this manner, Derrida secures his version of survival by annulling the lethal agon in which the singular, hysterical "I" stands no chance. Bloom, on the contrary, stays in the agon, endures it, and as long as his resistance lasts, he asks for nothing but a temporary displacement from deadly truths. Bloom's strong poet is not someone who would take command of language in the Nietzschean fashion (Nietzsche, after all, was a hysteric typically dreaming of becoming a master), but rather someone who would wrestle to survive in the murderous domain of language and use "the intricate evasions" of rhetorical tropes as defensive mechanisms against the always imminent danger of death. And if Bloom limits his speculation to strong poets it is certainly not because he is so damned "elitist," but because the strong poet is an emblem of what we could call, without too much pride, the *almost successful hysteric:* someone who did not submit to the dubious logic of self-renunciation and masterhood and gave a clear, if spiteful and ungrounded, *No* to the seemingly necessary. And this prolonged, obstinate nay-saying is as crucial here as was Nietzsche's postagonistic, half-ecstatic, half-resigned *Ja-Sagen* (Yeah-Saying):

> For every poet begins (however "unconsciously") by rebelling more strongly against the consciousness of death's necessity than all other men and women do. The young citizen of poetry, or ephebe as Athens would have called him, is already the anti-natural or antithetical man, and from his start as a poet he quests for an impossible object, as his precursor quested before him. (*AI*, 10)

The strong poet, therefore, is the embodiment of early Nietzsche's antithetical ideal, whose dignity rests in fighting the seemingly necessary, seemingly irresistible *Versuchung* of truth. But even more importantly and originally, the strong poet is also an incarnation of the unnatural man of Hebrew Exodus. Exodus, *yeziat mizraim*, was the revolutionary idea that promised to lead men out of the house of bondage, the dark Egypt of nature and its hopelessly circular laws, with their eternal, motionless return to themselves. The daring of the strong poet is based on pure hubris (or, if you like, chutzpah): he is willing to commit an error in order to escape what appears to be an inescapable truth. Will and error, combined in Bloom's favorite figure of a *willing error*—or, simply, a *lie*—constitute the gist of his "high argument," which is "that strong poets are condemned to just this *unwisdom*" (*AI*, 9–10). They cannot be too wise *too soon*, for this would amount to embracing the teaching of "happy substitution" and "second chance," which promises to free the subject from his impossible quest for "the real" and satisfy him with an achievable surrogate. "Poets as poets," Bloom writes, "cannot accept substitutions, and fight to the end to have their initial chance alone" (*AI*, 8).

The strong poet, therefore, is the Lacanian hysteric par excellence. He does not want to die. That is, he wants to come alive in his own sphere, made by him alone, in his absolute *priority*, which means, put on the proper poetic plain: he does not want to die in the language "as it is," as it "has been done"—the Nietzschean "it was"—but to come alive in his own language of here and now, in which he would be able to *name* himself without the alienating intervention of the Other, who wants him to follow the logic of initiation, based on self-sacrifice. In Lacan's system this wish can never be gratified because of the absolute intransigence of the logic of initiation into language: one must die as a living self and enter the symbolic sphere where he can eventually reconstitute one's lost sense of vital power by becoming a master. In Bloom, however, the ephebe-hysteric is less doomed, precisely because he can contest the very logic of initiation. Against the total seduction, he will "answer back with his own defensive discourse":

> I find it curious how many modern theorists actually talk about poems when they assert that they are talking about people. Lacan defines the Unconscious as the discourse of the Other. That is a fine trope, though probably it is gorgeous nonsense ... Had Lacan said that *poetry* was the discourse of the Other, he scarcely would have been troping. If I can invoke a somewhat greater and more central man, then I question also the grand formula that Poetry is a man speaking to men. Poetry is poems speaking to a poem, and is also that *poem answering back with its own defensive discourse.* (*KC*, 108; my emphasis)

This leads Bloom to a less static picture than what we find in Lacan. For Lacan, desire is stuck in the hopeless repetition of its own apriorical failure: it negates itself the very moment it gets articulated. The sooner it moves beyond that stage, the better from the therapeutic point of view. Bloom's strong poet, however, *uses* repetition as the vehicle of his stubborn subversion, which Bloom calls a process of revision: "Conceptually, the central problem for the latecomer necessarily is *repetition*, for repetition dialectically raised to re-creation is the ephebe's road of excess, leading away from the horror of finding himself to be only a copy or replica" (*AI*, 80). Repetition, the ephebe's "royal road," expresses both "stuckness" and a move forward, a certain Kierkegaardian "recollection forward" that constantly works on and for the difference. Here, repetition is a sign of resistance to the logic of initiation that demands self-sacrifice for the sake of sublimation. As we have already suggested in the previous chapter, Bloom's scene of instruction differs from Lacan's scene of initiation because of the ambivalence of the message; the ephebe is being instructed by the precursor who himself refused to walk the ordinary path of renunciation and obedience in order to safeguard his living singularity. The ephebe's instruction comes not from the Nobodaddy of the abstract *ça parle* but from the singularized other who spoke a powerful idiom. Lacan's scene of initiation, however, also contains ambivalence, but of a different kind: it points to a lack of authority in the real other the child is being subjected to, which can be reinforced only by revealing its continuity with the true Other Lacan calls, after Hegel, "Death, the absolute Master."

LANGUAGE AS A DEATH KIT

> This is the tremendous power of the negative; it is the energy
> of thought, of the pure "I." Death, if that is what we want to call
> this non-actuality, is of all things the most dreadful, and to hold
> fast what is dead requires the greatest strength. Lacking strength,
> Beauty hates the Understanding for asking of her what it cannot
> do. But the life of Spirit is not the life that shrinks from death
> and keeps itself untouched by devastation, but rather the life that
> endures and maintains itself in it. It wins its truth only when, in utter
> dismemberment, it finds itself . . . Spirit is the power only by looking
> the negative in the face, and tarrying with it.
> —Hegel, preface to *Phenomenology of Spirit*

> In fact, Man is only too well aware that he is condemned to death,
> but not to suicide. Yet this philosophical recommendation can
> truthfully recommend only suicide, not the fated death of all.
> —Franz Rosenzweig, *The Star of Redemption*

Is the strong poet doomed to failure the moment he begins his resistance, or does he stand a chance? Indeed, the whole setup of contemporary, mostly post-Heideggerian philosophy seems to write off the existence of a strong poet as an a priori impossibility. The "I" must die in language, lose itself in signifiers, and complete the work of mourning over its eternally lost referentiality, also abandoning the hope that it will ever regain itself as the power of fresh and generative name giving. This issue becomes particularly pressing—at least for us, more or less successful hysterics, who still care about the fateful question of the subject or what comes after it—if we concentrate on one special and philosophically privileged case of the deixis, the naming of the "I," the indication of the existence of the singular living self *in speech*. In fact, the vicissitudes of this one special case of reference may be responsible for the development of all of contemporary post-Hegelian thought. Hegel writes in *Phenomenology of Spirit*, in the chapter on the French Revolution called

"Culture," which deeply influenced Hegel's reception in twentieth-century France:

> In speech, self-consciousness, *qua independent separate individuality*, comes as such into existence, so that it exists *for others*. Otherwise the "I," this *pure* "I," is non-existence, is not *there*; in every other expression it is immersed in a reality, and is in a shape from which it can withdraw itself ... Language, however, contains it in its purity, it alone expresses the "I," the "I" itself ... The "I" is this particular "I"—but equally the *universal* "I"; its manifesting is also at once the externalization and vanishing of *this* particular "I," and as a result the "I" remains in its universality. The "I" that utters itself is *heard* and *perceived*; it is an *infection* in which it has immediately passed into unity with those for whom it is a real existence, and is a universal self-consciousness ... *This vanishing is thus itself at once its abiding*; it is its own knowing of itself, and its knowing itself as a self that has passed over into another self that has been perceived and is universal. (1977, 308–9; my emphasis).

This fragment contains in a nutshell all the problematics we have discussed thus far: the subject cannot content itself with sheer self-affectivity; it cannot, the way the beautiful soul does, contemplate its *Seinsgefühl* (sense of existence) mutely; it has to plunge into the intersubjective realm of speech, in which it becomes "infected," or "contaminated." Its particularity has to pass the test of death, only to be reborn as a universal, infinite pure "I." In his analysis of hysteria, Lacan repeats Hegel's diagnosis, introducing at the same time, however, a temporal difference that really makes the difference: unlike in Hegel, the lethal test of language does not purify the subject of its particularity. In fact, language does not allow the singular subject to constitute its particularity in the first place. There is no *Aufhebung* (sublation), for there is simply nothing to be sublated, and, simultaneously, nothing to be *regained* at the higher level of linguistic expression. The truth of the subject is the moment of its birth in death. In its beginning is its end.

Hegel was the first thinker to notice the strong connection between the natural law of death, which governs the universe of material things, and the non-natural law of reason, which rules the world of Spirit. In Hegel's system, the former was nothing but an alienated form, or the *Anderssein* of the latter. Death, by returning all particulars to generality, performs in the sphere of matter the same function language fulfills in the universe of rational thought.[10] Here, rationality is nothing more than the passage from the world of lively and direct, sensual experience to the icy realm of conceptual abstraction: the chaotic richness of *sinnliche Männigfaltigkeit* (sensuous manifold) has to die if it is to be resurrected in the order of concept. And this resurrection is as important as death, which serves here as a ritual of linguistic initiation. In Hegel's proud account, man is "the master of death": he manages to tame its power of negativity, which destroys the immediately given, and to subordinate it to the process of restoration, crowned by an emergence of the historically rich, concrete concept, which, indeed, will regain the creative power of the Adamic original name. Death, once it is mastered, emancipates man from the passivity and the oppression of the fallen senses by granting him access to the universal from before the Fall. The true reality of reason can only reemerge from the ruins of the sensual.

Since Hegel, the close identification of death and language has become a staple of modern philosophy. It has been reinforced by the decline of Hegel's own positive dialectics in the strongly deidealized reading of *Phenomenology of Spirit* undertaken by Alexandre Kojève, on the one hand, and on the other by the emergence of Heidegger, who had shifted death into the very center of his philosophical thought. Now, however, man cannot portray himself any longer as a "master of death"; quite the contrary, after Heidegger's intervention, it is death which gains "absolute mastery," commanding only one attitude of man—equally absolute *Gelassenheit* (releasement), a resignedly affirmative acceptance of death's "truth-saying" final *ver-dict*. The pupils of Alexandre Kojève (who will soon become the leading voices in contemporary continental philosophy) fuse two visions of death—Hegel's and Heidegger's—into one, which proves to be a truly "lethal" combination: Bataille explicitly praises "dying" as the only sovereign moment of human existence; Blanchot and de Man after him talk about the death of the author as the prerequisite of getting into a postmortal "space of literature"; Derrida deconstructs the Husserlian notion of an immortal "transcendental life" by claiming that only experience of death can lead to the activity of representation; and Lacan advocates the destruction of the individual ego as the necessary condition of reaching the truth of our "subjection to the Other" who is nobody else but "Death, the absolute master." Here, the thanatic tendency of late, posttriumphant modernity reaches its extreme. Modern life discovers its own irreversible finitude—*die Endlichkeit*—only to find itself totally "arrested" by its verdict (like in Blanchot's famous story *L'Arrêt de mort*, meaning both "arrest" and "sentence" of death). It begins to perceive itself as nothing but an error, an unjustifiable delay in face of the pressing, overwhelming truth of death which is always already there, from the very beginning, ready to terminate life's aberration. It is as if this deathbound thinking rediscovered Schopenhauer saying: "At bottom every individuality is only a special error, a false step, something that would be better had it never existed; indeed, it is the actual purpose of life for us to recede from it" (1958, 491–92). It is precisely here, in this shock of finitude, that the second-wave, death-driven deconstruction we have mentioned in our introductory chapter truly originates.[11]

Two words occur most frequently in Blanchot's writings. One is "death," as in *Arrêt de mort*, or *L'instant de ma mort* (*The Instant of My Death*). The second is "step," as in *Faux pas* (*The False Step*), *Le pas au-delà* (*The Step Not Beyond*), but also, as the ambiguous French *pas*, in *Celui qui ne m'accompagnait pas* (*The One Who Does Not Accompany Me*). The ambiguity of *pas*, both "step" and a negating particle, is highly significant. For *pas* in Blanchot is necessarily paradoxical: it is at once a dance move and a move of withdrawing from the dance, an act of thrusting forward and an act of immobilization. Here, every *step* is immediately a *stop*—as indeed in Schopenhauer, a *faux pas* and simultaneously an error, a tactless overstepping of order and etiquette. Once it recognizes itself as blunder, it immediately freezes. Every step is thus an impossible *pas au-delà*: the futile effort of "stepping beyond" that automatically "stops" and turns into its own inhibition—"nothing beyond."[12]

This paradox of false stepping results from the highly significant inversion of Heidegger's concept of death; *Being and Time* defines death as the "possibility of impossibility," whereas Blanchot reverses the formula and redefines it as the "impossibility of possibility." Heidegger writes, in reference to the ultimate *Möglichkeit*, which is death:

> The more unveiledly this possibility gets understood—the more purely does the understanding penetrate into *Dasein as the possibility of the impossibility of any existence at all.* Death, as possibility, gives *Dasein* nothing to be "actualized," nothing which *Dasein*, as actual, could itself *be* . . . Being-toward-death, as anticipation of possibility, is what first *makes* this possibility *possible*, and sets it free as possibility. (1962, 307)

Prima facie, it would appear that death works here as a positive factor of authenticity, even a form of heroism, in conducting one's life as the persistent and resolute realization of one's *Vermögen* (potency) in the face of the final possibility of nonexistence. Death, the paradigmatic and primordial possibility, lies at the core of all other possibilities *as* possibilities: *Dasein* learns what it means to *be able* to become this or that by anticipating that it *can* die. The realization of its finitude motivates it to act and decide, that is, to plunge boldly into the modal universe of the possible.

But Blanchot reverses Heideggerian formula to show the essential ungroundedness of its heroic resolutness. The necessity of death cuts through all of *Dasein*'s projects and reveals their truth, as *mere* possibilities, as something possessing only a passing, modal, shaky kind of being that pales in comparison to what is truly unconditional. Death, therefore, is not something possible. It is instead a primordial necessity that manifests itself as the impossibility of any possibility. More than that, death signals an altogether different way of being (if this is still the right word), an alternative side of existence, which Blanchot designates in *Space of Literature* as a *nunc stans* (now) of "dying" in the never-ending present continuous:

> It is the fact of dying that includes a radical reversal, through which the death that was the extreme form of my power not only becomes what loosens my hold upon myself by casting me out of my power to begin and even to finish, but also becomes that which is without any relation to me, without power over me—*that which is stripped of all possibility*—the unreality of the indefinite. *I cannot represent this reversal to myself*, I cannot even conceive of it as definitive. It is not the irreversible step beyond which there would be no return, for it is that which is not accomplished, the interminable and the incessant ... It is inevitable but inaccessible death; it is the abyss of the present, time without a present, with which I have no relationships; it is that toward which I cannot go forth for in it I do not die, I have fallen from the power to die. In it *they* die; they do not cease, and they do not finish dying. (1982, 106, 154–55; my emphasis)

This reversal—not accessible to "me," but perhaps to what Blanchot in *La part du feu* (*The Part of Fire*) calls "consciousness without a subject," a fleeting, instantaneous consciousness of the Hegelian-Kojèvian master facing death, not yet encumbered by slavish subjectivity—shows the other face of death as the *nunc stans* of dying, the abyss of the present without a present. Its consequences are far-reaching. In Blanchot, already influenced by Heidegger's *Kehre* (turn), death becomes a factor that is decidedly less enabling and more disempowering, paralyzing. The impossibility of possibility announces from the start that all projects undertaken by *Dasein* are futile; the (non)presence of death discloses the fundamental impossibility of the moment of *decision* in which *Dasein* resolves to be something rather than nothing. This resolution appears insignificant when confronted with the verdict of finitude; death, instead of mobilizing *Dasein* to activity, reveals the irremovable *Nichtigkeit* (nothingness) that pervades and therefore *nichtet*, "annihilates," its inner possibilities. Hence the step *Dasein* takes to make its decision to be something rather than nothing is, in fact, impossible. Overshadowed by the higher truth of death, every step emerges as false, as an error needing correction. It becomes a paradoxical move of *passing*, of retreat and self-negation in the face of the higher *ratio*, according to which *there is nothing rather than something*. By problematizing every decision as decision, death invalidates every possibility as possibility, and above all else it negates the basic ambition of *Dasein* to lead *its own*, truly authentic existence. Death is an abyss of anonymity, in which it becomes impossible to say "I." This very step, the most fundamental among *Dasein's* projects, which strive to confirm the *Jemeinigkeit* (ever-mineness) of its *Angst und Sorge* (anxiety and concern), meets the strictest prohibition. "You shall not say 'I'" is the first and last of death's commandments, in light of which all other restrictions seem merely secondary, if not simply spurious. There is no escape from the verdict of anonymity: "'I' never die but 'one dies,'" Blanchot says (1982, 241).[13]

This Blanchotian revision of Heidegger's concept of death, which pushes it toward its implicit primordial negativity, reflects immediately on Hegel's theory as well. The triumphant assumption that man can master death, still vestigially present in Heidegger's heroic attempt to turn death into a crucial experience of authenticity, is rejected. We are now left with the bare destruction of *das Diese*, the sensual content of experience, together with the concrete presence of the one who speaks, without any hope of their future resurrection. "How can I, in my speech, recapture this prior presence that I must exclude in order to speak, in order to speak it?" Blanchot asks in *The Infinite Conversation* (1993, 36). I cannot, there is no such possibility. "When I speak," notes Blanchot in the essay "Literature and the Right to Death," "I deny the existence of what I am saying, but I also deny the existence of the person who is saying it . . . Language can begin only with the void: no fullness, no certainty can ever speak; something essential is lacking in anyone who expresses himself. Negation is tied to language" (1995, 324). But language not only begins, it also ends with the void: death, by definition, cannot be domesticated, mastered, or made instrumental. Once its absolute negativity is "let loose," it derides all efforts at control; it is the unmasterable per se. Just as in the dialectics of master and slave, any attempt to exploit death's negative power merely reinforces death's dominion over language. Language, instead of forming a newly resurrected order of things, becomes entrapped within the grip of death; instead of creating the new law of day, it remains for ever in the *nyx*, the law of night, ruled by the paradoxical non-*arche* (non-origin) of death, an element of entropy and dispersion. Death still has a liberating effect, for it leads away from the erring spectacle of false being. But with the demise of Western metaphysics, it shows no way toward resurrection. There is no longer any true reality behind the fallen one, just true nothingness; no true beings behind their appearances, only an *Abgrund*, the Heideggerian abyss of nonbeing.

Mastery is always on the side of death, which can never be forced into a positive form of *Setzen* (constitution). As in Blanchot's story, *The Light of the Day*, the Hegelian day of reason, seemingly so strong and autonomous, appears in fact to be maintained, encompassed, and pervaded by a strange, at once blinding and darkening radiance that comes from beyond it and has a capacity to subvert it at any time. Thus, when language names—this cat, or this woman, to use Blanchot's favorite examples—by the very act of naming it destroys what it names, without giving anything in its place. The words become funeral inscriptions of their designates. And while the writer can, with some degree of sorrow, accept the killing of "this cat," or even of "this woman," since every lost object may be forgotten sooner or later, the destruction of "the one who speaks" in the funeral inscription of "I" must cause him infinite and unspeakable pain. The deadly arrow of language hits where it hurts most: where the living, singular self desires, in Lacan's words, to "come alive in its own sphere," and thereby to secure its own, proper name. "I say my name," Blanchot writes closely echoing Kierkegaard, "and it is as though I were chanting my own dirge: I separate myself from myself, I am no longer either my presence or my reality, but an objective, impersonal presence, the presence of my name, which goes beyond me and whose stonelike immobility performs exactly the same function for me as a tombstone weighing on the void" (1995, 324). This notion of the experience of writing as the late modern version of the Hegelian "tarrying with the negative" will find a nearly verbatim reiteration in one of the catchiest phrases of Derrida's *Of Grammatology:* "Writing in the

common sense is the dead letter, it is the carrier of death. It exhausts life"
(1976, 17).

All of Derrida's work shows a never-waning fascination with the
Hegelian-Heideggerian conceptual—implosive rather than explosive—
mixture, which transforms language into a highly efficient "death kit."
As early as in *Speech and Phenomena*, Derrida develops this idea against
the Husserlian dogma of the "transcendental life" by ingeniously showing that the whole edifice of Husserl's transcendental construction must
crumble, for it cannot secure the full development of an intentional
meaning to its foundation, the transcendental ego. Saying "I" remains,
therefore, the most irritating misuse of language, which has to content
itself with *Anzeigen*, the lame and subservient linguistic function of indication, instead of evolving into a mature type of *noesis* (cognition). For
when scrutinized phenomenologically, the word "I," being the most general of words, immediately reveals its pathetic inadequacy: more than
any other *das Diese*, it clearly demonstrates what Derrida, after Hegel,
calls "the effect of inscription," that is, the effect of a lost reference, a
rupture and break with the phenomenal reality inherent to language
as language. "When we read this word 'I' without knowing who wrote
it," Husserl writes in *Logische Untersuchungen* (*Logical Investigations*), in
the fragment that Derrida turned into an epigraph to *Le voix et le phé-
nomène* (*Voice and Phenomenon*), "It is perhaps not meaningless, but is at
least estranged from its normal meaning." Performing a close reading
of the word "I," paying attention to the rhetoricity of language that de
Man would call "mere reading," pushes us away from the "normal sense"
we naively assume to indicate the concrete self that uttered the word "I."
In fact, it pushes us so far away that we are ultimately left with the very
opposite of its "normal" intention: a dreary general concept so sparse in
content that it is almost devoid of meaning.

This one case of naming, so crucial and fundamental, proved particularly resistant to Husserl's attempt at turning all deictic signs into
fully meaningful intentions. "I" has remained the most stubborn occasional token, refusing transformation into a living, concrete pleroma of
sense. Despite all the attempts to establish an immanent and discursively
autonomous sphere of the transcendental I, *this* I, says Derrida, by the
very persistence of its naming, remains linked to the psychological self,
which appears to be the most evasive of all indicated beings. It preserves
its vague occasional quality but, as in all cases of deixis and this one in
particular, this circumstance is rather what Lacan described as a missed
occasion or missed encounter (1979, 53): the phenomenal reality of the

self becomes erased the moment it is referred to. The erasing effect of inscription, which may pass unnoticed in more indifferent demonstrations of *das Diese*, is especially poignant here, since the word "I" appears as a blatant contradiction of what it pretends to stand for. Inscription becomes what it was originally: a funeral eulogy, an epigram that says, "It was, and it is no longer," or rather, because its lettering begins to blur immediately into a hardly recognizable trace, "It is not, so was it ever?" Derrida writes:

> Whether or not perception accompanies the statement about perception, whether or not life as self-presence accompanies the uttering of the *I*, is quite indifferent with regard to the functioning of meaning. My death is structurally necessary to the pronouncing of the *I*. That I am also "alive" and certain about it figures as something that comes over and above the appearance of the meaning . . . *The statement "I am alive" is accompanied by my being dead*, and its possibility requires the possibility that I be dead; and conversely . . . The anonymity of the written "I," the impropriety of the *I am writing*, is, contrary to what Husserl says, the "normal situation." (1973, 96–97; my emphasis)

For Hegel, this very contradiction was the positive moment of deliverance, as he made absolutely clear in his *Encyclopedia of Philosophical Sciences*, where he repeats the argument on *das Diese* in the chapter devoted to "Anthropology," in application to his three concepts of the human soul. The crucial stage of liberating self-erasure appears with the passage from *die fühlende Seele* to *die wirkliche Seele:* from the sensuous soul, which is already self-reflective but still bound to its physical existence, to the real soul, whose reality consists in identification with the free, purely negative energy of spirit. And the first, truly redemptive act of negativity, in which the newly born spirit asserts its power over the sensual world, is the negation of the physical, particular, here-and-now being of the sensuous soul. The *real* I is born the moment it *kills* its affective particularity. Either one lives—or one speaks; the gap between life and language is an abyss that cannot be bridged. "The death of the animal is the birth of consciousness."[14]

But of all thinkers who took this Hegelian sentence to their theoretical hearts, it is certainly de Man who went further than Bataille, Blanchot, or Derrida, Hegel and Kojève included. By engaging in a true *askesis*, he secretly aimed at controlling the incontrollable, that is, of assuming the position of death itself: an identification forbidden but, at the same time, perversely suggested by Hegel and Lacan, who talked about Death as the absolute Master. "But there is nothing false about the Law itself, or about him who assumes his authority," says Lacan in a divinely tempting fashion, drawing a thin line between *becoming the master*, which is forbidden, and *speaking in the name of the master*, which is encouraged (1989, 311). Bloom's prohibition of metalanguage in the cento quoted earlier can be said to derive directly from Lacan's additional restriction: "No meta-language can be spoken, or, more aphoristically, there is no Other of the Other" (ibid.), and it is openly addressed against those who, like de Man, toyed with usurping the Master position in the moment of the ascetic self-sacrifice, thus hoping for a reward—the masterly jouissance—that is strictly prohibited. "And when the Legislator (he who claims to lay down the Law)," continues Lacan, "presents himself to fill the gap, he does so as an impostor" (ibid.). For Lacan, therefore, we are doomed to err in language and produce figures of an infinite, unquenchable desire because *none of us* can ever assume the master position of death. De Man, on the other hand, who identifies with "deadly Apollo," acts precisely as an impostor: as a master of the sacrificial ceremony of language, he administers death of meaning and reference, turning language into a sacrificial body, an eerie "material event" which substitutes for the lost reality of representation. From Lacan's, as well as Bloom's, point of view, it is strictly impossible to take a stance that would stop the defile of signifiers and still the life of desire in language: even death, as in Falstaff's game of pretence, would be nothing but another figure of desire, another error of figuration. "One more 'turn' or trope added to a series of earlier reversals will not stop the turn towards error," says de Man seemingly in harmony with the Lacanian-Bloomian proscription of metalanguage (1979a, 113), yet, in fact, merely to suggest a forbidden way out—out of the labyrinth of tropes and straight toward death, which exposes the erroneous nature of tropological desire.[15]

De Manian pleasures are thus illegal jouissances of this impossible, self-defeating mastery: of crossing the thin line between humble submission to death's authority and triumphant identification with death's position, the ultimate vantage point of *imitatio mortis* (imitation of death). This is why de Man's language is so pervasively "thanatic," peppered with metaphors of death and deadness, obsessed with the "thingness" of language. In his characteristically strong misreading of Walter Benjamin's "The Task of the Translator," de Man praises the "killing" type of interpretation that should underlie every translatory practice, also offering a model for the practice of mere reading:

[Translators] disarticulate, they undo the original, they reveal that the
original was always already disarticulated ... *They kill the original, by*
discovering that the original was already dead. They read the original
from the perspective of a pure language (*reine Sprache*), a language
that would be entirely freed of the illusion of meaning—pure form if
you want. (1986, 84; my emphasis)

The "pure form" of language reveals itself after the ultimate sacrifice
of the deictic function; it is as if an astral body of language, a different, more sublime variant of materiality which becomes manifest only
after language had disentangled itself from the distraction of *showing*.
And in the course of the development of his theory, De Man's obsession with the Hegelian critique of deixis gradually becomes his leading
motif: "Literary History and Literary Modernity" from *Blindness and*
Insight, "Sign and Symbol in Hegel's Aesthetics" from *Aesthetic Ideology*,
and the latest "Resistance to Theory" and "Hypogram and Inscription"
are the crucial essays where de Man constantly returns to and reasserts
his radicalized version of Hegel's rejection of *das Diese* by turning it into
a general thesis of language's principal incapacity to capture the moment
of here and now. The lie of the "living metaphor" has to be exposed,
so the true, ascetic substitution can finally take place. Says de Man in
"Hypogram and Inscription":

> Particularity (the here and now) was lost long ago, even before
> speech. Writing this knowledge down in no way loses (nor, of course,
> recovers) a here and now that, as Hegel puts it, was never accessi-
> ble to consciousness or to speech. It does something very different:
> unlike the here and now of speech, the here and the now of the
> inscription is neither false nor misleading: because he wrote it down,
> the existence of a here and now of Hegel's text is undeniable as well
> as totally blank. (ibid., 42)

Although totally blank, the inscription is neither false nor misleading. It
substitutes for the real "here and now" not by representing it in a trope
but, precisely to the contrary, by renouncing and sacrificing any claim to
referentiality; it is what it *is*, in a pure form of language, and only for this
short instant *out of the labyrinth of tropes*.

But only death can give this vantage point, this privileged epistemological position where all rigor is ultimately a rigor mortis: a final
slumber that seals the spirit of living language and turns into a pure,

dead body that neither hears nor sees. De Man's practice of sacrifice is by far the highest achievement of the ascetic ideal and the most complete testimony of a thoroughly accomplished work of mourning one can encounter in today's humanities, plagued by the melancholy sense of loss—of God, man, and meaning. There is no trace of sorrow or concern left in his "apathetic formalism," which silently conducts its painstaking *work of death* by purging the act of reading of erroneous desires. Here, as in "whack the weasel," life is hit on its head the very moment it dares to emerge on the surface of language. De Man, to repeat again our opening theme, might have started with the traditional gesture of self-renunciation but, as Benjamin's paradigmatic "destructive character," rigorously accepted *nothing* instead. He turned the theme of loss into a theme of ultimate liberation, and opened himself to the initiating effect of death which sealed him in the *reine Sprache*, where only one voice can be heard: the voice of the Lacanian thanatic jouissance, clamoring that existence is nothing but an error in a purity of nonbeing.

What remained of Hegel in his contemporary revisionists, despite all the differences between them, is thus the sheer *effect of liberation*, but without its positive consequences. Death, as the driving force of language, offers no mastery over the truly real world of universal concepts, but it nonetheless maintains the power of initiation. The passage from the stage of *die fühlende Seele* to the stage of the pure, empty, and negative "I" releases the former's tensions and insoluble contradictions.[16] Hegel mocked the romantics, his greatest adversaries, for investing in the illusion of a "richness" suggested by their sensuous souls and their affective images, forever unable to comprehend the lethal negativity of language. The same can be said of today's deconstructionists, who deride the postromantic perseverance of the phantasm of authenticity as precisely *the phantasm*, a chimera engendered by a false totality of *die fühlende Seele*, which, like the camel of the Gospels, can never pass through the gates of enunciation. Unless it becomes free and is stripped of all its "riches," it will never enter the kingdom of language. There remains, as there had been in Hegel's time, a good reason for the deconstructionists' laughter, but then again, aren't they a little quick to situate themselves in the comfortable position of the master?[17]

Bloom obviously partakes of this "romantic," hysterical obstinacy; he *is* the camel who refuses to honor the Law of the Passage and insistently pushes his subjective *Belastungen* (encumbrance) into the eye of the needle, leading to the postmortal space of signs. The true romantic can thus be recognized by a stubborn repetition that "stupidly" renounces the higher truth of the linguistic initiation: "Monday—I; Tuesday—I; Wednesday—I . . ." This series, which Witold Gombrowicz wrote in his diary, is the perfect blueprint for such a bare, obsessive reiteration, which apparently conveys nothing more than typically hysterical anger, frustration, and despair. The longer the series goes on, the more evident its imminent emptiness becomes, its vain effort of "becoming alive in its own sphere." From the Hegelian point of view, this obstinate repetition merely strengthens the unbridgeable aporia with which the self clashes head-on, unable to find a detour that would circumvent the blockage. The moment of articulation here is automatically, in Lacan's words, the moment of decline and dispersion; the effect of inscription turns the singular self into what Kierkegaard called "the memorial volume," a token of absence and defacement with a quickly fading signature. But repetition means also—*taking time*. It means resistance in the face of the seemingly inavoidable, making a detour, postponing the verdict.

The Power of Error

> Making of the detour the temptation itself.
> —Maurice Blanchot

> Therefore Error became fortified. It elaborated its own Matter in the Void.
> —Valentinus, *The Gospel of Truth*

Is it possible to find a detour here, or is the self forever doomed to clash with the deadly aporia of its linguistic articulation? Can the self take a longer, lingering route that would save it, at least for a while, from the perils of language? Can it turn repetition, until now an expression of its paralyzing frustration, into a creative vehicle? Or, to shift this question back onto the Freudian plane, must the self be like the primitive life form that rises only in order to perish, to submit instantaneously to the highest law of death?

   Bloom, as a strong revisionist of Freud, begs to differ on this matter. Just like the others in the deconstructionist "crowd," he accepts the general frame of the whole debate about the aporetic relationship between self and language, but unlike them, he boldly plays Freud *against* Heidegger (and a Heideggerized Hegel), enhancing rather than effacing the differences. From a logical point of view, stating the aporia should be enough to relinquish all attempts of self-expression and dismiss them, in the de Manian fashion, as nothing but fiction. But from the ethical point of view—the peculiar ethics Lacan talks about when dealing with hysteria—logic proves to be insufficient. There appears a different *ratio*, a kind of Pascalian *raison du coeur* (reason of the heart), or, perhaps even better, Trillingian "reason of life" that at least allows us to postpone and complicate the verdict of logic. Moreover, as we will see, the difference on which Bloom insists is simultaneously the difference that allows for an ingenious retroping of the conflict between Athens and Jerusalem. Thanks to Bloom's emphatic effort to antagonize Freud and Heidegger, this clichéd opposition once again has a chance to come to light as a "vital hypothesis."[18]

It must be stressed again and again, however, that Bloom's defiance of the truth of self-renunciation does not necessarily lead him toward a radically opposite standpoint that naively invests in the self-expressive powers of the singular "I." On the contrary, his position is far more subtle, for what he rejects is not the very impossibility of self-expression but the a priori character of a predetermined, fated verdict discouraging any foray into the land of the impossible. Bloom's wisdom—which he likes to call "the wisdom of literature" instead of the dreary logic of philosophy, that "stuffed bird" (Moynihan 1986, 28), or even, as we have already seen, simply "unwisdom"—derives not so much from the total *rejection* of theory, but from a lingering, postponing *resistance* to theory where timing, neutralizing the horror of a priori, predestined aporias, plays a crucial role. Time, an ambivalent factor in Bloom's writings, is thus a two-faced cherub. It renders all contenders for the name "I" necessarily belated, arriving always at the moment when language has already belonged to others before them, but it also allows them to play with the strategy of belatedness and to accept the otherwise inevitable, though "only later." It is therefore time that creates a special dimension of the resistance to theory, of the "not yet" and "not now" that delay the moment of capitulation, of defying theory's apodictic and timeless truths. Time may thus be a Gnostic archon, forbidding singular selves their desired priority. But it is also, to use Shelley's subtler language from his *Defense of Poetry*, "a healer," which eases the tyranny of apriorical verdicts.

We learn more about impossibility, Bloom says, when we engage with it, that is, when we turn it into, in Emerson's words, "golden impossibility," a great, if not totally successful, occasion. For Bloom, saying "I," being able to utter this most occasional of words, is precisely such an adventurous, golden occasion, which simply cannot be renounced, even if it is ultimately doomed to failure. We thus learn about aporia not via theoretical, a priori insight into the nature of language, but always a posteriori, via "the path." The blockage has to be experienced as such, that is, as *trauma*. It is therefore not enough to reiterate, after Gombrowicz, "I, I, I . . . ," but it is also not enough to declare any attempt to close the discrepancy between the word "I" and the living self as a hopeless "fiction," a dualism that sounds suspiciously easy. "The path" Bloom talks about is more paradoxical than aporetic, in the crucial Blakean sense, turning paradoxes into the very opposite of "blockages," that is, into vehicles of dynamism and daring. "The Reflections upon the Path" that close *The Anxiety of Influence* mention that "in the story it only says one need come upon the place," and that "riding three days and nights he (the poet, the ephebe, the daring one who hasn't yet given up) came upon the place but decided it could not be come upon" (157). This "place," this here-and-now of the singular self that wished to name itself in a language no other self has ever used before, remains a missed occasion, a reference that can only be circumstantially hinted at, but never fully captured, though it also remains the dark center of all motion, without which it would not be discovered as *missed*, as a place that cannot be come upon. The difference, therefore, between de Man's sole statement of self-expressive fallacy and Bloom's painful conclusion is like the difference between indifferent *apatheia* and engaged *pathos*; between theory, which from the beginning assumes the futility of all resistance, and the resistance to theory, which stubbornly postpones the moment of surrender.

Timing allows a deferral that, prima facie, is nothing more than error. This is the crux of the difference between Bloom and deconstruction and, at the same time, of their closest, if agonistic, convergence. The use of deferral associates Bloom with Derrida, the use of error with de Man—although, deep down, Freud is the common source of this affinity. For Freud, life is both the postponement of nonlife and simultaneously an error, a defensive evasion of the traumatic ultimate truth. The deferral of life, therefore, takes place due to an error, a failure to face the truth, a swerve from the reality principle, but also a refusal to sublimate too soon, that is, to surrender by death to the powers of generality. Borrowing emblems from the Lacanian *bestiarium*, we could say that the strong poet begins as a hysteric but gradually develops into, alternately, a neurotic, constantly reexperiencing the power of repression, and a pervert, finding secret ways to satisfy his forbidden libido. Giving up sheer resistance, he eventually embarks on a complex play with the bequeathed language in which "the irregular intervals" (*AI*, 78) of his cunning detours create both a *dependent* and, at the same time, *singular* idiom. Bloom writes:

> Strong poets necessarily are perverse, "necessarily" meaning here as if obsessed, as if manifesting repetition compulsion. "Perverse" literally means "to be turned the wrong way"; but to be turned the right way in regard to the precursor means not to swerve at all, so any bias or inclination per force must be perverse in relation to the precursor ... To swerve (Anglo-Saxon *sweorfan*) has a root meaning of "to wipe off, file down, or polish," and, in usage, "to deviate, to leave the straight line, to turn aside (from law, duty, custom)." (*AI*, 85)

The strong poet, therefore, is an exaggerated version of the incurable "polymorphously perverse disposition," which Freud discusses in his *Three Essays on the Theory of Sexuality*, someone who, like Milton's Satan, rallies whatever remains to him—all pathologies at hand, all the power of the rebellious and the negative—and despite his better judgment demands his own share of enjoyment. He will summon all power of error to give himself enough time to survive. From the master's point of view, error can be nothing more than just error. Yet from the perspective of the oppressed singular self, error is anything *but* error, for it is the possibility of a new beginning, of a singular, distinct life. This is why, Bloom argues, "the strong poet's imagination cannot see itself as perverse; its own inclination must be health, the true priority" (*AI*, 85).

From the Gnostic perspective, the error of life partakes of the metaphysical scenario of all being, which comes into existence through a cosmic mistake. Here, the final say goes to Goethe's Mephisto, the purely rational spirit of negation who sees no reason for being and therefore speaks in the name of perfect nothingness. The very creation is nothing but error, *so wär's besser, daß nichts entstünde:* it would be better—wiser, purer, more logical—if no being emerged, so we, the rational minds, should act (Mephisto continues in his famous monologue) as if no being really, truly existed. We can thus deny, say no, and negate in the name of the highest logic, which gives no reason for the act of being; we can assume this sublimely aloof position and cease taking into account the fact of existence, which now erases itself as an error. *Der Geist, der stets verneint*, the spirit who says no, is therefore not just a minor spirit seeking perverse revenge against the splendor of God's creation, but a more primordial spirit of the pre-abyss who overrules the error of being. His authority is greater and more original. His is the primary way of nonbeing, the *nunc stans* of the present without presence, the never-ending "dying" in which absolute flux coincides with absolute stasis. Here, everything remains in constant motion, undercutting the stability of constitution and decision necessary for any being to emerge. Every constitution is nothing but a "disruptive *Setzen*," an act that automatically undermines itself, and every decision a faux pas, a false step/stop of immediate self-cancellation.[19]

It is, therefore, Mephisto who is the governing spirit of the Blanchotian postmortal "space of literature," in which every word is doomed forever to mourn the absence of what it stands for. He is the ruler of the mise en abyme, the Derridean, mirrorlike structure of language that dissolves its referentiality in self-effacement. And it is clearly for his benefit when Derrida says ironically, and cryptically, "I have never wanted to abuse the abyss, nor, above all, the *mise 'en abyme'*" (1987, 382). His is "the stony gaze" of the de Manian *Überleser* (Overreader), which hovers over the miscarried creation of texts and, by dispatching their constitutive errors, reverses their futile run toward being and returns them to where they came from and should have remained, to the abyss of undifferentiation.[20] And it is he who guards the impossibility of any possibility by fostering his sublime *ratio*, which Rodolphe Gasché, in the analysis of late Heidegger and his influence on de Man, has aptly called "the higher truth of the untruth" (1998, 56).

The structure of temporality, in which *being and time* are nothing but the *omission and oblivion* of the more primordial, abyssal truth of the essential impossibility of being, is the most characteristic feature of Heidegger's thinking. The error of existence stems merely from the fact of Being's own withdrawal, which allows itself to be forgotten by beings that can enjoy the illusion of their stability and separation only to the extent that they temporarily forget where they came from. *Seinsvergessenheit* (forgetfulness of being), which is the movement of *Seyn* (being) itself, and not just a mistake of Western metaphysics, is the forgetfulness of truth, which allows beings to be, that is, to endure, for a while, in their error: *Seinlassen* (letting be) is thus a purely negative gesture, a kind of an ontological negligence. Beings come to being when they forget Being as the impossibility of beings.

In Derrida's textual paraphrase, mediated by the works of Maurice Blanchot, this principle translates into the truth of the impossibility of writing: texts come to being only when they emerge from the oblivion of their purposelessness. Paradoxically, Orpheus, who should be constantly devoted to his orphic *nyx*, the poetic night of the senses, is able to write a song only in the instant of betrayal and "carelessness" dictated by his desire: his brief glance at Eurydice, whose presence is simultaneously captured and dissolved, is a generative moment of writing. The writing, says Blanchot, can be engendered only within the *nyx*, the abyssal matrix of texts, yet it also needs a seed of the external that is brought by forgetful, careless desire. And desire here *is* the synonym of Heideggerian oblivion; desire is nothing but a force of disregard for the paralyzing truth. The deferral of truth, momentarily blinded by desire, allows texts to be produced, but the act of reading, which is conducted simultaneously with the act of writing, returns them to their original night. As Derrida says about Blanchot's *Le pas au-delà*: every *pas*, "step," suggesting a move forward, springing "beyond" primordial nothingness, is immediately a *pas*, a "non" of the Mephistophelian *Verneinung* that erases and reverses, thus ultimately leaving only a trace of the aborted will to being. Like all beings in Heidegger, all Derrida's writings cancel themselves in the moment of reading, which is also recollecting. And the same motif is echoed by de Man's belief that only self-mystification on the part of the writer can lead to the act of writing; the writer who is, at the same time, his own reader would not be able to move. Being and writing are errors of oblivion. Nothing will save them once the truth is recollected.

There is something tautological about Mephisto's self-assuredness: his reasons are unimpeachable. He is well aware that he is right insofar as there are no convincing answers to the question of why there is something rather than nothing. His is the privilege of orthodoxy, that is, of rightness and straightness at the same time—of rectitude: his is the straight way, while being and life are on the Nietzschean "crooked path." His undoing of all existence is thus normatively justified, and death, as the final and sole possible meaning of life, without which it remains a meaningless error, is his closest ally and helper. His "straightening" practices lie behind, to use Milton's concluding lines from *Paradise Lost*, every "wandering step" of life, which they transform back into a negative faux pas that closes every possibility as possibility. Hesitancy is the attribute of life. When Adam and Eve, freshly expelled from the happy fields of their virtual nonexistence, "with wandering steps and slow, through Eden took their solitary way," they are not sure whether they should deplore or rejoice the opening horizon of the whole world before them. Dead assuredness is, on the other hand, the attribute of death.

Would it be an exaggeration to say that epistemology has always been thanatic and looked awry at the erring spectacle of life? It is precisely for this reason that Bloom, in his revelatory essay "Freud and Beyond," from *Ruin the Sacred Truths!*, reconfirms his dislike for philosophy, which has always been "interested in dying," and, by contrast, his sympathy for what he calls *speculation*, a different kind of wisdom that, in the Spinozan fashion, "meditates rather on life than death."[21] Freud, despite his postromantic, Schopenhauerian pessimism, belongs to the latter category of brilliant speculators, whose minds wander along the meandering, errant path of life. Rather dismayed than judgmental, Freud agrees that life is an error, but at the same time he draws no conclusion that would unambiguously privilege the truth. If anything, it is the other way around: he seems predisposed to save this error *as error* from the tyranny of truth and to stick loyally—as a speculator, and not as a philosopher—to the defenses of life. In *The Psychopathology of Everyday Life*, Freud openly calls these defenses *superstitions*, though without any intention to dispel them as mere errors: "My own superstition has its roots in suppressed ambition (immortality) and in my case *takes the place* of that anxiety about death which springs from the normal uncertainty of life" (SE 6, 260; my emphasis). To this, Bloom comments: "Against the literalism and repetition of the death-drive, Freud sets, so early on, the high figuration of his poetic will to an immortality" (*LF*, 27). Freud, therefore, *displaces* the normal anxiety about death with an erotic troping of a promise that can never be thwarted by anything literal, even the reality of his own death. Bloom concludes his reading of *Beyond the Pleasure Principle*: "A final sublimity is achieved, and though literal death is *accepted*, the figurative promise of a poetic immortality *returns* even as the figurative appears to be cast out" (ibid., 26; my emphasis). Should Freud's decision be regarded simply as a therapeutic concession in face of the acknowledged finitude of life? Or is there a new notion of temporality that gives chance to the errors of deferral, which would not be confused with mere oblivion or omission?

FROM ERROR TO ERROS: FREUD CONTRA HEIDEGGER

> Death is great.
> We are in his keep
> Laughing and whole.
> When we feel deep
> In life, he dares weep
> Deep in our soul
> —Rainer Maria Rilke, translated by Walter Arndt

After the exhaustion
Of all possibilities of non-being,
There emerged—being.
                    —Miron Białoszewski, "Nothing to Admire"[22]

It has become almost a matter of routine to talk about affinities between
Heidegger and Freud, between *Sein-zum-Tode* (being-unto-death) and
the death-driven life of *Beyond the Pleasure Principle.*[23] And indeed, the
analogy between the two thinkers seems absolutely overwhelming. Both
are obsessed with death and its various disguises. Heidegger thinks one
thought only, his compulsive *Seinsdenken* (thinking of being): a great
speculative tribute to the Novalisian "death in blue," the mother-abyss of
nothingness. Freud, if we are to believe Ernst Jones, wouldn't pass a day
without a nagging, depressive twinge of memento mori, which gradually
grew into his main obsession (1961, 279).

   Is this because they were both steeped in German Romanticism, in the
Rilkean images of the Great Death, to which "we belong"? Rilke's powerful short poem could easily work as an epigraph to both *Being and Time*
and *Beyond the Pleasure Principle.* In both Heidegger and Freud, death
is not just a marginal anticipation of doom: we belong to it, it is in us,
unforgettable, especially when we believe we are in the midst of life. In
Heidegger, death is ever-present from the beginning, as the basic token
of human finitude, *die Endlichkeit*, which blatantly contradicts Husserl's
dogma of the infinite "transcendental life."

   In Freud, the death obsession develops slowly. It first appears in
his reflections on "The Economic Problem in Masochism," where he
struggles to understand how pain and fear can bring pleasure. Then it
reemerges in *Three Essays on the Theory of Sexuality* (1905). Finally, after
a long period of latency, it resurfaces with the force of great revelation in *Beyond the Pleasure Principle* (1920). Jean Laplanche, offering a
seminal reading of this most philosophical of Freud's essays in *Life and
Death in Psychoanalysis*, says that "we find in this text a new, entirely original, and even unheard-of conjunction of the different modes of what
might be designated, in all its generality, as the 'negative': aggression,
destruction, sadomasochism, hatred, etc." (1976, 106–7). Indeed, here
the power of the negative breaks through all the barriers of Freud's
earlier enlightenment progressivism, turning his neat, therapeutically
responsible universe upside down: the death-drive, until now tamed and
minor among other psychic energies, suddenly becomes "a universal
force largely transcending the fields of psychology and even life itself: a

cosmic force that would irresistibly bring more organized forms regressively back to less organized ones, differences of level to a generalized equality, and the vital to the inanimate" (ibid., 107). Always there, contemplated and repressed on a daily basis, death suddenly comes back augmented and demonized, as Freud's most intimate *das Unheimliche* (the uncanny).

As the unstoppable, entropic drive within all beings, the death-drive certainly resembles the Heideggerian *Nichtigkeit*, the stream of nothingness flowing through everything that came to exist only for a short while. This certainly is the line of Laplanche, who, following (though also deviating slightly from) Lacan, assigns to Thanatos extraordinary prerogatives and calls it "the most radical—but also most sterile—principle of the logic of the unconscious" (ibid., 126). Death is the *sterile* truth of the unconscious, which is itself the truth, the real place, of the psyche. In a manner similar to Heidegger, who in *The Onto-Theo-Logical Structure of Metaphysics* conceived of Being as a continuous passage/translation (*übergehen/übersetzen*) from *Seyn* (being) to *Seiende* (beings), from primordial nothingness to the condition of ontological difference, Laplanche portrays the death-drive as the fundamental principle of *flow*: "The death-drive is the very soul, the constitutive principle, of libidinal circulation" (ibid., 124). Whatever becomes bound, fixed, constituted, the death-drive unbinds, liquidates, deconstructs; whatever comes to last as an entity, Thanatos translates back into the free motion of flux.

For Laplanche, therefore, the whole primary process and its jouissance, "the frenetic enjoyment," is on the side of the death-drive, which simply frees great amounts of psychic energy. And the primary process in Laplanche's interpretation is also primary in the deep Heideggerian (i.e., philosophical) sense, namely as *primordial*: it is privileged to the secondary process, which is created by "the exigencies of life," as the more fundamental order where, as Heidegger would have it, "truth resides." Life enters upon the stage only later, as a latecomer that has to struggle against the "primacy of the zero principle" to survive (ibid., 117). That is, it must struggle against the overruling tendency toward Nirvana, a free, unbounded flow of energy that creates no tensions and no fixations, and thus promises a state of (non)being where absolute flux and absolute stasis coincide in the perfect *nunc stans*. Life, therefore, creates its own "principle of constancy" that imitates and rests on the "principle of Nirvana," but with one significant difference: it tries to maintain minimal tension, "the reserve of energy," which becomes fixated on the narcissistic object—the ego.

This binding, however, is weak, for the libido prefers to be free and unbounded, and to resolve itself in the jouissance of the death-drive. The secondary process is thus secondary also in the metaphysical sense of a later, essentially lesser order of emanation, initially deducible from and ultimately reducible to the primary one. The conservative element of Eros belongs to death, which remains the basic truth of all drives: all they wish is to return, that is, to *repeat* the initial state of nothing, or a free flow. And if the principle of constancy is set on repeating a certain amount of bound energy, it is only *because of an error within the reproductive system of death*. Hence, Eros is not really the second principle of being but merely a bungle—or, as kabbalists would have it, a cosmic catastrophe. It would therefore appear that life as such has no life of its own, and that is why it cannot come to life in its own, proper sphere; it wholly belongs to its mighty Other, Death. Eros, then, is not so much an opposite cosmic force but only a subservient archon, a subforce we might appropriately call: an *Erros.*

Laplanche's brilliant rendering of Freud's *Beyond the Pleasure Principle* has only one drawback: it is too philosophical. That is to say, it implicitly privileges monism over dualism, one governing principle over two. Dualism, philosophically speaking, is not a particularly comfortable position, and it usually tends to collapse into a more or less implicit kind of monism. And yet—and this is the point on which Bloom stubbornly insists—the speculative originality of Freud's doctrine consists precisely in maintaining this dual, conflicting structure. Why? Because such duality does not allow us to prescribe final verdicts, so highly valued by philosophy's quest for certainty: two different principles mean two different truths, which eventually cancel one another out *as* truths.[24] While it may be "hard to imagine what could possibly restrict the 'universal' of death" (ibid., 107), Freud nevertheless posits a second force—the life-drive, or Eros, and with it a primordial conflict between the two. Laplanche may be dismissive about Eros's origins in "the optimistic ideology of progress or evolution" (ibid., 108), but it is, at least in Freud's intentions, a second, equally mighty principle whose role is to bind energy and keep it on a higher level of configuration.

Even if Eros cannot be maintained as a separate principle—for its conservative, repetitive nature indeed points to its genetic dependence on the death-drive—the dual structure can still be preserved if we turn Eros into *Erros:* not so much a principle, but, in fact, the very opposite of principality, a disturbance within the *arche* itself, a chance for deviation (*clinamen*, swerve) from the arche-truth. We might even call it, partly after Derrida, an anti-*arche*, whose sole role would consist in disordering and differing the reproduction of the source. We could even venture so far as to call *Erros* a force within death itself, indicating its inner impossibility to reproduce itself faithfully. *Erros* would be the very reverse of the law of entropy, seen no longer as decay but as a generative source of difference.

Perceived in this reversed perspective, death, though seemingly primordial, cannot maintain the privilege of being the supreme truth philosophy desires, for it necessarily fails to reproduce itself as such. The free flow by sheer error, necessarily inscribed in its "freedom," becomes *something*. As in the epigraph offered here by Miron Białoszewski's short poem "Nothing to Admire," nicely suggesting an absence of any metaphysical mystery: "After the exhaustion of all possibilities of non-being, there emerged—being." Error is thus as primordial as the truth of *flux* and cannot be made subordinate to it. Since the *arche* fails by necessity to reproduce itself as such, beings are equally justified and "authentic" ontologically as Being itself (precisely because Being can never be itself "in itself"). Shifted again into the psychoanalytical idiom, this would mean that the secondary process is, in fact, as primordial and inevitable as the primary one, and not just its accidental offspring. Life may be a latecomer, a late compromise formation between Thanatos and its erring offspring, Erros, but this condition of belatedness does not compromise life as a new quality: since it cannot be deduced from one single truth, which cannot maintain itself as truth, it cannot be reduced to it either. The *Setzen* might not be intended or carefully planned, but this does not mean automatically that it has to be as "disruptive" or "illegal" as a bad Heideggerian *Übersetzen*, a false copy or unfaithful reproduction. There is no obligation and no reason to return to such a source. Life may not have a sound metaphysical reason on its side, but it can always answer back with the defiant Nietzschean question: *Warum nicht?* (Why not?).

Positing a conflict, an opposite principle of the life drive—or, as we have translated it here, at least an instability within the seemingly monistic *arche*—radically changes the picture. The whole question of truth, which traditionally derives from the solidity of "the origins," begins to waver: the origins are themselves in conflict, unstable, and one cannot derive from them a single, unambiguous message. All one can do, as Lévinas would say, is to "walk away from the origins," that is, to *forget*, but this time in the fully positive sense of the term, as in giving up futile nostalgia—their impossible, archetypal, fundamental, universal, ever-binding truth. Or even to forget the truth altogether, accept the "why not" as life's only legitimacy—and begin to err, wander, explore the "vast open land."[25]

Only the conflict, which allows us to forget the ultimate truth, permits us to develop a notion of temporality, by which I mean *true* temporality: not just a display of one eternal, principally timeless truth, but the real time of the conflict, unresolved, vast, and open. What Derrida calls "the Freudian scheme of temporality" is therefore precisely such a *time of conflict*, in which death functions as a form of *Nachträglichkeit*, afterwardness or late revision, the emergence of which does not cancel, sublate, or annul previous positions. Here, death is not "the higher truth of the untruth" that would correct, that is, literally straighten the erring path of life; it does not give, as Werner Hamacher would have it, "the unsurpassable interpretation, which in every surpassable it must already be at work" (1996, 22). Death does not spell the supreme Heideggerian illumination that denounces life's self-understanding as a mere illusion. Rather, as in Kafka's parable of Moses, beautifully analyzed by Bloom in *The Strong Light of the Canonical*, death indeed takes away the hope to enter Kanaan, but it has no power to invalidate Moses's life spent on an errance in the desert (*SLC*, 41).

A DEATH OF ONE'S OWN

> A Death of One's Own
> Adventure most unto itself, The Soul condemned to be . . .
>   —Emily Dickinson

Another point of simultaneous affinity and difference between Heidegger and Freud refers to the fundamental question of the *Meinigkeit* of death. Seemingly, Heidegger and Freud say something very similar. The former says that death is the most fully possessed possibility of *Dasein*, while the latter claims that the life of an organism consists in dying its own death. Both these statements involve the suggestion of personal ownership, an intimate relation between death and the self at the apogee of its individuation. This diagnosis, however, develops toward two radically divergent conclusions.

If we follow the Blanchotian revision of Heidegger, we will see that his reading of *Sein-zum-Tode* chimes closely with the evolution of

Heidegger himself, who would quickly give up the remnants of the singular self still constituting his early project of *Dasein* and make a "leap" into the abyss of *Seyn*, a neantizing matrix of all beings, prior even to ontological difference. Blanchot's paraphrase, which pushes the concept of death toward neutral anonymity, merely reveals the tendency that was present in Heidegger from the very beginning, the obvious reverse of his early heroic investment in "resoluteness." Let us repeat: the sources of post-Heideggerian deconstruction lie in the other of decisionism, in the "disruptive *Setzen*," which is fully aware of its arbitrariness.[26] In the shadow of every step, which knows that it is merely passing from one nothingness to another, death always lurks with its higher truth of *Abbau* (deconstruction).[27] This is why later avatars of *Dasein* are no longer so bold and resolute; whatever is left of this early center of agency no longer relies on death as an enabling and mobilizing force. On the contrary, this center of agency becomes an empty clearing, full of a resigned *Gelassenheit*, always ready to receive the annihilating (*nichtende*) impact of Being.

In late Heidegger, therefore, the anticipation of death works in the same way as it did in *Being and Time*, that is, as the highest intimation of the truth of Being, but this time as if from the other side of decisionism. Here, every decision of self-constitution loses its autonomous power by "turning on itself" (*verwinden*) to the source of nothingness from which it sprang and to which it dutifully returns. *Nichtung* (annihilation), the category that steadily gains significance in late Heidegger, is the mode in which Being manifests itself in the world of beings. Whatever comes to Being in the act of *Setzen*—a thing, a phenomenon, a singular life— never acquires ontological autonomy; it is as though always kept in check by the all-pervasive power of *Nichtung*, the neantizing umbilical cord that closely ties beings to Being. Whatever becomes constituted has no chance for ontological emancipation: the mother-abyss is always there, ready to correct the errant insubordination of its progeny. Therefore, if "belonging to Being" appears as the highest truth, then any act of positive constitution on the part of singular beings, by necessity involving a moment of emancipation, separation, and disobedience, is nothing but error and scandal crying out for immediate rectification.

Blanchot's revision of early Heidegger was not merely a blunder or whim. If anything, it was rather a *clinamen* following the logic always implicitly inherent to the Heideggerian *Todesdenken* (thinking of death). Death is the highest law and the highest truth, in light of which, as Blanchot says, "I become aware of the illusion essential to all possibility"

(Holland 1995, 48). If death in Freud, conceived within the model of *Nachträglichkeit*, is truly one of the possibilities for its authority and does not overrule previous interpretations, in Heidegger death is a "possibility" only in name, covering the imminent truth of the necessary. Moreover, by stating that "Death is *Dasein's ownmost* possibility," Heidegger does not say that *Dasein* dies its ownmost death; he merely says that its life must take into account a possibility of death that puts an ultimate end to all its projects (1962, 307). Heidegger adds:

> Death does not just "belong" to one's own *Dasein* in an undifferentiated way; death *lays claim* to it as an *individual Dasein*. The non-relational character of death, as understood in anticipation, individualizes *Dasein* down to itself ... *Dasein* can be *authentically itself* only if it makes this possible of its own accord. (ibid., 308)

In writing this, Heidegger by no means suggests that death itself can be individuated. On the contrary, it is precisely death's pondering presence as the law that turns every life into solitary and singular *Sein-zum-Tode*. It is because of death's generality that *Dasein* can fully experience its own mode of finitude. It is the imminence of death as something immediately invalidating ordinary illusions of selfhood that gives *Dasein* an intimation of its highest truth, that is, an insight into the essential futility of its *Entwürfe* (projects), in which it also projects itself as a separate being. Memento mori reminds *Dasein* that no deceit and no detour is ultimately possible; here, death signifies the Law itself, the paradigmatic force of which lies precisely in its making no exceptions. This paradoxical "possibility" appears to be absolutely certain, which is not exactly an attribute of the merely possible.[28]

Compared to Heidegger's intransigence, Freud's verdict sounds more muted, especially in that it is stated antithetically: all living organisms strive toward death, *but* they die—or at least, they *want to* die—a death of their own. Laplanche comments:

> Every living being aspires to death by virtue of its most fundamental internal tendency, and the diversity of life, as observed in its multifarious forms, never does anything but reproduce a series of transformations determined in the course of evolution, a series of adventitious detours provoked by any one of a number of traumas or supplementary obstacles: *the organism wants not simply to die, but to die in its own way.* (1976, 107; my emphasis)

Strangely enough, Laplanche does not engage in a closer analysis of what it means to "die in one's own way": this *Meinigkeit*, just like life itself, appears to him as yet another mistake in the series of detours provoked by disturbances within the reproductive system of death. But Freud invests a lot in this singular figure, even more than in the hypothetical dualism of Eros and Thanatos. We could even risk a thesis that it is precisely in *the figure of a death of one's own* that his intended speculative dualism comes to the fore in the strongest. It is here that life, as a latecomer, asserts its autonomous position in relation to the universal principle of death.

Freud's argumentative meandering in *Beyond the Pleasure Principle* is notorious, but, in fact, there is a clear cadence governing his line of thought. First, he tells us that "the aim of all life is death" (1984, 311), a sentence that already sounds like a *sentence*, a concluding adjudication from which there is no appeal. This apparent ending line, however, is where the whole detour of Freud's speculation is just beginning. His argumentation runs according to the musical rhythm of *da capo al fine* (from the beginning till the end): the "yes, we must die" is the finale from which Freud's speculative repetition evolves into a story full of "intricate evasions":

> For a long time, perhaps, living substance was thus being constantly created afresh and easily dying, till *decisive external influences* altered it in such a way as to oblige the still surviving substance to diverge ever more widely from its original course of life and to make ever more complicated *détours* before reaching its aim of death. These circuitous paths to death, faithfully kept to by conservative instincts, would thus present us today with the picture of the phenomena of life. (ibid., 311; my emphasis)

Freud never explains what he means by "decisive external influences": they are mysterious factors of disturbance, disordering the free flow of energy that wants to return to its previous state. They are, to use Blanchot's wonderfully ambiguous formula, a kind of "arrested death."[29] They present deadly dangers for an organism but, instead of killing it instantaneously, they "catastrophically" alter its way of functioning (*kata-strephein*, meaning a sudden turn), which from then on becomes increasingly defensive. A singular organism will, obviously, die, but *not now*; surrounded by death, it challenges and postpones its coming. The self-preserving instincts, says Freud, emerge not to negate death but merely "to assure that the organism shall follow its own path to death, and to ward off any possible ways of returning to inorganic existence other than those which are immanent in the organism itself" (ibid., 311). "The circuitous path to death" becomes synonymous with the organism's individuation: its own immanent evasions of death, which constantly endanger it, compose a singular signature, a singular arabesque—not so far, indeed, from Friedrich Schlegel's favorite trope of life—which defies the straight, orthodox law of instantaneous dying.

In the next step, a truly "wandering step," Freud takes is an even more surprising turn, since "the own path to death," which thus far has individuated only the evasions of death, becomes transposed into a singular way of dying itself: "What we are left with," he concludes, "is the fact that the organism wishes to die only in its own fashion" (ibid., 312). The deepest desire of every living being is thus to die in its own way, not just to postpone for as long as possible the universal, hovering presence of death, which comes in the inalterable guise of natural necessity, but to *change* the very nature of death, to make it singular, personal, one's own. That is, to render it less fatal and more chancy. In this openness to chance, which challenges the law of death in its most legalistic, law-constituting essence of exceptionless generality, one can easily hear the cry of a deeper, almost totally suppressed desire to conquer death altogether. And even if this cry for immortality cannot be satisfied—Freud fully accepts the fact that we no longer live in the happy metaphysical universe of a triumphant, infinite, transcendental life—it can still be answered, and the validity of its demand at least partly maintained. Among all modern thinkers, Freud is probably the last one who made an effort not to give in completely into the disenchanting discovery of man's finitude.

In Heidegger, the sudden remembrance of death ends all anecdote, peripety, and irony. In light of the paralyzing truth, life's strivings become arrested: *Gelassenheit* means liberation from desire which finally learns how to no longer want anything, purify itself of negativity, and in its stillness imitate death. In Freud, on the contrary, the whole *Sinnwandlung* (wandering of meaning) only begins with this knowledge, which, in fact, can never be brought to light as *knowledge*. It is always partly repressed, and this is precisely why the death-drive can only manifest itself in a chiasmatic entanglement with Eros, in repetitions that are constantly worked upon by defenses that turn them into something "new": new anecdotes, new events, new cunning ironies of life. The detour ends the way it must, but—again, *but*—this end is not just the dreary, mechanical eternal return of the same; rather like the end of a story that tries to terminate itself in its own right. There is an element of chance here, the singularity of an accident that softens the iron rule of *Ananke* (fate).

In Freud, therefore, death makes allowances for an exceptional way of dying. This difference may seem negligible, prima facie, but it eventually makes all the difference. For the right to die one's own death is at the same time the right to acquire a name of one's own. This is, after all, the sense of Jacob's duel with the Angel of Death, whom he wrestles till he gets the blessing of a new, this time truly proper, name—not merely the mocking "heel-clutcher," but the truly grand "Israel": "the one who fought with God." The blessing, which says that you will die your own death, also promises that your name shall not be forgotten. In the end, what this blessing bestows is not death but "more life." Thus, when Freud quotes one of his favorite lines from German romantic poetry—*Die Schrift sagt, es ist keine Sünde zu hinken!*[30]—he *secretly* sides with Jacob and his struggle for the postponement of death, which the Hebrew hero agrees to accept, but only later, and only on his own terms.

Jacob's Way

> Let us recall that although Freud did indeed say that "the aim of all life is death," the course of his argument leads him to the statement that "the organism wishes to die only in its own fashion," only through the complex fullness of its appropriate life.
> —Lionel Trilling, *Beyond Culture*

> Human life, like a poetical figure, is an indeterminate middle between overspecified poles always threatening to collapse it. The poles may be birth and death, father and mother, mother and wife, love and judgment, heaven and earth, first things and last things. Art narrates that middle region and charts it like a purgatory, for only if it exists can life exist; only if the imagination presses against the poles are *error and life and illusion*—all those things which Shelley called "generous superstitions"—possible.
> —Geoffrey Hartman, *The Fate of Reading*

In his wonderful book *On the Psychotheology of Everyday Life*, Eric Santner observes that Harold Bloom is probably the only contemporary thinker who remains faithful to "early Hebrew vitalism," which expects only one promise of thinking: *the blessing of more life*.[31] This vitalistic line is also clearly present in Freud's peculiar scheme of temporality, which in Bloom's revision emphasizes and makes central what has been left hesitant and ambiguous in Freud himself, namely the creative *potential of deferral*. Bloom's famed contrariness, his resistance to epistemological theory, his reluctance to face the semitautological truths of deconstruction, are all deeply rooted in the essentially Freudian belief in the beneficiary effects of all sorts of delays. And these delays cannot be reduced simply to blank errors, as sterile as the truth from which they deviate, for Bloom insists that they produce their own, glorious quality.

Time, which Bloom takes to resist the preestablished impossibilities of theory, defers and complicates the moment of achieving the destination and thus changes the goal, although, from a purely theoretical perspective, the goal may seem the same. Even if all living beings, according to Freud, meander toward death, struggling for the delay of the sentence, it is nevertheless death that they encounter in the end. In Bloom's parallel, death is also ultimately a failure, "a ruined quest" at which the poetic self finally arrives. *Yet such a purely conceptual approach would cancel life altogether:* it would have to conclude, after Mephisto and some of his deconstructive followers, that there is a primordial "rule of death" underlying life, turning it into a game of false pretenses. Death is the end, but it is also already "in the beginning," as in Schopenhauer's famous pun—*Natus est denatus* (the just born is already dead). Whatever happens in-between, "in the midst of life" (*in mitten des Lebens*)—or, after Hartman, "in an indeterminate middle between overspecified poles always threatening to collapse it"—is merely deviation, blunder, failure in reproducing the original state, nothing more than a "poetical figure." Can *taking time* change anything in this chillingly motionless picture?

Those who believe it can belong to the Party of Eros, or rather, as we have already established, *Erros*. For this would be a peculiar Hebrew *Erros*, a unique force of life as latecomer and survivor, lying behind the act of errance that struggles to acquire a right of its own, and to turn what initially appears as a blunt error into a new principle. Once again, we could evoke Lévinas who, in *The Trace of the Other*, differentiates between two types of journey, which can serve us here as metaphors for two opposite ontological models. He contrasts Odysseus's striving to reach home with Abraham's impulse to leave the place where he was born and start to wander "away from his origins." Heidegger's vision of beings, forever tied by the umbilical cord of *Nichtigkeit* to the abyss of *Seyn*, keeps them close to their source; merely half-constituted, half-existent, ontologically "weak," they never properly leave the home of *die Erde* (earth), and if they do, it is only because of their deplorable alienation and "forgetfulness of Being," which then have to be corrected by vigilant poets and philosophers. Freudian beings, on the other hand, are "posted" by the initial conflict—or catastrophe—on their circuitous path of life, which sends them "away from their origins" into the desert of errant wandering. Heidegger's beings are always already "dying" in their *Andenken* (thankful commemoration), the nostalgic, mournful remembrance of their true abode, whereas Freud's beings may be pathetic in their attempt of emancipation, but at least they try to "get out" from their paralyzing house of bondage.

Erros is the driving force behind the Exodus, the great Hebrew leaving-of-Egypt, *yeziat mizraim*, where *mizraim* represents the dark thanatic powers of myth, the eternal subordination of life to death as the highest Law. By wandering into the desert, the Hebrews challenged the natural Law and made the first *clinamen* from its authority: they walked away from their origins, tore the umbilical cord from the mythical mother-abyss, and entered the path of *error*. And it does not matter in the end if Kanaan, the promised land truly free of death's reign, is available. What counts is the decision to wrestle with death, delay its final verdict, and create a space in which error can be coined into a new principle, "the middle of life." Moses, who never entered Kanaan, but, as Kafka says in his parable, "sensed its smell through all his life," is only apparently death's victim: his surrender to death does not cancel his life as the mistake and faux pas of a senseless wandering in a desert. He is not reminded of anything higher and truer he had forgotten; he dies his own death, which makes his life stand out as a separate, solitary decision that deserves a name of its own just as much as the wrestling life of Jacob.

If *thaumazein* (wonder) is the Greek moment of passage from myth to philosophy, an experience of wonder in the face of *singular things*, just being there, clear and distinct in their own strong light of "appearing," their *phainesthai*—then the Exodus, *yeziat*, serves as its Hebrew equivalent, leading to a similar sense of astonishment in the face of *singular lives* that have resisted obliteration strongly enough to be called forever by their proper names. The Greek, horizontal plane of metaphysical wonder, facing distinct, particular beings "here and now," meets its alternative in the Hebrew vision of History, "the time without boundaries," in which it is temporal resistance, the skill of endurance and survival, that truly entitles one to wonderment and awe. The Greek wonder is an instantaneous, atemporal illumination of *it is*, while the Hebrew wonder refers to *it was*, taking into account the temporal horizon of historical emergence and disappearance in which the singular stands out as powerfully memorable and, as in Kierkegaard, "unblurred."

Zakhor (remember), the most fundamental Jewish imperative of remembering, is thus a counterpart of the Greek insistence on staying amazed at the spectacle of being.[32] And this remembering works in the direction precisely opposite to Heidegger's remembrance: instead of paying tribute to the primal night, which first gave and then took away, it praises singular lives for their capacity to "walk away from their origins" and single themselves out, to differentiate, to stand distinct. The only immortality these lives can aspire to is the potentially infinite amazement of *zakhor*. Yet, on the other hand, it is precisely their finitude that is a cause for wonder at all: they lived, they died—*but*—something happened *in between*, something amazing and irreducible to the economy of the cycle, something that managed to get beyond the wheel of nature.

I do not wish to appear as someone kicking in an open door, and present as brand new what has already been to some extent successfully assimilated by contemporary thought. My sole ambition here is *to reintroduce the difference* which has been partly lost as a necessary prize of this appropriation. Thus, although the "Jew-Greek" strategy proved to be extremely efficient in demonstrating philosophical significance of Hebrew motives, it happened nonetheless at the expense of their alternative speculative potential. For instance, Blanchot wrote copiously and affirmatively about Exodus, especially in *L'indestructible, être Juif* (The Indestructible, Being Jewish), but his remarks, inadvertently with Heidegger in the background, sound almost always out of tune. "What does being Jewish signify?" he asks, quoting Pasternak. "'Why does it exist?' . . . It exists so the idea of exodus and the idea of exile can exist as a legitimate movement" (Holland 1995, 230). But, as we have already seen, in Blanchot, the faux pas of existence and life never acquires a strength of a new principle, "a legitimate movement," for it is still only a negation of the higher truth of un-truth, the abyssal primary *arche* of death. This reproach applies all the more to Lévinas's commentary on Blanchot, "The Regard of the Poet," in which he attempts to reconcile the Hebrew "error of existence" with Heideggerian-Blanchotian "ultimate un-truth." Yet, such reconciliation completely ignores opposite vectors of these two "movements." While the Hebrew "error of life" stumbles *forward*, away from the origins, the Heideggerian "un-truth" is regressive and *abbauend* in its constant effort to return beings to the matrix of *Seyn*. Putting it bluntly, *error* is boldly constitutive, while *un-truth*, though seemingly means the same, merely negative, derivative, secondary, and thus lacking legitimacy. In all those analogies, where death remains, as Celan once put it, *ein Meister aus Deutschland* (the master from Germany), the meaning of Exodus, which is most of all walking away from the universe of death, is irretrievably diminished, if not simply lost.[33]

This peculiar wonder of Exodus echoes in Bloom's Jewish-Gnostic description, inspired by Ferenczi's *Thalassa*, of the initial condition of thrownness-fallenness that he wishes to transcend in the radically anti-Heideggerian move of *yeziat*, "getting out":

> The ephebe's first realm is ocean or by the side of ocean, and he knows he reached the element of water through a fall. What is instinctual [i.e., *natural*] in him would hold him there, but *the antithetical impulse will bring him out and send him inland*, questing for fire of his own stance. (*AI*, 79; my emphasis)

Here, the antithetical impulse—in the previous chapter we have called it metaphorically a "dry spot"—is yet another trope for error, or Erros, the force that pushes away from the "watery" truth of origins. And the greatest error the ephebe, this singular being single-mindedly pursuing the goal of separation, can commit is *the negation of origins:* "The largest Error we can hope to meet and make," Bloom continues, "is every ephebe's fantasia: quest antithetically enough, and live to beget itself" (*AI*, 79). The fantasy of self-generated life may thus be a blatant falsehood, yet it is necessary for the singular being to "get inland," to find its own stance, and the opposite of watery, abysslike undifferentiation, to find the singular spark, pneuma, fire. From this primordial fantasy of self-generation, there soon springs another that dares to impeach the lawlike character of death itself and trope it into a matter of contingency. As Freud writes in *Beyond the Pleasure Principle:*

> We have drawn far-reaching conclusions from the hypothesis that all living substance is bound to die from internal causes. We made this assumption thus carelessly because it does not seem to us to *be* an assumption. We are accustomed to think that such is the fact, and we are strengthened in our thought by the writings of our poets. Perhaps we have adopted the belief because there is some comfort in it. If we are to die ourselves, and first to lose in death those who are dearest to us, it is easier to submit to a remorseless law of nature, to the sublime *Ananke*, Necessity, than to a chance which might perhaps have been

escaped. It may be, however, that this belief in the internal necessity of dying is only another of these illusions which we have created *um die Schwere des Daseins zu ertragen* [in order to stand the burden of existence]. It is certainly not a primeval belief. The notion of "natural death" is quite foreign to primitive races; they attribute every death that occurs among them to the influence of an enemy or of an evil spirit. (1984, 316–17)

This evasion, however, is precisely what happens to Bloom's strong poet, whose fate, seemingly necessary, gradually turns, in the course of his struggle, into a *chance;* whose line of fortune, first tinged by fatality, almost imperceptibly opens itself to *tuche* (accident), the different, truly accidental, nonnecessitarian aspect of *fatum* (fate), the anarchic left hand of the goddess *Ananke.* The strong poet is thus like a child, the primeval "father of man," or the Vichian severe divinator who challenges, or disregards, the laws of nature. He stubbornly perceives the allegedly "internal cause" of his failure as a result of the *influence* of the precursor's spirit. To the serene comfort that issues from sublimation, a surrender to "the remorseless law of nature," he prefers the equally remorseless anxiety that accompanies the unpredictable trajectory of chance. His *clinamen*, therefore, is what it originally meant for Democritus: an *error*, certainly, but at the same time the actually occurring fall of an atom that has deviated from the straight line of necessity by chance, the *tuche*. Thus Bloom writes in *A Map of Misreading*:

Shelley understood that the *Intimations* Ode, and its precursor, *Lycidas*, took divination as their true subject, for the goal of divination is to attain a power that frees one from all influence, but particularly from *the influence of an expected death*, or necessity for dying . . . Take the darkest of Freudian formulae, that "the aim of all life is death," reliant on the belief that "inanimate things existed before living ones." Oppose to it the inherent belief of all strong poets, that the animate always had priority, and that *death is only a failure in imagination.* (13; my emphasis)

"Literally, poems are refusals of mortality" (*MM*, 19), but what really counts is the very act of refusal itself. In his essay "Poetic Origins and Final Phases," which opens *A Map of Misreading*, Bloom sketches an outline of a "poetic life" he imagines as a Freudian meandering that refuses to reach its final destination in death *too soon*. The poetic life is spun between two deaths, two giant seas: the sea of origins, which spits out a new life seeking its fortune on its way "inland," and the sea of return, which closes in the end upon the solitary wanderer. Bloom compares the antithetical impulse, causing the new life to leave the maternal universe of waters and emancipate itself from mother/abyss/nature/death, to Ferenczi's metaphor of a catastrophe, which he himself renames "catastrophe of vocation," thanks to which the poet—the emblem of every bold new life—is given his Second Birth *as a poet*.

Shifted back to the Freudian perspective, this is the moment when life, due to some "decisive external influence," instead of dissipating immediately, hardens into a sudden singularity, for this one special influence "alters it in such a way as to *oblige* the still surviving substance to diverge ever more widely from its original course of life and to make ever more complicated *détours* before reaching its aim of death" (Freud 1984, 311; my emphasis). What is so decisive and obliging about this one unique influence that, instead of killing the organism immediately, turns into a trauma, a *near-death experience that nevertheless lets its subject survive*? Is this yet another instance of error, in which death fails to reproduce itself correctly and, instead of killing, offers life? One way or another—for Erros moves in mysterious ways—this traumatizing influence results in such an accumulation of protective energy that life, now given its singularity, begins to pave its own, circuitous way to death. Death is arrested and, as such, postponed. The conservative instincts will now reproduce the habit of protection and repression, instead of returning the living organism back to the sea of the inanimate. "'Protection against stimuli is an almost more important function for the living organism than reception of stimuli,'" Bloom repeats after Freud, adding, "it is a fine reminder in *Beyond the Pleasure Principle*, a book whose true subject is influence" (*MM*, 12).[34]

A QUARREL IN THE FAMILY OF GNOSTICS

> We have become Freud's texts, and the *Imitatio Freudi* is the
> necessary pattern for the spiritual life in our time.
>   —Harold Bloom, *The Breaking of the Vessels*

> Life is born in sin only in the sense that sin is death and all life
> proceeds to death. The *sin* in the sex act, then, is not that of love but
> that of parentage, the bringing of life into time.
>   —Jacques Lacan, *Four Fundamental Concepts of Psychoanalysis*

Life, like the glass of many colored dome,
Stains the white radiance of eternity.
                    —P. B. Shelley, *Adonais*

The puzzling allusion to "the decisive influence," which sets the primitive life-form off the course and pushes it toward its involuntary development, is the main theme of Derrida's and Bloom's interpretations of *Beyond the Pleasure Principle*. Both critiques were written at about the same time, and both emerged in a clear apposition to Lacan's rendition of Freud's major essay in his 1954 to 1955 seminar, *The Ego in Freud's Theory and in the Technique of Psychoanalysis*. Together with Lacan's text, these critiques constitute a threefold effort to gnosticize Freud, whose "Gnosticism" appears very different in each case.[35] But only Bloom appears to be fully explicit about this project, noting in "Freud's Concepts of Defense and the Poetic Will":

> From a Gnostic perspective, catastrophe is true creation because it restores the abyss, while any order that steals its materials from the abyss is only a sickening to a false creation. Freud's materialistic perspective is obviously neither that of normative theism nor of gnosis, yet his catastrophe theories unknowingly border upon gnosis. For what is the origin of Freud's two final drives, Eros and Thanatos, if it is not catastrophe? Why should there be urges innate in us to restore an earlier condition unless somehow we had fallen or broken away out of or from that condition? *The urges or drives act as our defenses against our belated condition;* but these defenses are gains (however equivocal) through change, whereas defenses proper, against the drives, are losses through change, or we might speak of losses that fear further change. *Change is the key term*, and every cosmic origin of change is seen by Freud as having been catastrophe. (*LF*, 20; my emphasis)

Unhappy with the notion of the drive, just as Freud himself was, Bloom proposes to replace the dubious primordiality of *der Trieb* (drive) with a more original pair of concepts, which he draws straight from the Gnostic cosmogony: *catastrophe* and *defense*. Catastrophe is the source of every happening, coming-to-being, becoming, of every change that disturbs the cosmic Nirvana of the abyss. Defense, on the other hand, is a move against change, an urge toward restoration that would undo the catastrophic results. Bloom notes cautiously:

> I am not a psychoanalyst, but as an amateur speculator I would ask whether defense is not *the* most fundamental concept of psychoanalysis, and also the most empirically grounded of all Freud's pathbreaking ideas. Repression is the center of Freud's vision of man, and when a *revised theory of defense broke open the white light of repression into the multicolored auras of the whole range of defenses*, then Freud had perfected an instrument that even psychoanalysis scarcely has begun to exploit. (*LF,* 5; my emphasis)

This beautiful image of the white, monotonous light of repression breaking into a colorful halo of manifold defenses comes from kabbalah, in which the blinding light of the godhead breaks the vessels it was supposed to fill, and is sent in the form of separate sparks, together with the *quelipoth,* the scattered fragments of matter, far away into the void and away from the center, the God himself. Bloom's unmistakable religious intelligence reads Freud into this old, Gnostic pattern, and the result is surprisingly adequate and enlightening. First, the trauma is too intense to be experienced (i.e., maintained by the psychic vessel) and thus causes a catastrophe. Second, the catastrophe creates the hollow center of repression, which cannot be represented as such because, by definition, *it breaks every form.* And third, a representation of this white-black, blinding (and therefore invisible) light can be given only *in defense* against it, in a distant realm of confusion in which the spark gets caught in matter, and insight gets mixed with resistance, precisely the compromise formation that Freud refers to as *Abwehrmechanismen* (defense mechanisms).

Defense, therefore, is not just an undoing (in fact, it never manages to undo anything), but, most of all, an *apotropaic representation,* or—to come closer to Bloom's idiom—a trope and a figuration of the original catastrophe. Again, precisely as in the Lurianic Kabbalah, every attempt at representation is always an attempt at restoration, and the other way round: a figure does not undo the change, it cannot compete literally with time's "it was," but it can undo it *in effigy* by troping the moment of the catastrophe in the hope of moving beyond it, to reach the blessed time of before. By first calling drive an original defense, and then by conflating defense with restoration, and restoration with representation, Bloom can now introduce his own trope of the master drive, *the poetic will,* which closely resembles our Erros. Poets are masters of figuration, which, Bloom insists, also makes them adepts in the realm of psychic defense: "To defend poetry, which is to say, to defend trope, in my judgment is to defend defense itself. And to discuss Freud's concepts of defense is to discuss also what in Romantic or belated poetry is the poetic will itself, the ego of the poet not as a man, but of the poet as poet" (*LF*, 2).

The poetic will is neither Schopenhauerian will nor representation, but a *will-to-representation*, a drive-defense against the primary catastrophe, an urge for reparation against the original crisis, a lie against time's irreversibility. Bloom, again:

> But *can* they [the poets] cease to lie, and particularly *against* time's "it was"? *What is the poetic drive, or instinct to make what can reverse time?* Freud ended with a vision of two drives only, death-drive and Eros or sexual drive, but he posited only a single energy, libido. The poetic drive or will is neither masked death-drive nor sublimated sexual drive, and yet I would not assert for it a status alongside the two Freudian drives. Instead I will suggest that the creative will or poetic drive puts the Freudian drives into question, by showing that those drives themselves are defenses, or are so contaminated by defenses as to be indistinguishable from the resistances they supposedly provoke. (*LF*, 3–4)

Sharing Freud's uneasy mistrust of the possibility of maintaining the dualism of the drives—first, the sexual and the self-preserving instincts, then, Eros and Thanatos[36]—Bloom proposes his own, more secure version of dualism based on the dual movement of the Lurianic Kabbalah: contraction and restoration, catastrophe and defense, trauma and figuration. The poetic will driving toward figurative, defensive representations, which hope to reverse and undo time's merciless "it was" in the process of *nachträglich* understanding, is here as primary as the catastrophe itself. And the catastrophe is precisely the mysterious "decisive influence" Freud introduces at one point in his speculation in order to explain the equally decisive change that turned life into a more durable, more complex adventure. In describing this intermediary form of organic life, Freud uses the term "vesicle," which is not very far, in fact, from the Lurianic "vessel." This time, however, it is a vessel that *almost* got broken. Bloom, not very convinced by Freud's scientific backup of his hypothesis, writes:

> This grotesque organism is a kind of *time-machine*, because its "protective shield" precisely does the work of Nietzsche's revengeful will, substituting a temporality that does not destroy for one that would, if mortal time were not warded off. (*LF*, 16; my emphasis)

"If it cannot be evaded, then it must be repressed" (*LF,* 12) is the golden rule of psychoanalysis: "the decisive influence," which is the *almost* deadly danger, the death itself that somehow—Freud, or any other Gnostic, does not know why—failed to kill, is too strong to be experienced or avoided. What happens in between these binary possibilities is, precisely, *repression.* The breaking of the vessel is thus delayed, postponed, deferred; the vessel takes time to work against time, to avenge itself against its lethal verdict. This means at the same time that breaking *does* happen, but merely on a figurative level that starts the whole series of repetitions in which the vessel will partly reenact and partly repress its own moment of breaking until it breaks for real. The organism does not die here and now, but at the same time it *does* die, by incorporating the trauma of death, isolating its destructive energy through the field of *Gegenbesetzung* (countercathexis), compressing it in a neat package, and sending it off, until the moment when it will be ready to do it "from internal reasons," *aus den inneren Gründen.* From the very first moment, therefore, "the decisive influence" is never death itself, but always a figure of death, a death defended against and simultaneously represented by a swerve from its lethal literalness.

In shifting the Freudian dualism toward the dualism of catastrophe and the poetic will—or, the dualism of free, unbounded, lethal energy, which can hardly be contained in its "packet," and figurative representations, which try to bind and withhold it—Bloom makes a move that clearly privileges the works of Freudian Eros. It is Eros that tries to defend, represent, and restore, by maneuvering away from the place of trauma, while Thanatos insists on the literal repetition of the catastrophe, which, this time, should do its job, that is, kill the organism with no further ado. "Eros or libido *is* figurative meaning; the death-drive *is* literal meaning" (*LF,* 22), Bloom writes, and this equation will become a guiding motif in all his books on poetic revision. Like Freud, who felt fine with the fact that his "superstitious" ambition for immortality took the place of the normal, prosaic anxiety of death, Bloom also believes that these Erotic lies constitute a value in themselves, even though prima facie they may appear weak and infantile:

> A person tropes in order to tell many-colored lies rather than white lies to himself. The same person utilizes the fantasies or mechanisms of defense in order to ward off unpleasant truths concerning dangers from within, so that he sees only what Freud once called an imperfect and travestied picture of the id. Troping and defending may be much

the same process, which is hardly a comfort if we then are compelled
to think that tropes, like defenses, are necessary infantilisms, traves-
ties that substitute for more truly mature perceptions. (*LF,* 1)

Still, this description becomes highly ironic once we recognize that the
most mature of all mature perceptions is death itself in all its naked literalness. Then the "necessary infantilisms" of defensive mechanisms begin
to appear as truly necessary and no longer so infantile, and the whole
life as such becomes one ceaseless process of defense. Thus, when Freud
speaks about *der eigene Todesweg* (one's own way to death), does he mean
the final failure of the system of defense, or on the contrary, its ultimate
triumph? Or, in other words, is "dying my own death" just a return of
the repressed trauma that once *almost* killed me and now comes back to
do the job properly, a return that finally puts an end to all my ruses and
detours, or is it the last of these turns and meanderings, the last and the
best of these figures in which I diligently repeat my own act of dying?
Poetically speaking, is my-own-death a fiasco, or a victory?

This is the question we pose again and again, for it formulates precisely the alternative that causes the rift in our family of Gnostics. Bloom
believes that he follows Freud in his feel for "poetic justice," which gives
a final say to the power of figuration.[37] "Drive, for poets," Bloom writes,
"is the urge for immortality, and can be called the largest of all poetic
tropes, since *it makes even of death—literal death, our death—a figuration
rather than reality*" (*LF,* 6; my emphasis), which is the greatest imaginable
Erotic accomplishment. As Emily Dickinson would have it, figuration
tells all the truth, but tells it slant, and its success lies in the circuit. The
life may be finite but it will not allow itself to be a priori determined by
its finitude.

But Lacan, and to a certain extent Derrida as well, tend to devalue and
doubt Eros's figurative efforts. In his defense of poetry, Bloom criticizes
Lacan's psychoanalysis for its furious literalism, a disbelief in the power
of figuration or, as we have called it here, "the power of error," which,
for Freud, was characteristic of such regressive libidinal formations as
sadomasochism: "We might speak of a 'regression of libido,' a fall into
metonymizing, as being due to *a loss of faith in the mind's capacity to accept
the burden of figuration*" (*LF,* 22; my emphasis). The priority of metonymy
before metaphor, so typical of the "French Freud," automatically means
the priority of Thanatos before Eros, the priority of literalness before
troping, or, even more bluntly, the priority of truth before error. Bloom
firmly states: "Forgetting that only Eros or figuration is a *true* revenge

against time, the sadomasochist overliteralizes his revenge and so yields to the death-drive" (*LF*, 23).

We will deal a little later, in the section concerning Bloom's "Sixfold Confrontation with Lacan," with Lacan's notion of "the real" as a hyper-literalization that transcends and, at the same time, ultimately thwarts all attempts to catch it in the Erotic net of the symbolic. But what about Derrida? He would certainly agree with Bloom's critique of Lacan's obsession with *le réel* (the real) as a case of "furious literalism" that devalues the symbolic and refuses to accept any displacement of the real in the realm of writing. Derrida always insisted that "there is writing in the Voice,"[38] which, translated into our idiom, simply means that the experience of death/trauma/catastrophe is impossible in its bare, literal form, and that it can only be "experienced" later on as its own "trace," or, as we call it here, its own defensive figuration. So, there is nothing to return to, even if, as in Lacan, the place of return is a lack, hollowness, a black hole. There is nothing literal that could circumvent the chain of signifiers and secure its own return in the end, as though no change whatsoever had occurred in between. On the contrary, everything, with no exception, must be submitted to the law of writing and get "disseminated en route" (Derrida 1987, 464).

But it can be argued against Derrida that he himself overliteralizes this *nothing*, which is supposed to return but cannot because it—literally—is nothing. While Lacan treats this "nothing" as if it were something capable to return as a guardian of the truth, Derrida treats this "nothing" as if it never existed. The "nothing" of repression, however, is but a metaphor that clumsily tries to approach the unmentionable X, the lethal "decisive influence" of the initial trauma, which, just like the Kantian X, has to be simultaneously included and excluded from all epistemological equations. Derrida's depiction of the Freudian dualism does not differ much from Bloom's: they both boil it down to the opposition between the "catastrophic," that is, thanatic, free-floating energy of excitation, and the "defensive," or erotic, tendency toward binding (*Binden*). But Derrida does take up his position from the other side of the Kantian fence. While Bloom tries to include this psychic *Ding an sich* (thing in itself) in a theory of defenses that tells all the truth but always slant, in the multicolored light of apotropaic figuration, Derrida fights this Lacanian residue of *das Ding* (the thing) with all the determination of the Hegelian dialectic, which famously believed that Kant's notion of the thing in itself was nothing but a "philosophical scandal." Since the great X is unmentionable, there is no reason to mention it at all: *worüber man nicht sprechen kann, darüber soll man schweigen* (Whereof one cannot speak, thereof one must be silent). The thanatic flow of free energy is "mute" (*stumm*) and leaves no archives; it is, as Derrida says in *Mal d'archive* (*The Archive Fever*), "archiviolithic" by definition. It is a silent drive and should best be left in silence—as, precisely, *nothing*:

> The death-drive is not a principle. It even threatens every principality, every archontic primacy, every archival desire . . . It is at work, but since it always operates in silence, it never leaves any archives of its own. It destroys in advance its own archive, as if that were in truth the very motivation of its most proper movement. It works *to destroy the archive: on the condition of effacing* but also *with a view to effacing* its own "proper" traces—which consequently cannot be called "proper" . . . the death-drive is above all *anarchivic*, one could say, or *archiviolithic*. It will always have been archive-destroying, by silent vocation. (Derrida 1996, 12, 10)

This silent drive can be seen only thanks to a figurative disguise in which it paints itself (in Freud's words: *ist gefärbt*), in Eros's colors; the thanatic ray has to cut through the defensive schemata of erotic imagination in order to show itself. Yet, while this black-white light shows, while it leaves visible traces, while it is bound and fixed in a steady shape, it is no longer this *destrudo* whose sole work consists in effacing its own manifestations.[39] This X, therefore, is not just the Kantian *Ding*, which silently—but also indifferently—submits to the operations of the intellectual apparatus. The thanatic X is not *indifferent*: its only "proper" characteristic is that it does not want to leave anything "proper" of its own—no form, no concept, no idea.

This, too, is a form of Gnosis, a deeply negative version true only to the pure negativity of Mephisto and to his cosmic *archiviolence*, which would wish to "unbind" the whole universe into a flow of intense, eternally self-destructive energy. There is, as usual in Derrida, a mute (*stumm*) normative hint emphasizing, as though in passing, the death-drive's "silent *vocation*," which is to set free by destroying and destroy by setting free, to reenact the moment of original catastrophe, which this time around would not be *arrested* (both stopped and bound, halted and resisted), but rather turned into what Walter Benjamin used to call "a permanent catastrophe," a *nunc stans* of self-annihilating ecstasy. What, then, is this erotic coloring if not a meek, sheepish defense in the face of the real-real, the truth, the only true origin? What, if not a garrulous "clamor of life" trying to cover up death's "unspoken curse"? Doesn't this sound too Lacanian? If so, where is the difference between Lacan and Derrida?

The difference lies not so much in the defense of defenses, which is the Bloomian route, but in a different perspective on the works of Eros. Lacan has nothing but contempt for its "sheeplike conglomerations" (1989, 105), while Derrida, more cunningly, simply does not regard them as *works* at all. For him, the whole dualism of energy and binding, self-effacement and work (as oeuvre, *Werk*), or jouissance and work (as *Arbeit* and *Durcharbeitung*) sounds suspiciously traditional and, in Kantian terms, precritical. The big work of Eros—figuring, supplementing, substituting, displacing, representing, and restoring—is Eros's self-delusional bad faith, which merely keeps it going but has nothing to do with what it really does. *Binden* is a role assigned to Eros but not necessarily the true outcome of its functioning. It therefore binds

> that which is as original as this function of stricture, to wit, the forces of excitations of the drives, the X about which one does not know what it is before it is banded, precisely, *and* represented by representatives. For this early and decisive function consists of binding *and* of replacing: to bind is immediately to supplement, to substitute, and therefore to represent, to replace, to put an *Ersatz* of that which the stricture inhibits or forbids. To bind, therefore, is also *to detach*, to detach a representative, to send it on a mission. (Derrida 1987, 393)

The Freudian division between the primary and the secondary process is, therefore, highly misleading. In fact, both tendencies, to maintain free energy and to bind energy, are equally original: the supplement is as primordial here as what it supplements. "The secondary process," Derrida adds, "is the supplementary *sending* (*envoi*). It transforms freely mobile cathectic energy into immobile cathectic energy, it *posits* and *posts*" (ibid., 394). Positing and posting are intertwined as one and the same process, which seemingly echoes Bloom's vision of representation as always simultaneously a defense: to posit (*setzen*) an energy in a figure means automatically to post it (*senden*) in a future, so its terrifying immediacy can be postponed, differed, and deferred, until it can be experienced again, in the safety of *Nachträglichkeit*. This is the work of Eros, whose binding and taming are all in the service of what Freud called a mastering repetition, a repetition in the therapeutic function of *Durcharbeiten* (working-through).

But Derrida does not endorse this process himself: he reproaches Eros for not being bold enough, for being, in Lacan's words, too "sheeplike." For Eros does not see the chance that opens itself in the very act of *detachment;* it is so busy with defending itself, and at the same time substituting for the traumatic impact, that it eliminates an opportunity for freedom, which lies dormant in its symbolic productions. Eros is so blinded by its *work* of positing and posting that it cannot actually see that it is all *play*, play that is bound and determined by *nothing*. While Eros pictures itself to be only work, a serious restorative effort of defense against *something*, it detaches itself even further from the primary energy, whereas, when it loses its "seriousness" and begins to enjoy its sense of detachment and indeterminacy, it paradoxically gets closer to what it wished to represent: it starts to lose itself in its figurations, efface its traces, unbind the meanings, just like the original *nothing* of the "archiviolithic" death-drive. When Eros forgets that its duty is to posit and post, it begins to *disseminate*, and in this manner it achieves a freedom that is *almost* the freedom of the unmentionable, free floating X.

The general thrust of Derrida's reading of *Beyond the Pleasure Principle*, therefore, is to undermine Freud's effort to maintain metaphysical dualism and collapse it, if not into monism, then into a deconstructive, postdualistic kind of dynamic disorder. Here, Derrida obviously differs starkly from Bloom, for whom the Freudian dualism (which he translates into a dualism of catastrophe and defense) offers the only chance to see the poetic will as a constitutive force of its own autonomous value. Operating within the Kantian, semitranscendental perspective (as does Lacan, although differently), Derrida cannot see anything positive in the "autonomous value" of the works of Eros; since they are bound by *nothing*, they may just as well detach themselves completely from their origins and start a disseminating play. While Bloom, by moving away from the epistemology of X and its appearances, can perceive the relation between catastrophe and defense in a different light, where the latter is no longer determined by its representational "truth." Quite the contrary: it is set free to *lie* against its own, catastrophic origins—at the same time, however, it remains attached to them via this apotropaic relation.

The drive that bothers Derrida most, however, is not so much Eros, but a deeper drive that renders both Eros and Thanatos subservient. The moment in which this drive, which Derrida calls "the drive of the proper," comes to the fore is the crucial story of "the vesicle" overwhelmed by an almost deadly experience:

> The topology of the vesicle at least has permitted the definition of trauma. There is trauma when, at the limit, on the frontier post, the protective barrier is broken through. In this case the entire defensive organization is defeated, its entire energetic economy routed. The great menace of the *return* makes its return. The PP is put out of action. It no longer directs the operations, it loses its mastery when faced with the submersion, flooding (*Überschwemmung*); great quantities of excitation whose inrush instantaneously overflows the psychic apparatus. Panicked, the latter apparently no longer seeks pleasure. It is occupied only with *binding* (*binden*) the quantities of excitation and with "mastering" (*bewältigen*) them. (ibid., 348)

Fort—away—with the pleasure principle: the vesicle has now to deal with the unbearable *da*—here and now—of the trauma. The binding and mastering of too-intense excitations is more important than experiencing pleasure: "there is *already* a tendency to binding, Derrida continues, "a mastering or stricturing impulse that foreshadows the PP without being confused with it. It collaborates with the PP without being of it" (ibid., 351). What it binds, compresses in a package, and sends into the future is the death itself, which will be "unpacked" only in its due, adequate, *proper* time. From this, Derrida concludes: "The drive of the proper would be stronger than life *and* death ... the most driven drive is the drive of the proper, in other words the one that tends to reappropriate itself. The movement of reappropriation is the most driven drive" (ibid., 356).

Yet, the drive of the proper—in Derrida's reading of Freud, the only real drive—seems strong as death only within "the game of life-death," as long as it lasts. Once the game ends, it has to give in to Thanatos, which only then reemerges in its absolute universality as a force "so general" (ibid.) that it cannot be reappropriated by any particular "drive of the proper." Derrida reverses here to the already familiar Heideggerian motif: *Death cannot be appropriated.* Death is law itself, generality, the universal justice of fate, ruthless fairness, the very opposite of the proper name, or the signature in which the drive of the proper tries to accommodate the necessity of its own dying. The drive of the proper emerged only as a mistake when the first catastrophe occurred and death failed to kill "the vesicle"; it is thus nothing but an error, which also derives its force—or at least its appearance, a fake mobility—from being an error. To use Hartman's topology, the drive of the proper as error occupies the middle, which has no standing of its own and can be collapsed any time into one of its extremes: the first death, which did not manage to kill, and the second death, which returns to finish the job. The attempt to make this second death *mine*—to work on it, to appropriate it in an idiomatic figuration—is nothing but a lame excuse to keep the verdict at bay as long as possible. Derrida, once again making the connection we would like to sever, writes:

> The desire for the idiom—nothing is less idiomatic. I have indeed spoken, I believe, of Freud and Heidegger, of their irreplaceable signature, but the same is said, in another way, according to another proper treading, another step [*pas*], under the signature of Rilke or of Blanchot, for example. The proper name does not come to erase itself, it comes by erasing itself, to erase itself, it comes only in its erasure . . . *It arrives only to erase itself.* In its very inscription, *fort:da.* It guards itself from and by itself, and this gives the "movement." (ibid., 360)

It is no accident that Derrida puts the word "movement" in quotation marks: these arrivals/erasures, this "coming into one's own"[40] and immediate disappropriation, this barren child's play of self-projections and self-contractions does not create a personal history, a labyrinth-arabesque of a single signature, but merely an oscillation that comes close to "paralysis." The erroneous drive of the proper makes only "retreats, *faux-pas*, false exits, this imperturbably generalized *fort:da*" (ibid., 377). Despite all the ruses to get away from the place of the catastrophe, the drive of the proper, says Derrida, can only achieve more of the same: it can only cause the *return* of the trauma which, this time, *will* kill. Its appearance of movement, therefore, is a constant self-cancellation:

> What goes on and what does not? Who marches or does not march, works or does not work [*marcher*], with Freud? What makes him march/work? What prevents him from marching/working? Who? And if it were *the same* which gives and suspends the "movement" that "there is" (*es gibt*), if there is? The same step [*pas*]? (ibid., 337)[41]

Indeed, there is hardly any movement here, and hardly any work (*marcher* means both "moving forward" and "working"). One wonders, however, if this standstill is not due to Derrida's willing conflation of Freud and Heidegger, the consequence of which is that there is ultimately no difference between the drive toward autodestruction and the drive toward my-own-death. They merge together under the general auspices of

Sein-zum-Tode: "The death-drive pushing toward autodestruction, toward dying-of-one's-own-proper-death, the proper is produced here as autothanatography" (ibid., 393). But this equation is deeply misleading, because once all other more striking dualisms are brought down, even by Freud himself, this one difference, between the sheer drive toward autodestruction and the circuitous drive toward dying-one's-own-proper-death, serves as the final opposition.

"My-own-death" is not the return to the literal occurrence of death, but the last figuration, the ultimate trope, a turn and meandering on the circuitous path of life, in which the death-experience meets its conclusive elaboration. In Bloom's terms, this last trope is more like the final, sixth ratio of poetic revision, which he calls *apophrades,* "the return of the dead," and in which the poet dies "of internal reasons," that is, by identifying in the end with the precursor, the source of his deadly anxiety. What Derrida dismisses as an abortive (non)stepping and the dysfunctionality of the whole arrangement of the drive of the proper (*qui pas marche,* "does not function") is, in fact, an enormous *work* of appropriation and identification, or, to put it in Hegelian terms, almost a reconciliation, in which death, the very externality of the initial catastrophe, becomes one with the most inner tendency of the organism itself, with its *innere Gründe* (inner reasons). Without the power of figuration this enormous *demarche,* signifying both work and advancement, could not be done. But by equating this specific drive simply with the will to self-destruction, Derrida loses all its operative *différance* and turns all the figures that have emerged from it into an illusion of "the middle." Eros either plays or works, but in the latter case it merely strains itself in vain.

Like Lacan, therefore, though for different reasons, Derrida participates in what Bloom calls "a loss of faith in the mind's capacity to accept the burden of figuration" (*LF,* 22). Not because he would like to guard *the real,* forever concealed behind "the sheep-like conglomerations of Eros," but because he puts in doubt the whole construction of psychic history that might make use of the works of Eros. Once the symbolic is properly understood, says Derrida, that is, once it is understood beyond paralyzing oppositions caused by the most driven drive of the proper— of the literal and the figurative, trauma and defense, the unspeakable X and representation—it can begin to *move on* freely. Free at last, toward play and dissemination. Only ecstatic *fort!,* finally without any retentive, anxious, appropriating *da.* Freud's favorite *Spielzeug* (toy), therefore, has to be cast away: no more narcissistic strings pulling back the spool, no more drive of the proper to hold down its rolling motion.[42]

For Bloom, the metaphor of the spool is equally crucial, yet he would use the game of *fort:da* neither as a model of return (which, in Lacan's manner, annuls the *fort*, making *da* inescapable and ubiquitous), nor as a trope prefiguring dissemination (which, as in Derrida, annuls *da* for the sake of *fort*), but as the scheme of a patient, hardworking, slowly advancing, almost *limping* displacement, in which the thread pulls both ways, *zurück und vorwärts*, back to the center of trauma and away from it, but never returning exactly to the same place. The dualism is maintained, and with it all the dilemmas and problems life has to resolve, however imperfectly. This limping, *das Hinken*, is therefore never simply a "paralysis." This is the Jacob's way to which Freud appeals as a last resort, trying to excuse, first, his own, and then, life's hesitant meandering. Limping is far from faultless, but, as the Scripture says, it is no sin either. Jacob's is the way of walking *after the Fall*; one has fallen, one tries to get up, one limps.

Jacob is the silent hero of *Beyond the Pleasure Principle;* his story is the first narrative comprising everything Freud wished to say in his great speculation.[43] Jacob encounters death and wrestles with it; he does not die, he prevails, though he saw death face-to-face, and he goes on limping, however damaged, till the blessing is passed on and he is ready to die *aus den inneren Gründen*. Putting it in Bloom's Gnostic terms, the story would mean that the way to cure the catastrophe of life is not to return, undo, or literally to reverse it but, on the contrary, to *intensify* the cataclysm by turning it (Benjamin again) into a permanent catastrophe, a crisis piled upon crisis, and defense grafted upon defense. It would mean that the only way to cancel the scandal of life is to win the blessing of more life. To turn an apparent vice into a possible virtue; to turn an error into a glory.

This is precisely what Bloom tries to say when he deliberately mixes defense with representation and representation with restoration, while claiming that the latter is not a simple reversal or return but a move that is displacing and thus proleptic; a future-oriented act of redemption. In *A Map of Misreading*, Bloom writes in reference to Lurianic Kabbalah:

> Tikkun is restitution or restoration, man's contribution to God's work. The first two stages can be approximated in many of the theorists of deconstruction, from Nietzsche and Freud to all our contemporary interpreters who make of the reading subject either what Nietzsche cheerfully called "at most a rendezvous of persons," or what I myself would call a new mythic being, clearly implied by Paul de Man in

particular, the reader as Overman, the *Überleser*. This fictive reader simultaneously somehow negatively fulfills and yet exuberantly transcends self, much as Zarathustra contradictorily performed. Such a reader, at once blind and transparent with light, self-deconstructed yet fully knowing the pain of his separation both from text and from nature, doubtless will be more than equal to the revisionary labors of contraction and destruction, but hardly to the antithetical restoration that increasingly becomes part of the *burden and function* of whatever valid poetry we have left or may yet receive. (*MM*, 5; my emphasis)

Thus, one can also limp because of the "burden and function," because all of the erotic-erratic work of a death-inflicted life that needs to be done by the poetic saving lie, which tries to trope us out of our Fallen condition.

The Call of the Distant God: Lacan

> The fear of the lord is indeed the beginning of all wisdom.
> —G. W. F. Hegel, *Phenomenology of Spirit*

> And unto man he said, Behold, the fear of the Lord, that is wisdom.
> —*The book of Job*

Our discussion of how to place Harold Bloom in relation to "the deconstructive crowd" and expose his vitalistic "high argument" against their overwhelmingly thanatic tendency could not be complete without Bloom's juxtaposition with Lacan, whose psychoanalythic theory offers one great hymn to the death-drive.

Die Entstellung (meaning both "distortion" and "dislocation") involved in Lacan's apparent "return to Freud"[44] is in many ways parallel to Kojève's "return to Hegel." In both cases, the key maneuver consists in a restitution of the "proper" position of the master who, in modernity, this Age of the Slave, had become unjustly forgotten.[45] Lacan's message is thus analogous to that of Heidegger, who also struggled with what he called a "European nihilism," plagued to the same extent by the harmful fantasy of emancipation. For Lacan, subject is constituted by his *total subjection to the Absolute Master, which is Death*. In front of death, we are all but slaves—some, however, can become more "lordly" in boldly recognizing their syndrome, and some, persisting in self-lie of their apparent autonomy, only exacerbate their "slavish" condition. The alienated subject, therefore, *does not know that he is already dead* and goes on living its zombielike life with its futile hopes of happiness and freedom—while the dealienated subject enjoys his symptom, that is, delights in the experience of its own death, which is precisely the idea of jouissance. In Lacan's view, all psychic pathologies come from the essential *méconnaissance* (misrecognition), which erroneously insists on *dialecticizing* the relation between master and slave, that is, on imagining the Dead Other as someone with whom one can enter into a relation, negotiation, mediation, agon, or dispute, as though it were possible to wrestle something from Him, to win. Neurotics, obsessives, perverts—all of them somehow fail to get the message that "God is dead, and his tomb is empty": *the Other does not exist.* Death is the only true Other, "the absolute Master." As Lacan puts it in "Aggressivity in Psychoanalysis": "Here—that is, in the Master and Slave encounter—the natural individual is regarded as nothingness, since the human subject is nothingness, in effect, before the absolute Master that is given to him in death" (1989, 26).

For Lacan, who faithfully follows Kojève's *Introduction to the Reading of Hegel*, modern individualism is thus nothing but a laughable phantasm. In the Kojèvian Age of the Slave, the self-preserving instincts get the better of the courageous risking of death, and, together with "the promotion of the ego" (ibid., 27), the unhappy triad emerges: frustration, aggression, regression. The ego "is frustration in its essence" (ibid., 42), for it cannot accept the condition of being enslaved by the Other, which manifests itself primarily in an impossibility to express oneself as oneself in a language that always belongs to the Other.[46] The ego, therefore, is the unconscious, unknowing product of the subjection to the master, which it represses to assume a position of false sovereignty: the identification with cogito—the transparent stream of consciousness, whose constant activity veils its inherent lack of substance—allows the ego to pretend to be, as Freud described it, "a master in its own home." But the ego, in fact, is nothing but a metonymic chain of the imaginary, a bricolage of signification that begins with the specular image of the mirror stage, passes through the ego ideal, and ends with the final "subjectification by the signifier" (ibid., 307). It is an "alloyed" subject masking its opacity by using the privileges of the word "I" as a blank, empty, agile shifter. Here, "*Bewusstsein* [consciousness] merely serves to cover up the confusion of the *Selbst* [the self]" (ibid., 307), which will sooner or later have to undermine the ego's delusory sense of intrapsychic omnipotence.

In Lacan's thoroughly Gnostic and iconoclastic system, the ego is so false and remote from the "truth" precisely because ego is only an *image*. It emerges in the mirror stage, when the enchanted child contemplates his image as an integral, whole being, simultaneously corresponding and not-corresponding to his inner experience of a mutilated body, *le corps morcelé*, a body fully dependent on maternal care, already wounded by the fear of dispersion. In the order of the real, therefore, "the subject is no one. It is decomposed, in pieces" (Lacan 1991, 54). Compared to this, the autonomous ego is nothing but a *fiction of the imaginary*, which has nothing to do with the real of the subject. And this fiction proves totally helpless in light of the "truth," the ever-returning place of truth, *wo es war*, "where it was," where the traumatic encounter with it—*das Ding*, the castrating presence of the Other—occurred, and with "it" the experience of one's own death. Between the order of the real, that is, trauma, anxiety, death arrested, body in pieces, and the order of the imaginary—ideal fiction of fullness, distinctness, and autonomy—there is no mediation, only a stark dualism. The psyche, torn between its fallen reality and sublime ideal, finds itself in the state described by Hegel as the unhappy consciousness characteristic of the slavish soul. It is only thanks to the order of the symbolic that the subject will be able to transcend this unhappy dualism and give voice to the "truth," so far mute. For it is only in the symbolic that the psyche begins to achieve a "masterly" rank by coming into a deep and intimate relation with death.

Thus, following Hegel, Lacan will say that at the bottom of human symbolization there lies a deeply internalized experience of death. The great ode to death, which concludes Lacan's "Function and Field of Speech and Language in Psychoanalysis," praises its power of pure negativity, without which no sign could ever emerge. In referring to the famous game of *Fort! Da!* played by little Ernst, Freud's grandson, in *Beyond the Pleasure Principle*, Lacan extols the death-drive lying behind the birth of the symbol:

> These are the games of occultation which Freud, in a flash of genius, revealed to us so that we might recognize in them that the moment in which desire becomes human is also that in which the child is born into language. We can now grasp in this the fact that in this moment the subject is not simply mastering his privation by assuming it, but that he is raising his desire to a second power. For his action destroys the object that it causes to appear and disappear in the anticipating *provocation* of its absence and presence. His action thus negatives the

field of forces of desire to become its own object to itself ... *Fort! Da!*
It is precisely in his solitude that the desire of the little child has already
become the desire of another, of an *alter ego* who dominates him and
whose object of desire is henceforth his own affliction. (ibid., 103–4)

Ernst, faced with the absence of his mother, does more than just therapeutically attenuate her disappearance in his little game: he throws a
Nietzschean "so be it" to her departure and wraps himself in a solemn
solitude. Now, his sole companion is his *alter ego*, a paternal ideal that
wishes of him one thing only: to kill his immediate desire for the mother
and, at the same time, die for a life filled, guided, and wholly determined
by this one demand. The birth into language, the initiation into the symbolic, cannot occur without the gesture of self-renunciation. Lacan,
again:

> Thus the symbol manifests itself first of all as *the murder of the thing*,
> and this death constitutes in the subject the eternalization of his
> desire ... The first symbol in which we recognize humanity in its
> vestigial traces is the sepulture, and the intermediary of death can
> be recognized in every relation in which man comes to the life of
> his history ... This is the only life that *endures and is true*, since it is
> transmitted without being lost in the perpetuated tradition of subject
> to subject. (ibid., 104; my emphasis)

Lacan goes on to distinguish three related figures of death, which all
derive from Hegel's Master and Slave dialectics. The first kind of death
poses the menace, which prohibits the slave to enjoy the fruits of his serfdom, always belonging to the mighty Other. The second figure, which
is that of the Master, results in a consent to sacrifice one's life "for the
reasons that give to human life its measure" (ibid., 104). And the third
and highest figure consists in total self-denial, "the suicidal renunciation
of the vanquished partner, depriving of his victory the master whom he
[the subject] abandons to his inhuman solitude" (ibid., 104):

> Of these figures of death, the third is the supreme detour through
> which the immediate particularity of desire, reconquering its ineffa-
> ble form, *rediscovers* in negation a final triumph ... This third figure
> is not in fact a perversion of the instinct, but rather that *desperate
> affirmation of life that is the purest form in which we recognize the death
> instinct.* (Lacan 1989, 104; my emphasis)

But, how can the death-drive be the final, however desperate, affirmation of life? We are swimming here in the uncontrollable sea of equivocations in which Lacan's style abounds, oscillating between many different O/others and M/masters, big and small. The life affirmed in the death-drive is the "human life" that acquires its measure via death, and not the "animal life" in which—Hegel, again—"the individual disappears into the species, since no memorial distinguishes its ephemeral apparition from that which will reproduce it again in the invariability of the type" (ibid., 104). The animal life is nothing in its "inconsistent passage from life to death" (ibid., 104), and so is, as we already know, a "natural man." The difference that allows man to establish his "human life," and thus to exit the world of nature, is to accept this nothingness, or rather, as Lacan cryptically suggests, to *rediscover* it in the negation of his immediate desire:

> The subject says "No!" to this intersubjective game of hunt-the-slipper in which desire makes itself recognized for a moment, only to become lost in a will that is will of the other. Patiently, the subject withdraws his precarious life from the sheeplike conglomerations of the Eros of the symbol in order to affirm it at the last in *an unspoken curse.* So when we wish to attain in the subject what was before the serial articulations of speech, and what is primordial to the birth of symbols, we find it in death, from which his existence takes *all the meaning* it has. (ibid., 104–5; my emphasis)

And death, as the final sense of the subjective life, means first of all that the ego is nothing but a hopeless *liar:* there is no being, no separate existence of the "I," no "stuff" that would fill its fantasy of autonomy. On the contrary, there is only absolute dependence, in which desire, once it leaves the animal kingdom of simple need, becomes inadvertently mimetic, mirroring the will of the other. It means secondly that also Eros is a *liar:* the symbol not only does not preserve the thing in its "sheeplike conglomerations," but "murders" the object and turns it into its "memorial." And thirdly, it means that there is a release from these *lies* that offers the *truth:* man is nothingness, which never really becomes "something," and the whirlwind of beings is but a veil of Maia. If the subject stops *lying* to himself, and agrees that while he gives birth to the symbol he engages in a "suicidal resignation," he can be cured: he can rediscover himself in the universe of death, which he never truly abandoned.[47] Solitude, renunciation, and *askesis* lead to the silent pleroma of "the unspoken curse," which says "No" to the noisy universe of beings and opens a gate to "the place called *jouissance*," the place of the ultimate truth, of "I am." In one of his most convoluted Gnostic phrases, Lacan says, "I am in the place from which a voice is heard clamoring 'the universe is a defect in the purity of Non-Being'" (ibid., 316). Free of hope, compassion, and fear, free of the sheeplike superstitions of Eros, this pure voice, which the Gnostic tradition names "the call of the distant God," says: I have come to life only in order to die. I hail death by returning to it right now, as I speak and as you hear me. I am but an error in the order of things, which I dutifully correct by stating this eternal truth. I exist only to be the witness to this truth which otherwise, without the witness, could not be a truth. *To be for nonbeing* is the only justification, sole legitimacy of my existence.

The true desire therefore desires its own negation and annihilation by considering itself cursed, that is, belonging to the fallen region of being, but able at the same time—unlike animal need and demand—to rise above it, into sublime Nothingness. It is called from afar by the voice that declares existence to be nothing but error, and its jouissance is the mystical bliss that accompanies a correction of this "defect," a sign of final Gnostic fulfillment, the homecoming to the House of the Father. The only meaning the being can find is to become *the witness to the truth of death*, and it is precisely this *rediscovery of death* that coincides with Lacan's conception of "happiness."[48]

Lacan's story of the formation of desire—that is, of a fall into the bad infinity of life and redemption through a death that brings another, truer life—reads like many Gnostic narratives of fall and return. The subject renounces his demand for love and dies for the erotic game of impossible fulfillment. The moment his desire "reconquers its ineffable form," it rediscovers its true nature, that is, that it desires no object, no thing— that, in fact, it desires *nothing*. Lacan elaborates in "Subversion of the Subject and the Dialectics of Desire" that "castration means that *jouissance* must be refused, so that it can be reached on the inverted ladder of the Law of desire" (ibid., 324). Desire, therefore, has a vector opposite to demand and climbs back on the "inverted ladder." The Law draws desire back home to its true form of jouissance, to the house of the Father, where it rediscovers that it never wanted anything, or that all it ever wanted was the perfect purity of nonbeing.

The ego, which believes only in its own perfect image, forgets that the subject has been created in the image of the Word (which, in this iconoclastic Gnosticism, is strictly *not* image). But the subject can rediscover its sense of singularity when it, in turn, forgets the illusory association of individuality and autonomy, and finds it in the midst of his deepest destitution. This is how Lacan interprets the fragment from the *Upanishads* he has taken from "What the Thunder Said," the fifth part of T. S. Eliot's *The Waste Land:* "That is what the divine voice caused to be heard in the thunder: Submission, gift, grace. *Da da da*" (ibid., 107). The Thunder of revelatory trauma conveyed the voice of the real, the call of the distant God: *da da da.* But what the subject heard and how he heard it remains absolutely his own. The subject may be "nothingness," but what makes it singular is not just a resistance to submission, but the *tuche:* the accidental, contingent character of the traumatic scene in which the voice is heard and obeyed.

It may well be argued, however, that this unique moment of singular submission gets lost in Lacan's rhetorical hyperglorification of the act of self-offering: the potentiality is there, but somehow overlooked. Lacan, struggling with the Anglo-American variation of the psychoanalysis of the ego, which, in his opinion, perpetuated the worst illusions of modern individualism, pushed to the other extreme[49] and perversely elevated the most traditional of premodern institutions, *the initiation through death.* The rite of passage of the nameless one to the social existence of the proper name, being always the name of the dead ancestor, forms the general scheme of Lacan's reflection, which he borrowed from anthropological discourse, most of all from Lévi-Strauss. The nameless one dies for his "liminal"—that is, in Victor Turner's interpretation, nondescript, anarchic, and unruly—life of immediate desire, and enters a new, postmortal space of linguistic order in which he acquires the name of the dead father, from this time on remaining in the grip of "what He wants." "Man speaks, then, *but* it is because the symbol has made him man" (ibid., 65), Lacan writes, completely disavowing the active side of the subject, which received so much emphasis in the modern philosophy of cogito, and making it disappear in the passivity of necessary submission.

This rigid scheme, self-evident in archaic societies, becomes problematic in the Age of the Slave, which abhors death and preaches the virtue of self-preservation, direct desire, and survival. It may thus well be that the rediscovery of this scheme in the twentieth-century continental philosophy, so clearly marked by its antimodern attitude, derives from its contempt for the "vulgar" vitalism of modernity. Shifting the whole problematics into the sphere of language—turning the initiation through death into the prerequisite of the access to the symbolic—is an ultimately *anti-moderne*, radically reactionary gesture for it undermines modernity as simply contrary to logic. Lacan argues that the real cause of suffering in modern society comes from the clash between the inevitable scheme of initiation, which always has to lead through symbolic death and self-renunciation, and its contemporary, vitalist rejection; the main discontent of our culture is its disagreement with itself *as culture*. The very idea that the subject might somehow *survive* in language and, despite his initiation, evade death is nothing but a harmful illusion, merely adding to the general modern *Unbehagen*. For what the modern subject takes for his survival is nothing but *the unrecognized death:* "Who knew, *then*, that I was dead?" he asks, pointing to our common slavish fantasy of life (ibid., 300). Psychoanalysis, therefore, conceived as science, ethics, and religion at the same time, has only one purpose: to return the subject to the moment of his death so that he can act it out and relive it without fear and trembling. And the tough law of initiation allows only one course of action: rediscovery, recognition, and acceptance. *Submission, gift, grace.*

THE SEA OF VOICES: BLOOM'S CONFRONTATION WITH LACAN

> But the one who works hard enough, begets his own father.
> —Søren Kierkegaard, *Fear and Trembling*

> But there is no human voice. There is no voice that could be ours . . . Language is always a "dead letter" . . . The logic shows that language can never be my voice.
> —Giorgio Agamben, *Language and Death*

We have now mapped Bloom's vitalistic position from all possible sides, juxtaposing it with major continental trends in philosophy, psychoanalysis, and history of ideas, only to conclude that Bloom begs to differ in practically everything these trends assume as their most cherished dogmas. One of them claims that vitalism is an *impossible* position, contradicting the very logic of the initiation into language: to paraphrase Derrida, one has to be already dead to say, "I am alive." Bloom's contrariety in this particular respect makes him a truly "odd fish" in the deconstructive company, but not completely beyond dialogue. The sources—most of all *Beyond the Pleasure Principle*, to which we have devoted this whole part—are, at least partly, similar. Like Lacan, Bloom places this work at the very center of Freud's achievement, but unlike him, he emphasizes what had been understated by Lacan, namely, the notion of one's own death. The subject dies in language, all right, but he dies there in his own way, which constitutes a not-so-small victory over death: and he submits, but this submission has agonistic overtones that, although present, tend to sound rather low in Lacan's monotonous funeral symphony.

Yet, the most critical difference lies in their approach to language: for Lacan the symbolic sphere belongs to the nonexistent Great Other, the Nobodaddy of the linguistic Ulro, while for Bloom language is pimarily "the wealth of ocean, the ancestry of voice" (*MM*, 17). What Bloom thus proposes is a strategy we could call a revitalization of the dead fathers, a deliberate prosopopeia. He insists on a literal reading of the Freudian dream-formula that "these fathers don't know that they are dead" and makes them appear "outrageously more alive than the ephebe himself" (*MM*, 19). But in choosing this particular line of defense against "the ancestry of voice," he cannot help but see that the "French Freud's" choice of the Dead Father; that is, a shift from prosopopeia to allegory is also a trope of defense, although, perhaps, not as effective as it would seem. By suggesting that it is less disgraceful to lose with Language as Such than with the powerful precursory idiom, it offers an instantaneous a priori apology for the poetic failure. Bloom throws a belligerent stone in *Kabbalah and Criticism:*

> When current French critics talk about what they call "language," they are using "language" as a trope ... To say that the thinking subject is a fiction, and that the manipulation of language by that subject merely extends a fiction, is no more enlightening in itself than it would be to say "language" is the thinking subject, and the human psyche the object of discourse ... The obsession with "language" is one of the clearest instances of a defensive trope in modern literary discourse, from Nietzsche to the present moment. *It is a latecomer's defense, since it seeks to make of "language" a perpetual earliness, or a freshness, rather than a medium always aged by the shadows of anteriority.* Shelley thought that language was the remnant of abandoned cyclic poems, and Emerson saw language as fossil poetry. Is this less persuasive than the currently modish view that literature is merely a special form of language? (104–5; my emphasis)

For Bloom, language is not a dead thing of, as de Man would have it, "inhuman origin" (1986, 101), but rather a "fossil poetry," a petrified memorial of a once vital struggle. And the choice between these two visions of language is for him not so much a choice between truth and error but a choice between two different *tropes* (and thus two different *errors*): enlivening prosopopeia and deadening allegory, which amount simply to two different *defenses*. Once we agree, with Freud and Bloom, that all our mental life is made up of defenses, and that the white radiance of truth glimmers only through its multicolored lies, we enter a pragmatic domain in which only one question is worth asking: Which one is more efficient from the poetic point of view? Bloom tries to convince us that, in the long run, the better defense is the one that *vitalizes*. Only strong poets, to paraphrase Wordsworth, can *look into the life of this thing*, which is our language, and make it come alive again in their agonistic efforts to resume the fight. Only they can see that language is a "fossil poetry": not a straightforwad "negation of the voice" but a gradual *fading of the voice* the idiomatic timbre of which can nonetheless still be heard.[50]

In other words, Bloom dares to say that Hegel was wrong, at least in his conception of language—and he, indeed, must say it, for otherwise all his project would be doomed. If language were *only* this "inhuman thing," governed by the intransigent, absolutely universal law of death that orders all concrete living existence to vanish and be replaced with abstract concepts, the poets would have to capitulate in face of this merciless logic and give up their idiomatic voice. But the purely conceptual idea of language is not a final say in poetic matters. The role of the poet consists not in glorifying the deadness of language, in which all names faded into concepts, the way worn coins efface their inscriptions—but in forcing the language to reveal its most archaic layer, the paradisiac "pure language of names." And even if he cannot reach the Adamic speech directly, he nonetheless can reach the residues left in language by others—other Adams-to-be—who failed in their quest, but not without trace. Theologically speaking, Bloom's catchphrase—*lying against time*—could thus be interpreted as the poets' effort to revert the flow of time and stop language from falling from the poetic Eden into the Ulro of Hegelian abstraction. If language is rather a "fossil poetry" than the thanatic device bringing all creation to the Eleusian night, then there is still hope to regain, at least partially, its lost power of naming. No poet, who would read Hegel and understand him, could continue as a poet.

The idea of survival in language is therefore more complex in Bloom than in his post-Hegelian deconstructive contemporaries. The poet does not die in language the moment he enters its anonymous *neutrum*, he is rather traumatized by "the decisive influence" of the powerful pre-cursory idiom, which first chooses and then haunts him. This is the gist of the catastrophe Bloom so often talks about, the lowest ebb of the ephebe's creative powers: he is suddenly instructed that he is *not* young Adam early in the morning, spontaneously diffusing names, and, at the same time, imprinted with the "ibid.," which, at this very moment, he can only literally repeat. As a poet, therefore, he dies, or nearly so. Hence the second intervention: in order to secure the possibility of individual survival in language, Bloom has to invest in what, for Lacan, was never anything but the phantasm of the imaginary—the idea of autonomous self-constitution. This investment, however, is not as straightforward as it is in the psychoanalysis of the ego, in which autonomy is treated as the subject's real and inalienable asset. Instead, rather, it will be the invest-ment in the imaginary, precisely *as the imaginary*. And this fantasy will not be just a "plague," covering the essential nothingness of subjective desire, but a constitutive phantasm allowing the subject to counteract the effect of his offering to language, turning it into an *agonistic submission*. After all, agon could not take place without the rhetorical reinforcement of the narcissistic fantasy of self-constitution, "the great Oedipal proj-ect," which finds its best articulation in the sublime self-description of Milton's Satan, Bloom's favorite phrase: "self-begot, self-rais'd / By our own quick'ning power."

Also, the notion of trauma is played out very differently here. While Lacan describes trauma in terms of symbolic death, Bloom reinterprets trauma in terms not so much of death per se, but more as *korban:* "almost-death" or "death arrested." This is precisely the Freudian "decisive influence," which does not cause immediate death, but, by catastrophe or mistake—which is yet another meaning of Lacan's ominous *tuche*, the incomprehensible event—inflicts the individual life with "sickness unto death" and sets it on a meandering errand to its own way of dying, the mysterium of *apophrades*.[51]

The concept of trauma focusing on survival also emphasizes the aftermath of trauma: the attempt of *Durcharbeiten*. Hegel's belief in the power of the Slave's work to resolve the initial traumatizing situation corresponds with Freud's—and also Bloom's—belief in the power of *working-through-figuration*. And vice versa: Kojève's disbelief in the alter-native way of the Slave corresponds with Lacan's and, then, Derrida's disbelief in the works of Eros, those sheeplike, escapist, *herdisch* (gregari-ous) conglomerations of metaphors. More faithfully to both Hegel and Freud, the Slave for Bloom is not the subject who simply *withdraws from initiation*, unable to face the risk of death, but the subject who, to use Kierkegaard's formula, "works hard enough to beget his own Father." By shifting the Hegelian Slave into the realm of psychoanalysis, as well as Kierkegaard's "experimental psychology," Bloom regains the original dialectical movement of Hegel's crucial relation: he will invest in the Slave's *work*, which marks his initial submission, and show that even dead masters can be wrestled with in an endless, unstoppable struggle for recognition.

And finally, last but not least correction: Bloom takes a much more welcoming stance toward the peculiar linguistic distortion that Lacan calls "the poetic function of language."[52] For Lacan, as a psychoanalyst, the purpose is to reveal "the primary language" of an analysand and expose the moment of his submission to the signifying order. For Bloom, as a strong poet himself, the purpose is to reveal the primary language of the poetic ephebe and expose the moment in which his own desire got entangled in the idiom of his precursor. Hence Bloom provides his own version of the Freudian formula: "Where the precursor was, the ephebe should emerge." For Lacan, the figures of speech, though interesting for a psychoanalyst, are nonetheless just defensive mechanisms of the ego that have to be broken in order to reveal "the unspoken curse" of the real underneath them. For Bloom, on the contrary, these very figures, serving as defensive mechanisms, allow the individual subject to survive poetically in language, or, in other words, to die in language in his own fashion, always stressing the particular occasion of his Scene of Instruction. Lacan writes:

> Periphrasis, hyperbaton, ellipsis, suspension, anticipation, retraction, negation, digression, irony, these are the figures of style (Quintilian's *figurae sententiarum*); as catachresis, litotes, antonomasia, hypotyposis are the tropes, whose terms suggest themselves as the most proper for the labeling of these mechanisms. Can one really see these as mere figures of speech when it is the figures themselves that are the active principle of the rhetoric of the discourse that the analysand in fact utters? (1989, 169)

This question is also the starting point of Bloom's analysis, but, unlike Lacan, he will be content to stay at the level of those hardworking, slavish defenses whose function is to "mediate" desire in language and thus actively hinder the direct *return* to the first revelation of the Word and its elusive, nihilistic "truth." For Bloom, the defenses are not merely reactive protections, but also means of working through the initial trauma of submission, which he prefers to call—less oppressively—The Scene of Instruction. Instead of simply rediscovering "where it was," the Bloomian subject is given a chance to shift this "place" a little in his own direction, and—to use the fortunate Lévinasian formula once again, chiming well with Freudian "displacement"—to "walk away from his origins." The ephebe emerges *almost* in the place where the precursor was because, in fact, he is unable to return simply "where it was"; even in his effort at return, as in the last Crossing of Identification or in *apophrades*, he will be necessarily displaced, for he still will be troping deeper and deeper, willingly, into the world of artful lies.

But who is speaking here? Who pushes "it" in his own direction? In a way, also in Bloom, the subject of speech is a space of "inter-diction" between "the thing," which submitted to the Word, and "the ego," which pretends it never happened. But instead of emphasizing the split and dualism (*déchirement*), he treats the speaking subject as a compromise between the two. The figures the subject uses by virtue of "the poetic function of language" are not to be dissected into the literal real and the defensive figuration: they are integral and nonreducible. They neither return to the place of "truth" (Lacan), nor disseminate blindly away from the place of "truth" (Derrida): they patiently displace, creating for the singular subject a space of its own. So, while in Lacan the subject emerges only in the act of "subjective destitution," that is, only after he disposes of the narcissistic illusions of the ego and returns to his primary symptom, in Bloom, the subject constitutes himself with the help of the ego's defenses, fuelled by what in the romantic phase he calls "the new version of the id" and later on a "poetic will."

This confrontation with Lacan should finally explain why Bloom's interest in poets exceeds the field of literary criticism and cuts straight into modern speculative thought. This is because the Bloomian strong poets are the only survivors in the domain of language, the most lethal area of post-Hegelian philosophy.

It is time once again to shift our whole argument, which developed around differing readings of *Beyond the Pleasure Principle*, back to where we started: into the sphere of language. This is where poets, those privileged, romantic-Emersonian "representatives of mankind," plunge in, have a near-death experience, struggle to survive, and, in their secret hearts, long for a forbidden, impossible immortality. The sea from which the poet emerges *in spe* is, indeed, "the wealth of ocean, the ancestry of voice" (*MM*, 17). We already know that "the sea of poetry, of poems already written, is no redemption for the Strong Poet" (*MM*, 16). On the contrary, it is the night of an anonymous influence that "kills immediately" by returning every new life to the waters of undifferentiation. If the poet is to be born he needs one "decisive external influence," which, instead of engulfing him in the generality of words, will become his ownmost, singular and singularizing, *trauma:* "the influence of an *expected* death." From the dark sea of the ancestry of voice, *one* voice will have to spring forth, singling itself from the oceanic anonymity of the Lacanian *ça parle:*

> To the poet-in-a-poet, a poem is always *the other man*, the precursor, and so a poem is always a person, always the father of one's Second Birth. To live, the poet must misinterpret the father, by the crucial act of misprision, which is the re-writing of the father ... A poet ... is not so much a man speaking to men as *a man rebelling against being spoken to by a dead man outrageously more alive than himself.* (*MM*, 19; my emphasis)

It is precisely this *outrage* that causes the hysterical reaction that concerned us at the beginning of this chapter. And hysteria, as we have already demonstrated in reference to Blanchot, de Man, Lacan, and, partly, Derrida, has its reverse in a powerful, equally primordial wish to surrender and make happen now, without delay, what is doomed to happen later anyway. The arrested death is, after all, only a death, and the single traumatizing influence is, after all, an influence whose primary function is to "kill." These are the moments of "weakness" in which the finite life deeply doubts its own sovereign quality, and the poet, the very emblem of life, resigns himself to the solace of a straightforward return. The shortest way possible, the paralysis of self-canceling oscillation, is always a temptation even for the strongest poet. "Every strong poet in the Western tradition is a kind of Jonah or renegade prophet," Bloom writes. "Call Jonah the model of the poet who fails of strength, and who wishes to return to the Waters of Night, the Swamp of Tears, where he began, before the catastrophe of vocation" (*MM*, 14). He continues:

> If not to have conceived oneself is a burden, so for a strong poet there is also the more hidden burden: not to have brought oneself forth, not to be a god breaking one's own vessels, but to be awash in the Word not quite of one's own. And so many greatly surrender, as Swinburne did. (*MM*, 15–16)

While poems may be "refusals of mortality" embodied, all that even the strongest poets—these Swinburnian "weariest rivers" winding somewhere safe to sea[53]—can do is to drift off toward the ocean, that is, "surrender, [though] only at the end" (*MM*, 16). Yet this surrender, though always tempting, both contemplated and evaded throughout the poet's life, does not come without a final surprise, which is as astounding as Freud's conviction that the ownmost possibility of every living organism is not simply to die but "to die in its own fashion." *Apophrades*, the final phase of the poetic life, "recollects forward" poetic origins in the Kierkegaardian manner: "Particularly the strongest poets return to origins in the end, or whenever they sense the imminence of the end" (*MM*, 17). The ephebe undertakes the idiom of his precursor but, via the metaleptic trick, he now sounds more precursory and original than the real voice of the ancestor himself. The "weary river" of the poetic life winds off to the sea, and though the poet loses the battle for absolute priority, "the hard, partial victory had been won" (*MM*, 26): he changes the "sea of Word," leaving in it his own signature. From now on, he can become the deadly "decisive influence" for new latecomers in the future; and he will need them to secure his "hard victory," for without their agonistic struggles against him his own voice would inevitably fade. His victory is not only hard and partial—it is also relative. Unless his voice has a power to haunt the living, his poetic self will not survive.

"Nobody wants to be his own memorial volume," Kierkegaard writes in *Repetition* (1983, 132). Yet, if we stick to the seemingly slight, yet decisive, difference we have discovered between Heidegger and Freud, we would have to tame Kierkegaard's ambitions and say that all the living individual can actually want is to *be* his own memorial volume, with a strong emphasis on "his own": a memorial volume with an unblurred inscription. The opposition here is not as striking as it was for Blanchot when he formulated his theory of *neutrum* in contrast to the traditional vision of the writer's immortality; it is not a simple immortality, as opposed to anonymous neutrality, that is at stake in this game, but *a* different mode of mortality, a mortality tinged with a narcissistic signature, an effort of survival meriting a symmetrical effort of *zakhor*, or remembrance. A mortality which agrees with life's finitude but rebels against presenting *Endlichkeit* as a final say or a verdict which spells the ultimate truth of a finite existence, its "final interpretation." A mortality which invests in the power of error and displacement from the preestablished place of truth, seeking constant movement "in the midst of life" instead of the "paralysis of artificial death." For while the Heideggerian inscription turns resignedly the word "I" into an anonymous grave, sheltering within the undifferentiated element of *die Erde* all those who ever spoke it in vain, the Freudian inscription wants at least to preserve the singular story of its own, long-resisted, failure.

"Death is the most proper of literal meanings, and literal meaning always partakes in death," Harold Bloom writes in *Poetry and Repression* (10). Bloom shares the deconstructionist belief that figuration, which creates literary writing, somehow always emerges in "postmortal space." Yet, in Bloom's account, "the one who writes" does not become either the Hegelian *master of death* or the Heideggerian *shepherd of death*, but rather the Freudian *wrestler with death*, who looks out for wayward methods of outwitting the Law. Blanchot, de Man, and Derrida are thus absolutely right when they say that there is no writing without "the night of the senses," but this relation to death, which constitutes language, can be conceived in a more dialectical and antinomian way than the straightforward Hegelian *Meisterschaft* (mastery) or the equally straightforward, symmetrical, Heideggerian *Gelassenheit*. The wrestling-with-death resembles a maneuver that Michel de Certeau called "a tactic behind the enemy lines" (1984, 12): a deceptive, cunning subversion of the greater power from within its dominion. Life leads a guerilla war against death, leaning on death's stronger economy and subverting its strategies for life's own sake. Figurative writing is thus a conscious lie, a "willing error" whose desire is, first of all, to escape the death of literal meaning. Here, *Sinnwandlung* is not so much a dissemination of a literal source as a "wandering away from the origins" that offers a chance for the singular desire to "come alive in its own sphere."

The greatest apology for Error appears in Bloom's description of the third revisionary ratio, *kenosis*, which is strung along various metaphors of night and death: "Night brings each solitary brooder the apparent recompense of a proper background, even as Death, which they so wrongly dread, befriends strong poets" (*AI*, 78). Here, the orphic *nyx*, the Blanchotian "night of the senses," the Heideggerian abyss, and the Hegelian death of mastery come forth in the poetic dance of tropes, nonetheless subordinated to the higher trope, the Freudian death of one's own, which, unlike the others, is not to be dreaded. Quite the contrary, in Bloom's troping, night-death does not spell a dissolution of everything singular but "befriends poets" by offering them a chance of *discontinuity*, of turning away from the spell of instruction, from which something new, a "new beginning" can emerge:

Critics, in their secret hearts love continuities, but he who lives with continuity alone cannot be a poet. The God of poets is not Apollo, who lives in the rhythm of recurrence, but the bald gnome Error, who lives at the back of the cave; and skulks forth only at irregular intervals, to feast upon the mighty dead, in the dark of the moon. (*AI*, 78)

Chapter 4

The Davharocentric Subject, or Narcissism Reconsidered: Bloom Versus Derrida

The *moi*, the ego, of modern man ... has taken on its form in the
dialectical impasse of the *belle âme* who does not recognize his very
own *raison d'être* in the disorder that he denounces in the world.
> —Jacques Lacan, "Function and Field of Speech and Language
> in Psychoanalysis"

We have examined the dangers the poetic self encounters in his potentially lethal confrontation with language, but only from the one side of
this phenomenon; we showed how the deconstructive conception of
writing as the "postmortal space" bars the self, as a concrete living entity,
from entering the symbolic sphere. This time, however, we shall look
at the other aspect of this aporetic relation: the deconstructive conception of the subject. It will, I hope, soon become clear that the aporia
is, at least, partly caused by an obsolete and, in fact, very traditional
notion of the subject the deconstruction wants to shake off but rather
unsuccessfully: it always returns, under various disguises, as the only
possible model of subjectivity. The eccentric term "davharocentric subject" will soon find its explanation too. Bloom's proposition to substitute
the Hebrew name for "word," *davhar*, for the Greek *logos*, which he formulated in his commentary on Derrida, will appear to have significant
consequences in transforming our conception of the self, which—quite
suprisingly—will suddenly emerge as a valid contender for the missing
"deconstructive subjectivity."

The aim of this chapter is thus mainly critical: it intends to demonstrate that despite all the promises to give account of a "deconstructive
subjectivity," Derrida failed to do so, postponing the moment of positive

delivery and providing in the end only excuses. This charge relies on the thesis that Derrida—again, despite his overt declarations—proved unable to rethink critically the concept of narcissism which he himself saw as crucial for the future philosophical understanding of subjectivity. And although Derrida draws the concept of narcissism from the writings of Freud, it can be nonetheless easily shown that the meaning he attaches to this notion is much older: its true source appears to be Hegel's famous critique of the beautiful soul. My purpose here will be to show that what Derrida calls the aporia of narcissism is, in fact, nothing more than the deconstructive version of the Hegelian dilemma of the beautiful soul—and, theoretically speaking, a rather "defunct" one, for it explicitly prohibits any dialectical procedure that could lead us out of this aporetic predicament.

The Aporia

> Everything we thought of as a spirit, or meaning separable from the letter of the text, remains within an "intertextual" sphere; and it is commentary that reminds us of this curious and forgettable fact.
> —Geoffrey Hartman, *Deconstruction and Criticism*

The whole discovery of Derridean deconstruction could be summed up in one sentence: "The referent is in the text." Just like Heidegger's *Dasein* "is-in-the-world," the referent "is-in-the-text"; this phrase builds a uniform whole and cannot be dissociated into separate elements. In an interview, Derrida scolds those "naïve" followers of deconstruction, who think that it is a method allowing one to eliminate the question of reference, and insists that deconstruction has only wanted to reconsider "the effects of reference" as they appear in writing: "The referent is in the text," he concludes (1985, 15). "Everything we thought of as a spirit, or meaning separable from the letter of the text, remains within an 'intertextual' sphere," says Geoffrey Hartman (*DC*, xiii), adding that we constantly need a *commentary* which would remind us, as if from offstage, about this "curious and forgettable fact." For we, the readers, seduced by the *effect* of writing, tend to forget about it, and, led by appearances to the contrary, imagine that spirit or subject can exist separately in its own kingdom of privileged self-presence. Just as we tend to forget about Being, which throws *Dasein* in the primordially alien *Weltlichkeit* (worldliness) and thus never allows it to constitute itself in a full, monadic autonomy, we tend to forget about the nonsovereignty of the subject which, by analogy, can prove its reality only by entering the realm of the other in the scene of writing. After Lacan—who used an analogous phrase, *en souffrance*—Derrida would say that the subject always lives in a state of *suspension*, which means simultaneously "suspense, but also dependence"[1]: it is both bracketed and pending, both absent and present in the form of a delayed arrival. Derrida would create innumerable descriptions for this paradox of being-in-the-text of which the best one comes under the familiar name of *différance:* a mechanism of deferring and delaying a presence which can neither come to a full expression nor be simply put by. It cannot be completely forgotten or cut off, but it cannot be made fully present here and now either. It thus runs through the text in the *rhythm* of a never-ending hide-and-seek, almost here, almost now—always there, always later: always promising itself, and never fully arriving.

The *différance* runs according to a familiar motion of the idealist subjectivity which was first framed theoretically by Fichte: its endless oscillation is nothing but the Fichtean *Schweben* in which the I can never become truly present to itself and spins away from itself in a process of constant self-alienation. *Schweben,* this movement of infinite oscillation, fascinated Friedrich Schlegel, who attributed the same movement to irony, and then was taken up with an equal allure by Paul de Man, who turned Schlegelian irony into his own version of parabasis, a ceaseless game of "here and gone," where statement and reflexivity, performance and commentary oscillate in the quasi dialectic of mutual deconstitution.[2] *Schweben,* not surprisingly, appears also to be the model movement of the deconstructive aporia where the *effect* of inscription, the seemingly tangible presence of the referent, is always checked by the reflexive *truth* of inscription which immediately puts in doubt its external and sovereign status. Derrida, therefore, would say that the subject becomes present only in the moment of arrival and an immediate self-erasure. Or, as de Man would reformulate it in *Allegories of Reading*, the writing subject promises to show itself in the end, but since the final word of *écriture* never comes, it always has to excuse itself for its absence (1979, 299–301). Arrival and erasure, promise and excuse constitute two sides of one and the same, always oscillating, aporetic, self-canceling motion.

Schweben can either be sealed by paralysis, or become a beginning of a dialectic. The idealist solution preferred, obviously, the dialectic. Fichte and Hegel, each in his own way, reinterpreted this initial oscillation as a pregnant contradiction producing a story of progression: the

final act of conquering self-alienation in the triumphant return to the
self, which fully recognizes itself in its objectifications, ends the dialectic and stills the tension of the original *Schweben*. But the deconstructive
aporia is strictly nondialectical. More than that: it is *fundamental* and, as
such, it does not await any solution. It cannot be broken down, analyzed,
and replaced by something else; it belongs to what Rodolphe Gasché,
generalizing Derrida's term from *Of Grammatology*, had called "infra-
structures": peculiar quasi transcendentalia which are as much conditions
of possibility as conditions of impossibility, both enabling and disabling
(1994, 4). Aporia, therefore, is not a *problem* which can be solved and
sublated, *aufgehoben*, on a higher level of questioning. "It is not necessarily a failure or a simple paralysis, the sterile negativity of the impasse,"
says Derrida in *Aporias*. "It is neither stopping at it nor overcoming it"
(1994, 32). And then he adds, clearly with a didactic purpose in mind:
"When someone suggests to you a solution for escaping an impasse, you
can be almost sure that he is ceasing to understand, assuming that he
had understood anything up to that point" (ibid.). Aporia, we are led to
believe, does not still the movement; at the same time, however, it is final
and unsurpassable, which means that every *pas* taken within its vertigi-
nous oscillation must automatically be also the Blanchotian *pas* in the
sense of "no," a *pas* which steps forward and cancels itself in the very
motion of advancing. Arrival and erasure, promise and excuse, advancing
and regressing—all this happens at once in one act of *Schweben* which
cannot be *aufgehoben* (sublated, sublimated, substituted) by any other
course. It is neither paralysis, nor movement; neither the sterility of an
impasse, nor a solving illumination. Aporia is what it is, fundamentally,
and all other names merely push us away from the understanding of it.[3]

But why not, indeed? What is the reason for this indictment? Is it
because any substitution of *Schweben* would have to mean the sublation, and with it taking for granted the whole inventory of the Hegelian
dialectic? When translated into the crypto-theological idiom we have
employed in the last chapter, the choice between the idealist dialectic
and the deconstructionist aporia boils down to the choice between the
Hegelian, essentially Christological belief in the subject's capacity to
resurrect after he had been annihilated by the act of entering the alien
medium of writing—and the deconstructive, essentially tragic skepsis,
which denies the subject any possibility of resurrection and forces him
to face death as the ultimate horizon of *écriture*. In Derrida's account,
aporia is explicitly a *thanatological* trope, modeled on the "awaiting (at)
the arrival of death": "Death, as the possibility of the impossible *as such*,

is a figure of the aporia in which 'death' and death can replace ... all that is only possible as impossible, if there is such a thing: love, the gift, the other, testimony" (ibid., 79), and—last but not least—the very act of writing. Aporia, therefore, indicates "the singular motion ... , the pene-trating advance, which gives or pre-gives access to the meaning of dying. Thanks to it, *Dasein* is as if in accord with its own death" (ibid., 71). This *accord*, in which the subject reconciles himself with the impending necessity of his death, is in fact the same as the gently suicidal gesture of Heideggerian *Gelassenheit:* the subject agrees to enter the postmortal space of writing, accepting the fact that for him to be means at the same time to be dying. Knowing that with this acceptance the subject "arrives at the limits of truth" (ibid.) is precisely the essence of aporia.[4]

But, is this "arrival at the limits of truth" really the final say? It would be only on one condition: if we were to maintain the course of classical epistemology, which perceives the subject as a logocentric and egological stronghold of inner truth and absolute certitude; in such a case, noth-ing could save us from the discovery of deconstruction, which made the subject merely a barely surviving effect of language, a "referent-in-the-text." The clash between the dogma of subjective self-enclosure and the imperative to confront the subject with otherness in the realm of writing indeed produces an aporia which cannot be transformed into a problem, that is, into a question awaiting an answer. If ironic oscillation of the romantic self between the delusion of autonomy and the truth of reality-testing is indeed the ultimate predicament of the writing subject, then there is no hope for it—or rather, as Derrida tries to convince us, its only hope lies in *understanding the aporia*, that is, in "living in accord" with its lethal verdict.

THE BEAUTIFUL SOUL IN WRITING

> The soul is superior to its knowledge, wiser than any of its works.
> The great poet makes us feel our own wealth, and then we think less
> of his compositions. His greatest communication to our mind is to
> teach us to despise all he has done.
> —Ralph Waldo Emerson, *The Oversoul*

This constant reference to Hegel is not at all accidental. As much as deconstruction relies heavily on Heidegger's critique of Husserl's tran-scendental consciousness, it also relies on Hegel and his critique of all post-Cartesian avatars of self-enclosed subjectivity: most of all, the beautiful soul. One closer look at the aporia, which constitutes the deconstructive subjectivity, is enough to see that it is simply Hegel's description of the beautiful soul, with this one and only difference that, unlike in Hegel, her indecision is turned here into a permanent fix from which there is no escape.

The beautiful soul lives in the state of a ceaseless *Schweben*, and her natural expression is irony. The beautiful soul is "unhappy," though she may not know it, because she cannot identify herself with her actions: as it was put by Lacan, who claimed that modern ego never managed to pass the stage of the Hegelian *belle âme*, her dialectical impasse comes from the fact that she refuses to "recognize her very own *raison d'être* in the disorder the she denounces in the world." She lives in a state of dissociation, torn between her narcissistic self-image of absolute inner freedom and the humiliating condition of limitation coming from the external world. But, says Hegel, it is only the world of action which constitutes true reality; the inner kingdom of thoughts and feelings only has the status of a fantasy. The beautiful soul, therefore, is isolated from real existence she perceives as alien and hostile; she is self-enclosed and perfectly transparent to herself, but has to pay for it with the loss of reality. She may revel internally in her consummate monadic existence, yet, at the same time, she might as well not exist at all. She lives the Cartesian *dream of separation*, free of influences and anxieties—but this is precisely what makes her *unreal*. Thus, the only way for the beautiful soul to become real is to plunge into the world of action and—Hegel uses this word himself—be "infected" or "contaminated" by otherness and tarry with inescapable alienation. The moment the beautiful soul decides to allow herself to be contaminated, she loses her self-present, pure, subjective life; at the same time, however, she gains—the sacred word for Hegel—*reality*. The beautiful soul has to speak out—express herself in speech and in writing—in order to come into existence and become *die wirkliche Seele*, a "real soul." Says Hegel:

> In speech, self-consciousness, *qua independent separate individuality*, comes as such into existence, so that it exists *for others*. Otherwise the "I," this *pure* "I," is non-existence, is not *there*; in every other expression it is immersed in a reality, and is in a shape from which it can withdraw itself . . . Language, however, contains it in its purity, it alone expresses the "I," the "I" itself . . . The "I" is this particular "I"—but equally the *universal* "I"; its manifesting is also at once the

externalization and vanishing of *this* particular "I," and as a result the "I" remains in its universality. The "I" that utters itself is *heard* and *perceived;* it is an *infection* in which it has immediately passed into unity with those for whom it is a real existence, and is a universal self-consciousness . . . *This vanishing is thus itself at once its abiding;* it is its own knowing of itself, and its knowing itself as a self that has passed over into another self that has been perceived and is universal. (1977, 308–9)

This image of the beautiful soul is an obvious point of departure for all deconstructionists. The confrontation with otherness, the necessary influence, the inevitable contamination are the fundamental conditions of *becoming real,* yet they immediately clash with the most cherished prerogatives of "egological" subjectivity, as they are stated in the Emersonian motto, which constitutes the ultimate, romantically naive praise of the beautiful soul: tautological self-enclosure, self-certitude, self-transparency, full existential self-reliance. Derrida restates the same diagnosis in *Of Grammatology,* yet without the dialectical hope of Hegel, who believed in the "abiding" of the particular self-consciousness in the universality of reason. For Derrida, the subject, conceived by him as a "substantiality of a presence unperturbed by accidents," can never make it into the world of *écriture,* which is the very opposite of the narcissistic "self-sameness." Says Derrida:

> Constituting and dislocating it at the same time, writing is other than the subject, in *whatever sense the latter is understood.* Writing can never be thought under the category of the subject; *however it is modified,* however it is endowed with consciousness or unconsciousness, it will refer, by the entire thread of its history, to the substantiality of a presence unperturbed by accidents, or to the identity of the self-same (*propre*) in the presence of self-relationship. (1976, 68–69; my emphasis)

When juxtaposed, these two quotations form the whole of the problem, in which there evolves the issue of the "promised" deconstructive subjectivity. The subject, says Hegel, *must* plunge into the world of otherness to become real—the subject, says Derrida, *as* subject, can never become contaminated by anything alien to itself. However we try to modify the subject, whatever sense we attempt to bestow on it, it is doomed to clash with the radically dispossessing realm of writing in which it can only *die:* erase itself, vanish, disappear.

The question now is how we intend to deal with this clash: whether we want to solve it in the dialectical manner, that is, hope for a reconstitution of subjectivity after it was negated in the moment of expression; or freeze the paradox of *Schweben* and give it a mysterious conceptual halo of aporia; or—still another option—rethink the notion of the subject in a truly heterological way, that is, in a manner radically opposite to the image of the beautiful soul. My thesis here will be that Derrida, indeed, *intended* to rethink the subject in a thoroughly heterological way—in the end, however, merely recapitulated the Hegelian dilemma, without following Hegel's dialectical solution. He wished to find a new conceptual scheme for subjectivity conceived as a priori "infected," but merely ended up by reformulating the paradox of *Schweben*—disappearing in self-expression— in terms belonging to his late favorite, deeply *gelassen* (quietistic) idiom of reconciliation with the impossible. In consequence, we cannot find in Derrida a true "subject-in-writing," only a traditionally autonomous subject constantly being crushed by the heteronomy of *écriture;* not a new way of subjective being—only the old one, merely turned into less solid, more fragile, aporetic and self-canceling. In this manner, the critique of the subject as untenable crux of the phallogocentric philosophy, characteristic of Derrida's early deconstructive endeavour, gradually becomes a canvas for a more positive—though always hesitant—description of subjectivity as submitted to the law of *Schweben*. What first appeared to be a dysfunction disqualifying the subject from existence, now turns into an aporia which presents the subject as a mode of being verging on impossibility, constantly oscillating between emergence and obliteration. Never able to pass beyond the idiom of the beautiful soul, Derrida merely changes its vector and, instead of refuting subjectivity altogether, allows for a "lame" existence of the subject which must confront itself with otherness but is not capable of surviving in the alien medium.

Miscalculations of the Subject

> The right to narcissism has to be rehabilitated.
> —Jacques Derrida, *Right of Inspection*

> It is consequently impossible to construct a noncontradictory or coherent concept of narcissism, thus to give a univocal sense to the

"I." It is impossible to speak it or to act it, as "I," as Baudelaire put it, *sans façon.*
        —Jacques Derrida, "Passions: 'An Oblique Offering'"

The promise, however, was much more ambitious: what Derrida wanted was neither a total destruction of the subject, nor its dubious maintenance as a quasi-transcendental condition of writing, but a new language in which he could present the subject as "situated" firmly within the text. "*I don't destroy the subject: I situate it* . . . It is a question of knowing where it comes from and how it functions," goes the famous reply in which Derrida defended his position against the critics who reproached him for his too radical antisubjectivist bias (1972, 271; my emphasis).[5]

This is precisely why Derrida's late writings about subjectivity are visibly plagued by a lingering, vague sense of unease: he seemed not to be able to find a way out of the aporia of the beautiful soul, and was clearly displeased with the results. For the last, almost four, decades, Derrida has been continually promising to appoint a new candidate for subjectivity—but somehow failed to deliver the promise, and, just like de Man's Rousseau from *Allegories of Reading,* always had to excuse himself in the end. Far from being a simple subject-basher, Derrida sought to square the circle of the "deconstructive subjectivity" by saying, simultaneously, that deconstruction is unthinkable without some notion of a subject, but also that the subject is unthinkable without a reference to "egological" tradition, which, via the critique of the metaphysics of presence, became the first target of deconstruction. Caught in the vicious circle of two contradictory "unthinkables," he could thus only assert that deconstruction is a work in progress which still has to rely on the categories it deconstructs.

Much of his later work centers around the possibility of a new "situated" subject, and the concept he chooses as the most promising for his revisionist prospects is the concept of narcissism: this is where, he thinks, the logocentric subject finds its roots—and this is also where it can be, at least, partly amended. The reason why Derrida picks up this concept is quite obvious: narcissism, the way it functions within psychoanalytic tradition, is both a defensive strategy and a delusory self-image of the psyche as hermetically self-enclosed and autonomous. As such, the concept of narcissism seems dialectically "double-bound": narcissism is already a reaction to otherness, although an apotropaic one, for it produces the appearance of a perfect monad which enjoys no relationships with anything but itself. Narcissism, therefore, is both heterological as a defensive reaction—that is, already implying an encounter with the other—and tautological in its unconscious delusory result, while it immediately constructs an illusion of self-sameness. It is, as Derrida says in "Passions," contradictory and noncoherent: it appears to contain in itself the whole dilemma of the beautiful soul.

So, why should the right to narcissism be rehabilitated? What is so philosophically promising about this "contradictory" predicament? In the interview "There is No *One* Narcissism (Autobiophotographies)," Derrida, asked about the "provocation" of his perplexing attempt to reintroduce the notion of narcissism, exclaims:

> Narcissism! There is not narcissism and non-narcissism; there are narcissisms that are more or less comprehensive, general, open, extended. What is called non-narcissism is in general but the economy of a much *more welcoming, hospitable narcissism, one that is much more open to the experience of the other as other.* I believe that without a movement of narcissistic reappropriation, the relation to the other would be absolutely destroyed, it would be destroyed in advance. The relation to the other—even if it remains asymmetrical, open, without possible reappropriation—must trace a movement of reappropriation in the image of oneself for love to be possible, for example. Love is narcissistic. Beyond that, there are little narcissisms, there are big narcissisms, and there is death in the end, which is the limit. Even in the experience—if there is one—of death, narcissism does not abdicate absolutely. (1995b, 199; my emphasis)

There is, therefore, no one narcissism; there are little and big ones, and it is rather a question of the degree of the narcissistic recentering which causes the "egological" problem that needs to be deconstructed. To some extent narcissism is indispensable to keep up a meaningful relation with the Other which otherwise, that is, without a countermovement of reappropriation, would sink into complete indifference. Love, being the very opposite of indifference, is after all narcissistic too. It has to involve both vectors: "falling in love" with the alien object as well as the defensive checking which secures this fall by a moment of assimilating withdrawal into oneself.

Here, love is not just an accidental example but a psychic situation chosen by Freud himself to describe the mechanism of a narcissistic phobic defense which intervenes from a fear of being completely lost in otherness, however alluring or attractive.[6] Death, too, is another

Freudian example: "Even in the experience of death, narcissism does not abdicate absolutely," for it wishes to leave its singular mark on the process of dying, which then would become "dying in one's own fashion." The self, therefore, in the very motion of being drawn out of itself, defends its integrity by dying in the alien medium—in Derrida's favorite case, the medium of writing—but preferably "in its own way," that is, by leaving there its own signature. As Derrida says in another interview from the same collection, "*Eating Well*, or the Calculation of the Subject":

> The relation to self, in this situation, can only be différance, that is to say alterity, or trace . . . [this is] a "who" besieged by the problematic of the trace and of différance, of affirmation, of the signature and of the so called proper name. (1995b, 260)

This narcissistic self, this "who" who cannot even be properly called a philosophical subject (being both its prototype and its late remainder, "what comes after the subject"), would thus be in a state of perpetual turmoil, agon, confrontation: "besieged" by conflicting forces—of sameness and alterity, identity and difference, rupture and affirmation—it could not achieve a state of rest: drawn out of itself, it would have to confront otherness, but in a defensive manner, hoping not so much for a triumph over its alienating power, but merely for a chance of marking it with its own signature, its own indelible proper name.

But this image is already very far from the "logocentric" starting point of the beautiful soul. For the notion of narcissism, when considered as a dynamic whole, suggests a way out of the "contradiction" it seems to pose at the very beginning: perceived as a *defense*, it offers a chance to reconcile the self's primary heterology with its tautological impulse to save the self's uniqueness against its complete "falling" into otherness, its—as Derrida would call it in *The Postcard*—"drive of the proper." For some reason, however, Derrida does not develop the notion of narcissism into this direction: he is willing to rehabilitate it as an aporetic, double-bound, "non-coherent" move of expropriation and reappropriation, but he is never willing to rehabilitate it as a *defense*. Understanding narcissism in terms of defense offers a dynamical solution to its initial aporia—but giving up on such reconceptualization means pushing it back into the already familiar idiom of the beautiful soul and its self-canceling motion of *Schweben*. So, why this reluctance to follow to the end the Freudian idiom of *Abwehrmechanismen*?

Our thesis here is, indeed, not very far from Derrida's intuition that there can be no "deconstructive subjectivity" without a thorough deconstruction of the concept of narcissism. Yet, we do not mean here a simple *destruction* of the concept of narcissism, but rather a reworking, a *Durcharbeiten* of this concept so that it can begin to mean something else that it used to in the philosophy of consciousness, or rather that it can begin to display its neglected heterological side, so far conceptually overshadowed by the logocentric tradition. We have suggested that this transumptive rescue of the notion of narcissism should occur along the concept of defense: so far we have thought about the subject in triumphant terms—either absolute success, or equally absolute failure; either full undisturbed self-presence, or total absence and alienation—now we shall try to think about it as a predominantly defensive mode of being that lives in the world of compromises, half measures, and insoluble negotiations. We should, therefore, move it once and for all away from Hegel—and closer to Freud.

Yet, this is precisely the move which Derridean deconstruction never really completed, feeling strangely uneasy about Freud's legacy.[7] This unease derives mostly from the fact that it is impossible to reconcile Freud with the radically ethical idiom Derrida embraced in his later writings due to the influence of Lévinas: the idiom which overemphasizes the effect of alterity, and is peculiarly marked by a relative omission of the sober, decidedly nonutopian Freud. When we say "relative," we do not imply a complete omission: rather, a hierarchy in which some fundamental findings of psychoanalysis have to surrender to the overruling language of this primarily ethical and *sacrificial* perspective. And seen in this perspective, the most crucial discovery Freud had ever made, the discovery about the essentially *defensive* structure of all mechanisms constituting "psychic reality," must be simply dismissed: they pose nothing but an unwelcome resistance to the gesture of self-offering which constitutes the Lévinasian idea of subjectivity as the "hostage of the Other." Thus, Derrida regularly links defenses to the psychoanalytic dogma of the supremacy of *ego*, and feels completely justified in rejecting them, together with the phallogocentric cargo of obsolete "egology." This sweeping dismissal, however, leaves him with "a 'who' *besieged* by the problematic of the trace and of différance, of affirmation, of the signature and of the so called proper name" (ibid., 260–61) who is simultaneously deprived of any means to *defend* itself against this *siege*. If there is any defensive capacity in the subject, it must be shattered and thus lead a way to the trauma of total "substitution for the Other." From the beginning, therefore, the concept of defense is conceived here as a merely negative condition: a resistance which needs to be broken to reveal a true meaning of subjectivity as giving itself away to otherness.

> Rethought in this way, the hostage is the one who is delivered to the other in the sacred openness of ethics, at the origin of sacredness itself. The subject is responsible for the other before being responsible for himself as "me." (ibid., 279)

In this act of radical—traumatic and sacred at once—expropriation, there is no room left for narcissistic defenses: the self has to discover its illusory status of autonomy and accept its total "subjection" to the Other (here one can also easily hear a distinct echo of the Lacanian theory of subjective destitution). Otherness takes all; just as in the image of the beautiful soul, which risks total destruction while confronted with the alien external world, the hostage-subject has to plunge into alterity without any hope for reappropriation. The right to narcissism, therefore, is granted here only as a negative condition of this sacredly purifying and traumatic experience—but not as a positive entitlement to pursue one's own interest, one's own "drive of the proper" as a separate singular being, bestowed with proper name and signature. Here, there is no place for a proper name spoken in the nominative—only an emptied place for an indefinite pronoun (*me*), spoken in the accusative by the Other. In the end, the gesture of total sacrifice for the Other merely repeats in the ethical idiom the gesture of the Hegelian beautiful soul who *dies* in the moment of her self-expression for others in the universal medium of language. There is no trace of "I" left in this "me" belonging wholly to the interpellating discourse of the Other.

In his attempts to find an embryo of the deconstructive subjectivity, Derrida, parallelly, tests also the idiom of early Heidegger. *Dasein* seems a promising candidate here for it is heterological from the start: thrown into the world, it is originally traumatized by otherness but tries to "stabilize itself" via *Angst und Sorge*. It can never reach the absolute balance of traditional subjectivity, appearing to itself as the unimpeachable foundation of everything that exists, but it can nonetheless strive for a relative recentering: "Not to be able to stabilize itself *absolutely* would mean to be able *only* to be stabilizing itself: relative stabilization of what remains *unstable*, or rather *non-stable*," says Derrida (ibid., 270).

This description is virtually crying out for its natural completion by the notion of defense: the relative stabilization, which can be achieved solely as an act of stabilizing itself *against* the traumatizing distractions of being-in-the-world, is understandable only as a working of a defense mechanism, exercising its positive "right to narcissism." But the word "defense" does not appear even once: Derrida's analyses of *Geworfenheit* (thrownness), expropriation and instability in face of the primordial being-in-the-world, overkill the effect of alterity to such extent that it becomes practically impossible to understand "who" is nonetheless trying "to stabilize itself," "assume presence," and generally counteract the impact of overwhelming otherness. How is this relative, minimal effort of stabilization achieved? "Who" is striving for it? What for? And why should "this situation" be called menacingly a "siege"? Yet, all Derrida can say in reply boils down to another dogma which simply has to be taken for granted: we must believe that the future subject lies under "the heading of *Jemeinigkeit* ... which amounts to an irreducible singularity" (ibid., 271). But what is this "irreducible singularity" if not the right to narcissism exercised positively, as the right to remain always "mine," despite all the inevitable contamination with otherness? How, then, can this position be reconciled with the self-sacrificial idiom of Lévinas?

It cannot. Once again, Derrida gives us the promise of a new heterological subjectivity (it would be only natural to complete *Dasein*'s *Jemeinigkeit* with the Freudian view of narcissistic defense), but backs down from it, falling into the familiar idiom of the beautiful soul whose defenses have to be shattered in the true, totally expropriating encounter with otherness. But this all-too-reductive account of psychical defenses as inseparably bound with the Freudian primacy of the *ego*, the last metaphysical instance of self-consciousness, self-immanence, and self-control, does not do a real justice to *Abwehrmechanismen*. In the approach we are trying to advocate here, the defense not only is not tautological by nature but, quite the contrary—it is originally and inescapably heterological: it is the only way for the subject to encounter and experience the other (that is, in a simultaneously apotropaic movement of reappropriation). The notion of defense transcends the realm of mere "psychology" and its traditionally "egological" background, for it is a philosophical requisite to understand the idea of *relative stabilizing*, on which Derrida grounds his last hope for the recovery of a deconstructive subjectivity.

Derrida's problem seems to consist in the fact that he cannot reconcile the right to narcissism with the presumed heterology of the new subject. In his curiously post-Hegelian manner, he insists on the radical either/or, where narcissism is portrayed always as an egological structure of self-sameness and heterology as an *arche*-trace which disrupts and destroys the self-enclosure of the ego. He somehow tacitly assumes that even if the ego never truly experienced a moment of the mythical selfsame stillness (for it *is*, in fact, heterological) this is nonetheless what it aims at—and this is also why it has to ward itself against alterity which arrives only to disturb it. For him, "the drive of the proper" would always remain on the side of reactive, logocentric forces which call for radical deconstruction; it cannot be rescued in the realm of heterology. This also explains why the story of an encounter with otherness has, in the end, to be told by him in a *sacrificial mode:* every time the wound of alterity opens itself, the ego has to sacrifice its autonomy and die. From the beginning, therefore, the subject comes to and out of existence in a ceaseless oscillation of *Schweben.* Either Narcissus—or the Other.

But, is this really what Narcissus wants: an absolute self-sameness at the cost of total exclusion of otherness? Or, perhaps, he only wants to defend himself against the onslaught of alterity which threatens to engulf his singularity, which is not, after all, so "irreducible"? Perhaps all he cares for is to encounter otherness "in his own fashion," leaving there his mark, his signature, a trace of his proper name? It seems that only if we understand narcissistic interest in strictly defensive terms—as an attempt to save my *Jemeinigkeit* against the "siege" of alterity—will we be able to pass beyond the aporia of the beautiful soul which creates a rigid opposition between the two. The notion of defense as a compromise formation, in which heterology is by definition already inscribed, offers a solution which has all the advantages of traditional dialectics, being simultaneously free of its vices: it allows to move further, beyond the aporia, without forcing us to assume the Hegelian teleology.

There Is No One Narcissism

> The mystery of poetic style, the exuberance that is beauty in
> every strong poet is akin to the mature ego's delight in its own
> individuality, which reduces to the mystery of narcissism.
> —Harold Bloom, *The Anxiety of Influence*

It would appear, therefore, that the deconstructive aporia of subjectivity as arriving only to erase itself, or as coming to one's own only to meet there an *arche*-trace of alterity, or, in yet other words, as always promising to be present and then excusing itself for its own absence, that this aporia not only is not fundamental, final, or in any way special, but results from Derrida's *inability to rethink narcissism* in terms different than "the substantiality of a presence unperturbed by accidents, or to the identity of the selfsame (*propre*) in the presence of self-relationship" (Derrida 1976, 68–69). Notwithstanding the stance of Derrida himself, who evolved from a rather nonchalant to a more concerned attitude toward subjectivity, his understanding of narcissism hardly changed at all. It always remained an essentially *reactive*, that is, recentering and reappropriating, force whose role he perceived first purely negatively— as a fixed point of origin designed to limit the freeplay of writing—and then, gradually, only slightly more positively, as a negative condition of a meaningful relation to the Other.

This inability to deconstruct narcissism into a heteronomical function of the subject was inscribed in Derrida's thinking from the very beginning. Already in one of his first deconstructive manifestos, "Structure, Sign, and Play in the Discourse of the Human Sciences," Derrida creates a strong opposition between subjectivity and writing, a model to be reiterated in numerous later texts, for instance, in the already quoted *Of Grammatology*.

> Structure . . . has always been neutralized or reduced, and this by a process of giving it a center or referring it to a point of presence, a fixed origin. The function of the center was not only to orient, balance, and organize the structure . . . but above all to make sure that the organizing principle of the structure would limit what we might call the *free play* of the structure. (1972, 247–48).

The reappropriating, narcissistic tendency of the subject, creating an illusion of "a fixed origin," is portrayed as reactive, for it ties down the freeplay of *écriture;* makes it, as Lacan would have it, *lesté,* encumbered by the heavy presence of a subject, or, in Foucault's words, the "ideological figure of an author."[8] The centering subject is the site of tautological certitude—whereas the liberated writing is the site of anxiety issuing from randomness and unpredictability:

> Thus it has always been thought that the center, which is by definition unique, constituted that very thing within a structure which governs the structure, while escaping structurality . . . The concept of centered structure is in fact the concept of a freeplay based on the fundamental ground, a freeplay which is constituted upon the fundamental

immobility and a reassuring certitude, which is itself beyond the reach of the freeplay. *With this certitude anxiety can be mastered, for anxiety is invariably the result of a certain mode of being implicated in the game, of being caught by the game, of being as it were from the very beginning at stake in the game.* (Derrida 1972, 248; my emphasis).

Subsequently, Derrida distinguishes two types of approach to the free-play of writing: "the sad, *negative*, nostalgic, guilty, Rousseaist" one, and the other based on "the Nietzschean joyous *affirmation* of the freeplay of the world and without truth, without origin, offered to an active inter-pretation" (ibid., 264; my emphasis), and adds that "this affirmation then determines the non-center otherwise than a loss of the center. And it plays the game without security . . . In absolute chance, affirmation also surrenders itself to genetic indetermination, to the *seminal* adventure of the trace" (ibid.). Center, security, presence, encumbrance are thus all located on the side of the narcissistic, centripetal, tautological subject— radical decentering, anxiety, indetermination, heterology, and adventure appear on the side of the writing finally freed from the subjective fixa-tion. As such, this affirmation of a freeplay "tries to pass beyond man and humanism, the name man being the name of that being who, through-out the history of metaphysics or of ontotheology . . . *has dreamed of full presence, the reassuring foundation, the origin and the end of the game*" (ibid., 264–65; my emphasis). Here, the role of the self, subject, and man is established from the start as purely reactive: binding, fixing, inhibiting, falsely reassuring.

At the same time, however, when reproached by Lucien Goldmann for being so "ultra," Derrida shrugs and replies that he had, in fact, "a much more humble, modest, and classical conception of what he was doing" (ibid., 271). Not deconstruction as destruction, disposing once and for all of such concepts as man, subject, and presence, but decon-struction as a reformulation, paraphrase, and translocation of the old concepts into wilder semantic areas where they would have to travel without a safety belt. Derrida replies:

> I didn't say that there was no center, that we could get along without the center. I believe that the center is a function, not a being—*a real-ity, but a function*. And this function is absolutely indispensable. The subject is absolutely indispensable. *I don't destroy the subject: I situate it* . . . It is a question of knowing where it comes from and how it func-tions. (ibid., 271; my emphasis)

Yet, even if we agree with the definition of the subject as a function, what could this function—of a center, of a subject—consist in *if not in limiting the freeplay*? What else could it possibly be? Or, in other words, how else could the subject be *situated* within the realm of writing; what other *effect* could it have on the stream of *écriture*? Perhaps it would be a "weaker," more permissive form of limitation but, still, it would have to pose some limits on the dissemination of signs; otherwise the subject would have nothing to do *in the text*, either as "being" or mere "function." Hence already in this early text of Derrida, there comes to the fore a pragmatic inconsistency which would seriously hinder his reception till nowadays: a very de Manian aporia, indeed, between what his texts say and what his texts really do. For, if there are truly two completely different types of interpretation—the nostalgic and the progressive— then his task as a philosopher, showing us this yet uncharted other shore, is anything but "humble, modest, and classical" (ibid., 271); in fact it is very "ultra," for it changes *everything* in our approach to reading. On the other hand, however, if this other interpretation consists not so much in the destruction as in the *deconstruction* of the center—that is, transforming it from "being" into "function"—then the difference should indeed be less radical and striking. In fact, instead of substituting a certain version of Nietzschean joyous fearlessness for metaphysical certitude, it should replace—more firmly and univocally—security with *anxiety:* the very anxiety of which Derrida speaks himself as the inevitable result of *being always implicated by the game,* but which, in fact, is the very opposite of Nietzsche's furious, desperate, rather manic *Ja-Sagen.*

Depending on which of the two Derridas we wish to follow—the "humble" or the "subversive" one: the one who wants to interpret the world of interpretation and the one who wants to change it—the effects will be very different. The "ultra" Derrida falls naturally into the idiom of the beautiful soul, which advocates absolute dissolution of the subject in the medium of writing, its complete—to use Freud's example—"falling in love" with otherness, closely resembling the Nietzschean *grosse Liebe* (great love) that lies at the bottom of his Yeah-Saying to alterity. The more "humble" Derrida, however, is the one who will later promise to rehabilitate the right to narcissism in a new, subtler language, where the subject could hope to survive—partially, heterologically, anxiously— in the sphere of *écriture*, and exercise his narcissistic entitlement as, in Harold Bloom's very Freudian formulation, "mature ego's delight in its own individuality." Only an "immature ego" would want to secure all the prerogatives of the logocentric subjectivity: "full presence, the reassuring foundation, the origin and the end of the game" (ibid., 265). The "mature ego," however, perceives its goals far more humbly: all it wants is the anxious pleasure of playing with the forces of alterity on which it hopes to leave the mark of its individual signature. It would seem, therefore, that when mature ego acknowledges the defensive nature of its narcissism, its interest changes distinctly. The ego no longer wishes to master the world of writing and triumph over alterity, but wants something far more "modest": only a *survival* of the proper name defending itself against anonymous dissolution.

We should now turn to Bloom, for his critique of Derrida, formulated in *A Map of Misreading*, makes, in fact, a very similar point to ours: Bloom is convinced that if we are to do justice to narcissism, especially the narcissism of strong poets, struggling to create their own idiom within the institution of literature, we cannot do it within the traditional philosophy of the subject with its "immature" egological and logocentric ambitions. On the surface of things, this also seems to be a claim made by Derrida—yet only in his more "humble" incarnation. Bloom takes over Derrida's idea that anxiety, which constantly accompanies the writing subject, issues precisely from "being implicated in the game"—that is, that subjectivity is indistinguishable from the reality of its actions, and there is no safe haven of cogito to which it could escape from the perils of confrontation with an alien medium. He attributes this position on the subject retrospectively to Emerson and his peculiarly American mixture of romanticism and pragmatism. Emerson differs from Nietzsche and Derrida (or, the Nietzschean, "ultra" Derrida), says Bloom, because he puts a limit on the motion of decentering and thus *saves* the subject, although merely as a function within the game, that is, no longer as what we could call in this gamester's parlance a *safe bet*, a sure asset beyond the hazard. In fact, this paradoxical *saving without safety*, or, even more perversely, *saving by anxiety*, results in the very opposite of the subject's traditional image of security and stability: here, the subject becomes the very source of anxiety, itself a high stake in the game. *The players are also the game*, writes Emerson in "Nominalist and Realist" (*MM*, 175), meaning that the subject as such is unthinkable without its immediate participation in the act of playing, in taking a risk of making itself known to others in writing. Yet, what matters here most is the *decision*—fully justified in the light of the "modest" variant of intratextuality—"to rally what remains": to rescue the subject from its idealist, philosophical implications and to *situate* it as the indispensable function *within* the game. Even if the cost of such translocation is the inevitable "gain of anxiety."

In *A Map of Misreading*, Bloom suggests that *différance*, when taken out of the radically deconstructive, antisubjectivist context, describes perfectly well the way of being of a subject "implicated" and "suspended" in the game of the text. Says Derrida in his celebrated definition:

> On the one hand, it indicates difference as distinction, inequality, or discernibility; on the other, it expresses the interposition of delay, the interval of *spacing* and *temporalizing* that puts off until "later" what is presently denied, the possible that is presently impossible. (1973, 129)

For Bloom, this "humbler" *différance* is a mode of manifestation of an *intratextual subjectivity*, which is the anxiety-ridden subject-player whose stake in the game, or its narcissistic interest, is to bring forward its singular presence. *Différance* is a quasi-transcendental mechanism which makes this presence both possible and impossible, or rather: possible only within certain limits as a presence tinged with a risk and hazard posed by the effect of inscription. *Différance*, therefore, "makes the presentation of being-present possible" (ibid., 134), but only as a gamble within the game, an act of bringing forward the presence coterminous with the time of the game. As long as the game lasts, the risks are taken, and the subject is in play; as long as it delays the verdict of "what is presently denied" and stubbornly sticks to the game, it defers the moment of its death. Delay, spacing, temporalization, and differing strategies which allow the writing subject to come forward, never as a direct "I" but only in cunning disguises—all this constitutes a complex defensive mechanism of subjectivity which, instead of withdrawing into the realm of false security and tautological self-sameness, pursues its narcissistic interest in the heterological sphere of "contamination."

In the meantime, however, we have changed the rhetorical register, and although we still talk about play, we do not imply the fearless, joyous, manically affirmative Nietzschean freeplay, but rather an anxious and caring game, gaming, and gambling: an altogether different thing, evoking a radically different frame of mind. Nietzschean freeplay, as well as the Nietzschean "ultra" incarnation of Derrida, knows no anxiety or encumbrance; no seriousness, no burden, no suffering can slow down its starry dance. As such, in fact, it is nothing but the universe of *logos* turned inside out, the world of epistemological certitude turned into fearlessness, equally free of anxiety: the ego, once a withdrawn, control-obsessed spectator, now plunges into a jouissance of ecstatic self-dissolution (which, again, is the version of *Schweben* or the narcissistic double bind as described by Freud). But if the play of *différance* is not a rapturous free-play but a serious game with serious stakes, in which we gain, instead of fearless joy, *more anxiety*, then Derrida is really talking about something completely else, coming from a far more "humble" tradition—something he himself calls the world of *negotiations*. Says Derrida:

> One does not negotiate between exchangeable and negotiable things. —Rather, one negotiates by engaging the non-negotiable in negotiation ... this means: *no thesis, no position, no theme, no station, no substance, no stability, a perpetual suspension, a suspension without rest ...* The suspension of negotiation I am talking about ... is a suspension that cannot be theoretical; theory is not possible, or rather, theoretism is not possible. (2002, 13–14; my emphasis)

It may well be that here, reaching the limit of "theoretism," we also reach the end of the philosophical approach to subjectivity. The notion of "anxiety" is, philosophically speaking, a homeless concept.[9] All philosophy knows is either certitude of self-sameness or the fearless jouissance of dissolution in otherness; in short, all it knows is the aporia of the beautiful soul and its endless avatars. In the realm of negotiations, however, this aporia shows its lively, dynamic side of a paradox. The subject "as function," that is, implicated in the game, the subject of narcissistic anxiety is beyond the strict, logical opposition of being and nonbeing; it is being *negotiated* within the game, as long as it lasts. It is, therefore, as we said at the beginning, both bracketed and pending, both absent and present in the form of a delayed arrival—but this time this description is no longer paralyzing. It spells not the end, but the beginning of movement.

In Derrida's writing, either early or late, one can easily detect an undercurrent thought which strives toward more "humble" solutions: with the help of the notion of narcissistic anxiety, it wants to depart from the paralyzing aporia of the beautiful soul and lead into a nontheoretical realm of defensive negotiations, suspensions, and compromise formations. This more "modest" enterprise consists in a process we could call a transformation of narcissism: a passage from the narcissism prone to delusion of absolute autonomy and dominion over alterity to the more "humble" narcissism whose consciousness of its merely defensive nature manifests itself in anxiety.

In the end, however, it is always the "ultra," the philosophical idiom which gets the upper hand in Derrida; the nondialectical image of the *belle âme* always bouncing back to reconstitute stark opposition with its unbridgeable either/or. Then, the only quasi solution to this aporetic diagnosis becomes not so much a "negotiation" but—quite the contrary—a version of Heideggerian, essentially passive *Gelassenheit* with its dubious wisdom of passing beyond the aporia in the act of "letting go." Says Derrida in an essay seemingly devoted to Angelus Silesius, but in fact totally concerned about the narcissistic implications of the name:

> What returns to your name, to the secret of your name—is *the ability to disappear in your name*. And thus *not to return to itself*, which is the condition of the gift but also of all expansion of self, of all augmentation of self, of all *auctoritas* [authority]. In the two cases of this same divided passion, it is impossible to dissociate the greatest profit and the greatest privation. (1995c, 13)

Whether big or little, therefore, Derrida's narcissism is stubbornly always *one:* it belongs to the economical calculation of the spirit whose internal paradoxes can be broken only by the *Gelassenheit* of letting go, of transgressing the circle of profits and returns and moving into the open world of magnanimous giving, where a gift means nothing more and nothing less than *dissemination*—and which constitutes precisely the other pole of the Freudian narcissistic aporia: falling selflessly in love. The two texts—"Structure, Sign, and Play . . ." and "On the Name"—are divided by almost thirty years, but the Nietzschean idiom of an originless, unencumbered freeplay comes back here with a vengeance, now disguised under the concept of *giving:* an already familiar, utopian gesture of generous, defenseless self-offering and self-resignation. "The ability to disappear in your name" repeats the Heideggerian, *gelassen* gesture of welcoming the verdict of death, this time however applied to the beautiful soul: she agrees to give up her isolation but also to let go her narcissistic anxiety in confrontation with otherness. She won't negotiate any profits or returns—only dissolve herself generously in the alien medium of writing. Her right to narcissism will thus be rehabilitated only to the extent of recognizing "the greatest profit" in "the greatest privation," that is, the final, fatal wisdom of giving herself away with *no return*.

Despite some moves to the contrary, narcissism appears to Derrida always in the form of a minimal necessary evil: a feeble impulse of reappropriation—an attempt to "return to itself"—which is doomed the very moment it emerges. Its only sense, therefore, is frustration—indeed, a

Hegelian beautiful soul turned permanently unhappy, or permanently and hopelessly "ill," as in Lacan's unfavorable image of the modern ego. Or, to evoke the sources Derrida refers to obliquely in the title of his interview with Jean-Luc Nancy, "Eating Well": it is a Nietzschean consciousness ready to devour the whole world, yet deliberately kept hungry. Derrida clearly cannot get rid of this digestive metaphor, which, in the French tradition, became only strengthened by Sartre's *Imagination* where the ego of idealist philosophy is portrayed as an insatiable glutton, capable of endless introjection. Thus, when he talks about "eating well" in the context of the "calculations of the subject," he obviously implies the conventional metaphor of reflective indigestion, which starts with Hegel, continues with Nietzsche, and revives in Sartre, at the same time sending a message that he himself is not going to pass beyond this tradition: the same critique of the ego's bad dietary habits reflects Derrida's concern about the metabolism of the psyche, always endangered by "not eating well," that is, by negating and assimilating everything else than herself. Or, when she is unable to do it—starving. The narcissistic ego in Derrida is still an "eating" one (i.e., one ready to triumph over reality, no matter how big or little, well fed or starved): as in the case of the Hegelian beautiful soul, its main attribute is appropriation, assimilation, and possession. Only sometimes, much too rarely: negotiation, compromise, anxiety. The guilt is always on the side of the subject, which cannot coherently state his "right to narcissism."

From the very beginning, therefore, Derrida had been testing many possible idioms to express his notion of a "situated subject," but with mixed results. He started with the Nietzschean idiom, rigidly dividing powers into active and reactive ones; in consequence, he proved unable to save the concept of anxiety which had to be replaced with the more radical notion of selfless joy. Then he tentatively borrowed the Lévinasian idiom, but only to come to a similarly negative conclusion and opt for a self-sacrifice of the subject in face of the Other. His parallel experiment with the Heideggerian *Dasein* also proved dissatisfactory, for it ended with the dogma of "irreducible *Jemeinigkeit*"—and, in a manner closely resembling the evolution of Heidegger himself, brought Derrida to the equally "sacrificial" idea of *gelassen* letting go of narcissistic anxieties. Only in his attempt to speak the idiom of "negotiations" did Derrida come close to Freud and his positive defensive notion of narcissism, but his own, partly private, "resistances to psychoanalysis" led him once again away from this, as we tried to demonstrate here, most promising project.

For it seems that only by rethinking narcissism in this latter, less triumphant, and more defensive, "mature" way, could Derrida pass beyond
the aporias of traditional philosophy of the subject and fulfill the promise
he gave at the very beginning of his deconstructive project: the promise of a situated, heterological subjectivity, able to confront otherness in
a negotiative mode, beyond the paralyzing opposition of self-enclosure
and self-dissolution. As we have tried to suggest here, this project, never
realized by Derrida himself, is exactly what Bloom has in mind.

IN DEFENSE OF DEFENSES

> A strong egoism is a protection against falling ill, but in the last
> resort we must begin to love in order not to fall ill, and we are bound
> to fall ill if, in consequence of frustration, we are unable to love.
> —Sigmund Freud, *On Narcissism: An Introduction*

> An Israelite would not be able to burst out contemptuously like
> Hamlet, "Words words, words!" for "word" is in itself not only sound
> and breath but reality.
> —Thorleif Boman, *Hebrew Thought Compared with Greek*

If Bloom can see in *différance* a mechanism revealing the true "function" of subjectivity in the game of writing, it is only because, according
to him, Derrida makes yet another significant departure from Western
philosophical tradition. He praises Derrida for giving up on the idea of
logos and bringing into play bold new semantic possibilities of its Hebrew
equivalent, *davhar*. Writes Bloom:

> Though he nowhere says so, it may be that Derrida is substituting
> *davhar* for *logos*, thus correcting Plato by a Hebraic equating of the
> writing-act and the mark-of-articulation with the word itself. (*MM*, 43)

Bloom never revoked his applause, despite many later fallings-out with
Derrida, and went on to think about this rediscovery of *davhar* as the
latter's main speculative achievement. Let us then follow, for a while,
Bloom's proposition, and see if it works, that is, if it clarifies some of
Derrida's notorious vagueness on the fateful question of subject.

We have already indicated that the main problem of Derrida lies in his
mistrust in the idea of defense that he always perceives as "egological"

and reactionary. For Bloom, quite the contrary, the subjective way is always and only the way of defense. Yet, it is crucial to understand the true target of this defense. Here, we will try to change radically the received understanding of the ego's defensive mechanisms, and show that they are not so much the defenses of the beautiful soul, who tries to seal itself tautologically in her inner kingdom, as the defenses of an already heterological subject who tries not to get *lost* in the realm of language and thus to *survive* the deconstructive aporia.

But the real question here is: is it possible to rethink the subject outside the traditional egological context? For Freud, the ego is predominantly the site of defense against disturbing onslaughts of both internal and external reality. As he asserts again and again, "the mental apparatus is first and foremost a device designed for mastering excitations" (1989, 553), and the ego, the privileged representative of the psyche, is nothing but an anxiously calculating logistic machine. Says Freud in *Inhibitions, Symptoms and Anxiety:*

> The ego is an organization ... whose desexualized energy *betrays its origins* in its striving for *binding and unification*, and this compulsion to synthesize increases in proportion to the strength of the ego. (1959, 24; my emphasis)

Ego "betrays its own origins" by becoming, first, desexualized, and second, oriented not toward a free flow of primary energy but toward "binding and unification," which throws over reality an immobilizing net of concepts and categories. In every attempt to theorize, therefore, Freud sees an extreme narcissistic syndrome of desire for total control, which can be detected already at the early stages of animistic thought. Comments Samuel Weber in his *Legend of Freud*, a book wholly devoted to the Freudian notion of narcissism:

> The animistic attempt to comprehend the external world in terms of unity and totality corresponds to the newly formed unity within the psyche: the narcissistic ego ... The "expectation of an intelligible whole" described by Freud, the expectation of a coherent meaning, appears thus to denote the reaction of an ego seeking to defend its conflict-ridden cohesion against equally endemic centripetal tendencies. *The pursuit of meaning; the activity of construction, synthesis, unification; the incapacity to admit anything irreducibly alien, to leave any residue unexplained*—all this indicates the struggle of the ego to

establish and to maintain an identity that is all the more precarious
and vulnerable to the extent that it depends on what it must exclude.
(1982, 13–14; my emphasis)[10]

Yet, if we compare these two quotations with probably the most famous
sentence from *On Narcissism: An Introduction*, which forms the epigraph
to this section, we shall see that things get much more complicated in
the process. The narcissistic ego not only is "precarious and vulnerable"
in its attempts to order the terrifying chaos of heteronomical data, but
is also caught in a dynamic double bind between two opposing *pursuits*,
and it is bound to "fall ill" whenever it fully accomplishes only one of
them. If it manages to subsume everything alien under "an intelligible
whole," of which it will make itself a solid center, it will collapse under
the weight of its own "strong egoism": it will turn into a dead black hole,
stagnant and opaque—hardly a match for the shiny beautiful soul of idealist philosophy. On the other hand, if the ego invests too much of its
narcissistic energy in *pursuing* an alien object, it will empty itself and
thus vanish, no longer able to sustain itself as a separate psychic instance.

Yet, there seems to be a way out of this aporetic predicament. Freud
suggests that, apart from the "unhappy" narcissism of a strongly egotis-
tic ego, which vainly tries to subsume all of reality under its rule, there
exists a "happier" version of narcissism he connects with a notion of creativity: not explanatory but creative pursuit of meaning, combined with
a pursuit of an object, remaining both alien and simultaneously related
to the ego itself. He thus quotes the final lines of Heine's *Schöpfungslieder*
(*Songs of Creation*), in which God himself declares that his illness, his
burning madness (*ein Flammenwahnsinn*), was the cause of the whole creation and that only thanks to the creative act could he finally be "healed,"
gesund. He was too full of himself, teeming with insane wrath, deeply
discontented with his original condition of self-sameness. Thus, by creating he "put himself out," but not completely, since he projected a new
meaning and established an intimate link with a work he created—the
world—whose existence was not simply reducible to God's inner representation of it, yet simultaneously not totally alien to him either. The
work, therefore, whose ideal paradigm is God's creation of the world,
appears as capable of squaring the circle of two contradictory pursuits—
the centripetal, self-enclosing pursuit of meaning and the centrifugal,
self-losing pursuit of object—by canceling the apparent opposition
of these two directions in one movement: the creative thrust forward
resulting in a *relation*, a vital singular link between creator and his work.

The creative act of thrusting forward and the vital link with something else other than the self, forming a privileged, singular relation, constitute two sides of this other, more dynamic and outgoing form of "healthier" naricissism. This is merely a suggestion, appearing at the end of Freud's essay, but it is precisely this alternative, simultaneously more sane and mature, notion of narcissism which we would like to develop here.[11]

This allusion on Freud's part leads toward a different, nonlogocentric understanding of what he himself calls a "pursuit of meaning." There are, fundamentally, two ways of interpreting this concept. One tradition, philosophical or "logocentric," would insist that this pursuit aims at an explanatory image of a seamless whole of beings which are subsumed under abstract, general categories; the other, that it aims at a different kind of command over things, which manifests itself in the power to name them in their singularity. The one tradition would like to see meaning as an effort of speculative integration of everything; the other—more primordial, biblical, or simply poetic—would like to see it as a force of giving names, especially for the first time.[12] This difference boils down ultimately to Bloom's favorite distinction, the fundamental difference between Greek and Hebrew understanding of the "word" and "meaning," which, throughout the whole history of the West, has made all the truly crucial differences. This is, again, the famous distinction between *logos* and *davhar:* between two types of sense-giving agencies— one based on the activity of conceptualization, the other based on the activity of singularized naming—which are both narcissistic, yet in a wholly disparate way.

The task of developing fully this critical difference would require a separate book,[13] but it will have to suffice here to give just an outline of the fundamental rift that opens between the two traditions. Greek *logos* tends to be "philosophical" in the absoluteness of its main driving ambition: going for a total epistemological victory over reality, it also risks a radical failure. While Hebrew thought never chose the path of philosophical certitude and thus never built a concept of a self-enclosed subjectivity, the Hebrew soul, the obvious precursor of the romantic *fühlende Seele*, is almost by definition "precarious and vulnerable," that is, a priori heterological, open to all sorts of revelatory traumas. She is defensive and anxious from the start; as Rosenzweig put it, always "in the midst of life," and thus never outside the world, in the safe epistemological haven of "the view from nowhere." The philosophical subject, therefore, thinks in an act of a silent logical process: its *logos* is tautological, that is, it wants to collect, preserve, and protect from the invasion of otherness. Whereas the Hebrew soul thinks in an act of a living speech: its *davhar* is heterological—it wants to mark itself, bring presence, manifest a difference. Thinking in terms of *logos* unifies, striving toward abstract totalities—while thinking in terms of *davhar* diversifies, striving toward singularized relations. *Logos* enhances generalities—*davhar* wishes for strong, singular presences. *Logos* subsumes particulars under general categories—*davhar* names things instead, and establishes between the namer and the named a singular relation. *Logos* is dualistic, and thus produces the fissure between the subject and the object, based on the logic of mutual exclusion—while *davhar* is agonistic and dialectical, driving toward a special relationship with the thing it names. *Logos* is theoretical—*davhar* rather visionary; *logos* is introjective—*davhar* expressive. Bloom writes in *A Map of Misreading*:

> *Davhar* is at once "word," "thing," and "act," and its root meaning involves the notion of driving forward something that initially is held-back. This is the word as a moral act, a true word that is at once an object or thing and a deed or act . . . In contrast to this dynamic word, the *logos* is an intellectual concept, going back to a root meaning that involves gathering, arranging, putting-into-order. The concept of *davhar* is: speak, act, be. The concept of *logos* is: speak, reckon, think. *Logos* orders and makes reasonable the context of speech, yet in its deepest meaning does not deal with the function of speaking. *Davhar*, in thrusting forward what is concealed in the self, is concerned with oral expression, with getting a word, a thing, a deed out into the light. (42–43)[14]

The ego of the logocentric order either wins or loses everything: its stake is the highest triumph—the whole chaotic, both external and internal, reality *negated* and thus subsumed under rational categories—or a total collapse, a complete dissolution in the disarray of the *flux*. The ego of the logocentric order is not implicated in the world, is not identical to the speaking subject, who lives in this world, but lies deeper than the speech act, in a transcendental realm of *beyond* where it cannot be touched by the contingencies of life: it can either rest totally outside or be destroyed by the exposition to the *flux*. But once we begin to conceive "the pursuit of meaning," which is the ego's part, in terms not of *logos* but of *davhar*, the stakes of the narcissistic game will appear in a different, in fact precisely reverse, light: not so much a totalitarian triumph of the subject over unruly reality, but as a successful defense against totalitarian reality which threatens to engulf, unify, and reduce the unruliness and difference of the singular self (for, we have to remember that no self can act with the innovative freshness of God's "first naming" and that it has to wrestle with the world as already created and the fallen language that preserved only traces of its original "name-giving"). The ego of *davhar*, in stark contrast to the ego of *logos*, does not seek triumph over reality, but merely a defense against reality as a reductive force; it does not wish to preside over the ego-centered order imposed on the manifold of sensations, it merely wants to cut into the order of things which threaten to destroy its precarious singularity. The ego's frustration and restlessness, as described by Freud, must hence appear as failure in the logocentric system, but they are completely at home in the vision inspired by a different, more Hebraic vision of the ego's narcissism, which is openly defensive and agonistic. The picture of the ego as constantly overlapping, negotiating, opposing, and dispersing itself and other psychic agencies in a "conflictual relation" is more true to the narcissism of *davhar* than the narcissism of *logos*, which apparently dreams only of peace, stillness, and everlasting sameness. There is clearly "no one narcissism" (as Derrida famously claimed), just like there is no one organization of the ego.

So, even if Freud's own interpretations may sound slightly misleading on this point, Bloom's Freudian revision makes it absolutely clear that the defense, which is synonymous with what Kierkegaard used to call "the subjective way," has nothing to do with safe-guarding the principle of homogenous self-presence. Thus, although he would endorse, in spite of the "French Freud's" open disgust for the mostly American "psychology of the ego," the significance of the book on defenses written by Freud's daughter, he wouldn't do it simply for the ego's peace of mind. After Anna Freud, Bloom also stresses the ego's "constant alertness to dangers from without and within" (Anna Freud 1996, 174), but he bestows a new twist on the final goal of all these defensive mechanisms which, in his case, is never simply a "self-preservation," never simply a sheer "existence," never just life, but—to leap again to Bloom's favorite Jewish idiom—*more life*, that is, life augmented and individualized, transcending the simple need of self-protection. The ego is indeed alert to all sorts of dangers, coming from without and from within, but not just because it wants to "preserve its existence" (ibid.), yet most of all because it wants to remain *distinct:* by protecting itself against deadly threats, it simultaneously shields itself against becoming one with the assaulting influences. It cannot deny the influence, but it can nonetheless defend against its literality, which means that the ego can *trope* it, thus

entering the path of creation: "a trope," he writes, "is just as much a concealed mechanism of defense, as a defense is a concealed trope" (*MM*,
77). Defenses are tropes, and vice versa; the psyche uses her defenses
as tropes, and the poem uses its tropes as defenses; trope and defense
is one and the same device. This is why Bloom will say in "Freud and
the Sublime" that "Freud's rhetoric of the psyche, as codified by Anna
Freud in *The Ego and the Mechanisms of Defense*, is as comprehensive a
system of tropes as Western theory has devised" (*A*, 98). Thus, if we forget that Anna Freud's therapeutic ideal consists in giving the ego of the
analysand a missing sense of safety, and read the following passage as a
description of a final and incurable predicament of the human psyche,
this portrait of the ego will come very close to the agonistic condition of
the poetic self, forever caught in its "dialectical relationship with another
poet or poets" (*AI*, 91). She asks:

> Whence does the ego derive the form of its defense mechanisms?
> Is the struggle with the outside forces modeled on the conflict with
> the instincts? Or is the converse the case: are the measures adopted
> in the external struggle the prototype of the various defense mecha-
> nisms? The decision between these two alternatives can hardly be a
> straightforward one. The infantile ego experiences the onslaught of
> instinctual and external stimuli at the same time; if it wishes to pre-
> serve its existence it must defend itself on both sides simultaneously.
> (1996, 174)

This agitated, chronically unsafe way of being which consists in oscillating—*Schweben* again—between two types of danger, in negotiating
a third place in between two contrary "onslaughts," is also the way of
being of the Bloomian subject, which finds itself in a constant motion of
displacement, that is, of fleeing from itself. It is not the "beautiful," pure,
and wholesome subject but a restless creature, torn and tense, which
defends itself against both internal and external danger, and escapes into
what may be called a *rhetorical asylum:* a language of figures lying halfway
between the internal and the external danger, the haunting vision of the
precursor, which "is in the id," and the inertia of words always belonging
to the anonymous Other. This subject—to paraphrase Derrida's famous
sentence on *Dasein* in "The Ends of Man"—is not exactly the Freudian
ego, but still, it is also not something completely else. It *is* an ego, but
without the "ego psychology" and the whole "logocentric" tradition
which engendered it: an ego freed from the conceptual pretences of

subjectivist philosophy, and thus freed to be what it is, truly *exposed*—vulnerable, shaky, and in a bad need of constant defense. Just like the bodily surface to which Freud compares it: equally prone to harm, laid bare, suspect to constant influences and irritations. Not a safe center lying in well-protected depths of psychic reality, but on the contrary—a moving, shifting, continually self-displacing, placeless place where it always hurts most.

Rethought radically in this new—Freudian, yet not necessary "ego-logical" or "logocentric"—way, the notion of defense opens up to theoretical perspectives which push the ego away from the classical subject and close to what, after Derrida, became known as a "deconstructive subjectivity." Here, first of all, defense is not just a secondary strategy of warding off otherness in order to secure subjective self-enclosure, but the ego's original mode of existence which makes it *marked* from the very beginning with a truly Derridean "*arche*-trace," a stigma of ever-present, imperishable alterity.[15]

Let's state it once again: Here, defense is not so much defending against alterity but, to the contrary, it is defending against *sameness*, which is implied in the twofold influence the ego is subjected to. The ego wants to be and to be distinct, which means that it only wishes to introduce difference where there is not enough difference, that is, where alterity, despite its name, not only does not constitute a source of difference but, quite the contrary, a major threat to difference. In its anxiety of influence, ego does not close itself off in the "egological" sameness but struggles against the pressure of identification which would produce only more of the same: either through the imitation of the precursor, or through the sublimation to the level of selfless, universal generality.

And the Freudian ego does not really know any of the "self-sameness" which the deconstructive critique of subjectivity targets as the most persistent residue of the metaphysics of presence: ego is a thin—as opposite to the fullness of the imaginary subject—and almost placeless *surface* which is in a ceaseless negotiation with hostile influences. As Derrida would have it, the ego permanently *negotiates*—in agon and in defense—and has no safe haven of sameness to fall upon; influence, anxiety, and defense form a triad which is present in the life of the ego from the very start, thus making it impossible for it to ever become self-present.

Thus, to use Derrida's phrase again, although not completely in harmony with his intentions, "there is no one narcissism" indeed, which means that narcissism cannot be simply identified with the ego's obstinacy to reduce everything different to the same; in the slightly perverse perspective we are trying to develop here, alterity is not so self-evidently *alter* after all. If there is a part of the psyche—Bloom would call it "a poet in a poet"—that begs to make the difference and break the spell of self-sameness, it can only be the narcissistic ego whose mature narcissism manifests itself in refusal to open completely and defenselessly to alien influences. For such unqualified openness would mean just one thing— *to imitate*, and with it: to perish as a distinct being, diminish one's life, and, worst of all, to lose one's name.[16]

And, last but not least, this defensive-agonistic notion of the narcissistic interest, which we have tried to champion here, completely changes the picture of the deconstructionist aporia from which we departed in this chapter. Instead of a "beautiful soul," whose sole ambition is to stay within herself and at all cost avoid the dissolution in the alien sphere of writing, we deal with an ego whose narcissism consists in precisely the reverse: in negotiating a vital link, a singularized relation with the universe of words. Its narcissistic interest drives this ego toward "putting itself out" and leaving "out there" a mark of its idiosyncratic signature. Although it cannot use words as if there were only names—given by it for the first time—it is nevertheless the unreachable ideal it wishes to achieve.

Tricks, Shticks, and Trafficking: Negotiations

> And yet there is suffering . . . there is suffering.
> —Jacques Derrida, *Negotiations*

It is always suffering which is the reason why we negotiate, that is, engage in a confrontation by wanting to make things a little bit better, but never ideal. The mode of negotiation, therefore, has less to do with the logocentric institution of questions and answers, and more with the hassling tradition of Hebrew heroes who, always more or less unfairly wronged, could not hope to win their appeal against God's verdict, yet could at least make themselves heard, raise their pained voice, and bargain for some degree of alleviation. The mode of negotiation, therefore, is used whenever we bring forward the singular presences of our *devarim* (words)—not as exchangeable, abstract *rationes* (reasons), which could be detached from our situatedness and weighed behind a veil of ignorance, but as concrete *voices* which expect perhaps pity, relief, or mitigation, but never an ultimate solution: "This means: *no thesis, no position, no theme, no station, no substance, no stability, a perpetual suspension, a suspension without rest*" (Derrida 2002, 13–14; my emphasis).

We have already noticed the change of rhetorical register in moving away from the Nietzschean careless, dauntless, lofty freeplay toward the anxiety-ridden, earthbound game of survival; now, in talking about "negotiations," Derrida explicitly confirms this change, which chimes with Bloom's insistence on radical "deidealization" of all our main speculative categories:

> This is why I prefer the word "negotiation" to more noble words . . .
> there is always something about negotiation that is a little dirty, that
> gets one's hands dirty. Once one negotiates, something is being traf-
> ficked, something in the order of a traffic, or the relations of force. It
> is a question of style, of social connotation: I prefer the word "nego-
> tiation" because it does not disguise the anxiety, about which I am
> speaking, with nobility. As a result, it seems more mediocre; one
> thinks of force, one thinks of compromise, one thinks of impure
> things. *Negotiation is impure.* (ibid., 13–14; my emphasis)

And one also immediately thinks of the other—less noble, less grand, merely defensive—narcissism of the real Freudian ego: indeed, with "no thesis, no position, no theme, no station, no substance, no stability, [in] a perpetual suspension, a suspension without rest"; the ego, which restlessly schemes to avoid being crashed by alien forces, is capable only of rotten compromises, and, driven by anxiety, avails itself of all possible dirty tricks to preserve its existence as a singular being: something unique, irreducible to surrounding forces and influences. Hubris and humbleness, a big cause and low measures; all this is combined in the impure, highly contaminated, decidedly nonutopian mode of *negotiation.*

There is nothing to boast about here, not much place left for the haughty Nietzschean pathos which Derrida, especially in his early "ultra" phase, so visibly enjoyed. The little essay by Derrida called "Che cos'è la poesia?" ("What Is Poetry?") is an enigmatic piece written in the "negotiative" mode, which, like Freudian dreams, seeks recourse to tropological disguises not for high symbolical reasons but, precisely the opposite, for shameful lack of nobility. But is it really true that Derrida "prefers the word 'negotiation' to more noble words"? Or, are we dealing here, once again, merely with declaration?

The first doubt emerges once one realizes that even here Derrida scrupulously avoids openly affirmative comments on psychic defenses

that lie at the background of his not very "noble" hedgehog figure, *le hér-*
rison. Recoiled in itself, down-to-earth, and fretful, yet at the same time
sovereign and defiant, the hedgehog, this traditional symbol of stubborn
self-defense, forms a perfect icon of a poem. Says Derrida, somewhat
immodestly:

> You will call poem from now on a certain passion of the singular
> mark, the signature that repeats its dispersion, each time beyond the
> logos, a-human, barely domestic, not reappropriable into the family
> of the subject: a converted animal, rolled up in a ball, turned toward
> the other and toward itself, in sum, a thing—modest, discreet, close
> to earth, the humility that you surname, thus transporting yourself
> in the name beyond a name, a catachrestic *hérrison*, its arrows held at
> the ready, when this ageless blind thing hears but does not see death
> coming. (1995b, 297)

The *hérrison* is catachrestic because it is not a simple metaphor whose
route can be traveled easily back and forward: it is a catachresis because
the image of the hedgehog is an uneasy, "barely domestic," distant projection, which bears all the features of *das Unheimliche* (the uncanny). It
cannot, therefore, be "reappropriable into the family of the subject," for
its vision of the subject is precisely *unfamiliar:* clandestine and uncanny.
It brings to the surface a murky secret of the psychic life, the "secret"
which, according to Derrida, is the source of the name (or surname) and
which is also a "knot" caught in what he calls "the paradox of narcissism": the dark entanglement of hubris and defense, warfare and anxiety,
humbleness and provocation, blindness and insight (1995a, 12). The
poetry, therefore, is this shadowy thing of uncanniness, the *unheimlich*
projection of the dark secret of the soul.

   The words with which Derrida describes the original condition of
poetry might have come straight from Bloom's *The Anxiety of Influence*
(and perhaps they did?). Every new poem, says Derrida, must meet the
same aporia in which it can only begin to *negotiate*, that is, switch to
the mode of dealing with hopeless, insoluble predicaments: it wants
to be original, singular, inimitable, safely beyond the rule of repetition
and generality. At the same time however—and here comes the already
familiar difference of valuation:

> Our poem does not hold still within names, nor even within words. It
> is first of all thrown out on the roads and in the fields, thing beyond

languages, even if it sometimes happens that it recalls itself in language, when it gathers itself up, rolled up in a ball on itself, it is more
threatened than ever in its retreat: *it thinks it is defending itself, and it
loses itself.* (ibid., 293; my emphasis)

Just like Bloom's poems, mean products of narcissistic anxieties, Derrida's
hérrison is not a noble animal either: "not the phoenix, not the eagle, but
the *hérrison*, very lowly, low down, close to earth. Neither sublime, nor
incorporeal" (ibid., 297), it is a *thing*, an artifact of negotiation which rallies whatever force it still has to withstand the impact of the surrounding
hostile reality. The poem, this blind thing of poetry, rolls itself up, and in
this ball-like, quasi-monadic state pretends to achieve a perfect discontinuity, which is, as Bloom asserts, the only dream of strong poets. Yet his
defenses, however admirable for their obstinacy, are countereffective and
thus completely futile:

> You must celebrate, you have to commemorate amnesia, savagery,
> even the stupidity of the "by heart": the *hérrison*. It blinds itself.
> Rolled up in a ball, prickly with spines, vulnerable and dangerous, cal-
> culating and ill-adapted (because it makes itself into a ball, sensing the
> danger on the autoroute, it exposes itself to an accident). (ibid., 297)

But it is precisely this exposure which makes the hedgehog poem defensive and provocative at the same time. It makes itself vulnerable by
showing its own spikes, it opens itself to wounding the very moment
it decides to wound: "No poem without accident," continues Derrida,
"no poem that does not open itself like a wound, but no poem that
is not also just as wounding" (ibid., 297). A poem, therefore, is a projection of the narcissistic self which casts itself obliquely in a form of
a "catachrestic *hérrison*," an "ageless blind thing," rolled in itself and
protectively sealed from the world of influences. But by doing this, by
committing such severe, such strongly willed error, the self also automatically projects a scene of a catastrophe (Bloom), or a necessity of an
accident (Derrida), in which this idiomatic reverie will have to crash
under the burden of the passing language. This Derridean pessimistic
image, nota bene, almost literally repeats the central motif of Shelley's
highly ironic *Triumph of Life:* the image of a heavy chariot, rolling down
the road to a doubtlessly bad infinity, rolling over everything singular which vainly tries to resist the all-leveling inertia of life. Whereas
Bloom would add immediately: all right, but at least *the poem will die*

pricking! It won't go unless it wounds the power that wounded it in the first place, unless it leaves a small indentation on the wheel of this old senseless chariot which rolled over it so indifferently. The familiar diagnosis resurfaces once again: the poem's success lies in dying its own death, in the singularity of its failure. It cannot win, but it must fail as no other poem dared to fail. But Derrida does not perceive it as success; "the death coming" simply annuls hedgehog's defensive maneuvers by exposing their seeming cunning as a touching "stupidity." No "negotiation" is possible where every resistance is doomed from the start.

Thus, if we recall what Derrida says about the "paradox of narcissism" in his essay on the name, we will see that this dark secret has only one strategy at its disposal; either it stays forever in the private depths of the beautiful soul, or it gets projected—and at the same time *sacrificed*—in the gesture which is only seemingly defensive but, in fact, comes much closer to a suicidal self-offering, once again, a Heideggerian *gelassen* letting go.

The Survival of the Effects, or *Not* Letting Go

> So shall my word be that "goes forth" from my mouth;
> It shall not return to me empty,
> But it shall accomplish that which I purpose,
> And prosper in the thing for which I sent it.
> —Isaiah, 55.10

Yet from the point of view of a poet—a point of view so well represented and defended by Harold Bloom—such "letting go" would mean nothing but a suicide. Derrida's analysis, revealing "the infinite paradoxes of narcissism," ruins the poet's dream and desire; hedgehog or not, he has no other choice but to try *not* to disappear in his name and *not* to offer his works as a gift for future generations. Thus, after all the talk about ignoble trafficking and dubious shticks, Derrida's "angelic" idiom bounces back at its worst (or rather, most noble), sounding no less "idealizing" than T. S. Eliot's praise of the individual talent which is supposed to win everything through losing oneself in the tradition. Nietzsche's bathos is back, and the uncanny moment of *le hérrison*—gone.

Is there anything left of the poet's singularity in his writing, once he "lets go" of his narcissistic "dark secret"? The subjective special effects that interest Derrida have no longer anything to do with the wretched paradox of narcissism (as he envisages it); they appear free from the self-defeating calculations of the egological order. Signature and date, says Derrida, are the only "marks" which indicate in *écriture* the singularity of the subject because only they can, partly losing themselves, and partly surviving, resist the contamination.[17] Other possible effects—most of all, *idiom*—rely on their "purity" and as such cannot survive in the contaminating realm of writing. Says Derrida:

> I do not believe in *pure* idioms. I think there is naturally a desire, for whoever speaks or writes, to sign in an idiomatic, that is, irreplaceable manner. But as soon as there is a mark, that is, the possibility of a repetition, as soon as there is language, generality has entered the scene and the idiom compromises with something that is not idiomatic: with a common language, concepts, laws, general norms. (1995b, 200)

And as he writes in "Psyche: Inventions of the Other":

> For there to be invention, the condition of a certain generality must be met, and the production of a certain objective ideality (or ideal objectivity) must occasion recurrent operations, thus a utilizable apparatus . . . once invented, so to speak, invention is invented only if repetition, generality, common availability, and thus publicity are introduced or promised in the structure of the first time. (1989a, 51)

But who would believe in *pure* idioms? Not even poets themselves who in their secret hearts know all too well that they are not young Adams in the morning of language. As usual, Derrida builds an opposition which is too stark and too simple and as such must lead to his preferred default mode of aporia: between desire for pure idiom and the institution of language as equally pure generality.[18]

As we already know, Bloom's favorite saying from *Pirke Aboth* is by the celebrated Rabbi Tarphon: "You are not required to complete the work, but neither you are free to desist from it" (Hertz 1945, 2, 21). Rabbi Tarphon and his concept of *work* as combining *in*-vention and *con*-vention, the moment of agon and the moment of consent—singularity and communality, newness and tradition, and, most of all, work as an always unfinished process, interminable, without beginning and without end, without *arche* and without *telos*—is the source of Bloom's dialectic which opposes the rigid, aporetic style of Derridean thinking. While

Derrida would emphasize the fatalistic nature of this paradox, saying that idiom has no other choice than to *surrender* to the context of tradition, Bloom embraces its implied dialectic and attempts to pass beyond the aporia of idiom and institution.

The double bind is only the beginning of the process, not its final characteristic: "In so far as a poet is and remains a poet, he must *exclude and negate* other poets," says Bloom. "Yet he must begin by *including and affirming* a precursor poet or poets, for there is no other way to become a poet" (*MM*, 121). The poet, therefore, cannot desist from struggling for his originality, but neither can he conduct this struggle in a vacuum. He has to admit the existence of what he at the same time longs to "exclude and negate." The Bloomian agon, therefore, works precisely the way of the Freudian *Verneinung*, which, in its dialectical and dramatic modernization of Rabbi Tarphon's wisdom, simultaneously affirms and undoes one and the same thing.

Thus, the ego, which is the subject of this agonistic denegation, cannot be conceived as the logocentric seat of "self-sameness" that finds its "proper place" in a quasi-transcendental *beyond*. It must be seen as a restless surface which, by its very nature, has no place of its own, and only wants to put itself in a place which always belonged to the Other.[19] The universe—as in the Koheletian picture we have already evoked—is already full of beings and full of meanings; there can never be anything new under the sun, unless through a trick or shtick. Beings and meanings have their places, but not the subject which can only come to existence by assaulting what already exists: by *cutting* into the body of language and by *slanting* the order of meanings. The subject, therefore, is a *stylus* which cuts, and thus leaves in the text a mark of an idiomatic indentation. It is, as Emily Dickinson would have it, *a certain slant of light* which allows to see what was, is, and will be *differently*, or as Stevens's necessary angel of imagination would say, "to see the earth *again*."[20]

This subject, living in constant overlapping, self-displacement, and agonistic negotiation with other influences produces a word, "a power-laden word," which cuts into language and slants vision, a word which does not convey the truth of an elusive inner presence but is a living performative of the presence which can be accomplished only in the game of writing. This *davhar* is a living proof of subjectivity, and, at the same time, its only "mark of survival." It does not return to the ego—for there is no safe place to return to—but, quite the contrary, *projects* "the subjective effect" onto the writing where it can stay, as Derrida would put it, "inscribed and monumentalized." It must become compromised and damaged, yet, at least relatively, it can be now *at rest*—like the Kierkegaardian memorial volume with an unblurred inscription.

Finally, the two types of narcissism come into a clear, open opposition. Logocentric narcissism wishes no contamination or confrontation with the other of writing, convention, and generality of signs; it wishes to stay pure, safe, and homogenous in the sphere of "self-sameness," evidently marked by its ownership. Whereas the davharocentric narcissism, hungry to "bring forward" the inner secret of singularity, longs for a performance and thus a test in an agonistic collision with "what already exists." A typical logocentric subject, therefore, would see its success in a beautiful self-enclosure, but such isolation would certainly indicate a failure for subjectivity conceived in terms of its uniqueness.

Part III

Wrestling Harold

Chapter 5

Intricate Evasions, or the Poetic Will-to-Ignorance

> Indeed, the most precious thing human beings possess . . . depends in the final analysis, as anybody can easily know, on some such point of strength that must be left in the dark, but nevertheless carries and supports the whole, and this force would give out at precisely the moment when one wanted to dissolve it through comprehension.
> —Friedrich Schlegel, "On Incomprehensibility"

We shall now resume themes we have already discussed in the first two parts, but this time develop them in Bloom's own idiom: highly idiosyncratic, deliberately "non-angelic" and "ignoble"; deidealizing, sobering, and disenchanting, yet not for a "reducing" or deadening but a "quickening" or vitalizing purpose (*MM*, 65) that puts its stakes on the defenses of the singular life. The first chapter will thus be devoted to the defense of the poetic self against the danger of reductionism; the canvas for our reflections will be delivered by the analysis of two of Bloom's famous ratios, *clinamen* and *kenosis*. The second chapter will tackle the crucial notion of antithetical vitalism, basing on another pair of *daemonization* and *askesis*. And the third chapter, evolving round the last duo of ratios, *tessera* and *apophrades*, will discuss the dialectics of the final outcome of the poetic struggle, this "hard-won, partial victory," which cannot be classified either as triumph or failure.

In Bloom's own rendering of the poetic agon, ratios form a linear story. Yet, the division of six ratios in couples is justified by the fact that they indeed can be systematized according to three types of defenses that govern the whole agon: *evasion* (first and third ratio), *life enhancement* (fourth and fifth ratio), and *reconciliation* (second and sixth ratio).

231

Thus, although Bloom's version of the agon may be more dynamic, this one is more systematic; by concentrating on these uniquely Bloomian types of defenses and their respective goals within the process of poetic singularization, it allows for a broader, more speculative approach we are championing in this book.

HUBRIS AND EXODUS: THE TRAGIC HERO OF OUR TIMES

> To be an artist is to fail, as no other dare fail.
> —Samuel Beckett, "Three Dialogs"

In the struggle to pave the meandering "subjective way"—simultaneously defiant and defensive, centripetal and centrifugal, retreating and advancing—Bloom is assisted by his two favorite tropes, deriving from both Hellenistic and Hebrew sources. Just like the romantic visionary company he has been writing on with such fervor for years, he seems to live under the spell of mixed influences. The numerous synonyms of his six revisionary ratios, in which he describes the structure of the poetic striving for originality, come both from the Greek and the Jewish tradition alike: *clinamen, tessera, kenosis, askesis, daemonization,* and *apophrades* meet their uneasy equivalents in many "Hebrew sixes" deriving from the Torah as well as from the kabbalistic *behinot* (revisionary tropes).[1] But here, we would like to point just to the two tropes, one Greek and one Hebrew, whose unique combination gives a peculiar flavor to Bloom's speculation on the agonistic nature of modern subjectivity.

These two tropes are: on the one hand, hubris, the conceit of singular being which refuses to be reduced to generality—and, on the other, the Jewish *yeziat*, the notion of Exodus, signifying a constant effort of getting out "into the wilderness" from all possible houses of bondage: systematic closures and universal truths which spell the tyranny of monotonous repetition. Bloom's notion of agon, in which modern poetic subjectivity fights for its right to be unique and singular, ingeniously juxtaposes these two splendid tropes of daring, which, although culturally distinct, unite in their powerful defiance against the reductive influence of "what already exists." And it is on their combined power that Bloom grounds his anguished hopes for the emergence of *the new:* a new poetic tone, a new voice, a new life that could not be easily reduced to the realm of the *already.*

The first appearance of hubris initiates what Hans Blumenberg aptly called "the work on myth," a process in which subjectivity defends its singular being against a return to the chaos of undifferentiation.[2] In Bloom's writings hubris likes to take on the Gnostic form of the pneumatic spark:[3] Lacan, himself deeply influenced by a mixed esoteric tradition, could have defined it as the typical hysterical hubris of an individual who anxiously refuses to sacrifice himself for the sake of the whole. The agon is therefore an intricate maturational process of the poetic hubris, which, by insisting on the Kierkegaardian repetition forward, refuses to be obliterated by the overwhelming power of generality. At the same time, however, the agon is yet another, particularly refined troping of Exodus-in-progress. The hubristic subject feels threatened by the modern, aggressively reductive incarnation of the reality principle and its thoroughly disenchanted influence; by fighting the united forces of generality—the burden of ever-growing history, the mechanistic impact of dehumanized nature, and the transience of everything singular in the face of the objective knowledge—it challenges "the myth of that which exists" to create its own counterreality.[4]

Bloom is not the first one to strike the connection between hubris and Exodus: this cross-cultural association is already a staple motif in Franz Rosenzweig and Walter Benjamin, who both attempted an ingenious "Jewish" reading of Greek tragedy.[5] Also, the reason for which he uses this conceptual melange in his notion of the agon draws from the same source: the belief in the primacy of *defiance* as the most primordial, and necessarily defensive, attitude of the singular self. According to Rosenzweig's *Star of Redemption*, defiance is a prediscursive symptom of the self's irreducible *Besonderheit*, "idiosyncrasy":

> The existence of man is the existence in the distinctive . . . He exists, not beyond the universal validity and necessity of knowledge, but *this side of it*. He exists, not when knowledge ceases, but before it begins. And it is only because he exists prior to knowledge that he exists afterward too, that he again and again announces his triumphant "I am still there" to all knowledge, no matter how completely it has deluded itself with having captured him in the vessels of its universal validity and its necessity . . . *His first word, his primeval Yea, affirms his peculiarity.* (1985, 64; my emphasis)

The singular self, therefore, has no theoretical grounds for its claims: quite the contrary, its hubris is unjustified in so far as it stems from an order, that is, in Derrida's words, "older than knowledge."[6] It says its "ancient Yes" to assert itself apart from any external predication and stamps its signature to defy the impact of a reduction which it simply *does not want to know*. This stubborn *Selbstheit*, the Rosenzweigian "selfhood," forms thus a nontheoretical ground of every effort of *yeziat*, "getting out" from all objectifying houses of bondage. It creates what Bloom, in his meditations on "the Jewish Negative," would later call a "radical inwardness": a realm of the self set apart from the pressures of external reality, yet not safely separated—the way Cartesian cogito would be—but always endangered and acutely aware of its agonistic, willfully lying, act of origin.[7]

Here, as elsewhere, I will try to misread deeper and deeper Bloom's favorite hero—his self-admitted obsession and synonym for the Gnostic pneumatic spark, *the poet in a poet*[8]—as an ingenious trope of this special part of the psyche that creates defensive mechanisms against influence, at the same time paving the necessarily wild and wayward "subjective way." This defensive-hubristic defiance comes to the fore mostly in two ratios of Bloom's revisionary sixfold scheme: *clinamen* and *kenosis*, and these only will be my concern in this chapter (the other four ratios, coupled analogically in doubles, will be the subject of the next two). *Clinamen*, the stage of the first "swerving," is the ratio in which the ephebe dares to challenge the authority of the poetic tradition, and does so on the ungroundable basis of narcissistic hubris, which allows him to imagine and anticipate his future greatness: the ephebe breaks the spell of "more of the same" by managing to get out into a broad, open land of his solitary vision. *Kenosis*, on the other hand, is the stage of humbling and emptying, in which the ephebe confronts the most reductive and reifying truths about himself: risking the loss of vision, he has to endure the knowledge about himself as an "objective man," subsumed under the same rules of existence that apply to everybody else. His hubris, so far fueling all his narcissistic fantasies, becomes challenged by a reality principle which leaves no room for self-flattering illusions; at that stage, the ephebe fights for the right to fantasize and thus to resist the universal truth. In both ratios, the gist of the defensive evasion consists in an effort *not to know*: to push away, relegate, defer, or postpone the knowledge which threatens to reduce the precarious singular to the status of a general concept. Both, *clinamen* and *kenosis*, are therefore based on the power of denial, the Freudian *Verneinung*, which, as we have already made it more than clear, comprises *the affective dialectic* of the romantic-psychoanalytic *fühlende Seele:* a dialectic of simultaneous acceptance and rejection, difference and repetition, continuity and rupture, recognition and negation.

Clinamen, or a Hell of One's Own

> Influence is a word that points to the stars; and literary history, as
> a history of the influence of an artist or culture on culture, often
> involves those theogonic bodies. Literature always contends with
> a star-system of some kind: with foreign inheritances, native debts,
> or an overhead of great works whose light still pulses though they
> existed long ago.
>> —Geoffrey Hartman, "From the Sublime to the Hermeneutics"

> God himself, if He wants to live for you, must die: how do you think,
> without death, to inherit his own life?
>> —Angelus Silesius, *The Cherubic Wanderer*

"Has anything more profound ever been written on inheritance?" asks
Derrida in *Sauf le nom*, his essay on *The Cherubinic Wanderer*. Well, perhaps yes. For it wouldn't be so tough to be an heir—*gefährlich ist es, Erbe
zu sein* (it is dangerous to be an heir), as says Nietzsche's Zarathustra—
if the precursor simply *died* to bequeath his life to a poetic progeny.
Thus, if it is so tough, it is only because the precursor refuses to die,
and continues to appear "outrageously more alive than the ephebe himself" (*MM*, 19). In the universe of death, brought by modern process of
Entzauberung (disenchantment), says Bloom, the one who lives here and
now seems less alive than the mighty precursor who has already proved
triumphant over the malaise of influence.

The disenchanted notion of influence as *influenza* is the major theme
of the first part of Bloom's *Anxiety*. In the modern "universe of death," the
once magical fluid sending inspiration on to the Vichian poets and divinators becomes an impersonal, strictly physical factor operating within
well-defined spatio-temporal dimensions.[9] This does not mean, however,
that the disenchanted influence loses its ominous power. Quite to the
contrary, it acquires all demonic aspects of what Girard used to call "the
corrupted myth." Max Weber, similarly, in his famous essay *Wissenschaft
als Beruf* (*Science as a Vocation*), called the era of *die Entzauberung* the time
of a bad spell in which all the advantages of a mythic universe vanish and
all its vices persist. That is, while all the reassuring aspects of mythical
belief are taken away from modern people, independence from the mysterious, influencing factors he called "the demons of our life" is not—and
probably will never be—achieved. Horkheimer and Adorno pointed
to the same impasse of modernity which failed to keep the promise of

autonomy: the disenchanted world with its monotonously homogenous, endlessly repetitive structure of terrifyingly infinite spaces not only does not offer freedom for singular subjectivity, but only spells reductive closures. The world of *influenza* therefore is even worse than Egypt, the bondage of primitive mystery; it is now the House of Reduction, the bad infinity of pointless numerical cycles.[10]

When translated into the sphere of poetic imagination, this means that the influence falls down from heaven to earth: it is now being exerted not between divine mediators—to recall Girard's idiom again— but between poets themselves for whom there is no escape from the hell of mutual rivalry. Influence is transformed into the pressure of the past, the burden of history, which no longer can be weakened by supratemporal, transcendent mediation. As a consequence, great cultural precursors appear as more alive than the actually living individuals who feel threatened by their, as Nietzsche would have it, "numinous shadow," semidivine by default in the increasingly secularized culture. The new-coming life can thus never "seize the moment"; it feels as if it was stolen by the ancestors whose spirits mercilessly haunt the present. Bloom calls it, after Nietzsche's famous essay on the uses and disadvantages of history to life, "the condition of belatedness," which causes the poet to "rebel against being spoken to by a dead man (the precursor) outrageously more alive than himself" (*MM*, 19). And romantics seem especially aware of this tricky predicament. Says Bloom, introducing his bold historicist thesis:

> Romantic tradition differs vitally from earlier forms of tradition, and I think this difference can be reduced to a useful formula. Romantic tradition is *consciously late*, and Romantic literary psychology is therefore necessarily a *psychology of belatedness*. (*MM*, 35; my emphasis)

Bloom thus follows Girard in demystifying the leading myth of modernity, which believes that, by annulling the impact of external mediators, it gives to the individual a chance of full autonomy, his, in Kant's famed words, *Ausgang aus der selbstverschuldigten Unmündigkeit* (exit from the self-inflicted immaturity). In fact, it is the other way round: the more modern *Entzauberung* progresses, the more the degree of dependence increases, which hinders the process of emancipation. The individual may no longer bother about the disarmed majesty of transcendent gods; now, however, he has to deal with new, even more possessive candidates for the glory: *precursors*.

And although Bloom swears that all he has in mind is merely "a theory of poetry," his analysis has a far more universal bearing: the relation of crippling dependence, which occurs between a late-born poet and his splendid dead ancestor, becomes a general predicament for all participants of modern culture. The "poet as a poet" is thus, as in all romantic writings, a pars pro toto of all humanity: what we all, moderns, undergo, he or she experiences with exemplary intensity. This suggestion appears very clearly in Bloom's recent preface to the new edition of *The Anxiety of Influence*, where he states that his theory of poetry "may also be read as an allegory of any writer's (*or person's*) relation to tradition, particularly as embodied in a figure taken as one's own forerunner" (xiii; my emphasis). And it is precisely this allegory that allows us to broaden the philosophical scope of Bloom's seminal insight into the nature of poetic influence. In Bloom's writings the poet's predicament is a *synecdoche of the modern condition.*

In the disenchanted, post-Cartesian "universe of death," culture, instead of offering a chance of instant emancipation—Kant's liberating "exit from the self-inflicted immaturity"—turns into a substitute source of oppression.[11] The weak, half-formed individual stands in front of beauty, truth, and goodness impersonated by the greatest representatives of his tradition. From the onset, therefore, his creative impulses would be checked and inhibited by the "earthly powers" of internal mediators whom he admires and envies at the same time. The ephebe—as Bloom, after Stevens, likes to call the young latecomer—has no choice but to try to equal the power of those who, by very definition, cannot be equaled: he is a weakling, while they personify everything that is the best in tradition, or—to evoke Scholem's fortuitous phrase, not so completely at odds in this seemingly secularized context—"the strong light of the canonical." The ephebe, therefore, is like Jacob who wrestles with one of the Elohim Angels, for he has nothing to lose anyway. Or, he is like David who marches against Goliath with his pathetic little sling—unless he resorts to some cunning trick, he will be done.

Jacob the desperate, and David the sly—these are two real heroes of Bloom's poem (as he himself likes to call his "theory of poetry"). The former represents pure will of life: the only thing he wants from Yahweh is his blessing, which in Hebrew means simply *more life*.[12] The latter represents what Hegel, if he ever turned into a romantic, could have called a pure cunning of life, *List des Lebens:* the indispensable Nietzschean "vital lie," or the Freudian "ruses of the unconscious," without which the individual could not escape the overwhelming power of generality, the deadening impact of systems and values that form the heavy shield of the "objective spirit." For, if Aristotle is right in saying that truth is one, but blunders many, then the essence of particularity and diversity must lie in the *willing error*—in deceit. The individual, who wants to confirm his right to singularity in front of the "splendor of culture," must choose the crooked path of error which only leads toward individuation. Beauty, truth, goodness, and being already have their representatives—for the ephebe, there remains nothing else but deviation toward his own "subjective way": deceit, lie, appearance, error. Stanisław Brzozowski, in his *Voices in the Dark: Studies on the Crisis of European Romanticism*, calls this stage the "romanticism of negation": where no affirmation is possible, the individual has to negate, even against all odds, to break loose from the oppression of generality.

This is precisely why the greatest archetype of the romantic ephebe is the Satan of Milton's *Paradise Lost*. His descent from the "happy fields" marks a curved line, which is both fall and declension. And the only gain of the fall is, precisely, *the declension*. Says Bloom:

> Poetic Influence is the passing of Individuals through States, in Blake's language, *but the passing is done ill when it is not swerving*. The strong poet indeed says: "I seem to have stopped falling; now *I am fallen*, consequently, I lie here in Hell," but he is thinking, as he says this, "As I fell, I *swerved*, consequently I lie here in a Hell improved by my own making." (*AI*, 45; my emphasis)

"We, the late-born, ceased to believe in truth," said Stanisław Przybyszewski, a leading figure of the Polish modernist movement, in his *Psychologie des Individuums* (*Psychology of the Individual*)—written in German—and his aphorism very aptly expresses Bloom's intentions.[13] The condition of belatedness causes modern individuals to choose consciously a strategy of deceit (i.e., declension from truth). Przybyszewski's phrase reveals the modern version of the tragic alternative: either singular being with its right to one and only one life—or totality with its established pantheon of truth, beauty, and goodness. Either hell, horrible, humiliating but one's own—or heaven, wise and virtuous, but reserving the ultimate assertion of "I am" to the selected happy few.

Clinamen—the term coined by Lucretius to indicate the accidental deviation of the trajectory of atoms in an otherwise totally determined universe—becomes, in Bloom's language, a trope of romantic irony and its power of negation. The Miltonic Satan, falling and deviating at the same time, embodies all the antinomies of romantic consciousness which resorts to the strategy of fraud: its declaration of full autonomy and independence is a deliberately chosen rhetoric of hubris against the perfect world of precursors, so perfect and accomplished indeed that there is no place in their pleroma for a new member claiming his own right to glory. For when Satan proclaims in his famous speech to the angels who remained faithful to God: *We know no time when we were not as now*, he knows perfectly well that he is lying, that he is not *self-raised, self-begot*, but the son of the father against whom he rebels. But he has no other choice. The implacable logic of *clinamen*, the logic of *List des Lebens*, forces him to declare his fake perennial sovereignty.

The logic of *clinamen* bends every possible trajectory. Like Nietzsche, who in *Zarathustra* intoned his praise of "the bent path of eternity," Bloom also likes everything crooked. Deviation, diversion, swerving, declension, spite, and perversity are among his favorite expressions, always accompanied by equally beloved hyperbolic adjectives: wonderful, splendid, extraordinary. So, there is "splendid perversity of the spirit," "wonderful betrayal," and "magnificent deviation"—an inspired, vital rhetoric of crookedness which has become Bloom's trademark. What does this crookedness signify? Just as for de Man, the figure of all figures is irony, renamed as a "permanent parabasis of the allegory of reading"; for Bloom, such a hyperfigure is the very essence of figuration, namely, its meandrine, crooked wandering: the staunch unfaithfulness to anything literal and simple. This crookedness expresses the deepest lust for life—whereas the literalness of exact repetition spells deadness. "Death is the most proper or literal of meanings, and literal meaning partakes of death," says Bloom in *Poetry and Repression* (10).

Greek thought usually associated hubris with crookedness. Already Heraclitus speculated about the double meaning of the word *bios*, which means life, but also alludes to the bent shape of Apollo's bow, the symbol of individual creativity, always bordering on the hubristic defiance. In *Shelley's Mythmaking*, Bloom quotes Kerényi's famous work on Prometheus and says: "To this foolhardiness and impiety Prometheus adds a trait which Zeus does not possess, cunning, a useful gift but also a failing, not to be found in the highest of gods. Prometheus is of 'crooked thoughts,' *ankulometes*, a quality which Kerényi wisely notes as covering a range from deceitfulness to inventiveness" (*SM*, 56). Yet the most paradigmatic hero of crookedness comes from the Hebrew tradition where "more life" becomes the main pursuit: Jacob the lame, who won his "bent path" of life after the victorious struggle with the Angel of Death.

This "bent path," however, is not an art for its own sake. Its ultimate goal is to overcome "the universe of death," to wrestle life out of the cold legacy of Urizen, to outwit its straight angles by the serpent of a romantic arabesque. The triumphal poetic vision which bursts out at the successful end of the *clinamen* stage is thus based on the trope of reversal, the first "small" metalepsis anticipating the coming of the grand one which crowns the revisionary process: its aim is to reverse the proportions of the deterministic and the contingent image of reality. At first glance, or in the first stage of the romantic *via naturaliter negativa* (the naturally negative way),[14] the universe seems to be run by the iron rule of necessity, which only indifferently allows rare exceptions. Now however, in the radiant poetic vision, it is the other way around: *clinamen* becomes enthroned as the true ruler of the universe. Blake's singular Vortex, created by the power of the swerving fall, works like an imploding ebb in space which, in consequence, rapidly loses its sterile homogeneity. Suddenly, nature reveals its long forgotten primordial aspect of Spinoza's *natura naturans* (naturing nature), so deeply beloved by the romantics: here, the Titanic elements interfere with each other, creating singular vortices which remain in constant motion. Nothing seems done, static, determined and objectified, ready for inspection; quite the contrary, this is nature-in-the-making in which everything is still possible. Thus Bloom, as the paradigmatically exodic writer, describes the Cartesian-Newtonian universe in cyclic-circular terms, characteristic of all mythical thinking, and praises Blake for offering us moderns the chance of an ancient *yeziat*, "the getting out" of the modern version of *mizraim*, that is, nature mortified by science. Writes Bloom:

> In the Cartesian theory of vortices all motion had to be circular (there being no vacuum for matter to move through) and all matter had to be capable of further reduction (there were thus no atoms). These, to Blake, were the circlings of the Mills of Satan, grinding on vainly in their impossible task of reducing the Minute Particulars, the Atoms of Vision that will not further divide. In the Blakean theory of vortices, circular motion is a self-contradiction; when the poet stands at the apex of his Vortex the Cartesian-Newtonian circles resolve into the flat plain of Vision, and the Particulars stand forth, each as itself, and not another thing. (*AI*, 41)[15]

Clinamen, at first a shy swerve from the mythic domain of total determination, gradually marks its curved "way out" of a Newtonian Egypt into the "flat plain of Vision." The world it shows is no longer made of cycles and easily replaceable spare parts, but of singular, radiant, epiphanic beings, where every Particular stands distinct and erect, and can be only called by its proper poetic name. The blurring spell of reduction has been evaded once more.

KENOSIS, OR DARKNESS, IGNORANCE, AND SHAME

> Let us, as readers of poetry, be very wary about what Freud is saying, for he is destroying the whole enterprise of literary Romanticism, if we give him our entire allegiance, as surely we do not. He is coming to us here as the greatest of reductionists, wiping away moonlight like mud.
> —Harold Bloom, *Poetry and Repression*

> Our own great demystifiers, Freud, Marx, and Nietzsche, are much more naive than their romantic predecessors, especially in their belief that the demystification can become a praxis beneficial to the personality or to the society. In most romantic writers, this belief is overcome quite soon in their development.
> —Paul de Man, *Romanticism and Contemporary Criticism*

In Bloom's work, the strong poet plays the part of the Blakean emblem: he is an archetypal splendid hysteric who refuses to surrender to the already established, mythically self-enclosed system of "the already." Despite his being a "late-comer," he pretends to be the "first-born," in his priority equal to no one but Adam. So, while *clinamen* is the stage emblematically associated with Satan, who in the apogee of his narcissistic fantasy portrays himself as "self-raised and self-begot"—the ratio of *kenosis* proceeds under Adamic auspices: here, the stake of the game is *absolute priority*.[16]

In the stage of *kenosis*, the poet's main adversary is Fate, whose implacable temporal order pushes him away from the primacy he desires. Here, therefore, we deal with the temporal aspect of Exodus: the *yeziat* out of the Egypt of historical sequence into the sphere of anarchic, liberating "untimeliness." In Blake's poetic mythology, this natural order is represented by Tirzah, and in Freud by Ananke, whereas in Emerson, in *The Conduct of Life*, it appears as "Beautiful Necessity," the all-encompassing, fatal *anima mundi* (soul of the world), severely superb in her majesty. In

Bloom's mythopoesis, which follows closely Kierkegaard, this necessity takes on the form of repetition: the synonym of being, the very essence of "the system of existence." It is therefore in repetition, and not anywhere else, that the ephebe will have to exercise his share of freedom: he will thus diligently repeat the work of his precursor but, at the same time, treacherously try to "undo" the spell of his magnificent precedent. By seemingly complying with the fate of everything that exists, he will attempt an act of *poetic disobedience:* by repeating, he will try to perform the trick of separation. This is why the subtitle of this revisionary ratio is, apparently contradictory, "repetition and discontinuity."[17]

Bloom borrows the term *kenosis* from the letters of Saint Paul, where it is used to describe the self-humbling of Christ, who renounced his divine dignity to become one with suffering humans. Yet, in Bloom's wrestling vision, even this most lowly and unassuming of all images, acquires militant qualities: in consequence, this humbleness hurts the precursor more than the ephebe:

> *Kenosis*, in this poetic and revisionary sense appears to be an act of self-abnegation, yet tends to make the fathers pay for their own sins, and perhaps for those of the sons also. (*AI*, 91)

Psychoanalytically speaking, *kenosis* is one of the strategies used by the younger generation against the older one within the neurotic family romance. The son, weary of competing with his own father, pretends to surrender to his power, assuming an appearance of being "like him": yet, this appearance of submissive repetition barely hides a malicious parody which, in return, mocks the paternal original. Such *kenosis* often appears in Witold Gombrowicz, a literary master of family romance, especially in his *Pornography:* the hero, deeply entangled in an inferiority complex of "the young one," unknowingly repeats and at the same time grotesquely parodies a gesture of his father, thus combining obedience with an already rebellious ridicule. On the surface, he seems to relent in his efforts of rivalry, which only means that from this time on they will become even more subversive: cunningly hidden, silently reversing the tropes of submission. "You want a repetition? I'll show you a repetition. This is what you *really* are: an old pathetic phoney, a great example indeed!" says the son, in his derisive *imitatio patris* (imitation of the father). By resorting to *kenosis*, the ephebe does the same trick: he will emphasize his own misery as a poet, yet most of all to reveal the poetic misery of his prototype. His grotesque repetition of the paternal archetype will be deliberately crooked to help him "undo" its oppressive greatness.

Kenosis is thus the darkest of all ratios, for it truly is the time of the dirtiest (though still valid!) tricks against the precursor. The adjective "dark" is already one of Bloom's favorite key words, but in his description of *kenosis* it appears in unmatched abundance: *kenosis* is the true poetic "heart of darkness." The act of mocking separation, undertaken by our Adam *in spe*, occurs in an isolated, secluded space, in the "solitary confinement" of shame, guilt, and resentment. It isn't a dignified solitude, yet it is necessary to give the ephebe a semblance of total isolation, a primacy achieved in privacy. Says Bloom after Valéry:

> There are no names for those things among which a man is most truly alone; and Stevens urges his ephebe to throw away the lights, the definitions, in order to find identifications replacing the rotted names that will not grant a context of solitude. This darkness is a discontinuity, in which the ephebe can see again and know the illusion of a fresh priority. (*AI*, 86)

Kenosis, being the most malicious and crooked of all stages, is nevertheless indispensable for the sense of freshness—however delusory—it gives to the ephebe. Bloom's revisionistic rereading of Nietzsche attempts to prove that resentment, far from being simply reactive and impotent, is in the first place creative: that, in fact, without resentment there can never appear anything new under the sun. *Kenosis* is thus a stage which "undoes" the destructive findings of Nietzschean "genealogy" by retransforming them, once again, into a secret of creation. What was intended by Nietzsche as the ultimate denunciation of resentment as "the murky shop," the clumsy manufacture of values and ideals, in Bloom's account acquires a perversely positive meaning. Asks Nietzsche, provokingly:

> Would anyone care to learn something about the way in which ideas are manufactured? Does anyone have the nerve? ... Well then, go ahead! There's a chink through which you can peek into this murky shop. But wait just a moment, Mr. Foolhardy; your eyes must grow accustomed to the fickle light ... All right, tell me what's going on in there, audacious fellow; now I am the one who is listening ... —And the imagined interlocutor, who dared to boldly go where no one has gone before, answers:—I can't see a thing, but I hear all the more ...

—All the sounds are sugary and soft. No doubt you were right; *they are transmuting weakness into merit.* (1956, 180; my emphasis)

"I can't see a thing, but I hear all the more": this is precisely the darkness in which *new* names, words, and definitions proliferate. Here, indeed, the ephebe's weakness becomes transmuted into merit, his resentment into a promise of the new. Immersed in his own darkness, he feels free, for the first time, from the oppression of haunting images: he cannot see, but he can begin to hear *his own voice.*

This fragment from *The Genealogy of Morals* is the founding Scripture of all reductionisms, the very gospel of suspicion: it talks about darkness, which has to be enlightened, and the boldness of those who dare to step down into its murky manufactures.[18] It wants to bring brightness where dusk prevails; it wants to expose to the public light what has been kept secret. But this dark secrecy, which the genealogist wants to deny to all the perverse "manufacturers," is precisely what *kenosis* needs: otherwise the ephebe would not be able to transmute his latecomer's weakness into a fresh promise of priority. Here, one daring crosses with another: the enlightening boldness of the genealogist clashes with the secretive audacity of the would-be poet.[19]

This dilemma puts Bloom into a curiously aporetic position which draws us back to the very opening theme of this book: the threat of reduction, incipient in every critical enterprise, regardless of the sympathies of the critic himself, who may adore poets and altogether reject "the beneficial practice of demystification." What should the critic do when confronted with the ratio of *kenosis*? Should he follow the genealogical path and throw some light on the dark workshop of poetic resentment? Or should he rather resist the Nietzschean, voyeuristic temptation, and leave the poet's progress in its dark peace? It would seem, therefore, that *kenosis* is also a ratio in which the critic wrestles with his own, imminent tendency toward reduction. The critic's desire is to *know* everything about the poet—while the poet's desire is to prove, to evoke Rosenzweig again, that he is "older than any knowledge."[20]

Bloom is highly aware of this predicament. He self-ironically compares a critic to the Blakean Idiot Questioner who, instead of wanting to dissect and know everything, should ask himself what "uses" and what "advantages" his theory has for the life of poets. For if reductionism is the synonym for the idiotic inquiry conducted in a mortifying "spirit of gravity," then Bloom's own method, precisely *as method*, might also turn, despite his intentions, into a yet another Covering Cherub (*cherub mimshach*), the Red Dragon of Blake's vision, and the Enemy of any living creation. To use Nietzsche's formula, it may become yet another false "antiquarianism," with its industrious catalogs of all defense mechanisms the poet uses in the lonely struggle with his "toxic" family, a codification which will result merely in producing yet another toxin, yet another limiting obstacle.

This would really be a particularly painful irony: to classify all the defensive tropes of life with such analytical pedantry as to make life itself no longer possible. No wonder, therefore, that poets—*as poets*—don't want to know anything about their secret ruses against precursors and prefer to keep their "murky shops" in a safe hiding place.[21] Freud, by wishing to replace *id* by *ego*, and thus merely to increase the level of consciousness, is a notorious enemy of poets as poets, for he makes them chose a strategy of ordinary sublimation which is a synonym for poetic failure. But Bloom, the staunch adversary of sublimation, by wanting to replace impulsive defense mechanisms by his critical theory of influence, suddenly finds himself very close to an analogous danger. He thus feels obliged to emphasize that "the strength of any poet is in his skill and inventiveness at substitution, and *the map of misprision is no bed of Procrustes*" (*MM*, 105; my emphasis). Horrified by the mere chance that he might have procured a new *methodology* of reading, Bloom prefers to complicate his map of misprision to the point of such obscurity where it itself changes from a guide into a labyrinth. This, however, is a deliberately self-obfuscating maneuver on his part, a kind of final misguidance of the perplexed; it builds yet another "hedge about the poem" (the poem already being a "hedgehog"), which makes it impossible to be read *more geometrico* (in geometrical way).[22]

Yet, some inevitable doubts remain. Freud's is a typical enlightenment strategy: where there was *id*, the dark, secret, unique pathos of individual unconscious—*ego* must appear, with its consciously generalized and properly resigned feeling of "common human unhappiness."[23] And if Bloom ever comes close to repeating the same mistake (*kenosis* is, after all, a stage of repetition), it is precisely in this one respect: the poet who learns that his antiparental subterfuges have been, in fact, known for ages, that just like millions of other neurotic children before him, he also regards himself as a changeling and suspects his mother of infidelity, he will be crushed by a burden he won't be able to lift again. When Freud says that his therapy aims to transform narcissistic, secluded suffering into common human unhappiness, all he offers amounts to the substitution of hysteria for depression—nothing more, just a Schopenhauerian kind of consolation. Bloom, however, in defending the romantic right of the individual to break through the covers of the ever-recurring *das Selbe* (the same), cannot avail himself of the same strategy. He cannot offer poets a normalizing therapy of commonness for, by doing so, he would condemn them to the hell of depression, all the more terrible for the fact that, unlike in Satan's case, the hell not "of their own making": rather a communal, ordinary hell for everybody who has suffered *the same* from times immemorial.

There is, therefore, a danger—a danger not so much for the critics as for the poets—in bringing all those defensive, unconscious strategies to the light of the common day. The dark secrets of *kenosis* are dark indeed, but for the very reason that they must not become illuminated, or at least not *too soon*. Once exposed to the brightness of genealogical analysis, they lose their efficiency: as in Bloom's suggestive paraphrase of Stevens, moonlight turns into mud. Hence the child immersed in its family romance must come to all his strategic solutions *on his own*, without help and hints, in his shameful and resentful "solitary confinement." This is precisely his right of priority: all his maneuvers, when revealed and demystified as common to all his peers, become futile and laughable, and the child itself will be *caught:* exposed to its shame, and, at the same time, arrested in its secret strivings. Whereas the darkness in which it hides covers its narcissistic fantasies with a veil of protective ignorance that eases the pressure of objective knowledge.

Donald Woods Winnicott, the only truly self-avowed romantic adept of Freud, would probably say that *kenosis*, the ratio of beneficial darkness, corresponds to this stage in his scheme of maturational development, which is marked by the emergence of a "deep self." Unlike the *ego*, whose role is an "official" representation of the whole of psychic life, the deep self, the ego's secret shadow, rests buried in the folds of the unconscious until it feels ready to rise to the surface. "It is joy to be hidden, but a disaster not to be found," says Winnicott in *Playing and Reality*, pointing to the peculiar narcissistic game of hide-and-seek; the "deep self" is playing with reality (1971, 95). The self grows in hiding, and, as Winnicott goes on to imply, it has an explicit *need of noncommunication*. The self, therefore, is the instance which, psychoanalytically speaking, repeats the trauma of separation by simultaneously undoing its traumatic aspect: it breaks the continuity with the whole of the world, the pleromatic experience of the child's communion with the mother, to establish itself as a "unit," a singular distinct being. The self's concealedness is driven by a secret *timing* which governs its slow and delayed process of maturation.

It finds joy in being hidden and then suddenly found; in the *Schweben* of appearing and disappearing, or in the constant, playful oscillation of *fort:da*. The self does not want to be found *before its time:* to be found too early would mean to destroy "the murky shop" of its slowly ripening sense of distinction. Winnicott's findings, therefore, merely confirm our thesis from part 2, in which we praised the Bloomian strategies of delay and deferment. The "time of hiding," postponing the moment of the self's identification, enfolds psyche with a "protective veil" under which it may *take time* to mature.

And it is precisely this impatient "too-earliness," the disrespect for a psyche's dark inner timings, which is the common denominator of all reductionisms. The Nietzschean-Freudian genealogy deprives the psyche of her benign darkness *too soon*, and mercilessly brings to the light of day all her pathetic little ruses. It has no feel for the time which separates the joy of being hidden from the need to be found. Yet, although it was Nietzsche who invented this suspicious method, his own stand on this issue was, in fact, far more ambivalent; he also seemed to be highly sensitive to the demand of secrecy that conditions every maturational process as such. As he says in "On the Uses and Disadvantages of History for Life":

> All living things require an atmosphere around them, *a mysterious, misty vapor;* if they are deprived of this envelope, if a religion, an art, a genius is condemned to revolve as a star without atmosphere, we should no longer be surprised if they quickly wither and grow hard and unfruitful ... But every nation, too, indeed every human being that wants to become *mature* requires a similar *enveloping illusion*, a similar *protective and veiling cloud;* nowadays, however, maturity as such is hated because history [read: antiquarianism—ABR] is held in greater honor than life. (1997, 97; my emphasis)

The same ambivalence, pointing to the aporia between genealogical reduction and antireductionist, romantic respect for the secrecy of "maturation," can also be traced in Bloom. Bloom seems to be aware that it is impossible to create a *system* here, that is, to systematize and generalize all these defensive mechanisms whose role it is to defend—precisely— against systematic and universal generalizations. What is explicitly based on a *lie* cannot be easily returned to the realm of truth; what thrives on envelopes, veils, and secrecies cannot be expected to survive in full light. This is why, in the introduction to *The Anxiety of Influence*, he would say with cautious reserve that his own theory should be read "in ways that *need not be doctrinal*" (xxiv; my emphasis).

This delayed maturation can therefore be narrated only in a very specific genre that is particularly sensitive to the exigencies of good timing. It has to rely on the Winnicottian joy of being found *not too early, and not too late*, just in the right time, in the *kairos* (the right moment) of "the mature ego's delight in its own individuality." In this kind of narrative, every Particular, every singular subject, discovers *the same*, but always *afresh* and *in its own fashion*. All those mature egos eventually become (or not) singular beings—which, in the impatient perspective of reductionism, reads as nothing more than a banal contradiction, yet, in fact, it is neither banal nor contradictory: they merely need *time*, its subtle dialectical interplay of light and shadow which defers the ultimate moment of coming out. From the rash, reductionist point of view, poetic maturation stands no chance—for how can anything singular emerge out of the eternal return of the same ruses, maneuvers, and defenses? Yet, it all begins to make sense in the perspective of deferral in which the young psyche "takes her time": *kenosis*, whose psychoanalytic equivalent is Winnicott's "time of being hidden" is precisely a defense against all reductive factors of knowledge, reflection, and skepsis, threatening the becoming of the always precarious self. Thanks to this metadefensive mechanism, the singularity, which in the beginning is nothing but lie, fantasy, pure hubristic imagination, may gradually develop into a real object of the ego's justified delight.

Yet, it would be unfair to imply that Bloom fails to see in Freud the recurrence of the same terrifying specter that haunted Blake: the ultimate hypermodern incarnation of the Covering Cherub. He is certainly aware of such a danger: "Though I explore these *parallels*"—he says about the concept of family romance, carefully signalizing the distance between his theory of poetry and Freud's psychoanalysis—"I do so as a deliberate revisionist of some of the Freudian emphases" (*AI*, 8). Freud, the *cherub mimshach* of modern arts, stubbornly stands in the way which leads to the creative paradise: no fantasy, no illusion, no narcissistic dream of one's own originality can hope to enjoy a future under his thousand-eyed, petrifying gaze. Deep down Bloom *knows* that Freud must be treated with utmost caution, as an only tentative ally, for in the end, he *is* the master of Nietzschean antiquarianism in the domain of micropsychology and the author of the most disadvantageous use of numerous case histories for life, so he simply cannot be a friend of poets—or all those individuals who crave for their own names and lives. He is, after all, as Wittgenstein aptly observed, the maker of a "modern mythology": he offers us no hope of an Exodus from the Egypt of the relentless economy of drives.[24]

To Freud, therefore, all lies and subterfuges are merely illusions *ohne Zukunft* (without future): more than that, for Freud no *Zukunft* exists, no future in the sense of anything really new—every possible meaning is already there, in the past, in the eternal present perfect of the unconscious. Yet, the poet has to lie to himself and others to wrestle out the blessing of his own singularity precisely for the sake of the possibility of a future. He has to enkindle the spark of his hubris "in advance" to do the first step, the *clinamen;* he has to pretend that he is the incarnation of Adam in order to win separation in the act of *kenosis;* he has to fantasize about his unearthly charisma to counteract the power of a precursor in the moment of *daemonization,* etc. All these pathetic excuses *not* to face the poetic principle of reality are, to Bloom, vital, life-giving fantasies: false premises, all justified by the implication thanks to which only the singular, living truth can emerge.[25] Every bildungsroman is, in fact, an endless *catalog* of such cunning falsities which gain their rehabilitation only in hindsight as necessary stages in the process of the Nietzschean "maturation." Here, *Dichtung und Wahrheit,* "contrivance and truth," form an indissoluble whole. The self hides in temporal folds to protect its vital lies, and only when it is strong enough to withstand "genealogical" mockery of its unworthy origins does it dare bring itself forward to the surface and "be found." Freud, with his "mind of the moralist," never had time for the self's narcissistic whimsies. Yet, if it weren't for those whimsies, the whole secret universe of ingenious deceits, there would never have emerged a singular subjectivity, able to take delight in its uniqueness.

Thus, often the blessing of *more life* goes hand in hand with *less light:* the very reverse of enlightenment.

An Ambiguous Mythology

> "It's evident Crystalman has dug his claws into you pretty deeply,"
> said Krag. "The sound comes from Muspel, but the rhythm is caused
> by its traveling through Crystalman's atmosphere. His nature is
> *rhythm* as he loves to call it . . . or *dull, deadly repetition,* as I name it.
> —David Lindsay, *A Voyage to Arcturus*

This is also why Bloom's theory of poetry can only be a semitheory, highly aware of its speculative limitations; the aporia of the critic takes here the

shape of *das Schweben*, the favorite romantic movement of ironic oscillation between opposite poles. Bloom's "theory," therefore, constantly
oscillates between the respect for the veiled mysteries of the poetic initiate and the curiosity of the reductive demystification. By bringing two
opposite rhetorics into collision, it hopes to achieve a crossing from
which a new, more integral idiom can emerge. Writes Bloom:

> A theory of poetry that presents itself as a severe poem reliant upon
> aphorism, apothegm, and a quite personal (though thoroughly tra-
> ditional) mythic pattern, still may be judged, and may be asked to be
> judged, as argument. Everything that makes up this book—parables,
> definitions, the working-through of the revisionary ratios as mecha-
> nisms of defense—intends to be a part of a *unified meditation* on the
> melancholy of the creative mind's desperate insistence upon priority.
> (*AI*, 13; my emphasis)

The hint of both a personal and at the same traditional mythic pattern,
which nevertheless can be judged as an argument and present itself as
"a unified meditation," immediately suggests Friedrich Schlegel's idea
of a *new mythology*. Bloom's paratheoretical effort may be regarded as
a part of the project inaugurated by the Jena circle, which in Schlegel's
vision was already based on collisions of the incommensurate. The new
mythology was to bring together, in a dynamic, dancing unity, the *new*
as well as the *old*; the disenchantment of the modern and the magical
charm of the traditional world; the *sound* of distant gods and the *dull,
deadly repetition* of being; *playing* and *reality*. Schlegel's *neue Mythologie*
(new mythology) was thus devised as a bright, optimistic reverse of what
Max Weber had diagnosed as the worst possible combination of two
worlds. While in Weber's dark vision of the modern *Entzauberung*, we,
the moderns, were condemned to live under the spell of "disenchanted
demons," Jena's optimistic project aimed at the affirmation of a world
free of archaic mysteries, yet, at the same time, open to new kinds of
enchanting *Begeisterung* (wonderment). Bloom's mythic pattern is, in this
sense, also *new:* it is both personalized and argumentative, and, although
it plays with rhythm and repetition, it does not have the claustrophobic
tendency to systematize and reduce.

Yet, in the context of what we have already said, it would be a blatant contradiction to claim that Bloom's efforts simply belong to the
realm of "mythology."[26] The ambivalence with which Bloom uses the
word "myth"—on the one hand scolding Freud for having revived an

archaic form of reductive "mythicity," on the other perceiving his own
theory as grown on a "mythic pattern"—is something more than just his
private idiosyncrasy: it pertains to the rhetoric of romanticism as such.
Schlegel's *Speech on Mythology* is a particularly good illustration of this
partly deliberate confusion. On the one hand, it uses the word "myth" in
a loose and imprecise way as a vague negative contrast to all disenchanting practices of enlightenment; any word able to breath life back into
mortified nature deserves the praiseworthy name of "new mythology."
On the other hand, Schlegel is far from eager to assert the archaic features of old myths: he is as hostile as Schopenhauer will later be to the
repetitive toil of nature in its eternal return of the same cycle of life and
death. Quite the contrary, he wants nature to break free from the deadness of modern science and show its playfully nominalist side that, *unlike*
premodern mythical forms, would be friendly to what Blake called The
Particulars: singular beings proud of their singularity. The "new mythology," therefore, is anarchic rather than based on a solid, premodern
arche: its spontaneous arabesque form encourages lively paradoxes and
life-enhancing clashes of Particulars with each other and with nature as
a never-finished whole.[27]

Bloom's position on myth is similarly ambiguous: the word "mythology" appears in his writings rather misleadingly, both as a synonym and
an antonym of reduction. As a synonym of reduction it functions in the
Hebrew way: just as in Benjamin, Adorno, and Horkheimer, "myth"
equals the house of bondage of deadening repetition. Whether it is an
archaic belief or modern science does not matter, for the existential result
of total closure remains identical. But, in its romantic disguise, "myth"
emerges as an antonym of reduction: the idiom of life defying the gray
abstractions of "the objective way."[28] Following Schlegel, who in his
Speech on Mythology anticipated a synthesis of science and sensibility,
modern skepticism and premodern faith, Bloom also wants to give us a
new—although not as easily synthetic—idiom which will be able to put
on the modern languages of suspicion, most notably genealogy and psychoanalysis, a different, nonreductive spin. Instead of offering tools for
the School of Resentment, they could, as it seems in Bloom's treatment,
become the bearers of the Novalisian imperative of romanticization:
they could start to produce the "second charm" that, itself being a child
of modern speculation, would no longer perish under the cold touch of
philosophy.[29]

The motto from Stevens which opens *The Anxiety of Influence* could
not be any clearer on this issue: Stevens's hope that "a more severe, more

harassing master would extemporize subtler, more urgent proof that the theory of poetry is the theory of life" springs from the lineage of all those *new mythologists* who believed that they would be able to pass beyond the Goethean dualism of gray knowledge and evergreen life, and create one, integral idiom, which would allow to speak of life without immediately destroying it. This hope to get beyond pure objective knowledge which, according to Hegel's remark from *Phenomenology of Spirit*, is a substitute for immediate destruction—a recognition later explicitly confirmed by Nietzsche's complaint that life, once captured as our cognitive possession, "ceases to live when it is dissected completely" (Nietzsche 1997, 97)—this hope to pass beyond the traps of reductionism, or even to *redeem* reduction as a language potentially in service of "new mythology," remains the regulative idea of Bloom's stylistic efforts. His modernized "mythic pattern," when successfully achieved, has all the advantages of old mythologies—by introducing the factor of time and deferment, it surrounds the creative life with Nietzsche's "protective veil" or Benjamin's "aura"—at the same time, however, it does not leave us helpless in the face of the mystery. Far from giving up the task of knowledge, it makes a full, though at the same time skillfully timed, use of the combined explanatory powers of both major languages of suspicion: genealogy and psychoanalysis. With the determinacy of a true "strong poet," Bloom absorbs reductive idioms into the "subtler language" of his own romantic revision, which handles the mystery of poetic becoming tenderly in order to restrain their deconstructive impact.

The Critic's Hedge

> I want first to suggest that on a pragmatic view there is no language of criticism but only of an individual critic . . . A theory of strong misreading denies that there is or should be any common vocabulary in terms of which critics can argue with one another.
> —Harold Bloom, "Agon: Revisionism and Critical Personality"

Bloom is therefore a paradoxical critic, not because of his own maladaptation to the variety of critical schools, but because criticism as such is to him a paradoxical enterprise. Bloom's uneasy progress in this discipline demonstrates his acute awareness of its original, foundational aporia. The risky endeavor to speak in the name of those who wanted to leave the idiomatic mark of their names in the anonymous sea of language is always coupled with the inescapable practice of reduction: the typically critical *Haß-Liebe* (love-hate) consists here in a perverse fascination, manifesting itself in the first place in the deconstruction of what it admires (i.e., the authorial *claim to originality*). Thus, even if criticism wants to speak on behalf of singularity, it is still doomed to reduce it, in the fatal gesture of the all-leveling, almighty, and omniscient *Ananke* of current theoretical discourse. Bloom's extraordinary honesty lies in his readiness to admit that he, *as a critic*, is an inevitable victim of the Hegelian "unhappy consciousness," forever torn between its actuality and its longings.

Yet, says Bloom, most of the schools take this highly aporetic moment as a good point of departure—although, as aporetic, which originally means "blocking the way," it precisely *forbids* any departure. Instead of being a memento, the aporetic moment turns into a solid epistemological foundation, giving the advantage to a critic who prefers to take sides with the anonymity of *ça parle* and disregard the writer's aspiration to singularity. In the late preface to *The Anxiety of Influence* Bloom states explicitly that this difference became a true bone of contention between him and Paul de Man: unlike Bloom, de Man believed that there is a vantage point a critic can achieve via his higher rhetorical understanding of aporia, which allows him to become immune to the subjective seduction of an author (xix).

But this is precisely the hope of all schools which—*as* schools—take for a blessing what in fact is the critic's utmost misery: his "unhappy" compulsion to reduce. While Bloom, in his stubborn attempt to maintain critique as art, witnessing the singularity of works, loudly protests against any signs of mythological undifferentiation whose dull repetitiveness fuels all critical efforts of reduction. And it doesn't matter whether it is a magical myth of Northrop Frye's *great code*—or a thoroughly disenchanted, poststructuralist myth of Roland Barthes' *mythologies*. Bloom's faithfulness to the ancient project of Exodus forbids him to engage either with the sacred archetypes of the former or with the deconstructive patterns of the latter. His exodic, deeply Jewish angle allows him to express the critic's aporia in terms deriving directly from the Talmudic commentary, which saw itself as "building a hedge about Torah."[30] Instead of opening a wide road of accessible interpretation, of which reduction, social or philosophical, is the easiest one, the artful commentary rather *bars* the way, thus remaining true to its aporetic origins: "The literary critic, qua critic," says Bloom, "is not primarily an agent of social change. Her work is fundamentally to build a hedge about the aesthetic, and rise up disciples to it" (*AC*, vii). The

School of Resentment—"a sixfold movement," as Bloom calls it in one
of his Blakean visions of academic doom, "of Marxists, feminists, semi-
oticians, deconstructors, Lacanians, and Foucault-inspired, self-dubbed
New Historicists" (*AC*, viii)—reduces the critic's *Haß-Liebe* to a straightforward ressentiment, whereas "literary fictions continue to take place
between philosophy and history" (ibid.), that is, *between general concept and singular event*, thus by nature evading any direct attempt at
reduction.

Bloom's critical effort is therefore much closer to poetic activity in its
refusal to create a discursive *meta*-level; it resembles yet another revisionist spin put on the work of the writer, always within the same agon
and aporia of creation. Geoffrey Hartman observed once that romantic
poetry evolved from the epitaph beginning from the standard formula
siste viator, thus giving voice to the humble request of the dead, who do
not want to be passed unnoticed in their singular being that has become,
according to Hegel's famous formulation, "returned by death to generality." Gradually, this genre developed into a melancholy contemplation
of beautiful "spots of time" that are doomed to perish but can, nevertheless, last a little longer thanks to the visionary effort of poets. Hartman
proves his theory by quoting "the earliest genuinely lyrical poem of
Wordsworth" which appeared in *Lyrical Ballads* under the characteristically descriptive title "Lines Left upon a Seat in a Yew-Tree, Which
Stands Near the Lake of Eastwaite, on a Desolate Part of the Shore,
yet Commanding a Beautiful Prospect," where the traditional expression turns into "Nay, Traveller: rest!" "We are made to hear," he says,
"the admonitory voice of the deceased or of the living who speak for the
deceased" (1965, 389, 393).

This analysis of Hartman, although originally applied to the paradigmatic romantic poet, is fully, or even more applicable to Bloom's
paradigmatically romantic criticism. In reclaiming the right to singularity of all those *dead poets*, who are always in danger of being silenced
for the second time by critical reduction, Bloom listens to their weak,
pleading voices asking for a moment of attention, a moment of what
Jewish tradition calls *zakhor*, "remembrance"—and thus fights against
the Hegelian Thanatos, who mercilessly returns everything particular
to the abyss of undifferentiation. For, as Kierkegaard says, nobody, and
especially a poet, wants to be "a memorial volume with a blurred inscription." Surely, Bloom is one of these fiercely antithanatic, erotic figures
who keeps his stylus always sharp and ready to protect the epitaph from
vanishing.

CHILDE HAROLD

> I saw them and I knew them all. And yet
> Dauntless the slug-horn to my lips I set,
> And blew, "*Childe Roland to the Dark Tower Came.*"
> —Robert Browning

Every age sports its own image of Jacob's duel with the Deadly Angel. The first paradigmatic wrestler, Jacob fought against the vital order and the domination of nature. He outsmarted Esau, "the natural man"; won the blessing of priority despite the choice of nature which privileged his twin, and did the first "crossing" marking his own crooked way: he crossed Penuel after his fight with the Angel, thus anticipating the grand future crossing of Exodus.

The modern agon, as depicted by Bloom, is no more than a finely revised troping of this ancient motif. It is an esoteric misprision of *yeziat* where it is not directly nature as such, but *objective knowledge about nature*, with all its oppressive universality, which constitutes the real modern house of bondage, the *mizraim* of Western modernity. For Bloom, therefore, the agon is, first of all, an act of getting out of the leveling constraints of generality—be it truth, beauty, goodness, or even being, which together form the ultimate limiting fourfold of the modern *cherub mimschah*, the Covering Cherub. The Particular, with its unique, hubristic spark residing in a special place of the soul Bloom names "the poet in a poet," fights for what Kierkegaard, fully aware of the paradox, used to call "a singular truth": a state of individuation which can be achieved only due to a massive antithetical *evasion* and *revision* of the notion of truth offered by traditional epistemology.

The refusal to know, the refusal to give in to the temptation of "the objective way" and be seduced by truth, always fuels the agonistic effort, be it on a part of a poet, or a critic. The romantic poet begins his odyssey of individuation by refusing to accept the truth about the disenchanted, monotonously repetitive universe in which influence can only mean more of the same. His *clinamen* leads him out of the Newtonian cycles into the Blakean plain of Vision where things begin to shine anew with generative freshness. Later, however, he has to face the same skeptical truth about himself, as an ineluctable part of modern disenchanted reality. The stage of *kenosis* confronts him with the reductive threat of "genealogical" science he has to evade in order to save his power of Vision. And, finally, the "gracious" critic is the one who, in solidarity with the poet's solitary

agon, *refuses to know too much* about the poetic work; he rather joins it in
a horizontal commentary which "builds a hedge about the aesthetic" and
defends it against intrusions of hasty, reductive knowledge.

The main agon with reductionism, the personal agon of Bloom as a
critic, takes place between him and Freud. From the moment Bloom
uncovers the psychoanalysis of romantic consciousness he constantly
has to restrain himself from falling into the "covering" idiom of Freud's
"powerful mythology." In the never-ending cycle of revisions, it was
Freud who first fought with the Angel of Tradition[31]—now, however, it is
Bloom who has to wrestle with Freud. In Bloom's ingenious misprision,
the genealogical language of Nietzsche and Freud, the two modern masters of suspicion, offers not so much a reductive knowledge about poetic
origins but an opportunity for fruitful "crossings" which take us beyond
known boundaries into yet unmapped regions of ever-new "subjective
ways." Strong subjectivity, says Bloom, survives thus only as a *trope* and
only in these "crossings" which arise from initial aporias, "hedges," or the
wrestling points—yet the traces of strong subjectivity are also present in
those places where it sustained a failure. Asks Bloom in the theoretical
conclusion to his work on Wallace Stevens, "Coda: Poetic Crossings":

> What is a trope? It is one of two possibilities only—either the will
> translating itself into a verbal act or figure of *ethos*, or else the will
> failing to translate itself and so abiding as a verbal desire or figure of
> *pathos*. (*WS*, 393)

Thus, *in doing or in suffering*, strong subjectivity *or* the strong will of
strong subjectivity always makes itself present. And even if Bloom's figure ultimately turned out to be rather *pathos* than *ethos* (though I don't
think so), he would still command the respect with which chivalrous cul-
tures used to celebrate their battered warriors. For when Childe Harold
comes to the Dark Tower, he knows that he approaches it only to perish, surrounded by the countless hosts of those who vainly tried to reach
there before him. And yet, dauntless, the slug-horn to his lips he sets, and
blows: "Childe Harold to the Dark Tower Came." "To be an artist is to
fail, as no other dare fail," said Samuel Beckett, and this almost Freudian
remark, alluding to life's inevitable but always singular defeat in the face
of death, the most generalizing of all powers, offers a perfect summary
of all romantic efforts of redemptive individuation (Beckett 1983, 145).[32]

Bloom's epitaph, therefore, the ultimate Kierkegaardian place of
the proper name, could read as follows: he lived, he wrestled, and was

honorably beaten in a long struggle with the overwhelming forces of knowledge and reduction, always having taken the side of the weaker. Unlike the tumults of others, who surrendered immediately without even lifting their arms, he, at least, tried. And, perhaps, just by trying so hard, he managed to *transcend either victory or defeat* (*JY*, 224). Didn't he thus merit a memorial volume with an unblurred inscription, with a clear and distinct siste viator?

Chapter 6

Fair Crossings: From Mere Life to More Life

It is fair to be crossing
And to have crossed.
— John Ashbery

Harold Bloom has never hidden his dislike for Martin Heidegger. His introduction to *The Anxiety of Influence* almost begins with "Heidegger, whom I cheerfully abhor" (*AI*, xi), and the text itself is peppered with mocking references to "Heidegger and his French flock." Yet, as usual with Bloom, one of the most spiteful tricksters of contemporary humanities, the opening phrase, which ends with *nevertheless*, suggests some deeper affinity between the two thinkers, however inadmissible on the conscious level: an affinity of obsessiveness, of thinking "one thought and one thought only, and to think it through to the end" (ibid.). In Heidegger's case, it is the famous *Denken des Seins* (thinking of being), with its morbid twist of *Todesdenken*, where death, "the ownmost" possibility of *Dasein*, remains the only property of man. In Bloom's case, it's the very opposite: his fascination with Jacob's vital duel with the Angel of Death. Thus, what Heidegger hands over to Being in the act of *Ge-hören*, obedient submission, Bloom, like all his great Jewish precursors, wants to keep only for himself. Life, always *more life*, is for him what death is to Heidegger: "the ownmost," truly inalienable right of the single individual.[1]

DAEMONIZATION, OR "THE OWNMOST" SUBLIME

Monotheism seems to be closely linked to the name *I am*. Does not this name given to God reflect the danger that the individual feels

he or she is in reaching the state of individual being? If I am, then I
have gathered together this and that and have claimed it as me, and
I have repudiated everything else; in repudiating the not-me I have,
so to speak, insulted the world, and I must expect to be attacked. So
when people first came to the concept of individuality, they quickly
put it up in the sky and gave it a voice that only Moses could hear.
            —Donald Woods Winnicott, "Sum, *I am*"

Our typical experience of a work which will eventually have an
authority with us is to begin our relation to it at a conscious
disadvantage, and to wrestle with it until it consents to bless us.
            —Lionel Trilling, *Beyond Culture*

The question of life and vitality has always been absolutely essential for
Bloom, but the ratio of *daemonization*—the fourth one of the six revisionary stages—brings forth the idea of the vital power in a particularly
condensed form. The ephebe, in rallying what remains of his scattered
inner pneuma, begins to wrestle with the demonic aspect of his precursor. The paradigm of this stage, therefore, is Jacob's struggle with the
dark aspect of Elohim in which the former wins his new name and the
blessing. The new name is a sign of a true initiation, and the blessing,
according to the Hebrew tradition, always means *more life*. Says Bloom
in *The Book of J*:

> The Blessing gives more life, awards a time without boundaries, and
> makes a name into a pragmatic immortality, by way of communal
> memory. (*BJ*, 211)[2]

Bloom's fascination with ancient Hebrew vitalism, as exemplified by J,
the most enigmatic of the four writers of Torah—in *The Book of J* Bloom
imagines her to be a *Gevurah*, a lady of the King Solomon's court—is of
great importance for his understanding of the process of creativity. For
him, life, figuration, and vitality are synonymous. And *more life* is not
just a quantitative augmentation, but a radical change of quality: it is life
intensified, and transformed into a creative principle of expansion which
knows no boundaries or limitations (or rather, as we have already seen,
it does not *want* to know). It isn't a vegetative life of the mythic life cycle
which is all about boundaries and limitations, but a life in its pure quin-
tessence, extracted, purified, and transmuted into *will*: a completely new
category, for the first time sacredly represented by ancient Yahweh. This

vitalism has as its end not so much the "preservation of life" as "the burgeoning of life" (*BJ*, 303), a state of exuberance which reflects Yahweh's restlessly dynamic nature. A man touched by His Blessing—like Joseph or David, in Bloom's opinion the shiniest examples of Hebrew humanistic vitalism—is alive in a different sense than those who just live to survive. Says Bloom of his favorite Hebrew heroes:

> To be a lucky fellow is to be a charismatic, imbued with a strong touch of Yahweh's own passionate vitality. Vitality can be defined as the prime characteristic of J's Yahweh, since all life whatsoever has to be brought into being by him ... In J's version of the Commandments, there is no Sabbath. Her Yahweh is presence, is the will to change, is origination and originality. His leading quality is not holiness, or justice, or love, or righteousness, but the sheer energy and force of becoming, of breaking into fresh being. (*BJ*, 291–92, 294)

So, when in the opening to *The Breaking of the Vessels*, Bloom declares himself a "Jewish Gnostic" (3), it is precisely this intensified, almost demonical notion of life which forms the core of his peculiar, early Hebrew Gnosticism. But Bloom would not be himself if he did not put on the concept of Gnosticism his unique, revisionistic spin: the Gnosis he has in mind cannot be easily identified with anything we may find on this topic in the writings of Eric Voegelin, Gershom Scholem, or even Hans Jonas who, as Bloom frequently admits, introduced him into the world of Gnostic arcana. Propelled by the will to an intensified life, he takes many hubristic liberties with Gnostic belief itself, yet he is consistent with its very spirit, if not always the letter. And this spirit is nothing but the spark of rebellion against the tyranny of monotheism which, as Winnicott's epigraph reveals, demands *total sacrifice* and thus an internalization of death: in the universe created by one God, one Lord, and one King, all the highest and liveliest powers can be attributed to him only, there being no place any more for high-willed, high-spirited mortals.

The demand for total sacrifice may seem contradictory to the gift of the Blessing, yet it is, in fact, fully consistent with the nature of the omnipotent, vitalistic Yahweh. The God, whose name is "I will be present whenever and wherever I wish to be present" (this is how Bloom proposes to translate *ehyeh asher ehyeh*), gives and takes, bestows and deprives: the gift of life remains always at his mercy. Thus, Abram deserves his share of the Blessing, which forms the first covenant, only because he was ready to give up on the continuation of his life and sacrifice his son, Isaac, on the Moriah Mountain. This ambivalence of election could not be made clearer by J in *her* (if we follow Bloom's conjectures) description of the mysterious episode in which Yahweh, right after he appointed Moses for his task of "bringing my people out of the house of bondage," befalls him on his way back to Egypt and tries to kill him, and it is only thanks to Zipporah's cleverness that Moses can escape. Moses is dumbfounded and disoriented, yet Zipporah, by throwing to Yahweh her son's foreskin and declaring him to be her "blood bridegroom," knows exactly what he wants: he wants his share in what is most precious—the vital power symbolized by the male member—in order to remind "his people" that from this time on, he, Yahweh, is the only one who is in full possession of this power and can dispose with it as he pleases.[3]

Ancient Judaism, as represented by J and her ingenious misreader, observed this tension—between the capricious deity and clever humans who try to defend themselves against his whims—much more closely than the Judaism of the later, priestly revision which gravitated toward a more unequivocal, just and holy, image of God as *Melekh* and *Adonai*, the King and the Lord.[4] J's characters are never very pious: they are fascinated by this new God, the emblem of a new, high-willed, exhilarating vitalism, yet they never stop haggling and negotiating, as if unwilling to seal the final vow of obedience. Thus even Abraham—according to Kierkegaard, the very essence of blind faithfulness—has to rebound and assert his right as a separate, though mortal, being, and stands up to Yahweh, bargaining about the number of the righteous who might save the Cities of the Plain. This rebounding pattern forms the scheme of J's narrative repetition, from Jacob's exemplary struggle with Elohim to Israel's recurring acts of civil disobedience in the desert—with the single exception of Moses, who, not surprisingly after all, can be said to be punished for his lack of nerve and dies, as docile as ever, not having been allowed to enter the promised land.[5] The ability to bounce back, to renegotiate the covenant with the one and only God, whose power is just too big to be submissively endured, is often awarded by the zealous Yahweh, who seems to take a perverse liking in those who resist him in their striving for a more equal, less deferential deal. Here, the subversive principle of irreverence, comically oblivious to the disparity between Creator and his creatures, is clearly superior to the later "priestly" principle of the sublime, which seals the gap between the Ruler of the Universe and his humble subjects. Thus, when one reads this irresistibly funny divine comedy, which is Bloom's *The Book of J*, one is immediately reminded of a comment Benjamin made a propos Kafka in his letter to Gershom

Scholem from February 4, 1939: "I think the key to Kafka's work is likely to fall into the hands of the person who is able to extract the comic aspects of Jewish theology. Has there been such a man? Or would you be man enough to be such a man?" (Smiths 1989, 243). Scholem was way too serious, Benjamin in his own fashion, too—but if there ever were such a person, sufficiently human to see into the humor of the Jewish God, it is definitely Harold Bloom!

Of all the Hebrew heroes who haggle with God, Jacob is the most persistent struggler. He already fights Esau, his twin brother, in Rebecca's womb, but loses and comes second, clutching his twin's heel: hence his name, the heel clutcher. He is nevertheless determined to win Isaac's Blessing: by deceiving both him and his poor, nonsuspicious brother, he gains what he secretly wanted. Yet, from this time on, he is always in trouble, doomed to risk his life again and again. Just when he is about to lose everything and there is hardly any hope left for him to survive—for Esau is coming to him to take his revenge—he takes the step of his life: he *goes back* to the spot of the highest danger to confront his destiny. Instead of escaping, and thus letting himself become a passive victim of unfortunate circumstances, he sits and waits to ambush his own fate. And so the fate comes, in the demonic disguise of Elohim, one of God's Angels who wants to destroy him. Jacob, however, wrestles with the Angel till the break of dawn, and though his leg's ligament is torn, he does not relent: the Angel reveals to him his name, Israel, "may God persevere," which now becomes Jacob's new name, the symbol of his extraordinary perseverance and stubbornness.

This agon is the first archetypal instance of high, hubristic will displayed by a mortal: the first instance of what Bloom calls *theomorphism*, that is, an attempt to imitate Yahweh in his purest, most vitalistic essence of will.[6] Just like Abraham, who left his place of birth and hit the road "away from his origins," Jacob also performs the act of Exodus, pushing human possibilities beyond and out of the realm of myth and its non-ambitious pattern of life as sheer survival. Fate, the omnipotent ruler of the mythic paradigm, becomes challenged by the will, the very opposite of fatalism. Bloom is therefore right to emphasize that it is not Yahweh himself who fights Jacob but only one of the Elohim Angels, the divine attributes: Jacob wrestles not with his God but merely with his God's archaic, fatalistic aspect which becomes conquered and purified during the agon. He thus *helps* Yahweh to become what he really is: a nonmythical deity whose essence is not the crushing power of fate, but the pure energy of will.[7]

It may seem far-fetched to see in Jacob the founding hero of Gnosticism, but, then, what is Gnosis if not the emphatic revision of those features of monotheism which are always underplayed by pious orthodoxy? Bloom's strong misreading of the book of J is exactly this: it enhances what had been understated by the sublime Elohist, the pious Priest, and the scrupulous Redactor, the remaining three writers of Torah. It gives us a sudden, undistorted vision of ancient Hebrew vitalism in which mortals haggle with their God to become what they really are, that is, the *zelem*, God's image, entitled to their share in the divine *more life*. The Gnostic strain, the dark underbelly of monotheism, is thus nothing but the correction of the imbalance in which the whole of life and holiness is drained from the world toward God, King, and Creator; haggling, bargaining, disputing, negotiating is all mortals can do to decrease the scandal of this disparity and *hold back* their "ownmost" spark of life—or *keep* their Blessing despite Yahweh's threats of its always imminent withdrawal.[8] All the Gnostics, therefore, could be said to partake avant la lettre in Feuerbach's famous critique of monotheism: by protesting against the *drainage of the sacred* from themselves, against the call for sacrifice and deadly submission, they wish to participate in the same bursting energy that created the world. By insisting on their portion in the right to creation, which orthodox, priestly monotheism delegates to God only, they become an obvious blueprint for Bloom's "strong poets."[9]

In the ratio of *daemonization*, therefore, a poet is born in his new Gnostic incarnation: he will struggle with his precursor as his own Fate to conquer the fatalistic aspect of poetic succession and wrestle out of him a spark of charisma, a share of *more life*, which, as he is now convinced, should not be granted to his poetic father only. In *Violence and the Sacred*, René Girard identifies this spark of charisma with *kudos*, a sacred ingredient, not far removed from the Greek *pharmakon*, both demonic and beneficial, which travels from one lucky individual to another, never to be kept by anyone forever. Seen from this perspective, very Gnostic indeed, monotheism is a scandalous usurpation, which imparts the whole of *kudos* to one God who frequently admits himself that he is "jealous" and "possessive" of his holy power. The ephebe, therefore, is born as a Gnostic the moment he dares to redress this imbalance and reach for the elusive *kudos* of sacred glory. Writes Bloom:

> The ephebe learns divination first when he apprehends the appalling energy of his *own* precursor as being at once Wholly Other yet also

a possessing force ... To divine the glory one already is becomes a mixed blessing when there is a deep anxiety whether one has become truly oneself. Yet this sense of glory, should it prove to be an error about life, is necessary for a poet as poet, who must achieve imagination here by denying the full humanity of imagination. (*AI*, 101–2)

In Bloom's account, the two prototypes of the religious mentality—the submissive one represented by the obedient side of Abraham, and the rebellious one represented by the militant side of Jacob—are equivalents of two different strategies of identification. The first, more common one, is sublimation, which repeats the gesture of self-renunciation, that is, of offering the most vital part of oneself for the sake of higher values. Sublimation occurs when rivalry ceases and gives way to a sweet surrender: the ego comes to terms with its imperfection and begins to cultivate the distance between itself and its remote, unattainable ideals. The sublimating ego is humble, but not the cunning poetic self which cheats and calculates its gains and losses even in a moment of self-humiliation. No, this is just an ordinary, nonspectacular type of humbleness. Writes Bloom in *A Map of Misreading*:

> We move into the psychic area that Freud characterized as "normality," by means of sublimation, the one "successful" defense. My suggestion here is that psychic "normality," however desirable for persons, does not work for and in poems. (100)

And in *The Anxiety of Influence* he adds:

> Orphism, for latecomers, reduces to a variety of sublimation, the truest of defenses against the anxiety of influence, and the one most impairing to the poetic self. Hence Nietzsche, lovingly recognizing in Socrates the first master of sublimation, found in Socrates also the destroyer of tragedy. Had he lived to read Freud, Nietzsche might somewhat admiringly have seen in him another Socrates, come to revive the primary vision of a rational substitute for the unattainable, antithetical gratification of life and art alike. (115)

Bloom betrays his skepticism toward the "success" of ordinary sublimation by putting it in inverted commas. He is, in fact, tempted by a more risky variant of identification—always hesitant, deferred, and creatively repeated—in which the psyche becomes identified not with the ideal it passively admires but with the opponent against whom it fights (*BV,* 66). This identification is not accompanied by an ego's sacrifice of its own originality but, to the contrary, by the vital "quickening power" Milton had attributed to Satan in the apogee of his self-begotten pride. This, again, is Bloom's recurring motif, his ingenious retroping of the Lacanian concept of the hysteric, who delays the moment of self-offering to the Other, as well as the Derridean notion of deferment which, simultaneously, disturbs and propels the process of identification. Seen in this light, all six stages of "initiation" are, in fact, six strategies of delaying and complicating the act of maturation which, in case of the psyche striving for her singularity, cannot simply consist in a submissive attempt of imitation. But the mystery of this initial refusal—for how can an ephebe, who in himself is nothing, stand up to the precursor, who in himself is everything?—boils down to the "ownmost," inalienable spark of life the initiate refuses to sacrifice on the behalf of his all-alive, hyperpowerful deity, even if it proves nothing but "an error about life" (*AI,* 102).[10] Without this vitalistic residue, the "ownmost possibility of life," which, as a possibility, can always turn into "more life," there would be no hubris and no "quickening power" whatsoever: having nothing of her *own*, the psyche would be crushed under the burden of influence. And this inalienable power is, at the same time, the only source of all strong poems. As Bloom describes in *The Breaking of the Vessels*:

> The power I seek to gain over the text is what Milton's Satan called "quickening power," *the conviction of pragmatic self-engendering.* Such a power is parallel to any strong poem's power over its precursor poems. Power, in this sense, is neither the autonomous ego's location of itself in history, as in Abrams, nor the deconstructive process's demystification both of the ego and of history, as in Derrida . . . What concerns me in a strong poem is neither self nor language but the *utterance,* within a tradition of uttering, of the image or lie of voice, where "voice" is neither self nor language, but rather spark or *pneuma* as opposed to self, and act made one with word (*davhar*) rather than word referring only to another word (*logos*). A poem is spark and act, or else we need not read it a second time. (3–4; my emphasis)

Thus, the strength of a poem consists in its *presence*, or the way it makes itself felt as a powerful presence, imitating the divine manner of *davhar,* the creative word-act, or saying-as-manifestation. It isn't strictly *imitatio Dei* (imitation of God), rather a Gnostic attempt to become level with

God, yet not on the basis of God's creative powers, which cannot be matched, but, at least, on the level of the very fact of his *being:* for God's "I am," although mighty, is *not* the only "I am" in the world. "Monotheism," says Winnicott in the motto to this section, "seems to be closely linked to the name *I am*" (1986, 57), which also means that it begins to treat the assertion "I am" as a rare privilege, available solely to the highest being which truly can make itself present whenever and wherever it wishes.[11] The Gnostic intuition, however, challenges this restrictive use of "I am" and, although not fully democratic, reserves it for the chosen few "lucky fellows" who, in a manner precisely opposite to Job, became rewarded by multiple lives for *not* having been too obedient.

ASKESIS, OR LESS IS MORE

> The man of knowledge acts as an artist and transfigurer of cruelty in forcing his spirit to know against its inclination and often enough against the wishes of his heart—saying No where he wants to affirm, love, worship.
> —Friedrich Nietzsche, *Beyond Good and Evil*

Daemonization is the ratio in which the singular "I am" fights for its right to expansion and the powerful presence of *davhar;* however, just before the final outburst of energy, here comes yet another contraction. Right after the poet ventures into the area so far exclusively "controlled" by precursors, he once more has to "rally what remains" in order to save strength for his last, decisive jump. Thus, he has to inflict upon himself yet another painful limitation to see what truly "remains" of his "quickening power": what really can be named *his,* and what still belongs to his poetic father. This is the fifth revisionary ratio, *askesis,* which, in fact, is even more violent than the previous one:

> Intoxicated by the fresh repressive force of a personalized Counter-Sublime, the strong poet in his daemonic elevation is empowered *to turn his energy upon himself,* and achieves, at terrible cost, his clearest victory in wrestling with the mighty dead. (*AI,* 116)

This victory, it would seem, must be bought with self-offering, the same self-offering the ephebe defended himself against from the very beginning, delaying the moment of the necessary sacrifice. Yet—here comes another twist—this self-offering is as deceptive as all "humble" with-drawals the ephebe has made so far. This is, therefore, a Promethean sacrifice, which gives to God his due only in order to win independence for the mortals. The ephebe apparently accepts his failure before the precursor to whom he finally concedes the trophy of poetic priority; he knows that, despite the vividness of his narcissistic fantasies, he is not Adam after all, and that his narcissistic wish to name things for the first time is irreversibly wounded. Thus, he gives up the direct rivalry with the predecessor and represses his agonistic impulse, which, enjoying the vicissitudes of all repressed drives, emerges in the end as a *sublimated aggression*. This repressive limitation of the initial will to power is not, however, self-humbling, as it is in the case of "normal" sublimation; its goal is as antithetical as everything the ephebe has procured till now in his "murky shop" of poetic repression. Its aim is to *purge* the poetic drive so thoroughly that it finally becomes free of all alien contamination, of all the impurities coming from the will of the precursor, or, as Girard has it, from mediated, triangular desire.

Now, the desire and the drive are to follow the promise which has already dawned on the ephebe in the stage of *daemonization:* just as he can oppose to the precursor the countersublime spark of his "ownmost," inalienable "I am," he can do the same with his will, the rightful expression of his separate *sum*, and thus no longer want the same thing that the mighty mediator wants. This self-offering, therefore, whose function is to purify the poet's desire so it can truly become "his ownmost," is a fake sacrifice, not likely to please the poetic gods of T. S. Eliot's pantheon. In its cunning it resembles what Michel de Certeau used to call "a tactic behind the enemy lines" (1984, 12): as opposed to a fully developed strategy, which has autonomous means at its disposal, a tactic is a defensive-provocative maneuver which, left to alien devices, learns to appropriate and use them for its own purpose. All Bloom's revisionary ratios bear a close similarity to de Certeau's "tactics," yet the stage of *askesis* truly fits the description perfectly: it is a self-offering—as we have said, a long-expected one—a seemingly ultimate concession or admission of failure, yet done in such a way that the victorious trophy, the *kudos* of originality, has to pass hands and find itself in the possession of the ephebe. But the cost of this trick, even if it pays, is enormous. Writes Bloom:

> *Askesis* as a successful defense against the anxiety of influence, posits a new kind of reduction in the poetic self, most generally expressed as a purgatorial blinding or at least veiling ... Purgatory for

> post-Enlightenment strong poets is always oxymoronic, and never
> merely painful, because every narrowing of circumference is com-
> pensated for by the poetic illusion (a delusion, and yet a strong poem)
> that the center will therefore hold better. (*AI*, 121)

Within the family romance, which builds the canvas for Bloom's theory of
poetic formation, *askesis* is a stage in which the child tries to win independence by refusing to identify with the will of its parents. *You* want me to do
it, not *me!*—this is the most typical reaction of this phase. In consequence,
the child makes a self-offering: he renounces this part of his gifts that are
too contaminated by his parents' ambitions. The child becomes itself,
an isolated being, by thwarting parental hopes; he would rather give up
on his "natural" endowment than risk a failure of individuation. Wallace
Stevens was definitely one such neurotic child of post-Enlightenment
poetry. As Bloom says:

> In Stevens the reader confronts an *askesis* of the entire Romantic
> tradition, of Wordsworth as much as Keats, Emerson as well as
> Whitman. No modern poet half so strong as Stevens chose so large a
> self-curtailment, sacrificed so much instinctual impulse in the name
> of being a latecomer. (*AI*, 135)

Nothing is got for nothing, says Emerson, and this wisdom applies better here than anywhere else: individuation is gained at the horrendous
cost of the loss of spontaneity and mistrust of one's "natural impulse."
Askesis, by decreasing the circumference, promises that the center will
hold better, yet it is hardly a solution Yeats would have endorsed: quite
the contrary, this punctual isolation—the lesser the circumference, the
stronger the center—looses, in fact, mere anarchy upon the ephebe's
inner world, for he is now being cut off from what the romantics used to
call *die Spontanität* (spontaneity), the one, orphic stream of life flowing
through the poetic id and its impulsive drives. Yet, the ephebe is happy
with his precarious gain: for in this mere an-archy, he is cut off from his
poetic *arche* and thus at least left alone.

The ratio of *askesis*, therefore, is a site where the most crucial paradox,
on which the whole edifice of Bloom's poetic initiation is founded, may
finally emerge on full display: the paradox of "less is more." Bloom's revisionist theory of poetry reveals the mechanism of irreversible aging in
Western literary culture, its constant "falling into time." *Askesis* becomes
increasingly more important as a ratio in which every adept offers the

best part of himself in hope of getting back a little drop of fresh blood, a tiny portion of new vitality. The self-curtailment, which is the fate of modern poets who wish to survive *as poets* (and not just graphomaniacs), almost reaches its ultimate limits: the sacrifice takes gradually everything they have at their disposal. It is no longer a Promethean deceit, but an act Kenneth Burke called a "poetic suicide" executed in the name of poetic survival. Rigorous formalism leading to the final "dearth of meaning" (*DC*, 12) forces latecomers to speak in lower and lower voices about fewer and fewer subjects. Hence the "new tone" appears only at the expense of self-limitation and contraction, which borders on the edge of total ellipsis, silence, and demise.[12]

The Western literary tradition approaches the moment in which the very desire for the new, original, and singular begins to lose its initial, typically modern attraction: it is followed by such painful self-sacrifices that the stake, "the new tone," may seem no longer worth risking. Bloom does not hide his ambivalence in the description of the fifth, most fatal stage of his agon, in which the ephebe gambles to gain *more of himself*, yet this achievement is always bought with the loss, the decrease of the Blessing: *less life*. With tangible regret, Bloom mentions Wordsworth, who became less of a poet than he could have been had he not renounced his passion for an adventurous narrative, already "occupied" by others before him. And he pities his beloved Stevens, who curtailed his potentially loquacious Emersonian orphism to become more laconic than he himself would have wanted. Alas, *askesis* always consists in abandoning real passion—in, as Nietzsche tells us, "saying No where he (the poet) wants to affirm, love, worship"—and such must be the fate of poets who buy their *names* for the cost of their *lives*. The times of happy conjunction—the individual name easily coupled with more life in one act of Blessing—are long over; now has come the time of an excruciating *either-or*.[13]

Or, it would seem so prima facie. This paradox, with its apparently pessimistic conclusion, lies at the very core of Bloom's antithetical criticism. To combine vitality with revisionism resembles an attempt to square a circle: yet Bloom, more assertive than melancholy, never stops to convince us that the latecomer, even when he produces "the achieved dearth of meaning" à la Mallarmé, may still be as vital and powerful as Vico's primary divinators, the strongest and most spontaneous of all poets. Writes Bloom in "The Breaking of Form":

> From the poets of Sensibility down to our current post-Stevensian contemporaries, poetry has suffered ... an over-determination of

> language and consequently an under-determination of meaning. As
> the verbal mechanisms of crisis have come to dominate lyric poetry,
> in relatively fixed patterns, a *striking effect* has been that the strongest
> poets have tended to establish their mastery by the paradox of what I
> would call *an achieved dearth of meaning*. (*DC*, 12; my emphasis)

This "striking effect," however, requires a substantial revision of
Nietzsche's notion of vitalism, as well as a modification of Freud's economy of drives: the two sources Bloom wrestles with but still "props
himself up on" in *The Anxiety of Influence*. If we are to believe that *askesis*
and vitalism may go hand in hand in order to square the circle of Bloom's
antithetical criticism, we have to cross beyond Nietzsche and Freud or,
at least, submit them to powerful misreadings. For *unlike* Nietzsche, who
divides powers into active and reactive and calls only the former life
enhancing, Bloom does not hesitate to see more life where Nietzsche
would see merely passivity of decadence. With a sole exception, however,
and this exception is very significant for Bloom's implicit revision. In *The
Genealogy of Morals*, Nietzsche cannot but reluctantly admire the resoluteness with which the Hebrew priests turned the active power onto
itself in order to create consciousness and conscience:

> Whatever else has been done to damage the powerful and great of
> this earth seems trivial compared with what the Jews had done, that
> priestly people who succeeded in avenging themselves on their ene-
> mies and oppressors by radically inverting all their values, that is, by
> an act of the most spiritual vengeance. This was the strategy entirely
> appropriate to a priestly people in whom vindictiveness had gone
> most deeply underground ... It [the ascetic ideal] signifies, let us
> have a courage to face it, a will to nothingness, a revulsion from life,
> a rebellion against the principal conditions of living. And yet, despite
> everything, it is and remains a *will*. (1956, 167, 299)[14]

Bloom's revision begins with *tessera*, that is, an antithetical completion
of Nietzsche's ambivalent and aporetic fascination with this strange kind
of will which, "despite everything" he believes about health, power, and
beauty, stubbornly remains what it is: forceful, high willed, and boldly
oblivious to natural constraints of health and sickness. Nietzsche's genealogical rhetoric is unstable and clearly demands such completion:
stuck with his dogmatic naturalism, Nietzsche cannot find categories
that would descriptively follow his inexplicable attraction to this weird,

non-natural kind of will. It should be nothing but "sick" and "morbid," yet, at the same time, it somehow strangely *transcends* the naturalistic opposition of sickness and health. Nietzsche asks in one of the most hesitant passages in *Genealogy:*

> But what about the sources of man's morbidity? For certainly man is sicker, less secure, less stable, less firmly anchored than any other animal; he is the *sick* animal. But has he not also been more daring, more defiant, more inventive than all other animals together?—man, the great experimenter on himself, eternally unsatisfied, vying with gods, the beasts, and with nature for final supremacy; man, unconquered to this day, still unrealized, so agitated by his own teeming energy that his future digs like spurs into the flesh of every present moment. (ibid., 257)

In Bloom's interpretation, Freud's notion of the superego derives from the same indeterminacy between the active and the reactive, the same ambivalence of sickness and health, life and death. On the surface it might seem that it simply uses life against life; yet, in fact, the superego uses life in order to achieve a *different kind of life*, not the one associated with the id's spontaneous yet general *demands*, but the one enriched by the higher idea of *will*, teeming with future-oriented, proleptic energy and its infinite, singularized *desire*. This is why Bloom in *The Book of J* bases his "psychology of Yahweh" and his relentless vitalism not on the Nietzschean id but on the early Freudian paradigm of superego:

> And it is precisely here, in one of the greatest ironies, Freud is J's descendant and is haunted by J's Yahweh in the figure of Superego ... Poor Ego never will enter the Promised Land, because the personality of Yahweh is one with the daemonic intensity of the Superego. (*BJ*, 305–6).

And this is also the point in which vitality and revision can safely converge: we only have to remind ourselves of a *different* kind of vitalism that is offered by Bloom's misprision of the book of J. Renouncing one's spontaneous needs for the sake of will is not exactly the Nietzschean version of crippling morality in which one renounces one's desires for the sake of obedience to norms. This is precisely how the Promethean cheat can go on and on: "the achieved dearth of meaning," the subtle, ascetic dance of highly revised tropes continues still for the sake of life, although a different life than the life of "mere" instinctual demands. It is not a thanatic exercise of reactivity but a manifestation of life that has traveled far beyond the barbarian vitality of the Nietzschean *aristoi* (aristocrats). Vitality, therefore, may also lie in the power of repression, just as Jacob's high-willed vitality lies in his lameness, which signifies the cost of "mere life"—and the vitality of his children lies in the way they work hard to model the chaotic realm of their natural wants, as symbolized by the loss of their foreskins, the curtailment of the primitive phallic power.

It would seem, therefore, that once we shift from Nietzsche and his fascination with barbarian, naturalistic liveliness to early Hebrew vitalism with its "new version of the id," the paradox can be, at least partly, resolved. The simple Yes of the Nietzschean *Ja-Sagen* to the "physical" cycle of birth and death, repressed by the prohibition to participate in the repetitive "ring of being," does not produce an equally simple negating effect; rather, it dialectically dissolves into a subtler halo of "tender Yeses" (Nietzsche 1956, 122). It is, therefore, not life itself which gets negated, but only its natural, ringlike, hopelessly cyclical manifestation that binds its energy in a deadening compulsive repetition. It is not life itself which is "damned" or "wicked," but merely this mechanical form of the eternal return of the same that constitutes the rhythm of nature.[15]

A BETTER SIN

> It has all the vitality of error.
> —Oscar Wilde, *The Critic as Artist*

> One already understands me: this ascetic priest, this apparent enemy of life, this denier—precisely he belongs to the altogether great conserving and Yes-creating forces of life ... The No he says to life, his No, brings to light, as if by magic, an *abundance of tender Yeses;* yes indeed, even when he wounds himself, this master of destruction, of self-destruction—it is henceforth the wound itself that compels him to live.
> —Nietzsche, *Genealogy of Morals*

A more detailed discussion of Nietzsche is inevitable here, mainly for the reason that Bloom himself has blinded his sight by sticking to Nietzschean arguments for much too long. It is only later, in the '80s, that Bloom begins to work on the different, early Hebrew notion of vitalism, yet the retrospective projection we propose here is not completely unjustified. Bloom's growing impatience with Nietzsche, which culminates in "Freud and Beyond," the famous essay from *Ruin the Sacred Truths!* is mainly due to the aporias created by his own antithetical criticism that could not be resolved on the ground of purely Nietzschean vitalism.[16] Thus, although in *The Anxiety of Influence* Bloom continues to use Nietzsche's distinction of active and passive sin, coined by him in *The Birth of Tragedy*, which equals his own distinction of agonistic and "normal" sublimation, he already implicitly disagrees with him and perceives "the Semitic passive sin" as a refined and in consequence far more militant version of the Promethean deceit. Says Nietzsche in one of the most controversial fragments of *The Birth of Tragedy*:

> The legend of Prometheus is indigenous to the entire community of Aryan races and attests to their prevailing talent for profound and tragic vision. In fact, it is not improbable that this myth has the same characteristic importance for the Aryan mind as the myth of the Fall has for the Semitic, and that the two myths are related as brother and sister ... Man's highest good must be bought with a crime and paid by the flood of grief and suffering which the offended divinities visit upon the human race in its noble ambition. An austere notion, this, which by the dignity it confers on crime presents a strange contrast to the Semitic myth of the Fall—a myth that exhibits curiosity, deception, suggestibility, concupiscence, in short a whole series of principally feminine frailties, as the root of all evil. What distinguishes the Aryan conception is an exalted notion of active sin as the properly Promethean virtue ... The Aryan nations assign to crime the male, the Semites to sin the female gender; and it is quite consistent with these nations that the original act of *hubris* should be attributed to a man, original sin to a woman. (1956, 63–64)

Putting aside all the sexist and anti-Semitic innuendos, this passage tells us about two kinds of primal sin that begin the human odyssey. The Greek version of disobedience differs from the Jewish one in its tragic clarity: gods were cheated, gods want their revenge, and humans have to suffer either way, with or without the stolen fire. Whereas the Hebrew "passive sin" is "reactive" in creating a halo of mysterious, no longer conscious fear: the contradicted God, far from being the transparent agent of Greek tragedy, becomes internalized as a figure of moral commandment. Greek manliness, therefore, consists in brave fidelity to Prometheus: given the chance to repeat his sin, Aryans would have done it again. While Semitic cowardice lays in the repentance their passive, weak sin had created: if only they could, Jews would have piously revoked their trespass.

This is hardly an alliance for Harold Bloom. Everything Bloom tells us in *The Book of J* blandly contradicts Nietzsche's flippant dismissal of the non-Aryan, female passivity of "Jewish sin." In Bloom's account it isn't even a *sin:* first, it is childish misbehavior, which slowly and gradually matures into an agonistic attitude that finally surpasses everything the Greek hubris ever produced. Jacob's ambushing his own fate forms an image of a high-willed pride which is determined to crush the forces of destiny, and thus to *get out* of the tragic condition which is always a predicament of ultimate restriction.[17] The Greek active sin may therefore consist in tragedy, in which the singular outburst of life clashes with its inevitable limitation, yet the Hebrew sin aims at something else: it may consent to diminish the eruption of vitality by a sense of guilt and anxiety, created by the superego, but always in order *to cross a limit*, and to "pass forth."[18] The Greek sin inagurates the tragic scene where the same drama is played over and over again: the unrepressed life meets its inevitable doom in the blind, all-leveling verdict of *Ananke*. Whenever it says Yes to life, it is always in the same, repeatable form: birth, hubris, retaliation of fate; hence the Greek, "manly" *Ja-Sagen* lies in its power of endurance, in accepting the tragic predicament of life which inevitably closes itself in the naturalistic circle of *genesis* and *phtora*, "becoming" and "corruption." Whereas the Jewish sin internalizes punishment and thus changes the idea of life itself, by producing a whole new sphere of possibilities Nietzsche himself calls very aptly "an abundance of tender Yeses."[19]

This abundance of tender affirmations is precisely the goal of Bloom's antithetical vitalism. It would be a serious mistake to attribute to Bloom a straightforward belief in the ascetic ideal and to ignore the radical transformation it undergoes in the Bloomian revisionary system, where it is turned into an antithetical, life-affirming defense. Bloom deliberately collates two ideals Nietzsche himself kept apart—the ascetic and the antithetical, knowing well that this separation is the source of Nietzsche's insoluble antinomies. In the following fragment from *Kabbalah and Criticism*, which looks deceptively as a simple borrowing from Nietzsche, Bloom bridges this gap in one, seemingly innocuous maneuver:

> The ascetic ideal had kept man from nihilism, saving the will but at
> the expense of guilt, a guilt involving hatred of common humanity
> (with all natural pleasure). For the ascetic ideal is an interpretation,
> one that in turn inspires a change in the process of willing. This
> change signifies "a will to nothingness, a revulsion from life," *yet
> still a purposefulness. Life thus uses asceticism in a struggle against death.*
> Nietzsche, magnificently contrapuntal, attains a triumph in antitheti-
> cal thought by declaring that to be ascetic is thus to be life-affirming.
> The artist in particular transforms the ascetic ideal by incarnating
> "the wish to be different, to be elsewhere." . . . To be different, to be
> elsewhere is a superb definition of the motive for metaphor, for the
> life affirming deep motive of all poetry. (*KC*, 51–52; my emphasis)

What Bloom calls here Nietzche's magnificent contrapuntality, allowing
him to jump in one rhetorical move from the ascetic to the antithetical ideal, is, in fact, nothing more than Nietzsche's major contradiction
he himself could not resolve, getting stuck, rather unproductively, with
the traditional vitalistic notion of life as "natural life" (with all its natural, instinctual pleasures). The idea that "life uses asceticism in a struggle
against death" and that "to be ascetic is to be life-affirming" is Bloom's
(or, simply Jewish), and definitely not Nietzsche's, who, despite his incon-
sequential admiration for the Hebrew priests, would always maintain
that asceticism is the struggle of death against life, even to the detriment
of his own theory. But when *askesis* becomes antithesis, the image of life
torn between natural instincts and the artificial superegoic demands,
suddenly gains clarity: what initially (i.e., in the Greek eyes) appeared
as an oppression of natural life by the constraints of morals turns into a
Jewish vision of liberation of life from the oppressive bondage of nature.
Is is precisely this radical *Gestaltswitch* of perspectives that allows Bloom
to transform Nietzsche's incoherent notion of the ascetic ideal into an
antithetical life-affirming vehicle of restless "crossing," which produces
and then feeds "the wish to be elsewhere," the "exodic" desire of displacement. From the point of view of this liberated "more life," which
initiated a "change in the process of willing," the natural existence, which
lacks this sort of vitalistic inventiveness, seems nothing more than just a
contemptible "mere life," unworthy of any nostalgic glorification.[20]

The concept of "more life" that Bloom has in mind differs thus fundamentally from what Freud in his *Three Essays on the Theory of Sexuality*
used to call "the vital order," that is, the most basic natural system of
the instincts of self-preservation; it appears much closer to the originally

indeterminate and anarchic energy of libido, which cannot be contained within a well-defined, homeostatic system of needs and gratifications. From Freud's speculation in *Three Essays* follows that libido (i.e., human sexuality), precisely because of its indeterminacy, is always in danger of falling under the rule of the better organized vital order—but, at the same time, it can also use its original indeterminacy to free itself from the latter's mechanical functionality. Human sexual drive may be inchoate, premature, and deficient when compared to well-determined self-preservatory instincts—yet, this can also be seen as its advantage.

In the first stage of development, libido has to learn from the better-formed self-preservatory instincts and thus borrow their form of manifestation; it has to *lean on* (*Anlehnung*) the vital functions to use its objects for autoerotic purposes. Soon, however, this seemingly subservient "propping" turns into "wrestling," and anaclisis takes on the form of agon. In one of his best pieces, "Wrestling Sigmund," from *The Breaking of the Vessels*, Bloom boldly juxtaposes the story of wrestling Jacob from the biblical writer J with Freud's account of the beginning of human sexuality, thus giving a peculiar agonistic twist to the Freudian notion of *Anlehnung*. The picture that emerges out of the ingenious interference of two images—Jacob wrestling with the Angel of Death and human infant sucking maternal breast—presents human sexuality as a drive that fights with the vital order in refusing to be imprisoned by its mere natural functionality, the inexorable homeostasis of *phusis* (nature). It may thus seem that "wrestling a divine angel is rather a contrast to sucking one's mother breast, and achieving the name Israel is pretty unrelated to the inauguration of the sexual drive" (*BV*, 49), yet, Bloom insists, these two narratives tell the same story:

> *All human sexuality is tropological*, whereas we all of us desperately need and long for it to be literal . . . As Laplanche says, expounding Freud: "Sexuality in its entirety is in the slight deviation, the *clinamen* from the function." Or as I would phrase it, *our sexuality is in its very origins a misprision, a strong misreading, on the infant's part, of the vital order* . . . I call Freud . . . "Wrestling Sigmund," because again he is a poet of Sublime agon, here an agon between sexuality and the vital order. Our sexuality is like Jacob, and the vital order is like that among the Elohim with whom our wily and heroic ancestor wrestled, until he had won the great name of Israel. Sexuality and Jacob triumph, but at the terrible expense of a crippling. All our lives long we search in vain, unknowingly, for the lost object, when even that object was a

clinamen away from the true aim. And yet we search incessantly, do experience satisfactions, however marginal, and win our real if limited triumph over the vital order. Like Jacob, we keep passing Penuel, limping on our hips. (*BV,* 69–70; my emphasis)[21]

Bloom offers here a Jewish version of sublimation, which differs considerably from the teachings of "divine Plato" (as Freud calls him in the introduction to *Three Essays*). Instead of a winged Eros that flies above its abandoned, material objects to become unencumbered and purely spiritual, we get an image of an impaired, limping hero who managed to detach himself from the lethal embrace with the vital order and thus "passes forth," though damaged in his natural vitality. Instead of a Spirit, which rises above matter in a triumphant ascension toward the supranatural sun, we see an anxious quester, walking through a horizontal desert away from the Egypt of nature, but always "limping," always endangered by the fall into the snares of the "vital order."

In this version of sublimating *askesis*, nature is not so easily abandoned. The Exodus from nature, from the seduction of "propping" (*Anlehnung*) on the certainties of the vital order, is a hard-won victory that agrees with the fundamental dissatisfaction of the sexual drive: in not being able to find its true object (which, in fact, does not exist), it transforms everything natural into something figurative, that is, something else that it actually is, an eternally vague object of desire. In his strong misreading of Jean Laplanche's *Life and Death in Psychoanalysis*, Bloom adopts Laplanche's notion of *clinamen*, but gives it immediately a new twist. While Laplanche's vision of the wandering sexual drive is full of tragic lament on the hubristic "perversion" of the denaturalized human libido that can find no place in reality—Bloom embraces libido's lack of natural fit as a life-enhancing chance and opening of possibilities. While Laplanche sees libido as underprivileged in comparison to well-adapted vital order—Bloom goes beyond this traditionally tragic perspective and praises libido's original maladaptation for its figurative potential.

In Bloom's misreading, therefore, anaclisis appears as a moment both of the greatest danger and the greatest chance: it is an agon which may be either won or lost. Tendency for "propping" may either bow down the sexual drive and turn it into a quasi-natural force imitating animal instincts, condemned to their naturalistic model of "health"—or be overcome by the original indeterminacy of the drive, which will then begin to "trope itself" beyond mere functionality into the realm of more tender and more perverse Yeses. The drive may thus either fall into embrace

with nature, or, due to superegoic repression, give up on its early quasi-
natural fixations, renounce all (dis)satisfactions offered by real objects,
and expand into a figurative force, creating meanings in the domain
where previously there was nothing but pure, senseless functionality.
Once again: repression here is not the ascetic No said to life, but quite
the contrary, a negation which helps libido to detach itself from its quasi-
natural fixations and reclaim its original, nonteleological force.

This agonistic Eros, therefore, is not just an instinct of life as opposed
to the instinct of death, but a power of figuration wrestling both with life
and death as a cycle of mere functions. It is no longer sexuality forced to
conform with the natural need of self-preservation, but *Erros*, eros and
error combined: an energy of primordial libido that regains its original "erring" indeterminacy, which now serves not as its default but as its
main asset and advantage. For, once it detaches itself from the vital order,
it immediately begins to *err:* it crosses the limits of the functional system
of *physis* and wanders out from the Egypt of nature into the desert of
open possibilities. *Erros* refuses to be closed within boredom of natural
life, which just "piles life on life," unable by itself to produce one grain
of meaning, but, unlike in the more traditional, Greek-influenced teaching on sublimation and *askesis*, it does not reject life altogether. Quite the
contrary, instead of negating life, it reclaims its original anarchic libidinal form and, by liberating it from the confines of natural repetition,
transforms life into an exciting "quest romance" of continuous "crossing" and "passing forth" that began with the most paradigmatic of all
Shem heroes, Jacob at Penuel.

Eros, Thanatos, and Beyond

> As though to breathe were life. Life piled on life
> Were too little.
> —Alfred Tennyson, *Ulysses*

> The written questions addressed to literature . . . they are
> mortifications, that is to say, as always, ruses of life. Life negates
> itself in literature only so that it may survive better. So that it may
> be better. It does not negate itself any more than it affirms itself: it
> differs from itself, defers itself, and writes itself as *difference*. Books
> are always books of *life* . . . or of *afterlife*.
> —Jacques Derrida, *Writing and Difference*

Every ratio in Bloom's antithetical scheme opens a field of possible gains and losses. Every stage in his sixfold system has its victories which produce poetic strength and failures which produce poetic weakness. A miscarried *clinamen* bears a strengthless fruit of infinite irony; for Bloom, such failure would be represented by Friedrich Schlegel, especially when read via de Man—its main sin is impotency. An aborted *tessera* fails to restitute the sense of the whole: its main sin is lack of inventiveness, inability to continue the precursor's work. A failed *kenosis* produces a fake self-humbling: its main sin is inauthenticity. An unsuccessful *daemonization* inflates the ephebe with an empty hyperbole: instead of being tragic, he is merely pathetic. Bad *apophrades* turn the late poet into someone even more emphatically belated: their sin is secondariness.

But what happens when *askesis* goes wrong? *Askesis* is the stage of contraction, which "recollects forward" the ratio of *kenosis*, that is, self-humbling: its failures are, therefore, the recurring and augmented pathologies of the latter. Now, the passive-aggressive humbleness of *kenosis*, which aimed at emptying the power of precursor, becomes an overtly offensive stand against not only one's own creative efforts, but against the whole enterprise of creation as such. The paradigmatic gesture of such aborted *askesis* is Nietzsche's move toward genealogy: turning aggression from its antithetical sublimation back against the culture only because it makes this sublimation increasingly more difficult. If I myself cannot be a great writer, says the geneaologist, let nothing be great anymore. *Askesis* being repetition of *kenosis*, *kenosis* being repetition of *clinamen*—this highly developed Suspicion is nothing but the recurrent version of the initial irony, which now repeats its diffident cheat on the precursor in a far more grand and self-assured manner. Now it is an irony which is able to sweep away all edifices of meaning: an infinite parabasis floating free even of suspicion itself, the perfect deconstructive tool so eloquently described by de Man in his "Concept of Irony."

The topic of *askesis* brings us back to our meditations on life and death in deconstruction in part 2, in which we portrayed life as a ruse against death, played on death's own ground. This time this subtle, though crucial, difference between life and death boils down to two different approaches to the stage of ascetic limitation: one, "honest" and literal, consisting in accepting this limitation as the death-in-life, a lethal castration of one's natural vitality which leads toward *imitatio mortis* (as in Lacan)—and the other, "cunning" and figurative, consisting in using the limitation of life as a crossing which leads toward more complex, more individuated and perverse forms of life (as in Bloom). In the first case, death becomes literal, or, as Bloom once had it, acquires a force of "furious literalism." *Askesis*, which was supposed to be an ultimate ruse of life against frontiers and limitations, toying riskily with "un-deadness" and engendering truly infinite, singular and nonimitable poetic desire, loses its defensive character and turns into plain "death-in-life." A potentially strong poet releases himself from *Unbehagen in Kultur* (discontent of civilization), the source of permanent dissatisfaction, and becomes instead a strong critic, who, like the Nietzschean moralist, takes revenge on life he was forced to give up. The poet, therefore, who lapsed from *poesis* (creation) in the ascetic stage, tends to become a truly lethal critic, like Paul de Man: for reasons that might have been partly biographical, de Man indeed limited his creative vitality, yet what he imagined he gained instead was the power of seeing above the duality of blindness and insight, above all the necessary errors of life. He might have decreased his circumference and reduced himself to an immeasurable point, yet this point was precisely the precious "view from nowhere," that is, the epistemologically privileged vantage point of analysis which knows no temptations of misreading, for it is no longer interested in either mere or more life. This is precisely the difference between the Critic Bloom, who always used fake *askesis* as a complex life-enhancing device, and the Critic de Man, who treated the ascetic lure of death literally and seriously. Let us once again read this crucial quote from *The Anxiety of Influence*:

> Any stance that anyone takes up towards a metaphorical work will itself be metaphorical . . . Irony, in its prime sense an allegory, saying one thing while suggesting another, is the epistemological tropes of tropes, and for de Man constituted the condition of literary language itself, producing that "permanent parabasis of meaning" studied by deconstructors. (xix–xx)

So, while for de Man irony is the privileged trope of tropes which releases us from the traps of life, and, as a "death of meaning," allows us perfect contemplation—for Bloom, irony is just a minor lie in the long process of vital misreadings. Bloom, following Nietzsche, believes that "life is everything," so there is no escape from life even if life turns against itself—while de Man, more like Schopenhauer, believes in the blessing of death, that is, in the anticipation of a nirvanic deliverance from the dance macabre of pointless figurations which merely perpetuate the error of life. Bloom is happy to stay forever in the labyrinth of tropes; for him, *askesis*, although dangerously close to death, is never-theless only a *pretence of death*—precisely the kind of ruse that is used by Falstaff who simulates death in order to survive—and as such still in ser-vice of "assaulting the frontiers" and "crossing the boundaries" which belong to the realm of *more life*. Whereas de Man pushes *askesis* to the point from which there is no return, where he thinks to have achieved an epistemological nirvana of a perfect *indifferentia* (indifference); as a mod-ern incarnation of Thanatos he leads his free-floating signifiers out of the noisome chaos of life into icy domains of disinterested truth. Bloom believes that the strong poet can achieve life even in the close figuration of death and pass through castration even more vital than before—de Man, on the other hand, believes that he, as a strong critic, can achieve death already in life and take a position no poet *as a poet* can afford to assume. Bloom uses *askesis* merely as a highly deceptive strategic instru-ment in the ongoing vital agon, whereas de Man commits himself to his asceticism deeply and sincerely; one could even say, considering his ear-lier existentialist fascinations, with truly intense authenticity.[22]

The ascetic stage in which life so violently turns against itself reaches the point where the eternal dualism of Eros and Thanatos appears no longer valid or operative. There is a strange undecidability here which resembles only one figure from the Western tradition: the early Hebrew figure of J's Yahweh, whose capriciousness is a fabulatory equivalent of this fateful "crossing" between life and death that brings us into uncharted regions of existence, no longer intimated by "natural" life. A crossing, therefore, beyond which Eros may finally become a new, unpredictable power of *Erros*, forcefully driving from "mere life" to "more life."

The Paralysis and the Dance

> Tropes are perverse; they are *para-phusis*, unnatural, deviant.
> —Harold Bloom, *Wallace Stevens: The Poems of Our Climate*

> What holds together rhetoric as a system of tropes, and rhetoric as persuasion, is the necessity of defense, defense against everything that threatens survival, and a defense whose aptest name is "meaning." Vico named poetic defense as "divination," which in our vocabulary translates best as "over-determination of meaning."
> —Harold Bloom, *Poetry and Repression*

Bloom often quarreled with de Man's version of ascetic deconstruction, but the only place where his discussion takes on a fully systematic form is the famous coda to *Wallace Stevens: The Poems of Our Climate*, called "Poetic Crossings." It is here that Bloom fully asserts life's right tropological transgressions and perversions, in which it saves itself as a lie against the deadly literal return of the same. To the two already juxtaposed images of Jacob wrestling with the Angel of Death, and of an infant both leaning on and fighting the vital order of his needs, Bloom adds the third picture of a poem agonistically propping on its precursory texts. He could thus repeat after Ashbery: "It is fair to be crossing and to have crossed." It is fair to lie against aporetic cant and seek more life under however strict a prohibition. Writes Bloom:

> Deconstruction touches its limit because it cannot admit a question: why do we believe one liar rather than another? For the deconstructive critic, a trope is a figure of knowing and not a figure of willing, and so such a critic seeks to achieve, in relation to any poem . . . a cognitive moment, a moment in which the Negative is realized . . . but what can a cognitive or epistemological moment in a poem be? Where the will predominates, even in its own despite, how much is there left to know? How can we speak of degrees of knowing in the blind world of the wish, where the truth is always elsewhere, always different, always to be encountered only by the acceptances and rejections of an energy that in itself is the antithesis of renunciation, a force that refuses all form? (*WS*, 387)

If obsession with truth is, as Nietzsche claimed, the most characteristic expression of the "ascetic ideal," then, indeed, the de Manian deconstruction sticks firmly to this staple association: the persistent exposition of tropes as errors, that is, as epistemologically failed "figures of knowledge," completely disregards the conjecture that literature *as* literature could be nothing, in fact, but a cunning deviation from the demands of *askesis*. There is something almost tragically wrong, says Bloom, in such a straightforwardly "ascetic" approach to a literary text, demanding clear distinction between truth and error: a blindness toward the wayward—or *perverse*—nature of mimetic desire which struggles to want something else than was ever wanted before. How much, then, is there left to know in the blind world of the wish which always drives away from the reductive truth? "The issue of the limits of deconstruction," Bloom continues, "will be resolved only if we attain a vision of rhetoric more comprehensive than the deconstructors allow, that is, if we can learn to see rhetoric as transcending the epistemology of tropes and as re-entering the space of will-to-persuasion" (*WS*, 387–88). The tropes, therefore, have to be seen as most of all "figures of will" within a "diachronic rhetoric" which uses deconstructive tools in its own way. Says Bloom:

> Rhetoric, conceived as a text or system of tropes is an *ethos*, while rhetoric as persuasion falls under *pathos*, with an *aporia* between them as *logos* . . . Rhetoricity, in this sense, is a questioning on the poem's part of its place in literary language, that is, the poem's *own* subversion of its own closure, its illusory status as independent poem . . . To deconstruct a poem is to indicate the precise location of its figuration of doubt, its uncertain notice of that limit where persuasion yields to a dance or interplay of tropes. (*WS*, 382, 386)

"Variations are profuse, permutations abound, and yet there is a pattern to the dance" (*WS*, 405): a pattern which can be disclosed by the antithetical criticism that sees the poem as struggling against its own dependence on other poems; as turning its anaclitic relationships into agonistic ones. "A poem begins," writes Bloom, "because there is too strong a presence, which needs to be imagined as an absence, if there is to be any imagining at all" (*WS*, 375). Or, as he puts it in another text, "The Breaking of Form," a poem's referential signals are "disguises for darker relationships. A strong authentic allusion to another strong poem can be only by and in what the later poem *does not say*, by what it represses" (*DC*, 15). Tropes, therefore, dance away from the repressed truth about a poem's real point of reference, both absent and present—the poem of the precursor. Here, the conflict between rhetoricity and persuasion is not, as in de Man, between the history of literary language and an always thwarted will to *express* the "here and now" of direct experience,[23] but it is a conflict between the history of literary language and a will (not always thwarted) to *become* unique and singular in this very language.

In Bloom's view, therefore—contrary to what many critics say on this point—the poem is not at all about *expression:* or, rather, it is *not* about expression of any hidden experiential truth. For, once again, what is there to be known in this world of a blind wish, which does not know *what* it wants, merely wishing to be different from everything that is already (or, put in negative terms: merely instructed by the poetic superego *not* to be a copy or replica)? What truth can come forth and clash with the system of tropes if the only truth about the poem is that it imitates an already existing one? In de Man, who simply debunks the ideal of authenticity, an aporia appears when persuasion, which was supposed to be authentic, clashes with the existing machinery of language.[24] While in Bloom, there is nothing authentic about a poem's moment of origin: quite to the contrary, whatever *is* in a poet cannot be *authentic* and must be *mimetic*; whatever becomes *expressed* is never fresh, but always already *impressed* with a "commonplace." Truth is repetitive and full of sameness; the difference can come only with the blind wish to lie.[25] The influence—the primary impression—comes always first, and the conflict, which causes aporia, is not between the impossible will to expression and the system of tropes, but between the trope as commonplace and the trope as a "figure of will," attempting to sustain the singularity of poetic desire. The commonplace is a "place-of-voice," the spot where the seduction of the poet occurred, forcing him to repeat and imitate—the "figure of will," on the other hand, is a perverse twist executed on the former which realizes the poet's will to "slay the father," or, in other words, the will to difference. What was a "lie in the first place"—that is, once a vivid figure and now the commonplace which forms the *ethos* of language—can be once again lied against in this effort of singular *pathos*. Nothing protects the fathers who have already slain their fathers.[26] Says Bloom in "Auras":

> The gain-of-anxiety, for the strong poet and the strong reader, is the certain location of a place, even though the place be an absence, the place-of-a-voice, for this setting of a *topos* makes a poem possible . . . We mark the spot by *wishing to slay the father,* there, at *that* crossing, and we then know the spot because it becomes the place where the voice of the dead father breaks through. The marking, the will-to-inscribe, is the *ethos* of writing that our most advanced philosophers of rhetoric trace, but the knowing is itself a voicing, a *pathos*, and leads us back to the theme of presence that, in a strong poem, persuades us ever afresh, even as the illusions of a tired metaphysics cannot. (1981, 18–19)[27]

In Bloom's reading, therefore, the aporia will take on a different, more dynamic meaning: "Like a vision of the Gnosis, this aporia is a transgression, that leads from taboo to transcendence, or in the imagery of Romance it serves as the threshold between temple and labyrinth" (*WS*, 392). De Man's aporia is his rhetorical version of *askesis* in which desire has to die under the burden of castrating prohibition: the impossible wish of authenticity has to give itself away when confronted with the general system of tropes. Bloom's aporia is also his rhetorical version of *askesis*, but understood more cunningly as yet another ruse of life, which assumes prohibition-limitation only in order to become more perverse and thus, in its unique waywardness, more singular. The taboo of repression breaks into sublimity of desire, which has to become "perverse, *para-phusis*, unnatural, deviant" (*WS*, 388) in order to go on. For de Man, an aporia is taboo and temple: a place to worship the "nonhuman" superiority of language,[28] which put an indictment on our "authentic" desires. For Bloom, on the contrary, an aporia is a breaking of the form and a transgression into a labyrinth of tropes, which also happens to be—as in all mythological systems using the symbol of labyrinth—the way of a complicated, not just a "mere," life. This is why he will also say in *The Ringers in the Tower*, seemingly oxymoronically, about "the liberating burden of poetic influence" (9–10). This paradox once again points to the necessary stage of *askesis* in which poetic desire meets its prohibition and limitation and only thanks to them becomes the desire proper, that is, a desire breaking from the immanent circle of "mere life" into a transcendence of always wanting something else, singular, new.

The whole challenge, therefore, consists in properly understanding Bloom's ingenious misreading of the romantic expressivist paradigm. Modern thought has always been born out of some moment of immediacy, but, as we have already claimed in the second chapter of part 1, it does not need to be conceived in the strictly Cartesian way as a moment of knowledge; it does not have to come in the disguise of epistemological self-certain truth. It does not have to be "I think" and "I know"—it can also be "I am" and "I want." Every insight based on the belief in immediate, authentic self-knowledge, is bound to clash with the error of tropes—for, as Nietzsche rightly teaches, every concept is a metaphor, that is, an error and a lie in the first place. Veracity, therefore, cannot survive in language, and this is why de Man's ascetic resignation both fulfills and ends the tragic destiny of modern subjectivity, which cannot assert its truth in anything which implies mediation—most of all, in language. If we, therefore, approach the expressivist paradigm in the traditional way, it will locate the self in its deep, subjective, unique truth, which emerges on the surface of language as a confessional testimony. De Man's great merit lies in his radical translation of the figuration of doubt, which traditionally appears in the writings of the mystics (Bloom points to this source when he talks, after Scholem presumably, about the tension between orthodoxy and individual belief), into the confessional language of the modern self.[29] If the purpose of expression is to reveal the core of inner selfhood, then language—just like in the case of the most direct and intimate of experiences, the religious illumination—is more an obstacle than a help. The testimony turns into a testament: the self mounts a monument, which immediately becomes its tomb.

But, if we shift this point of anchorage from knowledge and truth into the realm of will, we shall obtain a different form of *assertion:* in Blumenberg's helpful idiom, the romantic *Selbstgewissheit* of "I am" rather than the Cartesian *Selbstbewusstsein* of "I think" (1979, 5); a type of certainty based not on knowledge but on an *urge*, the antithetical energy of difference, which refuses to take any stable form and thus swims like a fish in the unsteady waters of rhetoric, welcoming tropological errors as its true element. Perhaps, therefore, the modern self does not found itself on the subjective truth but on the *subjective lie*? Kierkegaard, who tarried with the paradoxical negativity of his own notion of "the singular truth," already came very close to Bloom's solution, which overtly renamed this antithetical, evasive "truth" as nothing else but "willing error" (*WS*, 394).

It may thus be misleading when Bloom asserts again and again that our strong misreadings issue from the "Will-to-Power over time and its henchman, language" (*WS*, 395), for such phrasing creates an unfortunate impression of will as, most of all, the will to control and master (this is precisely how de Man reads Nietzsche). This will-to-power cannot realize itself in mastery *over* language simply because—and this is the indisputable dogma of all deconstructions, Bloom's included—language transcends even the amplest grasp of any individual mind, but it can realize itself as a mastery *within* language, which is more like a mastery of *play*, an improvisatory *excellence*. The strong poet is not the one who holds language in the tight grip of Hegelian *Meisterschaft*, but the one who, like Nietzsche's Zarathustra, follows the dance of tropes. He wants to lie against anteriority—and here it is: language, the great accomplice, which was a lie in the first place, and is ready to lie and sin forever more. "One more 'turn' or trope added to a series of earlier reversals will not stop the turn towards error," says de Man in *Allegories of Reading* (1979a, 113), and, although he says it deprecatingly, this is precisely what the poetic self *wants:* for what truly counts is not the privileged experience, the insight, the confessional truth which vainly struggles to survive in language, but the *use* the poet makes of his singularity to twist and turn the already extant body of tropes. He does not want to *express* the truth of his own experience; his real purpose is to make himself alive in language by creating his own idiom, for which the original experience of "here and now" is just a pretext. The "treasure" of his selfhood, therefore, lies not in the depths of his experiential *Jemeinigkeit*, but on the surface of language which is the real target of his desire. He is not *coming back* to anything; his *Nachträglichkeit* is directed proleptically, like the Kierkegaardian recollection, forward; he repeats his "afterimages of voice" not in order to reveal the truth of the original trauma, but to make the body of language move by its dislocating *force*. There is a cunning and economy here—and not authenticity or sincerity, or at least, not in the first place. What the poet wants is nothing tangible or fixable, like the will itself—for he only wants *the difference*. Nothing more, and nothing less.

This retroping of the expressivist paradigm, which now consists not in revealing the inner truth but in releasing the urge of "expressive need" as a sheer energy of difference,[30] was approached by John Hollander in his preface to the *Poetics of Influence*, although perhaps not so successfully, for the moment he tried to squeeze it back within the traditional dualism of authenticity and textuality he immediately began to lose the originality of Bloom's invention. As he says about Bloom's misreading of the concept:

> A trope is a twisted strand of transformational process, anchored deep in the rock of *expressive need*, and stretched upward, taut, to a connection at the surface with a flat sheet of text. Formalist and structuralist readings would be like more or less detailed plans of the textual surface, affording a view of the end-section only of the tropical rope. Bloom is concerned with the length of the rope, the layers of whatever it is through which it passes, the ways in which, at any particular level, the strands may seem in their twisting to be pointing away from the determined direction upward, the relative degrees of tension and slackness and so forth. His is the most recent manifestation in a strange history of troping the concept of trope itself . . . He sees the war for authenticity and finality between surface (text) and depths (intentions variously clear and dark) as a true struggle of contraries . . . The conceptual rhetorician . . . does not interpret this war between text and intentions but fights instead on the side of text. (1988, xxx–xxxi)[31]

Yes, it's all true in a way, but the reintroduction of the notion of authenticity as Bloom's chosen idiom may be slightly deceptive. Rather, the key here is the intentions "variously clear and dark," which, in Bloom's account, are always, univocally and inadvertently, *dark*. The war deconstruction started to fight on the side of text was originally waged against *clear* intentions, the intentions hosted by "the subtle self" aspiring to hover above the text and control it in a quasi-providential way. Deconstruction rarely avails itself of psychoanalysis, and certainly not deconstruction of the de Manian variety. Bloom and de Man, therefore, talk about different wars, so they also fight on very different sides, in different conceptual universes. Does Bloom fight on the side of an expressive authentic self which struggles with the figurative obstacles of writing? I doubt it. If anything, he fights on the side of the unconscious subject of desire who cunningly uses the figurative instability of language to evade his traumatic instruction to imitate. For instance, how are we to read Bloom when he says that, despite all the possible poetic success, this fleshing out of the will into verbal acts is a kind of "translation that leaves the will baffled at the inadequacy of language to its desires" (*WS*, 402)? We can read it in a Shelleyan mode, assuming the traditional expressivist stance, which complains about the poverty of language juxtaposed with the richness of the inner self—or we can read it in a romantic revisionist way, which does not couple the will with a positive meaning, the Derridean *vouloir-dire* (literally, "wanting to say"), but, quite the contrary, with "the dearth of meaning" and the "absence of image" (ibid.). In this alternative interpretation, the inevitable failure to translate the will into act would be due not to the nature of language, but rather to the negative nature of will itself, forever "rampant with pathos" (*WS*, 402).

Yet, it is always will which pulls the strings of rhetorical figures: "What is a trope?" asks Bloom. "It is one of two possibilities only—either the will translating itself into a verbal act or figure of *ethos*, or else the will failing to translate itself and so abiding as a verbal desire or figure of *pathos*. But, either way, the trope *is* a figure of will rather than a figure of knowledge" (*WS*, 393). Bloom's revision of the expressivist paradigm is thus followed naturally by the claim "to revivify the ancient identity between rhetoric and psychology that is still being partly obscured by that endless clearing or curing of the ground now being called 'deconstruction'" (*WS*, 396–97). The ascetic purging of texts from life—the de Manian version of deconstruction—should now give a way to a revisionistic and more complex understanding of how the life of the will can make itself present in the world of texts. In this new "psychotextual" approach, there is no ready subject lurking behind the text with his darker or clearer, but always positive, intentions; there is no self-enclosed presence, which either succeeds or fails in expressing its inner truth in writing. There is only the murky, negative will, spawned by the contradictory instruction both to imitate and to cross beyond, *to lie against imitation*—and "the dance of tropes," which, being a lie in the first place, always "unnatural and deviant," helps the will to lie in its desired own, singular way. But these two sides are, in fact, one: the will to difference cannot exist without its displacement into writing, to which it escapes from the oppressive presence of the Voice. It is always already in-the-text, suffusing it with its "rampant pathos."

For, how can you tell the dancer from the dance?

Chapter 7

Tainted Love: A Psycho-Kabbalistic Reading of the Poetic Scene of Instruction

> The Cherub, in Ezekiel, is a guardian of Eden who has fallen into the role of Satanic hinderer. Poetic influence and Romantic love . . . may be the same process; at least they are similitudes verging toward an identity.
> —Harold Bloom, *Yeats*

> Wer war es, der zuerst
> Die Liebesbande verderbt
> Und Stricken von ihnen gemacht hat?
> —Friedrich Hölderlin, *Der Rhein*

The whole of Bloom's idiom is a living confirmation of the famous apothegm of William Blake, who claimed that it is wiser to be a tiger of wrath than a horse of instruction. It is through and through militant and agonistic—yet, being so tigerlike, it cannot always successfully avoid its uneasy place of origin: the Scene of Instruction to which he, as well as all the poets he writes about, are tied. Wrath is a dialectical denial of this primary encumbrance—but it also has a deeper and more rebellious meaning which Hölderlin, talking bitterly about Prometheus inaugurating the Age of Iron, called "shattering the bonds of love," a primary sin of modern *Entzauberung*. Is Instruction merely a source of bondage and burden the ephebe has to fight against to become free—or is it "the bond of love" which has to be cared for and cherished so it can grow into a mature form of dependence? Which language describes it better? The thoroughly disenchanted modern idiom of the struggle for emancipation—or the premodern, mythical speech of election and belonging?

Perhaps the Bloomian teaching on influence needs both: tigers of wrath *and* horses of instruction, the disenchanted discourse of agon *and* the archaic language of love, if only in order to pass beyond this opposition.

Just as in the last two chapters, we will focus our analysis on two revisionary ratios: the remaining ratios being the second, *tessera*, and the sixth, *apophrades.* They enjoy a peculiar, rather cumbersome position within the revisionary agon: *tessera* is the first attempt at completion, that is, of making whole again what has been broken by the first, aggressive ratio of *clinamen*, and *apophrades* is the final moment of identification between the ephebe and the precursor, which ends the agonistic cycle. Both these ratios seem, at least prima facie, reparative and as such *less* negative than the other four, which are propelled by open aggression toward the work of the precursor. Or, *are* they? Bloom's rhetoric admits the possibility of restoration and reconciliation with such slow reluctance, indeed with such "recalcitrance in the self" (*RT,* 22), that it allows the scattered sparks of love to show only in the midst of his deepest denial.

TESSERA, OR ANTITHETICAL COMPLETION

> It is difficult not to be unjust to what one loves.
> —Oscar Wilde, *The Critic as Artist*

> The North-American savages kill their parents; we do the same.
> —G. W. F. Hegel, *Jenenser Realphilosophie* (*Jena Real Philosophy*)

Bloom's style is the one of *stylus:* it is a battling instrument. He himself likes to portray his efforts in terms of "wrestling," which puts him in the same honorable line with Jacob and "Wrestling Sigmund": "Battle between strong equals, father and son as mighty opposites, Laius and Oedipus at the crossroads; *only this is my subject here*" (*AI*, 11; my emphasis), says Bloom, leaving no doubt as to his total immersion in the sphere of a never-ending agon. A few chapters later he will prove his point even clearer, by attacking the classical Freudian notion of the "normal" sublimation: "Whether sublimation of sexual instincts plays a central part in the genesis of poetry," he will say, "is hardly relevant to the reading of poetry, and has no part in the dialectic of misprision. But *sublimation of aggressive instincts* is central to writing and reading poetry, and this is *almost* identical with the total process of misprision" (*AI*, 115; my emphasis).

But the crucial word here is "almost." Is struggle really *the only subject* of Bloom's theory of poetic revision, or is there something else, suggested by the imprecision of the latter statement, some silent remainder? Bloom himself seems aware of the insufficiency of his wrestling rhetoric, for already in *A Map of Misprision*, the next work in the tetralogy written in 1975, this silent remainder finally gains voice. Bloom returns to the motif of *falling in love*, which occurs at the beginning of the agonistic relation between precursor and ephebe and, although unspoken, stays there till the end, taken for granted, but nevertheless delivering what Winnicott used to call a tacit "holding" for the whole relationship. The fight between "two mighty opposites" is, in fact, a kind of a love's labor—both, love and labor, or, in Freud's terms, seduction and its *Durcharbeiten*—whose aggressive overtone comes from the initial inequality between the lovers. Such is, after all, the meaning of Shakespeare's Sonnet 87 from where Bloom borrows his basic terms: "misprision" and "swerve." The lover, who cannot endure humiliation in a relationship with a person he feels to be far superior to himself, wants to return the gift of love, but since he is an unworthy receiver of such a gift, the reward, "upon misprision growing," comes home again, yet deeply transformed, if not simply deformed.[1]

So, it is rather this peculiar cycle of exchange, although disturbed and dialectically dynamized by the initial inequality between the antagonists, and not the struggle in itself which is the leitmotif of the poetic formation. *Clinamen* begins the cycle by starting the process of misprision, which is at the same time the process of "ripening" of the gift; toward the end, at the sixth stage of *apophrades*, the ephebe will feel strong enough to recognize the gift *as* gift, and return it to the precursor in reward for his not only threatening but also beneficial influence. Thus, indeed, "sublimation of aggressive instincts . . . is *almost* identical with the total process of misprision" (*AI*, 115), but it is by no means the whole story: the untold "holding" is as important here as the explicit content of the duel. Aggression *derives* from the unequal, difficult love, and *tessera* is, in a way, the first attempt of compensation: to make whole again, although on ephebe's own terms, what had been broken by the initial crisis caused by his violent swerve.[2]

In Bloom's narrative, this is a classic Nietzschean story of possession by a "numinous shadow." We don't find books we love, says Bloom, the books find us so we can fall in love with them: "We all choose our own theorists for the Scene of Instruction, or rather, as Coleridge would have said, we do not find their texts, but are found by them" (*BV,* 43). In consequence, the work of the precursor starts to haunt the mind of the ephebe, who is torn by its paradoxical message: on the one hand, it says, "be like me"—on the other hand, however, it says also, "you must not be like me." This is precisely the message Adam gets from his God who wants to be imitated, yet, at the same time, remain singular and unrepeatable. This ambivalent complexity is always present in Kierkegaard's notion of repetition: whatever is singular and original wants to repeat itself, so it can *exist,* and preferably exist forever—yet, at the same time, it shuns repetition, so it can stay singular and original:

> Indeed, what would life be if there were no repetition? ... If God himself had not willed repetition, the world would not have come into existence. Either he would have followed the superficial plans of hope or he would have retracted everything and preserved it in recollection. This he did not do. Therefore, the world continues, and it continues because it is a repetition. Repetition—that is actuality and the earnestness of existence. (1983, 133)

The earnestness of repetition, which is also a part of the wrestling ephebe, can only derive from the sense of obligation to repeat and to continue—that is, to *be*—despite the insoluble *aporia* hidden at the very core of the process of existence. It is difficult to be a *zelem,* precisely in the same way as Nietzsche says in *Also Sprach Zarathustra (Thus Spake Zarathustra)* that *gefährlich ist es, Erbe zu sein.*[3] Yet why carry this burden, if not in the name of something which escapes rational explanation, that is, the first *b'rit* (covenant) that was tied between the precursor and his latecoming image? This detour into Judaism is justified insofar as Bloom makes it himself in *A Map of Misreading* by giving us alternative six ratios, this time coming from a purely Hebrew source— *'ahabah, chesed, ruach, davhar, lidrosh, zimzum*—which are the subsequent metamorphoses of one of the major Jewish concepts, the love of election.

This eccentric group of six appears in the context of Bloom's discussion with Derrida, which we will once again resume, in yet a different context. While Derrida in "Freud and the Scene of Writing" claims that influence is but a mosaic of blind impresses, something we receive in the form of a random psychical "writing" due to which reality inflicts upon our minds durable traces, Bloom believes, in a truly Judaic manner, that influence is a matter of election. Or rather—that the only escape for the subject from the deadening universe of objectifying influences is election, that is, a situation of Freudian "decisive influence" which *turns one privileged impact into instruction*.[4] On this reading, the mind is not just a passive receiver of stimuli, not an indifferent surface on which world writes, equally indifferently, its random hieroglyphs, but a living system which from the very start finds itself in an intimate relation with its both choosing and chosen object.

In the Beginning Was the Voice

> Yes: writing has done much harm to writers. We must return to
> the voice.
> —Oscar Wilde, *The Critic as Artist*

The Scene of Instruction is a privileged, highly charged emotionally, and, indeed, *painful* object-relation. This pain, however, is not quantitative, measured by the surge of excitation, but irreducibly qualitative—a pain of *trauma*. Its power of "breaching" (Freud's *Bahnung*), therefore, derives from the pain brought by the inevitable "trespass" of love and trust brought by necessary inequality of the first object-relations. Says Bloom:

> I would venture that the artistic Primal Scene *is* the trespass of teaching. What Jacques Derrida calls the Scene of Writing itself depends upon a Scene of Teaching, and poetry is crucially pedagogical in its origin and functions. (*MM*, 32)

It does not mean, however, that the Derridean Scene of Writing does not exist; quite the contrary, without this intrapsychic script whose *Bahnung* cuts its way through the resistant layers, there would be no memory and, in consequence, no writing. Yet, what escapes Derrida is the crooked "pedagogy" behind the *écriture*, the painful trespass of teaching whose trauma constitutes one particularly strong Influence: from this time on, the original point of reference for all other "breachings," a Sevre model of influx, a painful heart of darkness. We may thus call this move a *re-personalization* of the primal scene, which, once again, must be seen not in terms of quantities, building a protostructuralist system of differences, but in terms of the irreducible qualities of a traumatic seduction:

> Jacques Derrida asks a central question in his essay on Freud and the
> Scene of Writing: "What is a text, and what must the psyche be if
> it can be represented by a text?" . . . My question can be rephrased:
> "What is a breath, and what must a weaving or a fabrication be so as
> to come into being again as a breath?" (*PR*, 1)

Here, psyche boils down to its original meaning of breath, text to its
original meaning of texture, and breath to its archaic equivalence with
word as voice: the weaving of the psyche has to be such that it can preserve the living presence of *davhar* so it will able to resurface later, not
as letter but again as breath. In Bloom's reading of Derrida, all these
clues leading to the "black pedagogy" of the Scene of Instruction are
already there, although implicitly. As we already know from part 2,
Bloom highly praised the author of *Of Grammatology* for his exuberant
kabbalist-baroque imaginary, which allowed him "to substitute *davhar*
for *logos*, thus correcting Plato by a Hebraic equating of the writing-act
and the mark-of-articulation with the word itself" (*MM*, 43)—even if the
full consequence of such substitution eluded him in the end. The change
from *logos* to *davhar* is of crucial importance here, for this is precisely the
meaning of the word as *voice*, *utterance*, and *stance*, which is Bloom's leitmotif throughout his analysis of the romantic poetic lineage:

> In the context of post-Enlightenment poetry a breath is at once a
> *word*, and a *stance* for uttering that word, a word and a stance *of one's*
> *own* . . . The strong word and stance issue only from a strict will, a
> will that dares the error of reading all of reality as a text, and all prior
> texts as openings for its own totalizing and unique interpretations.
> (*PR*, 1–2)

In the Bible the word "*davhar*," when spoken by God, bears the gravity of order and command issued by the master's voice. But the voice of
God, the source of living *davhar*, is too powerful to be endured by mortals. The Torah states clearly that only two first commandments could
be conveyed to the hosts of Israel directly by the voice of God, which
was too terrifying to be heard any longer; the rest had to be conveyed
in mediation, via the script brought down by Moses on his tablets.[5]
Writing, as contrasted with the living, expansive speech of *davhar*, is thus
associated with the act of restraining and repression, but also, simultaneously, with preservation; the script is the repository—safe *because*
hidden—of the oral word. Yet, no form can contain the power of *davhar*:

it is too creative, excessive, and "burgeoning" to be withheld in the vessel of writing. The constant breaking of these vessels, the most cherished esoteric image of the Lurianic Kabbalah, points to the inherent dialectic of the word whose power cannot be ultimately deposited in any kind of scripture, even the holiest. The tablets had to be broken and replaced by new ones—and this act is just a paradigm of an infinite series of subsequent substitutions, where "brokenness" means also "freedom": freedom to reinterpret and repeat in a new fashion, and thus bringing back the power of the original "word." The primary bonds have to be shattered to be reestablished as more equal, according to the logic of the *b'rit*.[6]

Let us now compare this biblical image—the incomprehensible divine Voice, deposited in the broken tablets of writing that open themselves to constant revisions—with the fragment from Freud's *Scientific Project* on which both Bloom and Derrida comment:

> The fact that pain passes along all pathways of discharge is easily understandable. On our theory that Q produces facilitation, pain no doubt leaves permanent facilitations behind in *psi*—*as though there had been a stroke of lightning*—facilitations which possibly do away with the resistance of the contact barrier entirely and establish a pathway of conduction there such as there in *phi*. (1966, 307; my emphasis)

This *as though there had been a stroke of lightning* is one of these Freudian metaphors whose occurrence immediately annuls any scientific project he could possibly have in mind: despite all the clever algebra of psychic quantities breaching through *phi* and *psi* types of neurones, we are suddenly in a different rhetorical register, resembling more the Hölderlinian idiom of election from *Wie wenn am Feiertage* (*As When on Holiday*). The stronger the influence, says Freud, the weaker it registers at the surface of the psychic apparatus, for it cuts straight into its deeper layers. Therefore, the paradox which underlies the Scene of Instruction consists in instruction both taking and *not* taking place. Acting through a thunderous Voice-Breath, hitting the ephebe with the force of a stroke of lightning, it is *too powerful to be experienced*. It is immediately repressed in a defensive gesture, protecting the brittle surface, and deposited in the deepest realms of the unconscious, that is—to go beyond Freud's idiom from his project and closer to Bloom's intentions—in the ephebe's id. This paradoxical location of the instructing Voice is responsible for the ephebe's dialectical relation to his own poetic origins that we may call an *apotropaic faithfulness*. Says Bloom:

> The last truth of the Primal Scene of Instruction is that purpose or
> aim—that is to say, meaning—*cleaves more closely to origins the more
> intensely it strives to distance itself from origins.* (*MM*, 62; my emphasis)

The ephebe's fidelity lies, therefore, not in his clinging to the very
moment of election, nomination, and instruction, but, to the contrary, in
his permanent attempt to escape, to displace himself from the spot, the
place "where it was." Here Bloom tries to restore the Hebraic ambivalence of presence which is too terrifying to be witnessed and too
traumatic to be experienced directly: instead, it has to be inscribed in
the reserve, *der Vorrat*, of inner psychic writing, which preserves it as a
source of constant anxiety. Then, whatever has been inscribed into an
ephebe's unconscious at that fateful moment, whatever deposit had been
left there, it has to be "broken" and transgressed in a flight from the
heavy presence of the original, fearful *davhar*.[7]

While Derrida, on the other hand, wants to convey a message that
would be less ambiguous: for him, the presence, which cannot be directly
witnessed, turns gradually into *nonpresence*. The whole story begins with
the act of writing, which marks the true point of departure, although it
is not the departure from the beginning, rather from the nonorigin of
the deferred trace. Writing is a repetition of a living presence, but since
this presence was immediately repressed from the start, the repetition no
longer repeats: in fact, it appears now as primordial. Says Derrida, referring to the system of "written" memory:

> All these differences in the production of the trace may be reinter-
> preted as moments of deferring. In accordance with a motif which
> will continue to dominate Freud's thinking, this movement is
> described as the effort of life to protect itself by *deferring* a dangerous
> cathexis, that is, by constituting a reserve (*Vorrat*). The threatening
> expenditure or presence are deferred with the help of breaching or
> repetition ... *Is it not already a death at the origin of a life which can
> defend itself against death only through an economy of death, through defer-
> ment, repetition, reserve?* (1978b, 202; my emphasis)

A seemingly similar maneuver was performed earlier by Derrida's precursor Lacan: seemingly, for in Lacan's deliberately antinomical logic,
the nonwitnessed, immediately repressed presence of the real—what he
calls a "missed encounter" or, more paradoxically, "an encounter which
never was"—cannot be simply reduced to nothing (or, as Derrida claims

in his critique of Lacan, it is, in fact, nothing which paradoxically works as something). The *nachträglich* repetition is obviously not a restoration—for it is impossible to restore what was never witnessed—yet, at the same time, it isn't just the Derridean moment *later* from which one can begin, regardless of the uneasy origin. There is a dark gravity here which does not allow repetition to turn into a free-floating trope of dissemination straight into the deadly economy of writing, a truly enigmatic "first time" of the "living presence"; the trajectory of repetition will thus always be bent and crooked even if it is impossible to return to the missed encounter.

Once again, therefore, we have to reiterate one of our main theses: repetition is neither dissemination nor return—it is most of all displacement. The erotic meandering of the *Bedeutungswandlung* (wandering of meaning) uses all the "differentiating" mechanisms of the *Bedeutungsflucht*, the flight of meaning, by turning them into means of figuration, preparing for the "coming home" of the original voice. Repetition, therefore, is not primarily a move which manages, at least partially, to break through resistance and return to the source of anxiety—but on the contrary it is driven and fueled by the very energy of displacement. The precursor, says Bloom, "is in the id," so the swerving spin of *Wiederholung* (repetition) can be due only to the power of repression: and the stronger the repression, the more creative, the more forwardly oriented the repetition. Yet, on the other hand, the vector of this displacement is not just the Derridean escape from the "living presence" into the economy of death that undermines life as such; all this intrapsychic work is undertaken in order for the *davhar* to rise up from the ashes of writing and reemerge as a "living presence" again, although this time issued from a slightly different place, a different "stance."[8]

Or, putting it more bluntly, without repression, terror, and anxiety, there would be no repetition in the Kierkegaardian sense. Instead of returning to the primal scene, it "recollects forward," that is, moves out of the fatal cycle, although in a crooked way that cannot escape the dark gravity of the original semipresence, the precursory "numinous shadow." This is precisely why the next ratio, *kenosis*, is called by Bloom repetition *and* discontinuity. For it is discontinuing (rather than continuing) repetition that constitutes the paradoxical mode in which the ephebe, both Tiger and Horse, remains ambivalently faithful to his origins. Despite the original bondage of Instruction, in the beginning is *not* his end.

THE HEBREW ALTERNATIVE

> Our capacity to love is frequently founded upon romance, which is
> necessarily the realm of imperfect knowledge; angels, like God, love
> with perfect knowledge.
> —Harold Bloom, *Omens of the Millennium*

Human love, and most of all the love of strong poets, is not only not built
on perfect knowledge, but on the very opposite of knowledge, which is
the strongest repression of all. Love founded on perfect knowledge can
last safe and intact for eternity—while love founded upon romance, the
gloomy play of seduction and inequality, must go through a rebellious
"shattering of the bonds of love," or breaking of the vessels in which the
trace of seduction had been deposited. Led by these theological metaphors, Bloom constructs the "romance" model of the Primal Scene of
Instruction on the basis of the alternative Hebrew six. The first stage
of this sequence, which starts with total inequality and then proceeds
to negotiate a more balanced covenant, is *'ahabah*, or the elective love
which caused Yahweh to choose Israel:

> *'Ahabah* is love unconditioned in its giving, but wholly conditioned to
> passivity in its receiving. Behind any Scene of Writing, at the start of
> every intertextual encounter, there is this unequal initial love, where
> necessarily the giving famishes the receiver. The receiver is set on
> fire, and yet the fire belongs only to the giver. (*MM*, 51)

'Ahabah is thus a stage of passive, presumably also reluctant, assimilation of the excess that flows over from the mighty *davhar*: it begins
the crucial interplay between the shadowy, unwitnessable presence and
the repression which leaves a deposit of the instruction in the form
of the intrapsychic, unconscious writing. Bloom calls it elsewhere a
spoken-trace.[9]

The next stage is *chesed*. As Bloom continues:

> Our model for the second phase is drawn from the same source.
> The model is Covenant-love or *chesed*, the Hebrew word that Miles
> Coverdale rendered as "loving kindness" and Luther as *Gnade*, which
> would make it *charis* or "grace." But *chesed* . . . is difficult to trans-
> late. The root means "eagerness" or "sharpness" and the word itself
> approaches what Freud meant by "antithetical primal words." For the

root meaning also embraces that kind of "keenness" that moves from "ardent zeal" to "jealousy," "envy," and "ambition," and so Covenant-love is uneasily allied to a competitive element. (*MM*, 53)

Chesed is thus the name of the love which leads God to lower himself and join the fate of his people in the act of covenant; yet the antithetical, complementary aspect of that same love, as felt by the elected, already bears a connotation of mimetic rivalry. When translated into the discourse of the Scene of Instruction, the stage of *chesed* means strengthening the power of defensive repression, which is also the first sign of activity on the part of the "flooded" psyche:

> The third phase in our Primal paradigm must be the rise of an individual inspiration or Muse-principle, a further accommodation of poetic origins to fresh poetic aims. Here the Old Testament *ruach* for "spirit" or "power of God's breath" can be a precise shorthand ... To differentiate such power from the precursor's source is to pass beyond the stage of assimilation once for all. (*MM*, 54)

Ruach is the spark of charisma that originally belongs to the precursor but can also be detached from his source and thus beget a new poet: this is why the moment in which the essence of *ruach* becomes extracted from its original bearer, the initiate can no longer bother about exactly *what* he had assimilated from his mighty antecedent. Now, if he is to repeat his Primal Scene of Instruction, he will not do it *to the letter*, but only *in the spirit* of his precursor. Here, repetition can truly move out of the house of bondage (i.e., literal mimesis) and rush forward into the sphere of bold figuration, or "supermimesis," of broken tablets, which is—almost—a freedom. Continues Bloom:

> With the fourth phase, the bringing forward of an individual *davhar*, a word one's own that is also one's act and one's veritable presence, poetic incarnation proper has taken place. (*MM*, 54)

Half unaware, out of the depths of his unconscious repressions, the ephebe finally produces what had been expected from him by the precursor: the living presence of *davhar*, the word of creative excess raising the precursor from the dead and allowing his to live again, in the ephebe's reincarnation. This compensation, however, is not conducted in the conscious spirit of gratitude (we are not dealing here with T. S. Eliot's individual talent willingly bowing to the splendor of tradition), and there is no hint of self-offering on the ephebe's part. Subsequently, says Bloom:

> There remains, in the fifth phase of our scene, the deep sense in which the new poem or poetry is a total interpretation or *lidrosh* of the poem or poetry of origin. In this phase, all of Blake or of Wordsworth becomes a reading or interpretation of all Milton. (*MM*, 54)

Lidrosh, or the trope of talmudic commentary which corresponds to the Latin *transumptio* (transumption), is a classical Jewish mode of bringing forth something *new*—yet not in opposition to the old but in an interaction with the traditional message (this is why the collection of most far-farfetched *lidroshim* could bear of all the names the title "kabbalah," which simply means "tradition"). *Lidrosh* is the perfect implementation of repetition forward, which maintains a dialectical balance between faithfulness to and the flight from origins, a dynamic negotiative interplay between separation and affiliation. Here, the initial gift has, indeed, grown on misprision by creating something else that is now worth returning. Concludes Bloom:

> The sixth and final phase of our Primal Scene is revisionism proper, where origins are re-created, or at least a re-creation is attempted, and it is in this phase that a newer practical criticism can begin ... Whereas the first five phases of my Scene of Instruction were canonical in their names and functions, the sixth phase, which is a wholly Romantic accommodation, needs an esoteric paradigm, for which I will turn to the regressive Kabbalah of Isaac Luria, sixteenth-century Rabbi and Saint of Safed. (*MM*, 54–55)

The final esoteric phase is thus *zimzum*, withdrawal and contraction. The precursor, the one who instructs, pulls back from the world he created—the interpsychic cosmos filled with his "spoken-traces"—and leaves it at the ephebe's disposal. Strong revision, says Bloom, which is the characteristic feature of modern creativity, is possible only thanks to this act of final separation. Yet it is an ambivalent gain: the adept enjoys more liberty, but it is bought by a simultaneous disenchantment, the loss of the magical link with the paternal pleroma. The Miltonian *Free at last!* is, inevitably, also a cry of the ones who fall down and out.

What is the place of the Hebraic six in relation to the six revisionary ratios from *The Anxiety of Influence*? Bloom is not at all clear on this subject: although he himself suggests that the Scene of Instruction is primal to any kind of writing and ends with the withdrawal of the precursor from his creation, some of the Hebrew stages chime closely with the Greco-Latin ones. For instance, *chesed* resembles *clinamen* in its ambivalent, aggressive, *Hass-Liebe* fascination; *ruach*, the phase of inspiration, seems analogous to *counterdaemonization*, where the adept tries to extract from the precursor the charismatic spark; and *lidrosh*, the Jewish transumption, may be easily associated with *apophrades*, the metaleptic, creative repetition of poetic origins. However, it is only in the sixth phase of the revisionism proper that the work of *die Durcharbeitung* (working-through), and its laborious negotiation with the initial dependence, really begins. Once the truly modern revisionary mode emerges, love and its vicissitudes, which wove their thread through the whole Scene of Instruction, give way to "battle alone" of the poetic agon. "Initial love for the precursor's poetry," Bloom says in *A Map of Misreading*, "is transformed rapidly enough into revisionary strife, without which individuation is not possible . . . Empedocles and Freud alike are theorists of influence, of the giving which famishes the taker" (*MM*, 10–11). The bonds of love finally shattered, the true fight for independence can commence.

APOPHRADES—THE FINAL FORM OF LOVE?

> The man prophesied by the Romantics is a central man who is always in the process of becoming his own begetter, and though his major poems perhaps have been written, he as yet has not fleshed out his prophecy, nor proved the final form of his love.
> —Harold Bloom, "The Internalization of Quest Romance"

> Nothing is less generous than the poetic self when it wrestles for its own survival.
> —Harold Bloom, *A Map of Misreading*

Would there be, then, an even more primal scene than the one, which had been detected by Bloom underneath the Derridean Scene of Writing: the even more deeply repressed, even more ambivalent, Scene of Love?[10]

This will be our guiding question in the analysis of the last stage of the poetic *Bildung*: *apophrades*, "the unlucky days" of the Greek *Antesteria*, when the dead return to their earthly homes to haunt the living. Actually, the very word "*apophrades*" is just the plural of *apophras*, which means "unlucky," "fatal," "misfortunate." And indeed, there is something very ominous about this ultimate ratio, which bestows a dark twist on the favorite trope of the romantics (i.e., the trope of return). From the very onset, writing about the antithetical romantic quest, Bloom puts himself in a safe distance from the mythic notion of full restitution, the full circle of, in Abrams's words, the "circuitous journey." *In my beginning is my end* is not exactly Bloom's formula, nor is any poetic or philosophical model of reconciliation. The agon with the mighty dead never stops, and the *apophrades* are but the last, triumphal display of the ephebe's quickening power. *Apophrades*, metalepsis or transumption, says Bloom militantly in *Poetry and Repression*, is "a trope that murders all previous tropes" (*PR*, 19).

At this stage, the ephebe's stubborn lying against time is finally rewarded. The adept opens himself once again to the unchecked influence of his precursor, but he does not assimilate it passively: now he is able to accept it on his own terms. He is no longer flooded by the Instructive Word; quite the contrary, he once again *repeats* the initial Scene of Instruction, but now it is he who returns the *davhar*, by speaking with the voice of his precursor. And it seems as if the apprentice speaks this voice louder and more distinctly than the master himself. The ephebe achieves thus a *metalepsis*, the trope of temporal reversal, which makes him sound, the real latecomer, more prior than the precursor: now the precursor's work seems but a pale copy of the metaleptic poem of the adept. The rule of the seemingly intangible order of time, the poetic *Realitätsprinzip* proper, becomes subverted, and this subversion is the final compensation for *die List des Lebens*, the restless and costly cunning of life which, from the very beginning, wished nothing else but to overthrow the necessitarian order of reality. Yet, the *apophrades*, the "unlucky" return, is by no means a happy end:

> The *apophrades*, the dismal or unlucky days upon which the dead return to inhabit their former houses, come to the strongest poets, but with the very strongest there is a grand and final revisionary movement that purifies even this last influx. Yeats and Stevens, the strongest poets of our century, and Browning and Dickinson, the strongest of the later nineteenth century, can give us vivid instances of this most cunning of revisionary ratios. For all of them achieve a style that captures and oddly retains priority over their precursors, so that the tyranny of time *almost* is overturned, and *one can believe, for*

> *startled moments*, that they are being imitated by their ancestors. (*AI*,
> 141; my emphasis)

A characteristic hesitation! Why does Bloom write "almost"? Why is
it only in those short *startled moments* that we begin to *believe* that the
tyranny of time is overcome? Bloom is far more uncertain and full of
reservations here than in the description of any other ratios. Is anything
really achieved in *apophrades*, or is it only a make-believe, a fragile illusion created only for the sake of a passing moment?

We could rephrase these questions into one: Is Bloom's refusal to end
the poetic formation happily due to something he discovered in the process, or is it his own, personal negative choice? I think it is both. We
should remember that Bloom's sixfold movement of initiation is not
just a simple repetition of a mythic paradigm but a modern, particularly
elaborate, Schlegelian-Blumenbergian instance of "the work on myth,"
which cannot fall back safely on the "happy field," where the triad of
fullness, estrangement, and restitution has its mythological dwelling.
The hesitation which always accompanies Bloom and his poetic initiates in manifold forms—as belatedness, deferment, procrastination, and
delay—is always there to remain; in fact, forever. The work on myth,
once started, cannot be stopped—but it also *cannot end*, unless it "brings
itself to an end," as in Kafka's astounding little mythological piece on
Prometheus, who becomes weary of his heroism, together with everybody else involved: the eagle, the gods, the wound, even the rock.[11]
The work on myth is thus very much like the effort of Exodus: getting
out, wandering, but rarely—or never—achieving the final destination.
Apophrades, therefore, is not a closure in any mythological sense. Quite
the contrary: the hesitancy with which Bloom draws his book toward a
conclusion, the visible uncertainty whether this is really the *last* stage,
points to the essentially unfinished and unfinishable project of the modern work on myth, *Arbeit am Mythos* (which can only end, as in Kafka, by
getting tired of itself).

Bloom's description of *apophrades* betrays a personal Gnostic bias we
have already discovered in his account of *tessera*: Bloom's all-pervading
militancy makes it difficult for him to think about all the restitu-
tive attempts within the agon as fueled by other motivations than just
the Nietzschean revenge on time, the scandalously assertive "It was."
"Retaliation," with its negative overtone of vengeance, collides here
with "compensation," overshadowing its slightly more positive connotation of "getting even." Yet, "getting even" suggests at least some sense

of obligation, if not exactly gratitude: and this is precisely the emotive mode for which there is not much place in Bloom's writings. The strong poet cannot indeed find means to prove his final form of love.

On the other hand, however, Bloom himself calls the agon a form of romance: "When a strong poet revises a precursor," he writes in *The Breaking of the Vessels*, "he re-enacts a scene that is at once a *catastrophe, a romance, and a transference* . . . Are these three categories or one? What kind of a relational or dialectical event is at once creatively catastrophic, incestuously romantic, and ambivalently a metaphor for a trespass that *works?*" (45; my emphasis). In Freud's description, family romance is essentially a labor of love which starts with the child's profound guilt, then affection for his parents, finally resulting in a "sense that his affection is not being fully reciprocated" and goes through the vicissitudes of this unequal, guilt- and wrath-ridden emotion. Says Freud in "Family Romances":

> If anyone is inclined to turn away in horror from this depravity of the childish heart, or feels tempted, indeed, to dispute the possibility of such things, he should observe that these works of fiction, which seem so full of hostility, are none of them really so badly intended, and that they still preserve, under a slight disguise, the child's original affection for his parents. (1950, 75)

Thus, if all those "works of fiction," which constitute the fantasies of the agon, are but the labors of ambivalent affection, then *apophrades* may—and perhaps should—also be read as a token of love, however repressed and reluctant. After all, the agon is also a *romance* and an affectionate *transference*, not only a traumatic catastrophe that has to be revenged.

We can thus read the final stage in Bloom's usual gloomy way, as the last Crossing of Identification, which is "the psychic act of so identifying oneself with something or someone outside the self that time seems to stand still or to roll back or forward. The dilemma here is the confrontation with mortality, with total death, and the prohibited instinct is the drive toward death, the self-destructiveness that Freud hypothesized 'beyond the pleasure principle'" (*WS*, 403). Or, we can venture a more cheerful idiom and say that, in the final metalepsis, the ephebe, already capable of "active love," allows the dead precursor to speak his own *voice*, his living *davhar* once more, thus letting him "come home again" (though this time a home owned already by somebody else), and enjoy the long-lost presence.

Is one of these phrasings truer than the other, or are they both equally justified?

BLOOM'S MYTHMAKING, OR THE DEATH OF LOVE

> The omnipotence of love is perhaps never more strongly proved than in such of its aberrations as these perversions. The highest and the lowest are always closest to each other in the sphere of sexuality: *vom Himmel durch die Welt zur Hölle* [from heaven through the world to hell].
>
> —Sigmund Freud, *Three Essays on the Theory of Sexuality*

The redemptive nature of *apophrades*, perhaps not so unlucky after all, comes to the fore more clearly in *A Map of Misreading*, where Bloom introduces the kabbalistic esoteric trope of *gilgul* (reincarnation) as the synonym of the final metalepsis, which allows "the reincarnation of a precursor through his descendant's acts of lifting up and redeeming the saving sparks of his being from the evil shells or broken vessels of catastrophe" (*MM*, 6).

These, however, are Bloom's later corrections and revisions, which merely testify to his own previous uneasiness about how to approach the potential moments of reparation. The last chapter of *The Anxiety of Influence* is steeped in a monotonous rhetoric of crisis: the Gnostic agon perseveres in the never-ending night, and not even a faintest light raises on the horizon to prophesy the break of dawn, or the coming of a poetic Sabbath. It would seem that Bloom's relentlessly bellicose rhetoric eventually begins to turn him into "a mere rebel," a figure whom he himself so eloquently criticized at the beginning of his book a propos Milton's mistreatment of Satan. Writes Bloom:

> Satan's later decline in the poem, as arranged by the Idiot Questioner in Milton, is that he ... ceases, during his soliloquy on Mount Niphates, to be a poet and, by intoning the formula "Evil be thou my good," becomes a mere rebel, a childish inverter of conventional moral categories, another wearisome ancestor of student non-students, the perpetual New Left. (*AI*, 22)

And although it may seem unfair to align Bloom with the "student non-students of the perpetual New Left" against whom he has always battled, one cannot help but see an obvious aporia in his own "poem," a danger of a similar "later decline" resulting from his unbalanced rhetoric.

This aporia was well spotted by Paul de Man in his review of *The Anxiety of Influence*, which he analyzed according to his aporetic model of discrepancy between persuasion and the system of tropes. Bloom, says de Man, wants to recreate the movements of the romantic "un-natural, deviant" imagination, which strives to get beyond any given, any natural boundary—yet the language he uses constantly pushes him back toward a gloomy naturalist reductionism. Writes de Man about Bloom's treatment of the romantic "anxiety of influence":

> In some respects this is a step backward. Just when we were about to free poetic language from the constraints of natural reference, we return to a scheme which, for all its generality, is still clearly a relapse into a psychological naturalism. (1983, 272)

It is an important point, even though de Man's intentions—to see the agon as a purely intertextual relation free of emotional encumbrances— are just the opposite of ours. Indeed, Bloom's "psychological naturalism" obfuscates the potentially redemptive content of the last stage, which simply cannot be properly formulated; too eager to avoid Frye's "angelic" and "concerned" influence, Bloom overkills the effect of deidealization. The orthodox Freudian rhetoric Bloom once fights against and then falls back into makes him obsessed with the economy of drives and the principle of exact, instantaneous retaliation, executed at every one of his six revisionary ratios. More than that, and perhaps also more significantly—it also puts in jeopardy the whole project of Bloom's agonistic, antithetical, and antinaturalistic vitalism, which, as we claimed through all this book, constitutes his greatest theoretical invention. The specter of naturalism, therefore, has to be chased away if we are to save what is most precious about Bloom's "theory of life."[12]

This aporia leads immediately to another poignant question, also brought about by de Man's critical remarks that one simply cannot avoid epistemology forever: what *is*, after all, the epistemological status of Bloom's artful lies? Walking the "crooked path" of Zarathustra, Bloom evades the Cherub of Epistemology in the constant Nietzschean *clinamen* from truth, yet, in the end there is no escape from the final confrontation. For, if Bloom doesn't lie that the poet's only weapon is "lying against time," then what is *the true nature of these lies:* literal or rhetorical? If we see in the sequence of six revisionary ratios a distorted, yet still redemptive story, leading from fullness, through loss, to restitution—then Bloom's "crooked path" is, indeed, *rhetorical:* deceit works as a defensive-provoking mechanism thanks to which life, despite all the obstacles, cunningly achieves its necessary goals. *Apophrades* is then a crowning ratio in which, as in Hegel's dialectic, the deceit is sublated in its negativity, for it reveals a new positive being: the adept, giving new voice to the dead precursor wins a victory which is no longer an illusion. This sublation of negativity equals the substitution of power—the real precursory power of priority—by *the representation* of power Bloom talks about in his essay on Browning's *Childe Roland to the Dark Tower Came.* Writes Bloom in *Poetry and Repression:*

> Roland learns, and we learn with him, that the representation of power *is* itself a power, and that this latter power is the only purposiveness that we shall know. (200)

This is precisely what Hans Blumenberg calls the creative potential of rhetoric, or what we have called the constitutive potential of fantasies: the representation of power *becomes* power itself, although it is not—and could not be—the very original power of poetic priority. The original deprivation breaks here into a new positivity—"a good moment"—yet, simultaneously, the quest itself, searching for the primordial source of power, is "ruined": the result is an ambivalent mixture of "good moments and ruined quests" (ibid.) which seems to be the most characteristic signature of Browning's poetry, so cheerfully self-reliant and so consciously belated at the same time. In Browning, Bloom continues, the sublation of negativity is indeed so convincing that his *apophrades*, in which he wrestles with Shelley, gain a "luckier" aspect of *gilgul*, the Lurianic trope of restitution: "There is a breaking-of-the-vessels," says Bloom, "but the sparks are scattered again, and become Shelley's *and* Browning's words, mixed together, among mankind" (*PR*, 204). The emphasis is not mine, it is Bloom himself who for once put the two wrestlers into peaceful conjunction, spelling the end—or, at least, a cease-fire—to the torments of agon.

But if we see in the six ratios not the figure of *Heilsgeschichte* but the Gnostic sequence of the fall—ever deeper into the abyss of time—then poetic deceit is nothing but a helpless defense, unable to create its own counterreality. Seen in this perspective, *apophrades* is the last ratio only by exhaustion: the adept knows that he reached the limit of his deceitful invention and cannot lie any more effectively either to himself or the others. No more tropes, turns, and twists. As in Kafka's *Prometheus: Die*

Götter wurden müde, die Adler wurden müde, die Wunde schloss sich müde
(the Gods became weary, the eagles grew weary, and the wound closed
itself weary).

This more pessimistic scenario coexists with the more uplifting version, but it is difficult to determine where Bloom's heart really is. Elisabeth
Bruss in *Beautiful Theories* goes even further than de Man and makes this
aporetic hesitancy a central *dunamis* of Bloom's own theoretical development, consisting in ceaseless self-revisions and self-misreadings, from
the *Anxiety of Influence* up to *Poetry and Repression*. In the end, she claims,
the reductive, soberly economic language of orthodox psychoanalysis
becomes so pervasive that the poetic revision finally *boils down* to a sheer
defense of a latecomer who merely *deludes* himself that he is able to beget
his own father. According to Bruss:

> In *Poetry and Repression* the defensiveness, the wholly nugatory qual-
> ity of revision is clearer than in any of Bloom's previous books; the
> wish to engender oneself or to be the sole possessor of poetic power
> reduces to a more or less tormented denial ... Whatever small or
> passing increments were possible in preceding versions of revision-
> ism are eliminated here. *To revise is to subtract from former glory, and
> troping can neither alter, undo, nor add to the true condition of the world,
> which is one of continual erosion and decay* ... In *Poetry and Repression*
> negative theology has become a kind of fundamentalism that may, in
> its literal-mindedness, do more to cloy than to increase our appetite
> for the Sublime. (1982, 342–45; my emphasis)

This may not be wholly fair, considering the fact that the essay on
Browning's "good moments" within "the ruined quest" comes from
Poetry and Repression, but the tendency to seal the subtle play of the
romantic *via negativa* with the fundamentalism of Gnostic negativity is
nevertheless a very real danger in Bloom's thinking, and already from the
very start.[13] Bloom seems to be torn between a fundamentalistically negative despair in the face of the futility of all our defenses as *mere defenses,*
and a shyly positive vision of an almost successful strategy of becoming
a singular subject, in which the Freudian *Abwehrmechanismen* evolve into
more defiant and effective tactics.

Thus Bloom "in negative" shows the sixfold revisionary process as a
ruined "cycle of reciprocity" in which the gift of influence is too traumatic and the costs of its return too high. Singular subjectivity is then a
fragile edifice *auf dem Nichts gestellt* (founded on nothing), a sand castle

built of defensive illusions, always endangered by the destructive clash with the principle of reality. It has neither the daring of a truly transcendental self, which boldly declares the secondary nature of the material world, nor the modest sobriety of the Freudian ego, who obediently bows to the *Realitätsprinzip*. It is stuck with its inefficient defenses and confused by its escapist illusions.[14]

According to Susan Handelman, such subjectivity is trapped, as Bloom himself, in the position of a hopeless, self-defeating gesture of rebellion that is characteristic of Satan-after-metamorphosis. Yet, in her "talmudic" rereading of Bloom's "Miltonic Kabbalism," she nonetheless proposes a reconciliation of "the prodigal son" with the Rabbinic Wisdom and claims that there is no such rebellion in Judaism that could not be incorporated into the tradition of interpretation:

> I suggest that especially in the cases of Freud, Derrida, and Bloom, there is tradition at the heart of heresy, a tradition that is compelling and reembracing. At the chiasmus, the crossing point, identities reverse. This would be a Seventh Revisionary Ratio (or perhaps Chiasmal Reversal), which Bloom does not mention—a return of the dead to *reclaim the prodigal sons*. (1982, 207; my emphasis)

The Seventh Ratio would be, therefore, like the seventh day after six tiring days of creation: a Sabbath of rest, armistice, repose; a climactic resolution to the qualms of agon.

Such a "reclaimed" Bloom, the prodigal son returned to the lap of Rabbinic tradition, or Bloom "in positive," would be less pronouncedly Gnostic-Satanic, and, at the same time, more romantic (or rather, simply Jewish, for Handelman is right when she points to the fact that Bloom's Hebrew version of the agon is, in the end, more "affirmative" than the original Greco-Latin one). His revised *Abwehrmechanismen* would show not only a defensive but also provoking side; his main weapon would not be the illusion, always bound to lose in confrontation with reality, but fantasy, challenging the very domination of *Realitätsprinzip* as such. The great boldness of fantasies would transform the poet's "lying against time" into a winning strategy whose final goal would be an actual reversal. And the *apophrades* would bring a moment of truce in which the ephebe would become what he really is, that is, *become his own influence* he no longer needs to repress—and the influence itself, originally traumatic, would be "redeemed," that is, accepted as the Shakespearean precious "gift" and the core of the act of identification.

Both these readings are equally justified, and it is also possible that Bloom maintains his ambivalence deliberately. For, as we have already suggested, this ambivalence belongs to the very enterprise of modern mythmaking.[15] This *mythopoiesis* wants to preserve all the disenchanted privileges of the modern individual—her Cartesian separateness, her monadic distrust toward influences—and, simultaneously, wants to incorporate her, the single unit, into a grand, metaphysical narrative of agon, crisis, and reparation. The practice of such mythmaking is and must be paradoxical, for it is doomed to "undo" constantly its own charm in the recurrent act of self-deconstruction. Every move of faith in the reenchantment of influence, in its transmutation into a beneficial gift, is checked by the counterpoint of skepsis, gravitating toward the economics of reduction and its naturalist idiom of power. Every approach to restoration and its asymptotic vision of redemptive harmony is immediately tainted with dissonance in which the individual all the more aggressively expresses her distinctness.

The ambivalence of Bloom's efforts makes the integrity of old mythoreligious narratives more problematic—but this is a purposeful stratagem. We will thus never know for sure what is the ultimate epistemological status of his lie against time and reality: whether it is a *mythos* of a modern man who managed to get out of the hell of pure individuation to tie with the world a new and free "bond of love"—or whether it merely expresses his *pathos*, the pain of the inachievable. Whether it is a real *doing*, or just a *suffering*.[16]

Perhaps this aporia would be at least partly solved if Bloom followed the critique formulated by Geoffrey H. Hartman, his best and most sympathetic interpreter by far. Hartman agrees with de Man that in Bloom we deal with the paradox of *misplaced naturalism* and that it is precisely this insoluble paradox which gives Bloom's style a flavor of permanent defeat. "There is nothing even faintly evangelistic in Bloom," says Hartman in his "War in Heaven." "He is totally a kaka-angelist, a bearer of bad news. For him the dynamic of history is governed by a necessary demon rather than a necessary angel—the 'demon of continuity'" (1975, 46). Yet, the connection he makes between these two aspects of Bloom's writings is far more interesting, at least for us here. In de Man's account, it is Bloom's pseudonaturalism that engages him in the spurious hysteria of interpersonal relations which otherwise could easily be toned down by choosing a more appropriate, sterile idiom of intertextuality. For Hartman, however, this is not an option: as we saw in our handling of the Scene of Instruction, he is not interested in reducing

Bloom to Derrida—the disseminating flight of meaning, or the free fall of signifiers is not a solution for Bloom, whose notion of the swerve tries to negotiate with "the unbearable presence" that looms at its origins. Hartman, therefore, is more sympathetic to Bloom's effort "to substitute *davhar* for *logos*," and to endure within this substitution—unlike Derrida, who, as we have already shown in a few places, very quickly lapses back into the world of *logos*. And if he has any reproaches to make against Bloom's theory, it is only on behalf of his even more persistent vision of the Hebrew *davhar* (i.e., the poetic voice) which is able to challenge the natural order and establish its *authority* regardless of the more naturalistic asset of *priority:*

> Bloom's theory is vulnerable because *priority* (a concept from the natural order) and *authority* (from the spiritual order) are not clearly distinguished; in fact, they merge and become a single, overwhelming *proton pseudos. By seeking to overcome priority, art fights nature on nature's own ground, and is bound to lose.* (ibid., 49; my emphasis)

What Hartman implies is that there is in Bloom, despite all his self-professed Gnostic Jewishness, a strong, destructive tinge of old Greek fatality for which all the efforts to get out of the natural order and to take revenge on the temporal verdict of "it was" must appear futile and absurd. *Nature cannot be fought on her own ground;* it can only be overcome if previously invalidated, stripped of her "natural" prerogative. It is only then that all the cunning, deception, and slyness can become something more than just a pathetic lie against the natural priority; it is only thanks to Exodus, which truly gets us beyond the vital order, that we may begin to consider Jacob's agon as victorious, and his loss of natural vitality, manifested by his lamed hip, as compensated by a gain of *authority*, already belonging to a different, non-natural realm.

In *The Anxiety of Influence*, however, Bloom makes a very strong connection between the Christian idea of Second Coming and the metaphor of Second Chance; he claims that second chance is but a poor consolation, which cannot be the concern of truly strong poets. By equating the second chance with the Christian Second Coming, he thus ties it with the resignation and surrender that are implied by the Freudian trope of "normal sublimation" whose unrebellious wisdom boils down to a passive acknowledgment that what cannot be cured must be endured, and what cannot be undone better be forgotten; the only thing that counts, therefore, is the future promise of a betterment and patient awaiting of its advent. Yet, if we look closer at Kierkegaard's notion of "recollection forwards," which constitutes the gist of his advancing repetition, we cannot help to notice that it *is*, in fact, nothing but a *second chance*, although a chance framed in more militant terms than the passive chance of the Second Coming. For, what else if not a second chance is Jacob's fight with the Angel of Death during which he is born anew, and this time not as a secondary twin, but as the winner of the name, the one and only founder of Israel—the truly firstborn in the order of spiritual authority? And what is the goal of this agonistic Scene of Nomination if not the defeat of nature with her false pretence to priority? Says Hartman in "The Struggle for the Text":

> Through this unmediated encounter, *everything shady in Jacob is removed:* the blessing he stole he now receives by right; and his name, tainted by his birth and subsequent behavior, is cleared. No longer will he be called Jacob, that is, Heel or Usurper, but Israel, the God-fighter—quite a title ... The name change denotes a character change, or the inner sense of Jacob's previous life breaking through. (1986, 8; my emphasis)[17]

Yet Bloom, Hartman says, "overcondenses," just as in the Freudian nightmarish dream work, where all the images collapse into one frightening message—and the result of this is homogenization: the dark *kenoma* of the same with no spark of hope or difference. We are suddenly back in the world of fatal, all-leveling influence, so horrifyingly diagnosed by Horkheimer and Adorno: the worst of all possible worlds, where every being wants to be singular but ends up becoming identical with everything else:

> Bloom's overcondensing *takes away the second chance:* literary history is for him like human life, a polymorphous quest-romance collapsing always into one tragic recognition. Flight from the precursor leads to him by fatal prolepsis, *nature always defeats imagination*, history is the representation of "one story and one story only." (Hartman 1975, 60; my emphasis)

Thus, Bloom's penchant for naturalistic rhetoric is ominous not only because it spells a "step backward" in the development of critical techniques, but most of all because it makes impossible a priori the adventure of Exodus, which promised to get us beyond the kingdom of natural priorities and to alleviate the rule of natural economy. Bloom, Hartman suggests, is thus endangered by an even more "powerful mythology" than the Freudian one: for in its insistence on natural priority, it cannot grant any separate place for anything so non-natural as "the psychic reality" and reopens the space for the intrusion of uncouth nature which threatens to get us back under her severe rule. Hartman is right when he points to the historical pattern in Bloom's own revision: the moment in which *The Anxiety of Influence* is written spells the perigee of Blake's influence and, at the same time, the apogee of Bloom's interest in Nietzsche. This means that Bloom's belief in romantic *mythopoesis* undergoes its true *Nacht der Erde* (night of the world), or, to use Bloom's own revisionary terms, passes through the stage of *kenosis* that, as we have already seen, is the ratio of doubting, emptying, and reduction in which the ephebe confronts his own nature he so long avoided thanks to the power of his fantasies. It is the moment of Bloom's Death of Love, or, to quote Michael Balint, "the extreme case of the loss of the erotic component" (1965, 33), which puts in doubt all the *errotic* efforts of figuration, absolutely expedient for romantic mythmaking. For, when authority is given to nature, every attempt to lie against her will come out as nothing but a childish and awkward lie, an infantile denial which will have to be corrected in the end. Where Egypt rules—the dark *mizraim* of death and death of love—the Exodus is nothing but an excursion, a futile escape, which is doomed to return to its place of origin. Nature, therefore, cannot be fought on her own grounds: it can only be fought against by a lie, which—narcissistically, errotically—believes in its own creative power to wander away from its origins and establish the alternative realm of the non-natural.[18]

On the other hand, even though Nature cannot be fought on her own grounds, she nonetheless *must* be fought against. Bloom, therefore, might have "overcondensed" his vitalistic language to emphasize the necessity to fight, yet this very emphasis, despite the sometimes unfortunate idiom, remains of the highest speculative value. It may thus be argued that Bloom's "naturalism" is not so much a firm theoretical position (as it is the case of Rorty) as a rhetorical device, designed to express the constant pressure for struggle and survival. Hartman is right when he differentiates between the order of priority and the order of authority; at the same time, however, he may be wrong pragmatically, that is, from the perspective of poetic practice. His vision of the Exodus, which leads us beyond the power of nature, may seem a little too secure, and the natural sequence of precursorship, correspondingly, too irrelevant.

While in Bloom, we are never safely out of Egypt, never fully in the hands of a transcendent deity whose authority invalidates the priority of natural gods. The drama of Exodus happens all the time, precisely as a *drama*, whose outcome is each time unknown. Egypt, the mechanical repetitive force of everything that already exists, is within us and without us, and the only counterforce is a sublime lie, which can either thwart itself from the start, by assuming the higher authority of nature, or persist, by lovingly investing in its own antithetical deceits. Yet, in the overemphatic naturalistic idiom, this lie stands no chances, for it is a priori marked by a masochistic loss of self-love which turns it into an immediate failure.[19] It has no "non-natural" backup for its restless work of negativity, no supranatural truth to pledge for it: neither the transcendent God, who is no longer present in the world, nor the transcendental spirit, the fountain of the negative in classical conceptions of subjectivity. It does not derive its power from a metaphysical realm beyond life, but is deeply, though antithetically, anchored within the vital element: the lie represents the negativity of life itself, which refuses to be fully contained by the vital order and restlessly drives from "mere life" to "more life." Hence, the lie, as nothing more than a *lie*, must be firmly narcissistic in order to survive—and this amour propre can come only from one source: the tacit "holding" of the whole agonistic process, which is the initial love of the election, bestowed on the ephebe by the precursor.

He, who was a liar in the first place, can only love other liars: the fresh adepts of the secret tradition of trespass. The precursor may thus "be in the id" and represent the force of nature for the ephebe, but in the end, the ephebe discovers the unnatural "lack" in his predecessor, his original *lie*, which was the loving cause of the election. In the last stage of *apophrades*, therefore, they are *both* out of nature, mutually enjoying their company of bold frauds.

Love, After All

> Riding three days and nights he came upon the place, but decided it could not be come upon.
>
> —Harold Bloom, "Epilogue: Reflections upon the Path," *The Anxiety of Influence*

But what is the final reason to fight against nature? Is it, as Horkheimer and Adorno assert, a first move of the enlightenment which disenchants the natural magic and seeks power over the natural, or is it a struggle whose meaning is more encompassing and redemptive? We can see that, in the end, the precursor, who was "nature" for the ephebe, shows a different, non-natural aspect of the "lack" which was his own, original lie against his Father he had to slay in order to become a strong poet. The initial ambivalence of the Scene of Instruction is thus resolved into one dialectical message: "be like me" and "do not be like me" come together into one imperative—"imitate me, but only in my struggle for non-imitation," or "repeat after me, but only my effort not to become a copy or replica," or "acquire, like me, a singular name." On this "redemptive" reading, the clue of the agon is not just separation and emancipation of the next individual, but a new bond tied on the higher level of mutual recognition of both, precursor and ephebe, engaged in the same struggle to lie, get out, individuate. This is also the moment, for the first time in the history of this battle, when Revision can also become a model for a Vision: an equally redemptive perception of nature which is also discovered as "lacking," that is, as wanting something else than the false fullness of the repetitive, vegetative cycle—something truly singular, particular, and transcending the sadness of "mere life." The saving lie of the strong poets, their restless romantic negativity, not only fights against nature, but also helps it to become what it could be, or what it was before the fall into a deadness of repetition: the kingdom of the original, still fresh creation. *Nature herself wants to be set free from her natural priority.*

It is true, then, that humans are not capable of the perfect love only God can feel toward his bride; the Scene of Instruction is not exactly the exalted subject of *The Song of Songs*, the perfect *hierosgamos* (marriage) between God and *Shekhinah*, the world as primarily created, for it takes place after—and thanks to—the catastrophe. In the ideal vision of creation, the original light of love radiates and reflects through the Channels of spontaneous and unrepressed communication between *sephirot*, the ten pillars of existence—and the catastrophe is always bound to what Gershom Scholem calls "The Breaking of the Channels," a blockage which stops loving light from flowing. It is precisely this blocked, repressed, tainted love that changes into its further "vicissitudes," unknown to God and his Angels: the strange, bitter fate tasted only by humans, inhabiting the lowest levels of the broken world.

Yet, it is still love, however crooked and disfigured by the blocked channels. The sparks are always there, ready to "come home again." So, it is true that in Bloom's agon "each slap is an antithetical embrace" (Hartman 1975, 49), but this is precisely how it must be, for it is in the nature of this perverse love to escape and, simultaneously, to bend the trajectory of its flight. It is, therefore, not just "the nightmare of always walking into parents," as Hartman says (ibid.), amazed by the shockingly reverse result of Bloom's quest for poetic originality; it is not *just* the nightmare, and it isn't so baffling after all. Or rather, it would be, if there were no love involved, if there were nothing redemptive to explain the "crooked" path of the wandering meaning, which cannot simply take the Derridean flight. For, as Hölderlin says in his *Lebenslauf*:

> Grössers wolltest auch du, aber die Liebe zwingt
> All uns nieder, das Leid beuget gewaltiger,
> Doch es kehrt umsonst nicht
> Unser Bogen, woher er kommt.[20]

Every lie is thus an "antithetical embrace" of the fallen truth it fights against, but perhaps it is not so completely *umsonst*, not so futile after all. For the place the lie comes back to is never exactly the same place where it began: the moment when Revision gives place to Vision, it suddenly sees that every truth, every priority it struggled against was also a lie in the first place.

Thus, "riding three days and nights he came upon the place, but decided it could not be come upon."

Notes

Introduction

1. In the most recent critical appraisal of Bloom's whole intellectual career, from 1959 (the date of publication of his doctoral thesis on Shelley) to 2005 (the editors called for contributions to commemorate Bloom's seventy-fifth birthday), Graham Allen and Roy Sellars complain in the preface that "while it may be true that Bloom's work is difficult to adopt as a methodology, and that it presents itself as a kind of literature, its unrepeatability does not, on its own, explain the lack of academic dialogue ... Kristeva, Barthes, Derrida and De Man are equally unrepeatable, for example, and yet their works, unlike those of Bloom, have been subject to a widespread and intensive (if not always successful) incorporation into academic discourse" (2007, xiv). My book can thus be seen as filling this lacune by delivering the discussion that should have happened in the '70s and '80s, but for many reasons, which I will also try to explain here, did not.

2. The term "counter-narrative" is used in this specific context by Michael Mack in *German Idealism and the Jew: The Inner Anti-Semitism of Philosophy and German Jewish Responses* as a revisionist response to David Biale's notion of "counter-history," which he created originally in reference to Gershom Scholem's work on the kabbalah, offering an alternative vision of the Jewish tradition. Mack's useful innovation consists in the fact that, contrary to the latter, the "counter-narrative" does not limit itself to telling the same story from a different perspective, but insists on the transformation of crucial concepts and ideas in which this story is told.

3. See most of all: Geoffrey H. Hartman, *Criticism in the Wilderness;* Susan A. Handelman, *The Slayers of Moses;* Norman Finkelstein, *The Ritual of New Creation;* Jean-Pierre Mileur, *Literary Revisionism and the Burden of Modernity;* Cynthia Ozick, *Art and Ardor;* and Moshe Idel, "Enoch and Elijah: Some Remarks on Apotheosis, Theophany and Jewish Mysticism," being his contribution to *The Salt Companion to Harold Bloom,* edited recently by Graham Allen and Roy Sellars.

4. As Franz Rosenzweig calls it in *The Star of Redemption,* pointing to an essential unity of the philosophical project from the pre-Socratics to Hegel.

5. To what extent Bloom truly is a "religious critic" will be a matter of a serious discussion in the following chapters of this book, for this is indeed a characteristic that may raise some protests, and not only on the side of the Jewish thinkers more favorably inclined toward orthodoxy. For instance, Leslie Brisman, in his

recent essay "Bloom upon Her Mountain: Unclouding the Heights of Modern Biblical Criticism," claims that Bloom is rather "a powerful and plain-spoken critic of religion—or, perhaps more precisely, of what happens to literary imagination when it degenerates into religious imagination" (2007, 336). On the other hand, Moshe Idel, whose essay figures as next to Brisman's in *The Salt Companion to Harold Bloom*, opens his reflections on the Bloomian "angelology" with the statement indicating the very opposite: "Among leading contemporary thinkers, Harold Bloom's interest in and contribution to a novel understanding of religion is outstanding" (2007, 347). This is not to say that these two opinions cannot be dialectically reconciled: for Bloom, every normative or—how he calls it after Nietzsche—"priestly" religion contains a vivid core of a "frontier speculation," which is still unencumbered by the pieties of dogmatic orthodoxies. This hot and fluid core tends to "fossilize" due to normative pressures and for this reason needs to be brought to life again in religious criticism. The religious criticism, therefore, is both criticism *of* religion and criticism *for the sake* of religion. One could thus say, paraphrasing Horkheimer's and Adorno's aggressive defense of Enlightenment, that Bloom tries to defend religion against itself.

6. In particular, see Peter de Bolla, *Harold Bloom: Towards the Historical Rhetorics*; David Fite, *Harold Bloom: The Rhetoric of Romantic Vision*; and Graham Allen, *Harold Bloom: A Poetics of Conflict*.

7. The motto taken from Stevens's *An Ordinary Evening in New Haven* is as follows: "A more severe,/More harassing master would extemporize/Subtler, more urgent proof that the theory/Of poetry is the theory of life,/As it is, in the intricate evasions of as."

8. In *Fallen Angels*, Bloom speculates on Hamlet as a literary figure anticipating the aporetic style of philosophical deconstruction: "Hamlet thinks too well, and thus perishes of the truth, pragmatically becoming a version of the angel of death. Hamlet is death's ambassador or messenger to us" (56). Convinced of the inhuman—and in this sense, perversely "angelic"—character of deconstructive thought, Bloom could thus paraphrase the famous saying of Kafka, which originally referred to the possibility of hope: "Yes, there is plenty of truth—*but not for us.*"

9. The criticism of asymmetry implied in Freud's dualism of Eros and Thanatos is well exemplified by this remark of Jonathan Lear: "In fact, Empedocles' choice of love or friendship (*philia*) and strife (*neikos*) is superior to Freud's love and death, precisely because strife stays at the same level of reality as love, whereas death is confined to the biological realm" (1998, 14f). What I perceive here as a speculative advantage, Lear interprets as Freud's philosophical sloppiness.

10. Bloom, whose favorite Gnostic text is Valentinus's *Gospel of Truth* (paraphrased by him in the opening to *The Anxiety of Influence*), became truly fascinated with Gnosis while reading the famous book of Hans Jonas: *The Gnostic Religion*. But he has deepened his interest and knowledge about Gnostic movements thanks to Bentley Layton, his Yale friend and translator of *The Gnostic Scriptures*, who once, in a private conversation, called Bloom "a native in the land of Gnosis," speaking its idiom naturally and effortlessly. Yet, what this exactly means has never been fully explained by either of them: "The word

'gnostic,'" writes Layton in the preface to his translations, "has two meanings. One is a broad meaning, denoting all the religious movements represented in this book, and many more besides. The elusive category ('gnostic*ism*') that corresponds to this broad meaning has always been hard to define" (1987, 5).

11. "Eternal return is the basic form of prehistorical, mythical consciousness," says Benjamin in *The Arcades Project* (D 10, 3).

12. The term "psychotheology," indicating a new mode of speculation that combines both psychoanalytical and religious insights, comes from Eric Santner's book on Rosenzweig and Freud, *On the Psychotheology of Everyday Life*. And although the very coinage is Santner's, we can say that in his theory of the poetic agon, stated for the first time in *The Anxiety of Influence*, Bloom pioneered *avant la lettre* this new psychotheological discipline, to which my book also wants to be a modest contribution.

13. See Gershom Scholem, "Über Klage und Klagelied" ("On Lament and Lamentative Song") (2000, 128–33).

14. As Mileur rightly observes apropos Bloom, meaning is the child of the Fall: "The exile that makes meaning possible manifests itself as belatedness, and the form of that belatedness, partially described by the revisionary ratios, is Bloom's own procedure of rhetorical substitution—his endless wandering from the language of religion, to psychology, to philosophy, to rhetoric—which rehearses a similar homelessness, since no rhetoric ever actually subsumes and becomes entirely sufficient to the purpose of any other. Being cut off from the substance, from the literal, is the price paid for meaning. But this suffering is also the freedom to trope and thus to be elsewhere—our defense against the literality of death" (1985, 58–59).

15. "Battle between strong equals, father and son as mighty opposites, Laius and Oedipus at the crossroads; *only this is my subject here.*" (*AI*, 11; my emphasis)

16. Scholem, in his *Ten Unhistorical Theses on Kabbalah*, says about Kafka that "he gave the best expression of the borderline between religion and nihilism" (1973, 271).

17. "Nahman's greatest originality"—says Bloom in the chapter "Yahweh's Psychology"—"his great swerve from Lurianic Kabbalah, was to deny the *reshimu*, the remnant of God's light that stayed behind in the void of the *tehiru*, the space vacated by Yahweh in the initial *zimzum*. Without the saving remnant of divine light, we stumble about in the void, beggars with amputated feet" (*JY*, 227).

18. To Finkelstein, therefore, Bloom's Jewishness, very much like Benjamin's or Kafka's Jewishness to Scholem, is the furthest outpost of Judaism in the world of the Fall, Exile, and Confusion, deprived of the reassuring props of Judaic orthopraxy, most of all the guide in the form of Law. Finkelstein describes himself in Scholem's words, originally addressed by him to Kafka, as "a rather pious atheist who brooded over the space He had vacated" (1992, 1). His, as well as Bloom's (and if I dare say, also my) Jewishness is thus self-puzzled, disoriented, stigmatized, with an acute awareness of exile, contamination, and a necessity of erring in the desert of doubts. Finkelstein enumerates three features characteristic of this posttraditionalist Jewishness: "1) the matter of secular literary activity; 2) the matter of 'wandering meaning'; 3) the matter of loss and exile" (ibid., 3).

In the introduction to Olivier Revault d'Allonnes's *Musical Reflections on Jewish Thought*, Bloom describes this "frontier" type of Judaism as particularly rich in consequences for the Western theory of interpretation: "The wandering people has taught itself and others the lesson of wandering meaning, a wandering that has compelled a multitude of changes in the modes of interpretation available to the West" ("I," 6). Moreover, they also taught itself the secret of *the Jewish metamorphose of exile into achievement* (ibid.), which consists in nothing else than the Freudian transference: the reorientation of the primordial libidinal investment in a lost object toward a new object, accessible here and now. Or, in other words: a shift from the original obsession with the Scripture, to which—in Benjamin's words—"the key has been lost," to a more general "text-centeredness" (*A*, 320) that can elevate any precursorial writing to the hights of a sacred Script.

19. The concept of the "hollow," which appears often in Bloom's writings, also comes from Ashbery's *Self-Portrait*; it is an emblem of a deadening imprisonment in which the soul is forced to "fit its hollow perfectly" and thus lose her "secret," or her inner spark: "The secret is too plain. The pity of it smarts,/Makes hot tears spurt: that the soul is not a soul,/Has no secret, is small, and it fits/Its hollow perfectly: its room, our moment of attention."

20. John Hollander, Bloom's friend and colleague from Yale, writes in his introduction to *The Poetics of Influence*: "Harold Bloom has always been an antithetical critic. Whether the primary system against which he was writing was the New Criticism . . . , or, whether at the present point of his career, he is melodramatizing . . . the originality of the so called 'J' author of the Hebrew bible, he has always written against his teachers" (*PI*, i). This characteristic mistrust against all schools as "parties of reduction," which absorb everything singular under general headings, was also nicely summarized by Graham Allen in his *Harold Bloom: The Poetics of Conflict*: "Bloom's presentation of his thesis in *The Anxiety of Influence* is bound up with a consideration of the possibility for a mode of criticism which might be able to respect the power of poetic utterance in its own terms. One might say that the undisclosed subject of that text is a defense against reduction, a desire, as Wordsworth puts it, to gain 'knowledge not purchased by the loss of power'" (1994, 15).

21. I borrow this term from Cornel West, who in his book *The American Evasion of Philosophy* claims that the tradition of American pragmatism simply cannot be regarded on the same footing as Continental philosophy from Plato to Derrida: "The fundamental argument of this book," he says, "is that the evasion of epistemology-centered philosophy—from Emerson to Rorty—results in a conception of philosophy as a form of cultural criticism in which the meaning of America is put forward by intellectuals in response to distinct social and cultural crises. In this sense, American pragmatism is less a philosophical tradition putting forward solutions to perennial problems in the Western philosophical conversation initiated by Plato and more a continuous cultural commentary or set of interpretations that attempt to explain America to itself at a particular historical moment" (1989, 5).

22. In his choice of life Bloom follows Spinoza, who in *Ethics* famously says: "A free man thinks of death least of all things; and his wisdom is meditation not of death but of life" (1951, 232).

23. And the continuation of this Orphic strain in the critical discipline is, as Bloom asserts in the coda to *Agon*, "The American Difference in Poetry and Criticism," "an antithetical criticism in the American grain, affirming the self over language, while granting a priority to figurative language over meaning" (*A*, 336).

24. Compare these two quotes on the separation of the self: "You think me the child of my circumstances"—says Emerson triumphantly in "The Transcendentalist"—"I make my circumstance ... I—this thought which is called I—is the mould into which the world is poured like melted wax. The mould is invisible, but the world betrays the shape of the mould. You call it the power of circumstance, but it is the power of me" (1990, 99). While Rosenzweig, in *The Star of Redemption*, draws on a more modest version of negativity: "In Judaism man is always somehow a remnant. He is always somehow a survivor, an inner something, whose exterior was seized by the current of the world and carried off while he himself, what is left of him, remains standing on the shore" (1985, 415).

25. This is why I cannot agree with John Hollander, whose critical remarks are otherwise usually very congenial to the Bloomian spirit: "I do not feel," he writes in the introduction to *The Poetics of Influence*, "that his contention with fashionable 'post-structuralist' writing has yielded him the same kind of rebound which his earlier revision of modernism, or of its scholastic form in New Criticism, or his fight against what he considers the facticious church of Freud (as opposed to the greatness of the writer himself), or against normative rabbinic authority over the text of the Pentateuch, have afforded. In the long run, his quarrel with the ephebes of Derrida and de Man may come to sound like so much static noise" (*PI*, xlvi).

26. The crucial works from this period (1973–82) that will be quoted most often in this book are the following: *The Anxiety of Influence: A Theory of Poetry*, 1973; *A Map of Misreading*, 1975; *Kabbalah and Criticism*, 1975; *Poetry and Repression: Revisionism from Blake to Stevens*, 1976; *Wallace Stevens: The Poems of Our Climate*, 1977; "Breaking of the Form" in *Deconstruction and Criticism*, 1979; *Agon: Towards a Theory of Revisionism*, 1982; and *The Breaking of the Vessels*, 1982.

27. In their preface to *The Salt Companion to Harold Bloom*, Allen and Sellars suggest that this is a period marked by Bloom's moving away from the anxiety of influence, as both the critical idea and the state of mind: "If we had to characterize Bloom's work since the mid-1980s, it would be in terms of freedom from influence, originality, authors who are influences rather than influenced, movers rather than moved ... Bloom has dramatically altered his orientation in the last twenty years, ceasing to describe and in some ways embody those who are belated and, instead, focusing on that small circle of authors who, as he now likes to put it, have made us all possible, whoever 'we' may be" (2007, xiv). Yes, but this seems to be only one, more serene and "Pateresque," of Bloom's later incarnations—whereas in his less known and popular, yet still abiding, Jewish-Gnostic mode of "religious criticism," he anxiously and persistently continues to "embody those who are belated."

Chapter 1

1. Bloom's disappointment with the model of "I and Thou" was also prompted by his reading of Scholem's critical essay on Buber, which criticized him for his ahistorical, antitraditionalist, and nonlinguistic type of self-enclosed mysticism. See Gershom Scholem, "Martin Buber's Conception of Judaism," in *On Jews and Judaism in Crisis*.

2. In Frye's *Archetypes of Literature*, myth and epiphany complement each other as narrative and meaning: they are "to borrow musical terms, the melodic and harmonic contexts of the imagery." Narrative runs according to "rhythm, or recurrent movement, deeply founded on the natural cycle . . . The pull of ritual is towards pure narrative, which, if there could be such thing, would be automatic and unconscious repetition . . . Patterns of imagery, on the other hand, or fragment of significance, are oracular in origin, and derive from the epiphanic moment, the flash of instantaneous comprehension with no direct reference to time . . . And just as pure narrative would become unconscious act, so pure significance would be an incommunicable state of consciousness, for communication begins by constructing narrative" (1972, 428–29).

3. "For the fact is," says Abrams, "that many of the most distinctive and recurrent elements in both the thought and literature of the (romantic) age had their origin in theological concepts, images, and plot patterns which were translated, in Wordsworth's terms, to men 'as natural beings in the strength of nature,' living in 'the world / Of all of us, the place in which, in the end, / We find our happiness, or not at all' (*Prelude*, III, 194; X, 726ff.)." Far from being a simple return to a pagan celebration of the natural, cyclic world, most of the "characteristic concepts and patterns of Romantic philosophy and literature are a *displaced* and *reconstituted theology*, or else a secularized form of devotional experience" (1973, 65).

4. Geoffrey Hartman, therefore, is right when he points to Bloom's tendency to break with Frye, already manifest in his book on Shelley, which must have appeared "too radical for a Christian-Humanist synthesis," but also too full of doubts to offer a complete "redemptive iconography" (1980, 102).

5. In *A Map of Misreading*, Bloom elaborates his criticism of Frye, putting him on the same plane with T. S. Eliot, the critic (though not a poet) he most dislikes: "Northrop Frye, who increasingly looks like the Proclus or Iamblichus of our day, has Platonized the dialectics of tradition, its relation to fresh creation, into what he calls the Myth of Concern, which turns out to be a Low Church version of T. S. Eliot's Anglo-Catholic myth of Tradition and the Individual Talent. In Frye's reduction, the student discovers that he becomes something, and thus uncovers or demystifies himself, by first being persuaded that tradition is inclusive rather than exclusive, and so makes a place for him. The student is a cultural assimilator who *thinks* because he has *joined* a larger body of thought. Freedom, for Frye as for Eliot, is the change, however slight, that any genuine single consciousness brings about in the order of literature simply by joining the simultaneity of such order. I confess that I no longer understand this simultaneity, except as a fiction that Frye, like Eliot, passes upon himself. This fiction is a noble idealization, and as a lie against time will go the way of every noble

idealization. Such positive thinking served many purposes during the sixties, when continuities, of any kind, badly required to be summoned, even if they did not come to our call" (*MM*, 30).

6. The whole paragraph sounds as follows: "The great critic Northrop Frye (who contaminated me) remarked to me that whether a later reader experienced (an effect of influence) was entirely a matter of temperament and circumstances. With amiable disloyalty I answered that influence anxiety was not primarily an affect in an individual, but rather the relation of one work of literature to another. Therefore the anxiety is the result and not the cause, of a strong misreading. With that, we parted (intellectually) forever, though in old age I appreciate the irony that my criticism is to his as the New Testament is to the Tanakh, which is spiritually the paradoxical reverse of our spiritual preferences" (*JJ*, 47).

7. In Frye's own words, enthusiastically endorsing Blake's thesis in *Fearful Symmetry:* "The life of Jesus is eternal joy and freedom; the death of Jesus represents the total achievement of that aspect of human life which consists of temporary painful necessities. But if we could escape from the necessity, we should also escape from time and pain" (1969, 400–401). "When we perceive as a mental form, or rather create, we perceive as part of a universal Creator or Perceiver, who is ultimately Jesus" (ibid., 108). "That is another reason why Jesus is called the Word of God. Reality is intelligibility, and a poet who has put things into words has lifted 'things' from the barren chaos of nature into the created order of thought" (ibid., 114).

8. See, for example, Gershom Scholem in "Toward an Understanding of the Messianic Idea in Judaism": "Yet the figure of Messiah, in whom the fulfillment of redemption is concentrated, remains peculiarly vague; and this, I think, has good reason ... Unlike Christian or Shiite Messianism, no memories of a real person are here at work which, though they might arouse the imagination and attract old images of expectation, nonetheless are always bound to something deeply personal. Jesus or the Hidden Imam, who once existed as persons, possess the unmistakable and unforgettable qualities of a person. This is just what the Jewish image of the Messiah, by its nature, cannot have since it can picture everything personal only in completely abstract fashion, having as yet no living experience on which to base it" (1995, 17–18).

9. Compare, for instance: "The quest of the hero," Frye writes in *The Archetypes of Literature*, "also tends to assimilate the oracular and random verbal structures, as we can see when we watch the chaos of local legends that results from prophetic epiphanies consolidating into a narrative mythology of departmental gods. In most of the higher religions this in turn has become the same central quest-myth that emerges from ritual, as the *Messiah myth* became the narrative structure of the oracles of Judaism" (1972, 429–30; my emphasis).

10. In his commentary on the negative, written on the margins to Lavater, Blake sounds very much like Nietzsche (and Frye only confirms this association by giving this chapter of his book the title "Beyond Good and Evil"): "But as I understand Vice it is a Negative ... Accident is the omission of act in self & the hindering of act in another; This is Vice, but all Act is Virtue ... Murder is Hindering Another. Theft is Hindering Another. Backbiting, Undermining,

Circumventing, & whatever is Negative is Vice" (Frye 1969, 55). Needless to say, all these "Hinderings" are high on the list of Bloom's tricks against anteriority: "backbiting and undermining not excluded . . . For Blake all negative evil comes from 'melancholy' of inaction that leads to 'jealousy' "; but for Bloom all poets are by necessity overburdened by melancholy and envious of their great predecessors. They are not solitary and powerful imitators of Jesus but rather minor prophets, competing for their place in the canon.

11. The term "antithetical" Yeats borrowed from Nietzsche, who in the *Genealogy of Morals* opposed the antithetical ideal to the ascetic ideal. In *The Will to Power* (no. 884) Nietzsche defines the new antithetical ideal as "existing blithely among antithesis, full of that supple strength that guards against convictions and doctrines by employing one against the other and reserving freedom for itself." In *Per Amica Silentia Lunae*, Yeats for the first time states his own formula of the antithetical: "The other self, the anti-self or the antithetical self, as one may choose to name it, comes but to those who are no longer deceived, whose passion is reality" (1998, 331). For Yeats, to be able to embrace reality means most of all to be able to face the inner reality of conflict: "We make out of the quarrel with others, rhetoric," he says in the same passage, "but of the quarrel with ourselves, poetry" (ibid.).

12. And earlier, while criticizing Yeats's typically esoteric inclination for natural religion: "For Blake, the body is flux to the imagination's force: the imagination's movement disdains the circular eddy that is the body's cycle. There is then no wisdom of the body, and if no natural wisdom is possible, then natural religion is pernicious error. Here is one of the fundamental points at which Blake and Yeats diverge, with important consequences" (*Y*, 67).

13. This defense, once again, aligned him closely with Frye, which he himself admitted in *A Map of Misreading*. Frye's new preface to *Fearful Symmetry*, composed in 1969, contains a great adage against the '68 revolt: "In his earlier work Blake thought of the essential 'Mental Fight' of human life as the revolt of desire and energy against repression, though even then he was careful to say that *reason was the form of desire and energy, which are never amorphous except when they are repressed.* Later he tended more to see this conflict as one of the genuine reason, or what he called intellect, against rationalization. 'The tygers of wrath are wiser than the horses of instruction,' but Blake thought of his own poetry as instructive, and the horses of instruction in their turn are wiser than the bulky mules of hysteria" (1969, iii; my emphasis).

14. Compare Goethe's *Prometheus*, where the hero says: *Hier sitz ich, forme Menschen nach meinem Bilde* (Here I sit, forming men in my image).

15. What Bloom proposes here is a curious romantic revision of Freud's own therapeutic imperative to strengthen the ego. As we shall yet see in part 2, this insistence on the ego as the only force capable of creating "a new version of id" determines Bloom's ultimate disagreement with Lacan: "In Freud the ego mediates between id and superego, and Freud had no particular interest in further dividing the ego itself. In romantic psychic mythology, Prometheus rises from the id, and can best be thought of as the force of libido, doomed to undergo a merely cyclic movement from appetite to repression, and then back again; any quest within nature is thus at last irrelevant to the mediating ego, though the

quest goes back and forth through it. *It is within the ego itself that the quest must turn, to engage the antagonist proper, and to clarify the imaginative component in the ego by its strife of contraries with its dark brother"* (*RT*, 27; my emphasis).

16. These are Bloom's own words: "Different as they are, Blake, Shelley, Balzac, and Nietzsche have an *apocalyptic vitalism* more or less in common" (*Y*, 33).

17. In *Yeats* we can find a passage which sounds indeed very Trillingian: "The most admirable restraint of imagination, in our time, is to be found in the writings of Freud, who does not quest after a cure that cannot be found. He offers neither Unity of Being, nor the simplicity of the Condition of Fire. Yet he understood that poetry might be a discipline roughly parallel to psychoanalysis, one in which the poet and his reader, like the psychoanalyst and his patient, would find not cure but a balance of opposites, not ultimates beyond knowledge but self-knowledge, not a control over fate but self-control. There are a few modern poets, of the highest achievement, who have the Freudian *wisdom that accepts limitation without prematurely setting limits*; Stevens, I think, is the major example of this diminished but authentic Romanticism, which might be called still a possible humanism" (*Y*, 215).

18. Still later in Trilling's thought there will appear yet another avatar of the antithetical-the adversary, namely "the opposing self," which, historically speaking, is responsible for the eighteenth-century turn toward authenticity. The opposing self, perfectly embodied by Rameau's nephew, who disbelieves culture for the sake of authenticity, is characterized by "intense and adverse imagination of the culture in which it has its being" (1979, x).

19. Brown's project can be called a naturalized regressive messianism which opposes itself to the bad infinity of Desire: "The reunification of Life and Death," he says, "can be envisioned only as the end of the historical process . . . For the restless pleasure-principle—which is the morbid manifestation of the Nirvana-principle—is what makes man Faustian, and Faustian man is a history-making man. If repression were overcome, the restless career of Faustian man would come to an end, because he would be satisfied and could say, *Verweile doch, du bist so schön* [Ah, linger on, thou art so fair!]" (1977, 91). Marcuse, too, sounds very Schillerian in his desire to return to a prehistoric world of nonrepressive sublimation where "the transformation of the libido" will eventually "engulf the Oedipal situation" (1966, 204).

20. And with it he would also go for always more repression, according to Freud's remark from *Inhibitions, Symptoms and Anxiety:* "It was anxiety which produces repression and not, as I formerly believed, repression which produces anxiety" (1959, 53).

21. "The essence of the Oedipal complex is the project of becoming God—in Spinoza's formula, *causa sui* [the cause of oneself]; in Sartre's, *etre-en-soi-et-pour-soi* [being-in-itself-and-for-itself]. By the same token, it plainly exhibits infantile narcissism perverted by the flight from death. At this stage (and in adult genital organization) masculinity is equated with activity; the fantasy of becoming a father of oneself is attached to the penis, thus establishing a concentration of narcissistic libido in the genital" (ibid., 118). And further: "The adult flight from death—the immortality promised in all religions, the immortality of

familial corporations, the immortality of cultural achievements—perpetuates the Oedipal project of becoming father of oneself: adult sublimation continues the Oedipal project" (ibid., 127).

22. "To equate emotional maturation with the discovery of acceptable substitutes—says Bloom in *The Anxiety of Influence*—may be pragmatic wisdom, particularly in the realm of Eros, but this is not the wisdom of the strong poets. The surrendered dream is not merely a phantasmagoria of endless gratification, but is the greatest of all human illusions, the vision of immortality. If Wordsworth's *Ode: Intimations of Immortality from Recollections of Early Childhood* possessed only the wisdom found also in Freud, then we could cease calling it 'the Great Ode.' Wordsworth too saw repetition or second chance as essential for development, and his ode admits that we can redirect our needs by substitution or sublimation. But the ode plangently also awakens into failure, and into the creative mind's protest against time's tyranny" (*AI*, 9).

23. In "On Language as Such and on the Language of Man," Walter Benjamin suggests that because nature became "over-named" by man, it fell into a mournful, nonresponsive silence: "Things have no proper names except in God ... In the language of men, however, they are over-named. There is, in the relation of human languages to that of things, something that can be approximately described as 'over-naming': over-naming as the deepest linguistic reason for all melancholy" (1978, 330).

24. It is thus not by accident that Bloom's favorite passage from Nietzsche is the one in which Zarathustra broods simultaneously on the limits and the limitlessness of the will, on the melancholy and mania of the will's revenge against time: "To redeem those who lived in the past and to recreate all 'it was' into a 'thus I willed it'—that alone should I call redemption. Will—that is the name of the liberator and joy-bringer; thus I taught you, my friends. But now learn this too: the will itself is still a prisoner. Willing liberates; but what is it that puts even the liberator himself in fetters? 'It was'—that is the name of the will's gnashing of teeth and most secret melancholy. Powerless against what has been done, he is an angry spectator of all that is past. *The will cannot will backwards; and that he cannot break time and time's covetousness, that is the will's loneliest melancholy . . .* This, indeed this alone, is what *revenge* is: the will's resentment against time and time's 'it was'" (1917, 53; my emphasis).

25. See Paul de Man, "The Contemporary Criticism of Romanticism," in *Romanticism and Contemporary Criticism: The Gauss Seminar and Other Papers.*

26. A very similar and, in fact, prior even to Girard, diagnosis of romanticism as a "valuable syndrome" emerged in the writings of Stanisław Brzozowski, a Polish modernist philosopher whose *Voices in the Dark: Studies on the Romantic Crisis of European Culture* brings the first definition of the romantic consciousness as dialectically self-deceptive. The eponymous "Romantic crisis" refers to the alienation of the modern individual unhappily confronted with the disenchanted world he no longer feels a part of; a true romantic knows the fact of his "conditioning" (Brzozowski uses here the German philosophical term *die Bedingtheit*), yet rebels against it in a hopeless impulse of clinging to the lost, spiritual depth of the desiccated reality. "Romanticism," Brzozowski says, "is the rebellion of a flower against its roots," which means that its deceptive surface is

kept alive by the very thing it attempts to repress. And this dialectics, diagnosed by Brzozowski as early as 1910, is already a psychoanalysis of romanticism in a nutshell.

27. Some commentators claim that this essay is the true precursorial text for Bloom's *Anxiety of Influence*, whereas, in its conclusions, it is as far from Bloom's speculations as Girard's book. Bloom, by psychoanalyzing first romantic and then modern consciousness, does something infinitely more than just adding a new touch to the de Manian aporia of the impossible *modo* (i.e., the creative moment of "here and now"). Applying Nietzsche's essay "On the Uses and Disadvantages of History for Life," as well as Baudelaire's "The Painter of Modern Life," de Man shows the paradox of modernist "forgetting," which gets implicated in history and memory the more it wants to break free from them. The more a modernist wishes "to suppress anteriority," the more he or she becomes dependent on the "literary form" which, almost via a malicious return of the repressed, betrays his or her unwanted relationship with the past. De Man, however, does not use the analogy with the return of the repressed content; this is already Bloom's invention which immediately electrifies and mobilizes the de Manian paradox, turning it into a truly Blakean "paradox of life," thanks to which there *is*, after all, movement and history—and not just, as in de Man's treatment, merely its empty "appearance."

28. The loyalty toward the romantic project of "getting away from the truth," which immediately translates into dislike for philosophy, is best visible in Bloom, who, despite high conceptual complexity of his revisionist scheme, maintains to be a philosophical virgin: for him, philosophy is nothing but a "stuffed bird," a dead thought fit only for contemplation of death, he himself never practiced and never will (Moynihan 1986, 28).

29. For Fichte, who embodies the transcendentalist creed even more perfectly than Hegel, there exists only the ultimate *either/or*: either one is an idealist and believes in the existence of an autonomous consciousness, or one is a dogmatist, that is, someone who "entirely rejects the self-sufficiency of the I, which the idealist takes as his fundamental explanatory ground, and treats the I merely as a product of things, i.e. as an accidental feature of the world" (1994, 16): "The dispute between the idealist and the dogmatist," says Fichte in his *Wissenschaftslehre*, "is actually a dispute over whether the self-sufficiency of the I should be sacrificed to that of the thing, or conversely, whether the self-sufficiency of the thing should be sacrificed to that of the I . . . the self-sufficiency of the I itself cannot co-exist with that of the thing. Only one of these two can come first; only one can be the starting point; only one can be independent. The one which comes second, just because it comes second, necessarily becomes dependent upon the one that comes first . . . *You shall not be able to obtain intellect unless you also think of it as something primary and absolute*" (ibid., 17, 22; my emphasis).

30. "Whether we are to attribute reality to unconscious wishes," writes Freud in reference to primal fantasies, "I cannot say. It must be denied, of course, to any transitional or intermediate thoughts. If we look at unconscious wishes reduced to their most fundamental and truest shape, we shall have to conclude, no doubt, that *psychical reality is a particular form of existence not to be confused with material reality*" (SE 5, 620; my emphasis).

31. It is also in this context that Bloom discovers the technique of *super-mimesis* (*MM*, 77) as a complex writing strategy which both represents and dislocates (i.e., refers to its literal sources by evasion and revision). Poems, he says, are "apotropaic litanies, systems of defensive tropes and troping defenses, and what they seek to ward off is essentially the abyss in their own assumptions about themselves" (*KC*, 111). This "abyss" is obviously the primal fantasy of self-constitution: the original lie against the literal truth which, as truth, could only result in reiteration of "more of the same," that is, in a mechanical repetition of the condition of absolute dependence.

32. We shall return to this topic later, especially in part 2, but already now it has to be said clearly that, despite a few common points, the romantic psychoanalysis we are trying to reconstruct here locates itself at the opposite pole of the Lacanian variation. The strong defense of the imaginary as a sphere which offers a welcome escape from the tyranny of truth is probably as non-Lacanian as it gets. In fact, Bloom has been often reproached for his investment in narcissistic images of the self that constitute the hubris of the strong poet, but these objections usually miss the point, for this is precisely what he wishes to assert *against* what he calls the "furious literalism" of Lacan's iconoclastic thought (*LF*, 22). For instance, Elizabeth Bruss writes: "If the theorist insists upon remaining in the Imaginary, or refuses to see the fruitlessness of inverted polarities, it is not because he has failed to understand their demystification. Rather, it is because to abandon them would be to lose their satisfactions" (1982, 328–29). And, in a way, rightly so: neither Bloom, nor any romantic whatsoever, would like to lose a promise of fantastical gratification for the sake of something so uncritically overrated as the "truth." Bloom's approach to Lacan in this matter is, to say the least, cautious and hesitant: "For the post-Enlightenment poet," he says in *Poetry and Repression*, referring to Lacan's concept of the mirror stage, "identity and opposition are the poles set up by the ephebe's self-defining act in which he creates the hypostasis of the precursor as an Imaginary Other. We can agree with Nietzsche that distinction and difference are humanly preferable to identity and opposition as categories of relationship, but unfortunately strong poets are not free to choose the Nietzschean categories in what has been, increasingly, the most competitive and overcrowded of arts. I am tempted to adopt here the notion of what Jacques Lacan calls the Imaginary Order, which has to do with a world of what Blake called the Crystal Cabinet, a Beulah-world of doubles, illusive images, mirrors and specular identification, except that Lacan says there is no Other in the Imaginary but only others, and for the ephebe there is always the imaginary Other. But I do find useful in poetic, rather than general human terms, Lacan's remark that ego, the *moi*, is essentially paranoid. The poetic ego is a kind of paranoid construct founded upon the ambivalence of opposition and identity between the ephebe and the precursor" (*PR*, 145–46). Bruss's comment suggests that Bloom's stubborn defense of the imaginary, against all knowledge of its "demystification," has no other goal than dubious "satisfactions" coming from the Crystal Cabinet of the psyche, whereas Bloom's point is that what she, faithfully after Lacan, calls "fruitlessness of inverted polarities" is not so fruitless after all, especially in the "overcrowded" realm of poetic competition. The fantasy of the self as strongly opposed to the Imaginary Other (instead of the Nietzschean symbolic mediation

of distinction and difference) has its useful function which consists in turning the poetic self-creative subject into a "paranoid construct." On my part, I would add that such "paranoization," however unpleasant it may sound, is also "useful in general human terms," for it keeps alive the crucial fantasy of self-constitution without which no sense of autonomy could ever emerge. It is, therefore, essential to understand that Lacan's attack on the imaginary order and his preference of the symbolic, where the "truth" of the overwhelming "belonging to the Other" takes place, cannot be taken simply as the final word of "demystification"; in fact, it rather reflects his disbelief in any sense of subjective autonomy, which he simply regards as a narcissistic illusion of the ego. Thus, while the Lacanians reproach Bloom for his investment in the Imaginary, he could reverse the argument and reproach them for a too one-sided investment in "demystification" and "truth," whose authority within the "psychical reality" may, in fact, be less obvious than it seems. For, if psyche is, as the romantics believe, originally based on *lie*—a willing error against the tyranny of reality principle—then such insistence on "truth," which occurs in Lacan's writings, would only demonstrate a lack of understanding for the antithetical rules governing psychic life.

33. The tarrying with the influence as both inevitable and threatening is an important leitmotif of Bloom's interpretation of Emerson, whom he sees a heir of the most urgent romantic question: How is it possible for a man who is a constant target of all sorts of distracting influences to become a self-focused, fully autonomous individual? And a skillful user of transcendental rhetoric? Indeed, Bloom suggests, Emerson is the most prominent thinker in the history of transcendentalism, for he did not accept its ideas as a philosopher but merely as a *rhetorician;* that is to say, he did not necessarily hold them to be true (as it was in the case of Fichte, who was probably the most consequential of all transcendentalists) but, in the pragmatic fashion, he treated them as handy, expedient tools for keeping alive their underlying fantasy. He was thus one of the first among the romantics to discover consciously the pragmatic use of rhetoric in making seem plausible the otherwise unfeasible ideal of full self-autonomy. The most characteristic feature of the Emersonian version of the grand Oedipal project is what Bloom calls "American Repression": "In Freud, the something evaded is any drive objectionable to ego-ideals, whereas in Emerson the something must take the name of a single drive, the thrust of anteriority, the mystifying strength of the past, which is objectionable to Emerson's prime ego-ideal, Self-Reliance . . . In the hour of vision there is nothing than can be called gratitude" (*PR*, 242). In Bloom's essay from *Poetry and Repression*, "Emerson and Whitman: The American Sublime," Emerson is portrayed as a "post-Christian" (ibid., 243) who no longer thinks according to the Puritan logic of "successive rebirths," but begins to perceive his self-reliant attempts of autocreation in terms of "successive *re-begettings of ourselves,* during this, our one life" (ibid., 243; my emphasis). The specificity, therefore, of the American Sublime consists in nothing less than in Emerson's conviction "that always he was about to become his own father" (ibid., 244): "Not merely rebirth, but the even more hyperbolical trope of self-rebegetting, is the starting point of the last Western Sublime, the great sunset of selfhood in the Evening Land," concludes Bloom (ibid.). This desire to shed radically all influences in the situation when the self crashes under "the burden of

influx" (*MM*, 167), this double knot of denial-avowal, constituting the defining feature of all fantasies, reveals Emerson's attachment to the primal narcissistic fantasy of a strong, autonomous self—precisely *as fantasy*.

34. Or, in the classical formulation from "On the Sublime": "The will is the genetic characteristic of human species, and even reason is only its eternal rule . . . All other things 'must'; man is the being that wills" (Schiller 1966, 193).

35. The deconstructive "logic" automatically produces here an argument, which says that such emphatic promotion of will does not free the subject from his incipient vicious circle: for, even if the subject is not present in the psychic life in its ready form from the start, then there must at least be *something* capable of wanting, wishing and desiring (i.e., some inchoate subject of desire). But, would this be a real objection to Bloom's romantic position? Not necessarily. First of all, the romantics do not assume a full *creatio ex nihilo* (creation out of nothing) of the subject, but merely a *crucial moment of subjectivation*, which has to pass from the extreme heteronomy of the dependent condition of the psyche in her initial state to a relative autonomy, however fantastical and unreal it may seem at the outset. Romantic point of departure is not "nothing," from which magically a subject emerges, but *die fühlende Seele*, the romantic heteronomous sensuous soul who is torn between her "weak" sense of herself and the threatening, dispersing influence. The only argument, therefore, is that without a strong fantasy of self-constitution, which rejects the initial state of dependence, this soul would stand no chance of enforcing her *Seinsgefühl* and would have to disintegrate. I argue here implicitly against Mikkel Borch-Jacobsen and his critique of "the Freudian subject," which, he claims, "like the fabled porcupine, is always there, and it stays the same, from the beginning to the end of the process, always in relation to an external model (outside-external or inside-external, it makes little difference) with which it has to conform but with which, as well, it never identifies *itself*" (1988, 123). The problem with Borch-Jacobsen's critique is that it gives Freud—or, for that matter, any "heteronomous," romantic or psychoanalytical, approach to the question of the subject—no chance, for it assumes the same intransigent Cartesian logic it tries to criticize projectively in Freud: it is not so much Freud, who treats his subject as "the fabled porcupine," as Borch-Jacobsen himself, whose reasoning follows exactly the Fichtean logic of the rigid either/or: either it is ready-made from the beginning, or "it is nothing prior to accepting in 'itself' a form that comes 'from without'" (ibid., 115); either influence is neutralized from the outset, or it cannot be called "influence," since in the primary state of subjective nothingness one cannot even assume any form of "relation." From this strictly transcendental point of view, the notion of influence is, indeed, a contradiction—but this is precisely why Freud and Bloom after him try to avoid its seemingly flawless logic.

Chapter 2

1. The following fragment from Christopher Norris's *Deconstruction: Theory and Practice* may serve here as a paradigmatic example of such treatment: "In Bloom's more recent writing *the personalist heresy* is pushed even further in

the direction of a full-blown Romantic myth of creation. Up to a point there is much in common between Bloom's 'revisionary ratios' and the practice of deconstruction. Both start out from the idea that literary history, in so far as it exists in any genuine sense, has to deal with texts in their relationship with one another, through a process of perpetual displacement which can only be described in rhetorical terms. Both dismiss the subjectivist illusion of the poet as self-possessed creator of meaning, an individual subject expressing the truths of his own authentic vision. To interpret a text is to seek out the strategies and defensive tropes by which it either confronts or evades the texts that precede it. Bloom is in accord with Derrida when he insists that textual origins are always pushed back beyond recall, in a series of hard-fought rhetorical encounters that make up the line of descent in poetic history. Where the difference emerges is in Bloom's countervailing argument that the 'strong poet' must always strive to create at least a working-space of presence for his own imagination. In other words, *Bloom wants to halt the process of deconstruction at a point where it is still possible to gauge a poet's creative stature in terms of his overriding will to expression"* (1982, 117, 118–19; my emphasis).

2. Here I will quote just one of the innumerable complaints Bloom has levied against Low Deconstruction, which now fuels New Historicism, a charge that is all the more bitter for referring to the reading of Shakespeare, Bloom's secular God: "In 'French Shakespeare' (as I shall go on calling it), the procedure is to begin with a political stance all your own, far out and away from Shakespeare's plays, and then to locate some marginal bit of English Renaissance social history that seems to sustain your stance. Social fragment in hand, you move in from outside upon the poor play, and find some connection, however established, between your supposed social fact and Shakespeare's words. It would cheer me to be persuaded that I am parodying the operations of the professors and directors of what I call 'Resentment'—those critics who value theory over the literature itself—but I have given a plain account of the going thing, whether in the classroom or on the stage" (*S*, 9). Having no objections to this portrait, I simply wonder whether this Shakespeare is truly "French," for no French theorist—including Foucault, who, like a black magnet, seems to attract most of Bloom's rancor—would allow himself such crude ideological reductionism. Low Deconstruction is, with New Historicism, mostly an American invention, or, to paraphrase Bloom, a secular American, academic religion that is itself a belated, puritanical version of a Marxism that America never really had. This quarrel, therefore, takes place not so much between "deconstruction" and "traditional humanism" as between reduction and aestheticism, that is, between "gender-and-power freaks" (*S*, 10) and a "hermetic aesthete" (*WSW*, 36). This confusion partly explains Bloom's ambivalence toward the deconstructive thought which he sometimes perceives as an easily dissmissible academic folly and sometimes as an interesting sparring partner in theory with whom it is productive to fight. Thus, on the one hand, he can say: "I have no relation to deconstruction. I never did have, I don't have now, and I never will have. Nothing is more alien to me than deconstruction"—and, on the other, he can also admit, referring to Derrida and de Man, that deconstructionists are "my remote cousins, intellectually speaking" (Salusinszky 1987, 68, 51).

3. A related opinion was uttered by Richard Rorty in *Achieving Our Country*, although in passing and in a way which lacks the philosophical substance we shall try to provide here. Rorty also carefully distinguishes between High and Low Deconstruction, treating the latter as a cynical, antiromantic, antivisionary stance of "knowingness," "a state of soul which prevents shudders of awe and makes one immune to romantic enthusiasm" (1997, 126): "Although I prefer 'knowingness' to Bloom's word 'resentment,'" Rorty continues, "my view of these substitutions is pretty much the same as his. Bloom thinks that many rising young teachers of literature can ridicule anything but can hope for nothing, can explain everything but can idolize nothing. Bloom sees them as converting the study of literature into what he calls 'one more dismal social science'—and thereby turning departments of literature into isolated academic backwaters" (ibid., 127). For Rorty—as for Bloom—the fundamental axis of all distinctions is "romanticism" versus "dryness." Romanticism is: "charisma, genius, romance" (ibid., 128), and an ironic vocabulary which is aware of its imperfection, issuing from contingency, individual bias, and the personal experience of hope, love, and awe. "Dryness," on the other hand, is: "logic, debunking, and knowingness" (ibid., 129), and a nonironic vocabulary which claims "to know it all" and see things to their true cynical core. Rorty is also quite unorthodox in the distribution of his sympathies: he reveres Bloom and Derrida for being "romantic utopians," while dismissing as "dry" de Man, Foucault, and Jameson. Though I rather doubt if Derrida is truly a romantic utopian, the axis Rorty proposes is worth maintaining, since it takes us out of the dreariness of so-called party loyalties. In the end, it seems true that Bloom and Derrida have more in common than Derrida and de Man, or Derrida and Fredric Jameson. This affinity, although approached from a completely different angle, was also remarked by Graham Allen, who in his *Poetics of Conflict*, a book devoted to Harold Bloom's critical theory, wrote: "If Frye can be said to have reintegrated the formalist project with its Romantic antecedents, then Bloom's work can be read as continuing that movement toward a Romantic formalism by dragging the Fryean-Eliotic emphasis on the dynamic function of interpoetic relations into a post-structuralist context. While the defining terms in Frye's criticism remain 'identity,' 'progression,' 'liberation' and 'similarity,' the key terms in Bloom's version of the 'literary universe' are the characteristically post-structuralist ones of difference, discontinuity and rupture" (1994, xxi).

4. A similar attitude was expressed recently by Martin McQuillan, who in his contribution to *The Salt Companion to Harold Bloom*, says: "The discussion which arises from Bloom's reading demonstrates a number of concerns about deconstruction which are only now beginning to become apparent to less perceptive readers of Derrida than Bloom" (2007, 236).

5. In an interview with Robert Moynihan (Moynihan 1986, 28).

6. "Unless we are philosophers, and I decidedly am not," writes Bloom in his latest book, *Where Shall Wisdom Be Found?* (50), we will not see any lure in Plato's *Republic*, which, for Bloom, is "the ultimate ancestor of all the current commissars of Resentment who throng our academy, and who zealously continue the destruction of literary study" (36). Plato is thus "fascinating bad news" (51), which attracts us perversely via his conceptual combination of ultimate

truth, death, and perfect order. "We cannot all become philosophers," Bloom continues, "but we can follow the poets in their ancient quarrel with philosophy, which may be a way of life but whose study is death" (62).

7. We should definitely count Richard Rorty among these dissenters: his antiphilosophical stance, though uttered within a philosophical discourse, is deeply indebted to Bloom's para-Nietzschean creation of the "strong poet" who says the ultimate *Yes* to his condition of contingency. "Contingency," Bloom says, "can be grasped only by poets, and not by philosophers, theologians, or historians, because only poets achieve self-creation by way of the recognition of contingency, whereas philosophers and historians lust to attain universality by transcending contingency" (in the foreword to Yerushalmi's *Zakhor*, xxi).

8. The best account of the hereditary link between Adorno and deconstruction is Peter Dews's *Logics of Disintegration*, which shows in detail the latter's moments of indebtedness to, as well as departure from, Adorno.

9. Indeed, the slightest implication of "psychologism" usually serves Bloom's critics to circumvent his arguments; once Bloom is declared to be "deeply psychological" and "personalizing" (Arac 1985, 349), or, worse, to have "psychological bias" (Perloff 1978, 372), it is somehow self-evident that he is excluded from *any* possible discussion within the deconstructive paradigm. This "self-evidence," however, is based on such theoretical shortcuts that it itself can—and should—be dismissed as a kind of ideological bias itself.

10. "I didn't say that there was no center"—said Derrida during the session following his presentation of "Structure, Sign and Play in the Discourse of the Human Sciences"—"that we could get along without the center. I believe that the center is a function, not a being—a reality, but a function. And this function is absolutely indispensable. The subject is absolutely indispensable. I don't destroy the subject: I situate it . . . It is a question of knowing where it comes from and how it functions" (1972, 271).

11. "There is nothing outside the text," a famous sentence-manifesto from *Of Grammatology* (Derrida 1976, 158).

12. These two disparate understandings of Derrida's celebrated saying are best reflected in the contrast between the bold metaphysical statement, which says that textuality is a universal *modus essendi* (mode of existence), i.e., everything exists as submitted to the law of *différance*—and the skeptical, cautious thesis which doubts expressive power of language itself and approaches texts as self-enclosed, nonreferential entitities.

13. See especially two essays from *Blindness and Insight*: "Ludwig Binswanger and the Sublimation of the Self" and "The Literary Self as Origin: The Work of Georges Poulet."

14. The metaphor of "living on" or survival in the contaminated, heterogeneous, endangering realm of textuality is very significant to Derrida: see, for instance, his "Living On: Borderlines" in *Deconstruction and Criticism*.

15. He was, as Christopher Norris rightly pointed out, deeply "unfair to Kierkegaard" and his anti-Hegelian attempts to find an existentially meaningful subject; see Norris 1988, 156.

16. On de Man's side: "The Rhetoric of Blindness: Jacques Derrida's Reading of Rousseau," an essay which was rightly summed up by Wlad Godzich as

"domesticating Derrida" (in *The Yale Critics*)—and on Derrida's side: *Memoires: For Paul de Man* above all, where Derrida stubbornly refuses to acknowledge the post-Hegelian, absolute negative of de Man's notion of aporia and tries to pull it to his own, more "playful" camp. It is clear that they both completely misrecognized their respective standpoint: de Man misinterpreted Derrida in his epistemologically rather traditional manner—while Derrida misrepresented de Man after his own image, that is, as a postepistemologist.

17. *Pirke Aboth*, 5, 25: "Ben Bag Bag said, Turn it (the Torah) and turn it over again, for everything is in it, and contemplate it, and wax grey and old over it, and stir not from it, for thou canst have no better rule than this."

18. With only one exception—that of Pete de Bolla, whose fine work on Bloom's diachronic rhetoric skillfully avoids any "personalist heresy" (see his *Harold Bloom: Towards Historical Rhetorics*)—all the other critics begin their analysis of Bloom's writings with the sacramental comparison to Freud's "family romance." Howard Felperin, much more sympathetic to Bloom than de Man, nevertheless states: "For Harold Bloom ... the text is the battleground of Oedipal agon" (1985, 31). The same description appears, less kindly, in Norris and Culler, where it immediately leads to another, even deeper confusion in which Bloom, with his "paternalistic scheme of poetic revision," seems to be sinning against feminist criticism. "Feminists critics have shown considerable interest in Harold Bloom's model of poetic creation," says Culler in *On Deconstruction*, "because it makes explicit the sexual connotations of authorship and authority. This oedipal scenario, in which one becomes a poet by struggling with a poetic father for possession of the muse, indicates the problematic situation of a woman who would be a poet. What relation can she have to tradition?" (Culler 1982, 60ff.). Commenting on Gilbert and Gubar's *Madwoman in the Attic: The Woman Writer and the Nineteenth Century Literary Imagination*, in which this confusion originates, Barbara Johnson confirms that, indeed, Bloom's "critical system is itself a garden of parricidal delights" and that his revisionary ratios are "dependent upon a linear patriarchal filiation" (1985, 105). Norris, in the same vein, asks rhetorically: "How this theory might apply to the *woman* poet—since its terms are *on the face of it* so exclusively Oedipal—remains very much an open question, and one which Bloom never addresses" (1982, 117). At least Norris has the good grace to imply the possibly metaphorical nature of Bloom's Oedipal idiom (which would make direct addressing of the woman-poet issue spurious) but somehow fails to make the connection. Needless to say, I regard these reproaches as gross misunderstandings. Probably the best way to see the Oedipal struggle as merely a metaphorical framework of the agon is offered by Gianni Vattimo, who in *The Adventure of Difference* talks apropos Nietzsche about "the Oedipal structure of time" (1993, 2). Such approach emphasizes the temporal dimension of the agon and refers it not only to the personal intricacies of the Sophoclean tragedy but also to the more original myth of parricide (i.e., to the slaying of Chronos, the Father-Time).

19. See, for instance, Frank Lentricchia's *After the New Criticism*, p. 347.

20. The first decisive rupture between cogito and sum is declared by Friedrich Schelling in his early text, *The First System of German Idealism* (an essay once wrongly attributed to Hegel). In criticizing Fichte, Schelling proposes to

concentrate not on self-consciousness but on the experience of one's existence, *Ich bin*, which, when chosen as a philosophical foundation, will lead toward different conclusions than the choice of *Ich denke*. This romantic *I am*, which has to fight for the right to self-assertion, lies at the very core of Bloom's poetico-critical enterprise: "Following Nietzsche," he says in "Freud's Concepts of Defense and the Poetic Will," "I have suggested that the poetic will is an argument against time, revengefully seeking to substitute 'It is' for 'it was.' Yet this argument always splits in two, because the poetic will needs to make another *outrageous substitution, of 'I am' for 'It is.'* Both parts of the argument are quests for priority" (*LF,* 6).

21. More on the narrating art of one's *Bildung* in the chapter "Intricate Evasions, or the Poetic Will-to-Ignorance."

22. "The individual cannot be deduced from thought," says Adorno against Hegel, "yet the core of individuality would be comparable to those utterly individuated works of art which spurn all schemata and whose analysis will rediscover universal moments in their extreme individuation—a participation in typicality that is hidden from the participants themselves" (2003, 163). Since no ontology can accommodate the paradox of the individual name—the universal moment in the extreme individuation, as well as the other way around: the singular moment in the extreme generality—it can only be approached via aesthetics, and Nietzschean aesthetics in particular, which openly endorses art as an error against the tyranny of truth. In order to bring down the sand castle of idealist philosophy, one should therefore not give up on the subject altogether, but *use its strength* to come up with a new, postphilosophical notion of subjectivity. And *the strength* of the subject, big enough to resist the pitfalls of theory, can only reside in the name: "The subject as ideology lies under a spell," continues Adorno, "from which nothing but *the name of subjectivity* will free it" (ibid., 182). This will also prove to be a natural choice for Bloom.

23. Felperin very aptly comments on this notion of displacement as a kind of a third way between Freudian return and Derridean dissemination: "But even if the wound inheres ineradicably, incurably in the word for Bloom and Hartman, they have none the less found ways of *deferring the presence of that pain* that are distinctly deconstructive" (1985, 121; my emphasis). I will develop this argument more fully in chapter 4 "The Davharocentric Subject."

24. See Harold Bloom, *Hamlet: Poem Unlimited,* as well as the chapter on Hamlet in *Shakespeare: Invention of the Human.*

25. Which, again, is the charge raised by Paul de Man in his review of *The Anxiety of Influence.* Clearly, the notion of vitalism has very different connotations for de Man and Bloom; while the former associates it automatically with the German tradition of *Lebensphilosophie,* with its ecstatic naturalistic overtones, the latter relates it to the Spinozian "meditation on life," which does not necessarily lead to the philosophical fetishism of nature, so typical for the post-Nietzschean continental life-philosophers. The idea of life that emerges from Bloom's writings differs radically from the metaphysical concept of *Leben* championed by Nietzsche, Dilthey, Simmel, Ernst Jünger, or Bataille: his notion of life does not imply a quasi-transcendental subject of nature or naturalized history, to which the individual human subject must subordinate to join "the stream of

life." Quite the contrary, in Bloom the bearer of life is always a living Particular which struggles to delay the moment of identification with *any* totality, nature and culture included. Whereas in the tradition of *Lebensphilosophie*—seemingly paradoxically but, in fact, in full harmony with its underlying Hegelianism—the elevation of Life as a philosophical category is always bought with the death of the concrete individual, putting an end to the "illusion" of its separation from the living whole.

26. More on the crucial difference between vitalism and naturalism in chapter 6: "Fair Crossings: From Mere Life to More Life."

27. I render this fragment in my own translation. The original runs as follows: "Die fühlende Totalität ist als Individualität wesentlich dies, sich in sich selbst zu unterscheiden und zum Urteil in sich zu erwachen, nach welchem sie besondere Gefühle hat und als Subjekt in Beziehung auf diese ihre Bestimmungen ist. Es ist in diese Besonderheit der Empfindungen versenkt, und zugleich schliesst es durch die Idealität des Bosenderen sich darin mit sich als subjektiven Eins zusammen. Es ist auf dieser Weise Selbstgefühl—und ist dies sogleich nur im besonderen Gefühl ... [Es ist] noch der Krankheit fähig, dass es in einer Besonderheit seines Selbst beharren bleibt, welche es nicht zur Idealität zu verarbeiten und zu überwinded vermag" (Hegel 1905, 360; §§ 407–8).

28. "Dies Fürsichsein der freien Allgemeinheit ist das höhere Erwachen der Seele zum Ich der abstrakten Allegemeinheit ... welche die natürliche Totalität seiner Bestimmungen als ein Objekt, eine ihm äussere Welt, von sich ausschliesst und sich darauf bezieht" (Hegel 1905, 369; § 412). This Hegelian picture of individual life as a contradiction which can only be sublated by death—or the negative thought imitating death—has its contemporary fascinating counterpart in Lacan's vision of human life as an error which can also be resolved by a kind of death, that is, the individual's submission to the Other of Language. The Lacanian error occurs at the cross-section of two fundamental fantasies that govern the primary imaginary sphere and inevitably clash with one another: the fantasy of one's mirror image and the fantasy of the cut-up body, *l'imago du corps morcelé*. Geoffrey Hartman, in "Psychoanalysis: The French Connection," combining Lacan with Derrida's *Glas*, ingeniously grafted on the mirror stage an "image of the proper name," *l'imago du nom propre*, expressing oneness, singularity, and integrity—as opposed to the picture of body dispersed, anarchic, manifold and nonunifiable. As long as these fantasies are both *images*, they are doomed to stay in stark opposition to one another; as soon, however, as they become *signifiers* within the symbolic order, their positions begin to shift in a process of endless mediation. The regulative ideal of this process is, of course, *nom-du-père*, the-name-of-the-father, which signifies the impossible: a perfect synthesis and reconciliation of the name and what it names, of the word and its reference. Lacan, following Hegel, discourages us from plunging into this desire and advocates "moving on"—but it would seem that strong poets are precisely those who refuse to relinquish the desire and long more strongly than others for the synthesis which has all the redemptive power of the biblical "scene of nomination." Once they become full names, not just empty tokens, they begin to heal by naming everything else, as in Stevens's definition of poetry as "health, both the healer and the namer of the thing healed."

29. Oscar Wilde, who deeply affected Bloom's mode of criticism, is in this respect even more antithetical than Nietzsche. In "The Decay of Lying" he openly opposes art to nature by saying that "art is our spirited protest, our gallant attempt to teach Nature her proper place" (1902, 2). Wilde is a romantic vitalist violently protesting against any form of naturalism with its positivistic cult of factuality: And if something cannot be done to check, or at least to modify, our monstrous worship of facts," he complains, "art will become sterile, and Beauty will pass away from the land . . . Certainly we are a degraded race, and have sold our birthright for a mess of facts" (ibid., 12, 26). Antithetical defiance against nature and its reductive, literal truths—note also the very Bloomian motif of contrasting Esau's sober "naturalism" with Jacob's heroic struggle against the natural—pushes Wilde to praise the skill of lying as the only way out of the naturalistic oppression: "The only form of Lying that is absolutely beyond reproach," he says, "is Lying for its own sake, and the highest development of this is, as we have already pointed out, Lying in Art" (ibid., 74).

30. His proposition, however, was quickly met with the symmetrical contempt of the other camp, and not so genial at that. In his review of Bloom's *The Breaking of the Vessels*, Daniel O'Hara could not restrain himself from pouring scorn on Bloom's pathos of originality, without giving a second thought to its philosophical foundations: "Poetry speaks the language of the will," he says, "with the will being an apocalyptic antithetical force at odds with all that is not itself, even with its own earlier representations, since this antithetical will desires the impossible: above all else to be itself alone, the great original to top all great originals, like that Alien God the Gnostics relentlessly attempted to envision." And he concludes, "The human-all-too human which would be a god—can we really afford this silly vision of literary creation any longer?" (1982, 101).

31. "The word *meaning*," says Bloom in the opening of his essay "The Breaking of Form," goes back to a root that signifies 'opinion' or 'intention,' and is closely related to the word *moaning*. A poem's meaning is a poem's complaint . . . Poems instruct us in how they break form to bring about meanings, so as to utter a complaint, a moaning intended to be all their own" (*DC*, 1).

32. The notion of encumbrance and and the lack of it in the manic episode, which bears some resemblance to Derrida's freeplay of signifiers, was the subject of Lacan's famous seminar on anxiety: "In mania," he said, "what is involved is the non-functioning of the *o*, and not merely its misrecognition. It is through this that the subject is no longer weighed down (*lesté*) by any *o*, and sometimes, without any possibility of freedom, is delivered over to the infinite metonymy and pure play of the signifying chain" (Weber 1991, 160). Samuel Weber, in his *Return to Freud*, comments: "The difficulties involved in the notion of the *o* are thus the measure of its importance. It holds the line, as it were, between the symbolic gone wild and the imaginary gone wrong, between the infinite metonymizing of signifiers and the unending mirroring of narcissistic identification" (ibid., 160). In the next two chapters, we will try to define this uneasy balance as the crucial difference between displacement on the one hand versus dissemination and return on the other.

33. Such is, according to Christopher Norris, the chief difference between Bloom and Derrida: "His argument," says Norris in *Deconstruction: Theory and Practice*, "shrewdly undermines the deconstructionist position by insisting on the

conflict of wills to expression behind the encounter of text with text. This struggle, he urges, must not be lost sight of in the undifferentiated merging of 'free
play' envisaged by Derridean deconstruction . . . Bloom is equally un-Derridean
in the use he makes of Freudian motifs and analogies . . . Derrida's reading of
Freud gives some idea of what Bloom most objects to in the practice of deconstruction. *It is a reading that totally discounts the psychic drama,* the conflict of will
and motive, which Bloom seizes on by way of analogy with the poet's 'anxiety
of influence' "(1982, 122–23; my emphasis). A similar protocol of difference was
drawn by Geoffrey Hartman in his already quoted preface to *Deconstruction and
Criticism:* "Derrida, de Man, and Miller are certainly boa-deconstructors, merciless and consequent, though each enjoys his own style of disclosing again and
again the 'abysm' of words. But Bloom and Hartman are barely deconstructionists. They even write against it on occasion. Though they understand Nietzsche
when he says 'the deepest pathos is still aesthetic play,' *they have a stake in that
pathos: its persistence, its psychological provenance.* For them the ethos of literature is
not dissociable from its pathos, whereas for deconstructionist criticism literature
is precisely that use of language which can *purge pathos,* which can show that it
too is figurative, ironic or aesthetic" (*DC,* ix; my emphasis).

34. We shall resume this difficult issue in the last chapter of the book, "Tainted
Love."

35. More on this in part 2, chapter 3: "Life and Death in Deconstruction."

36. "The arid wisdom which acknowledges nothing new under the sun," they
write in the *Dialectic of Enlightenment,* a piece of incantatory poetry deeply influenced by Koheletian pessimism, practically a book of Kohelet rewritten and
revised for our times, "because all the pieces in the meaningless game have been
played out, all the great thoughts have been thought, all the possible discoveries
can be construed in advance, and human beings are defined by self-preservation
through adaptation—this barren wisdom merely reproduces the fantastic doctrine it rejects: the sanction of fate which, through retribution, *incessantly
reinstates what always was.* Whatever might be different is made the same. This
is the verdict which critically sets the boundaries to possible experience. The
identity of everything with everything is bought at the cost that nothing can at
the same time be identical to itself" (Horkheimer 2002, 8). And Bloom's own
description of our modern world as a Gnostic *kenoma* fully converges with this
arid wisdom: "Our existing world," he says in *Omens of Millennium,* "is called the
kenoma, or cosmological emptiness, by the ancient Gnostics: a world of repetitive time, meaningless reproduction, futurelessness, Generation X; then, now,
and forever. What we have become is demon-ridden, trapped in a sense of fate
ruled by hostile angels called archons, the princes of our captivity" (*OM,* 239).

37. Lest this defense of solipsism should once again bring the charge of egoism, I will repeat that the solipsistic rhetoric on the part of the strong poet is
nothing but a precondition of a Vision which *struggles* to maintain all the "healing" properties of the Romantic Image. Solipsistic defense is simply a part of
the struggle in which the subject tries to "heal" his own ontological paradox and
become a true singular being surrounded by equally singular phenomena.

38. See his "On the Language as Such and on the Language of Man," in
Reflections.

39. Franz Kafka, *Die Aphorismen: Bertachtungen über Sünde, Leid, Hoffnung und den wahren Weg* (*The Aphorisms: Reflections on Sin, Suffering, Hope and a True Way*).

40. "Poetry whose hidden subject is the anxiety of influence," writes Bloom, "is naturally of a Protestant temper, for the Protestant God always seems to isolate His children in the terrible double bind of two great injunctions: 'Be like Me' and 'Do not presume to be too like Me'" (*AI*, 152). Bloom calls this predicament Protestant and not Hebrew, for the latter is, indeed, more dialectical; one could say that, by resorting to writing, a poet caught in the "Protestant" contradiction begins to avail himself of the "Hebrew" strategy.

41. In the preface to *The Western Canon* Bloom calls this will to displacement "a desire to be elsewhere": "Literature is not merely language," he says. "It is also will to figuration, the motive for metaphor that Nietzsche once defined as the desire to be different, the desire to be elsewhere. This partly means to be different from oneself, but primarily, I think, to be different from the metaphors and images of the contingent works that are one's heritage: the desire to write greatly is the desire to be elsewhere, in a time and place of one's own, in an originality that must compound with inheritance, with the anxiety of influence" (*WC*, 12).

42. In *Saving the Text* Hartman speculates about *imago du nom propre* as a secret fantasy of the writers who wish to give their names secret meanings, that is, to individuate them, but also to displace them from an often traumatic actual scene of nomination and to transform denunciation into annunciation. "The literature, he says, is the elaboration of a specular name" (1981, 111). This applies exceptionally well to the case of Jean Genet, to whom Derrida's *Glas* is devoted, but also to the case of Walter Benjamin, who, once gravely ill, wrote a feverish fantasy about his hidden "true" name—Agesilaus Santander—an angelic-demonic compound both deriving and not deriving from the imaginary scene of nomination Benjamin thought to have taken place in his early childhood when he was supposedly given a secret Hebrew name by his parents in the synagogue (ibid., 112–13; see also Gershom Scholem, "Walter Benjamin und sein Engel" ["Walter Benjamin and His Angel"]). Also, Derrida, in *On the Name*, suggests that fame— *renome*—is associated with the act of renaming—*renommer*—in which poets and writers manage to erase the initial, ambivalent scene of nomination and give to themselves a new name, a hyper-name, or a surname—*sur-nom* (1995a, xiv–xv). This act of self-nomination, overshadowing the original scene of instruction, is the clear analogue of the ruling fantasy of the Bloomian strong poet who wishes to be self-engendered, that is, "to be the father of oneself."

43. Compare also this fragment from *Poetry and Repression:* "I find useful enough," writes Bloom, "Paul Ricoeur's summary of primal repression, as meaning 'that we are always in the mediate, in the already expressed, the already said,' for this is the traumatic predicament that results in what I have termed the anxiety of influence, the awareness that what might be called, analogically, the infantile needs of the beginning imagination had to be met by the primal fixation of a Scene of Instruction" (*PR*, 232).

44. This ingenious punning was invented by Eric Santner, who, in his *On the Psychotheology of Everyday Life*, a book already inspired by Bloom's ideas, writes: "One might supplement Freud's structural model of the psyche with

another topology that I would like to abbreviate as the 'Ego and the Ibid.' What I mean by this bit of punning is that the *libidinal* component of one's attachment to the predicates securing one's symbolic identity must also be thought of as being 'ibidinal': a symbolic investiture not only endows the subject with new predicates; it also calls forth a largely unconscious 'citation' of the authority guaranteeing, legitimating one's rightful enjoyment of those predicates (that is at least in part what it means to 'internalize' a new symbolic identity). But because that authority is itself in some sense 'magical,' that is, unsubstantiated, without ultimate foundation in a final ground qua substantive reason, this 'ibidity' is, in the final analysis, a citation of lack, and so never settled once and for all" (Santner 2001, 50). We shall return later to the question of the precursory authority and its inherent "lack" in the last chapter of this book.

Chapter 3

1. In Marjorie Perloff's perhaps a bit too unkind words: "Then suddenly the bubble seems to have burst. By the mid-1980s, younger poets were no longer lining up to receive the Bloomian accolade, and graduate students seemed barely to know who Bloom was" (1992, 161). But also a much more sympathetic critic of Bloom, Peter de Bolla admits that "there has been no critical school or methodology developed in the wake of Bloom's work, no set of theoretical texts published in a series on 'Anxiety' or 'Influence,' no critical vogue called the Bloom School, no Modern Language Association panels on revisionism" (1988, 8).

2. I am grateful to Minae Mizumura for reminding me about the significance of the gesture of self-renunciation which runs through the whole of de Man's theoretical progress. In her eloquent article "Renunciation," she proves the central importance of such notions as "sacrifice" and "self-offering" for the formulation of de Man's unique technique of reading. She points to the tension between temptation and renunciation in which "renunciation is valorized not only as a 'difficult' act but also as a 'painful' act, the one that accompanies 'an infinite pain,' whereas succumbing to temptation is described through unflattering images of 'lethargy' and 'sleep,' which only evoke a vegetablelike obtuseness" (1985, 87).

3. We find an analogous critique of objective reason in Witold Gombrowicz, who at about the same time rebelled, with equal rancor, against the predominance of the "old and petrified Parisian culture" and sported the image of an "eternally immature youth," engaged in an agon closely resembling the one in which Bloom's ephebe wrestles with his dead precursors. "When I incessantly strive towards myself, they still, and for a long time already, want nothing else but self-destruction: to be able, once for all, to renounce themselves. Object. Objectivism. Some kind of askesis, almost medieval. Some kind of 'purity' they find so attractive in dehumanization. But their objectivism is not really ice-cold (though they wished it to be so), it stings with aggression. Yes, it is a provocation" (1988, 232; in my translation).

4. "Technically correct rhetorical readings," writes de Man in "The Resistance to Theory," "may be boring, monotonous, predictable and unpleasant, but they

are irrefutable. They are also totalizing (and potentially totalitarian) ... They are theory and not theory at the same time, the universal theory of the impossibility of theory" (1986, 19).

5. This untoward but pragmatically operative consequence was also confirmed by M. H. Abrams in his critique of the deconstructive method of Derrida, whom he reproaches for using a "doublespeak" which simultaneously undermines and asserts the possibility of having texts under control: "In this deconstruction of logocentric language," says Abrams in *Doing Things with Texts*, "he assumes the stance that this language works, that he can adequately understand what other speakers and writers mean, and that competent auditors and readers will adequately understand him. In this double process of construing in order to deconstruct he perforce adopts words from the logocentric system; but he does so, he tell us, only 'provisionally,' or *sous rature*, 'under erasure.' At times he reminds us of this pervasive procedure by writing a key word but crossing it out, leaving it 'legible' yet 'effaced'—an ingenious doublespeak, adapted from Heidegger, that enables him to eat his words yet use them too" (1991, 277).

6. This ambivalence was perfectly spotted by Carol Jacobs in her essay on de Man in *Telling Time*, where she—equally ambivalently—praises him for both being able and unable to withstand it; by making a witty association with Lacan's description of a symptom in his late seminar *Encore*, she spots this "encore" in de Man's writings as his own symptomatic compulsion to repeat. We are soon going to use this psychoanalytic association in a broader manner.

7. This is why Bloom would call de Man an "Over-Reader," thus paying him back for his dismissive description of himself as a "new vitalist": "Deconstruction is reading," says Bloom in *Wallace Stevens*, "but this is Over-reading, or the reading of an Over-Man, who knows simultaneously how to fulfill and to transcend the text, or rather how to make the text expose the *aporia* between its self-fulfillment and its self-transcendence ... Rhetoric, considered as a system of tropes, yields much more readily to analysis than does rhetoric considered as persuasion, for persuasion, in poetry, takes us into a realm that also includes the lie" (*WS*, 386). With no ostentation and backdoors, the master of reading, the Over-Reader himself, leaves the building of language and watches safely from outside as its ungrounded edifice is falling down.

8. The reference is to Derrida's critical reading of Lacan's "Seminar on *The Purloined Letter*" in his "Le facteur de la verité" (in *The Postcard*), otherwise known as "The Purveyor of Truth," the text we have already tackled a propos the difference (or the subtler, less evident *différance*?) between return, displacement, and dissemination. Here, however, we unambiguously side with Derrida's critique of Lacan as *le facteur de la verité* whose "letter always arrives at its destination." Barbara Johnson in "The Frame of Reference: Poe, Lacan, Derrida" tries to rescue Lacan from Derrida's assault by claming that the sentence "a letter always arrives at its destination" contains an irreducible polysemy: "It can mean 'the only message I can read is the one I send,' 'wherever the letter is, is its destination,' 'when a letter is read, it reads the reader,' 'the repressed always returns,' 'I exist only as a reader of the other,' 'the letter has no destination,' and 'we all die'" (1978, 170). Yet, in fact, all these readings can be shown to gravitate around the same, dark center and form one cluster, or a chain: there is only one

signifier which unlocks my trauma, which is strictly mine; the message which I send to myself is in the place of the real which is the only place which does not move; it is not me who reads this message but the other way around, for here it is truth itself which speaks; this truth reveals my absolute dependence on the other; there is no destination for there is no movement, no development, no psychic evolution; and the ultimate truth of all this is that we are, in fact, already dead. If this sounds a little cryptic at the moment, it will hopefully become clear in the course of this chapter.

9. Although it seems that among Lacanians, what exactly is the right question of the hysteric is a highly controversial issue. Daniel Lagache, for instance, as well as Laplanche and Deleuze, would argue that the problem of being dead or alive belongs rather to the obsessive, whereas the hysteric is concerned with the question of his/her sexual identification. This debate, however, is of no primary importance for us. Considering the fact—which will become clearer soon— that Bloom's strong poet goes through *all* possible "pathological" positions in order to postpone and complicate his relation with the Master-precursor, *all* the grand questions of the unconscious, including the sexual identity, become also his questions. Yet the most essential one is the issue which starts the revisionary duel, namely: *who is alive?*

10. "This universality," says Hegel in *Phenomenology of Spirit*, "which the individual *as such* attains is *pure being, death;* it is a state which has been reached *immediately*, in the course of Nature, not the result of action *consciously done*" (1977, 270). This state, however, can also be reached by an action consciously done, that is by an act of representation which imitates but also anticipates the course of Nature in depriving the individual thing of its particularity: "That it is perceived or heard," writes Hegel, "means that its real existence dies away" (ibid., 309).

11. This fusion of Hegel with Heidegger would not be possible, however, without a strong misreading of Hegel's phenomenology, which gave a peculiar twist to the figure of the Master as the only one who can truly experience death, accept the verdict of finitude, and carry this experience into the domain of pure thinking. Kojève's denigration of the Slave, as the one who shuns death and is thus forced to work, clearly conflicted with Hegel's own intentions, but at the same time chimed well with the decline of hope for a positive conclusion of the Hegelian dialectical process of history. In his *Introduction to the Reading of Hegel*, Kojève repeats now and again that the true realization of human life *as human* "is not possible without a Fight, without a social war, without the risk of life. This is true for reasons that are in some sense 'metaphysical'" (1969, 69). The Slave, therefore, if he is to emancipate himself from the condition of slavery, "*must* become a Warrior—that is, he must introduce death into his existence, by consciously and voluntarily risking his life, while knowing that he is mortal" (ibid.). And, probably in silent praise of the Soviet revolution, he concludes his reasoning with a disturbingly un-Hegelian note: "It is in the Terror that the State is born in which the 'satisfaction' is attained" (ibid.). In fact, not only this conclusion but the very structure of the whole argument is a severe departure from Hegel, who—as we yet shall come back to this—assigned to the Slave *his own* version of the awakening death experience, not through *risk* but through

fear. Nevertheless, it was the Kojèvian elevation of the Master and his fear-less tarrying with the deadly negative which left an indelible mark on Kojève's pupils, also partly for the reason that it could be well appropriated by the Heideggerian, equally "heroic" frame of *Sein zum Tode* (being-unto-death). This theme of double influence—of Kojève's *Denken des Herrn* (thinking of Master) and Heidegger's *Todesdenken* (thinking of death)—is very lucidly presented by Peter Bürger in his *Ursprung des postmodernen Denkens* (*The Origins of Postmodern Thought*), which nicely links surrealist glorification of suicide, Bataille's notion of expenditure, Blanchot's belief in the self-sacrifice of the writer, as well as Foucault's and Barthes' "death of the author" with the "masterly" strain devel-oped by these two precursors. On the strong connection between death and language in modern philosophy, see also a very instructive book of Giorgio Agamben, *Language and Death: The Place of Negativity*, in which he fully endorses the Hegelian-Heideggerian claim that, in human life, only death can deliver the negativity which is the necessary condition of thinking.

12. This is why the English translators of Blanchot's pun-title decided to enhance its negative side, and rendered it simply as *Step Not Beyond*. They have made this "step" probably in accordance with the suggestions of Derrida, who wrote on Blanchot's *Pas au dela* in three texts, coming from around the same period: Blanchot published his work in 1973, while "Pas," "Living On: Border Lines" and "The Law of the Genre" came out in 1975. Derrida emphasizes the aporetical nature of the Blanchotian *pas* as the nonstepping step, *pas sans pas*, "step, not" (1979, 103). He also finds *pas* as a hypogram interwoven as an obsessive phonic trace in other titles of Blanchot, like *Part de feu* (*Part of Fire*) or *L'espace littéraire* (*Space of Literature*).

13. In *Aporias*, a book explicitly devoted to the raise of *thanatology* as a prop-erly philosophical discipline, Derrida comments on the significance of the "turn" made by Blanchot: "Whan Blanchot constantly repeats—and it is a long com-plaint and not a triumph of life—the impossible dying, the impossibility, alas, of dying, he says at once the same thing and something completely different from Heidegger. It is just a question of knowing in which sense (in the sense of direc-tion and trajectory) one reads the expression of the possibiliby of impossibility. If death, the most proper possibility of *Dasein*, is the possibility of its impossibil-ity, death becomes the most improper possibility and the most ex-propriating, the most inauthenticating one" (1994c, 77).

14. Giorgio Agamben comments on this crucial moment in Hegel's dialec-tics in his *Language and Death*: "In dying, animal finds its voice, it exalts the soul in one voice, and, in this act, it expresses and preserves itself as *dead*. Thus the animal voice is the *voice of death*. Here the genitif should be understood in both an objective and a subjective sense. 'Voice (and memory) of death' means: the voice is death, which preserves and recalls the living as dead, and it is, at the same time, and immediate trace and memory of death, pure negativity" (2006, 45). And while an animal, which, dying, utters its final cry, its moment of death becomes immediately incorporated into natural process that abhors the vac-uum of negativity—man can separate and prolong this moment, this, as Hegel calls it, "vanishing trace," and turn it into principle of consciousness and speech: "Human language as articulation (that is, as arrestation and preservation) of this

'vanishing trace' is the tomb of the animal voice that guards it and holds firm (*fest-halt*) its ownmost essence: 'that which is most terrible (*das Furchbarste*),' i.e., 'the Dead (*das Tote*)'" (ibid., 46). And further: "If, already for Hegel, language was not simply the voice of man, but the articulation of this voice in 'the voice of consciousness' through a *Voice of death*, for Heidegger there is an abyss between the living being (with his voice) and man (with his language): *language is not the voice of the living man*" (ibid., 55).

15. As one of his students, Juliet Flower MacCanell, reminisces, death was a frequent topic of conversation with Paul de Man: "'Death interests me,' Paul de Man remarked as we walked last March in New Haven . . . He did not mind, he said, leaving life . . . Even here he showed a kind of intellectual appetite for the ultimate experience of otherness that death, in his thinking, was" (1985, 67).

16. And as Alphonso Lingis's *Deathbound Subjectivity* asserts, thanatism can also become a source of a new, quasi-religious ecstatic transports which exult death as the only law, imperative, ordinance, and verdict of human existence: "That the human spirit is mortal, deathbound, that death does not befall our existence by accident or as a catastrophe, but that our existence, of its own nature, projects itself, with all its forces, unto its death—this conviction is at the core of Heidegger's thought. Death is the law—the imperative—of our existence . . . that the deathbound propulsion of our existence is the spirit itself is what makes our movements comprehending and our existence exultant, ecstatic . . . Death is the law—the ordinance of our existence" (1989, 109).

17. Compare, for instance, this very apodictic statement of Werner Hamacher, a distinguished pupil of de Man, which reveals futility of any vitalism as a valid philosophical stance: "Speaking," he says in *Premises*, "is always also imparting to the dead and parting with them. Whoever speaks, whoever understands, dies— and, prosaically enough, does not stop dying. To use a word that was important to Nietzsche, Kafka, and Benjamin, one could say: whoever speaks, whoever understands, 'outlives' and is 'outlived' . . . Not even so-called 'life-philosophy,' which has been reputed—not without justification—to promote the ideology of immediacy like no other, could deny the part played by the mute, the departed, and the incomprehensible in understanding" (1996, 22).

18. This again turns Bloom against the mainstream of deconstruction, whose effort partly lies in bringing down the barrier between the Hellenes and the Hebrews. Derrida's position in "Metaphysics and Violence," deliberately mixing the Freudian and the Heideggerian heritages in the "Jewgreek—Greekjew" concoction of James Joyce's *Ulysses*, is clearly adversary to Bloom's attempt to maintain and retrope the difference.

19. I take this phrase, "disruptive Setzen," from Gasché, who, in his book on de Man, *The Wild Card of Reading*, describes by it the Heideggerian operation of Being. In *On the Origin of the Work of Art*, Heidegger introduces the metaphor of *die Erde*, the chtonic aspect of Being which shelters everything which emerged in order to return to its matrix. *Die Erde* shelters the constant motion of emergence and disappearance; provides a kind of an umbilical cord, the link of *Nichtigkeit* which ties all beings to their origins and pulls them back when the time is due. All *Setzen*, therefore, is like *Übersetzen*, a translation which inevitably loses something essential in the process and cannot stand as autonomous

NOTES TO PAGES 139–144

toward its original. In the process of *a-letheia*, of coming forth from uncon-cealedness, Being translates itself into beings, and, as if discontented with the product of such lame translation, withdraws them, thus retranslating them back into the original. This set of metaphors is absolutely crucial for us here, for it cuts straight into Bloom's fundamental opposition of the original and the copy, the source and its translatory replica, and shows how important is the prin-cipal choice of metaphysics. Certainly, if being is nothing but a badly drawn copy of the original of *Seyn*, then the whole revisionary process of emancipation makes no sense whatsoever. This one only would already turn Bloom fiercely anti-Heideggerian.

20. Among innumerable passages which make the connection between rhet-oric and death in de Man, see especially this one, from "Shelley Disfigured": "*The Triumph of Life*," says de Man, "warns us that nothing, whether deed, word, thought or text, ever happens in relation, positive or negative, to anything that proceeds, follows or exists elsewhere, but only as *a random event whose power, like the power of death, is due to the randomness of its occurrence*" (1979b, 69; my emphasis).

21. See Harold Bloom, "Freud and Beyond," in *Ruin the Sacred Truths!* On the other hand, compare the recent reconfirmation of the topos of death as philo-sophical muse in Derrida's *Donner la mort* (*Given Death*), in his meditations on Jan Patocka, the Czech Heideggerian: "Philosophy isn't something that comes to the soul by accident, for it is nothing other than this vigil over death that watches out for death, and watches over death, as if over the very life of the soul. The psyche as life, as breath of life, as pneuma, only appears out of this con-cerned anticipation of dying. The anticipation of this vigil already resembles a provisional mourning, a vigil (*veille*) as wake (*veillé*)" (1995c, 15).

22. In my translation.

23. The unquestionable authority in this matter is Lacan himself. Lacan was the first to strike and afterward to legalize the connection between *Beyond the Pleasure Principle* and *Being and Time* in regard to the notion of death: "The death instinct," he says in *Function and Field of Speech and Language in Psychoanalysis*, "essentially expresses the limit of the historical function of the subject. The limit is death—not as an eventual coming-to-term of the life of the individual, nor as the empirical certainty of the subject, but, as Heidegger's formula puts it, as that 'possibility which is one's ownmost, unconditional, unsupersedable, certain and as such indeterminable (*unüberholbare*),' for the subject—'subject' understood as meaning the subject defined by his historicity" (1989, 103).

24. In "Freud and Beyond" Bloom scolds those interpreters of Freud who polished down his essential dualism: Marcuse on the one hand, for privileg-ing one-sidedly Eros—and Lacan on the other, for resolving the conflict in the Heideggerian manner, that is, in favor of Thanatos. But the thanatic monization of Freud's system occurs far more often, and especially in the poststructuralist tradition of Lacan's disciples: Laplanche, Deleuze, and Derrida influenced one another strongly, coining among themselves a powerful trope of the primacy of the death-drive. Deleuze's *Difference and Repetition*, which had an obvious effect on Derrida's rereading of Freud in his *Writing and Difference*, goes as far in its mercilessly philosophical logic as to cancel Freudian dualism altogether

and reduce life explicitly to a blunder within "death's economy": the *units* of life appear whenever death fails to reproduce itself, that is, when it deviates from the "repetition in itself," a paradoxical static flow which produces pure difference. A similar thing can be said about Laplanche, who sees life as a trauma-induced failure in returning to the principle of absolute zero.

25. See Emmanuel Lévinas, "The Trace of the Other." In this short but crucial article from 1963, Lévinas contrasts two types of journey, turning them into two opposite philosophical models of approaching the question of otherness. The one type of journey is called "movement without return" (1986, 347) and is characteristic of Abraham, who "leaves his fatherland forever for a yet unknown land" (ibid., 348)—while the other is based on the "movement of return to the same" and is characteristic of Ulysses returning to Ithaca (ibid.). We admit, however, that we take this seminal distinction from Lévinas only in order to use it for purposes he himself would have never endorsed. What we need here is not his pious interpretation of the ethical encounter with alterity, but his emphasis on the philosophical significance of Abraham's "departure without return" (ibid., 349).

26. In a similar vein to Blanchot, also Hamacher radicalizes the idea of death as "the possibility of the impossibility of the existence as such," turning it against Heidegger's hermeneutic intention of rendering death enabling rather than disabling; against what Dolf Sternberg used to call the syndrome of *der verstandene Tod* (the understood death). In Hamacher's account, if death is enabling it is only through its being disabling, that is, by representing the nonrepresentable, by substituting for the absolute, ultimate otherness which tears apart the circle of self-appropriation. Death cannot be understood; it is forever left in the dark: "The postulate that 'death is, as long as it "is," essentially always my own' becomes untenable: the 'ever mineness' (*Jemeinigkeit*) of death withdraws into ever otherness (*Jeandersheit*). Death, the end, the most extreme and 'ownmost' limit of *dasein* and its possibilities, insofar as it is non-comprehended death, cannot be one's *own* death without at the same time being *another* death, a death impossible to appropriate" (1996, 32–34).

27. If we are to believe Daniel Lagache (1960), Freud's notion of the death-drive is also closely tied to the ambivalence implied by the concept of the Heideggerian *Möglichkeit*, possibility. Thanatos, driving toward a "reduction of tensions," comes forth as the opposite pole to the tendency toward "realization of possibilities," or perhaps, even more: it merely exposes the discouraging aspect of possibility as such, that is, its temporary and arbitrary side which paralyses the act of decision.

28. "The ownmost, non-relational possibility, which is not to be outstripped," says Heidegger, "is *certain* . . . If Being-certain in relation to death does not have the character of apodictic evidence, this does not mean that it is of a lower grade, but that *it does not belong at all to the graded order of the kinds of evidence we can have about the present-at-hand* . . . Holding death for true (death *is* just one's own) shows another kind of certainty, and is more primordial than any certainty which relates to entities encountered within-the world, or to formal objects; for it is certain of Being-in-the-World" (1962, 309).

29. Maurice Blanchot, *L'Arrêt de mort*.

30. "What we cannot reach flying, we must reach by limping ... The Book tells us it is no sin to limp." "Die beiden Gulden," Rückert's version of the *Maqāmāt* by al-Harīrī (Freud 1984, 338).

31. Harold Bloom, *The Book of J.* Eric Santner, combining Bloom's ideas from his two books dealing directly with Judaic thought (*The Strong Light of the Canonical* and *The Book of J*), comments: "In a brilliant and, I think, insufficiently appreciated essay on Freud, Harold Bloom situates Freud's conception of love somewhere in the interstices of Greek, Judaic, and Roman culture," but in the end makes Freudian Eros "more Judaic than Greek" (2001, 25). This means, he continues, that divine love, which passes on the elected ones as a "blessing of more life" (love as transference), allows the singular life to blossom as simply "lovable," that is, beyond the realm of justification, beyond the question of truth or error, and as such fully autonomously. Santner, therefore, would like "to view the blessing of more life ... as an opening beyond—as an *exodus* from—a life captured by the question of its legitimacy" (ibid., 30). Such life, freed for its singularity, would truly find itself in what Hartman designates as "the middle" and what Santner, after Rosenzweig, calls "the midst of life," that is, in a sphere of its own, able to suspend—or, *defer*—the pressure of "the beyond" and its "overspecified poles."

32. The best account of the imperative of *zakhor*, "remember!" appears in the acclaimed book of Yosef Hayim Yerushalmi, *Zakhor: Jewish History and Jewish Memory.* The specificity of Jewish memory lies in its flight from mythical origins (the Hebrew nation emerges "*in the midst of history* rather than in mythic prehistory" [1996, 12]), and in the individualization of its heroes ("Historical figures emerge not merely as types, but as *full-fledged individuals*" [ibid., 13]). "With the departure of Adam and Eve from Eden," writes Yerushalmi about the Hebrew *it was* as a miracle irreducible to the mythic return of the same, "history begins, historical time becomes real, and *the way back is closed forever.* East of Eden hangs 'the fiery ever-turning sword' to bar re-entry. Thrust reluctantly into history, man in Hebrew thought comes to affirm his historical existence despite the suffering it entails, and gradually, ploddingly, he discovers that God reveals himself in the course of it. Rituals and festivals in ancient Israel are themselves no longer primary repetitions of mythic archetypes meant to annihilate historical time. Where they evoke the past, it is not the primeval but the historical past, in which the great and critical moments of Israel's history were fulfilled" (ibid., 8–9). In the foreword to this edition of *Zakhor*, Harold Bloom recalls a similar juxtaposition of Greek and Jewish approaches to the question of origins and time which was done by Hannah Arendt in *Between Past and Future*, where she claimed that the Jewish version of memory was based "upon altogether different teaching of the Hebrews, who always held that life itself is sacred, more sacred than anything else in the world" (ibid., xv). Bringing Arendt into this picture is all the more fortunate for the fact that her longstanding obsession with the idea of "a unique life," as a separate autonomous whole made of historical contingency, became her more or less unconscious battle cry against the intellectual heritage of Heidegger, first her master and then, increasingly, the theoretical adversary she slowly learned to resist.

33. The analogous failure in retroping the difference between Athens and Jerusalem occurs in Derrida, and exactly for the same reasons. By writing on

Patocka's *Heretical Essays on the Philosophy of History*, Derrida speculates on the future of European thought and suggests that it would be shaped by the spirit of Christianity, which, so far, "has not yet come to Christianity" (1995c, 28): "What would be the secret," he asks, "of a Europe emancipated from both Athens and Rome?" (ibid., 29). Alas, not Jerusalem—rather, "Heidegger, and Heidegger alone," the only thinker able "to keep his reference to a supreme being distinct from all onto-theological meaning" (ibid., 33). And the key to this distinction lies in the properly understood notion of death as something both absolutely *given* and *giving*: "Death," continues Derrida in the already familiar, distinctly Heideggerian vein, "is very much that which nobody else can undergo or confront in my place. My irreplaceability is therefore conferred, delivered, 'given,' one can say, by death. It is the same gift, the same source, one could say the same goodness and the same law. It is from the site of death as the place of my irreplaceability, that is, of my singularity, that I feel called to responsibility" (ibid., 41–42).

34. In the second part of *Donner la mort*, which is devoted to Kierkegaard's *Fear and Trembling*, and particularly to the story of Abraham's near-sacrifice of his son Isaac, Derrida denounces the received Christian translation "sacrifice" for the Hebrew *korban*, which, in his opinion, "refers more to an approach, or a 'coming close to'" (1995c, 58), and as such it indicates not so much an experience of death per se, but an experience of a close shave which forms "the decisive influence" of the greatest trauma (*korban*, indeed, means in Hebrew "sacrifice," but the root $K o R a V$ indicates a movement of coming close to God, which, once we think of God as most of all *donnant la mort* (giving death), can also signify "coming close to death"). In this sense, *korban* is not so much *death accepted* as *death arrested*, though, at the same time, fully revealed in its destructive power; as such, it rather belongs to the vocabulary of *survival*, a strange, human kind of life which is from the beginning afflicted with death. What happens afterward, continues Derrida, is equally unique: the whole experience of *korban* plays itself out in silence, repressed speech. "All that goes on in secret. God keeps silent about his reasons. Abraham does also, and the book is not signed by Kierkegaard, but by Johannes de Silentio ('a poetic person who only exists among poets,' Kierkegaard writes in the margin of his text)" (ibid., 57–58). The Bloomian strong poet is also "a poetic person who only exists among poets," and who too must keep his reasons silent and repressed. Why? "Just as no one can die in my place," says Derrida about such poetic existence, "no one can make a decision, what we call 'a decision,' in my place. But as soon as one speaks, as soon as one enters the medium of language, *one loses that very singularity* . . . Speaking relieves us, Kierkegaard notes, for it *'translates' into the general*" (ibid., 60; my emphasis). Language "dissolves my singularity in the medium of the concept" (ibid., 61); therefore, it is only in the medium of the religious decision, in its silence and secrecy, that absolute singularity, "nonsubstitution and nonrepetition," can flesh itself out. "Speaking relieves," for it *releases* us to death in the moment of sacrifice, whereas *korban*, the decisive influence of a deadly trauma, wants us to evade death and *survive*, though always "with the fear and trembling" of losing our singularity.

35. There is only one explicit reference to Derrida's "To Speculate—On Freud" (which appeared in English for the first time in *Oxford Literary Review* in

1978) in Bloom's text, and there is no mention of Bloom in Derrida's Freudian speculation, yet the sense of mutual contamination is very strong. For instance, in Derrida, the very theme of legacy in Freud reads like a travesty of Bloom's notion of the precursor whose authority grows *in time*, not despite but thanks to his real absence: "No legacy without transference," says Derrida. "Which also gives us to understand that if every legacy is propagated in transference, it can get underway only in the form of an inheritance of transference. Legacy, legation, delegation, *différance* of transference: the analyst himself, not even his generation, does not need to be 'there,' in person. *He can be all the stronger in not being there.* He sends himself—and the postal system forwards" (1987, 339). This, obviously, echoes Bloom's claim that dead precursors appear to be outrageously more alive than any actually living person, and that their authority depends on the temporal operation of transference. Or, an even closer echo of Bloom's conviction that "precursor is in the id": "But the demonic (that which haunts, coming back from the past and producing the effect of *das Unheimliche*) is not more or less inherited, like one content or another. It belongs to the structure of the will" (ibid., 353). Or, in the deeply dramatized portrait of the scene of instruction and the issuing process of revision as "this immense chain of an inheritance that is negotiated, received and rejected, incorporated or denied, an abyssal scene of a legacy, of delegation and denegation, this traffic of influence" (ibid., 375).

36. On Freud's aggressive attempt to ward off the vision of the approaching monism, which would put his position in an undesirable proximity to Jung's, Bloom comments: "The dualism of the drives is stated here with a singular and positive harshness" (*LF*, 21)—a harshness, which, obviously, merely shows Freud's deep theoretical discomfort.

37. "What begins to be clear," writes Bloom, "is that the drives and the defenses are modeled upon poetic rhetoric, whether or not one believes that the unconscious is somehow structured like a language" (*LF*, 22).

38. "Things would be quite otherwise," admonishes Derrida, "if one were attentive to the writing within the voice" (1987, 465).

39. *Destrudo* is a term Freud invented as a counterpart to libido but gave up on it in later drafts of *Beyond the Pleasure Principle*.

40. Under the title "Coming into One's Own," in *Psychoanalysis and the Question of the Text*, Derrida published an early, shorter version of the second chapter of "To Speculate—on Freud," which later became a significantly longer text: "Freud's Legacy."

41. This very Blanchotian motif is elaborated by Derrida with great detail in "Living On: Borderlines," an essay devoted to the double reading of Shelley's *Triumph of Life* and Blanchot's novel *L'Arrêt de mort*: "Survival and *revenance*," writes Derrida, "living on and returning from the dead: living on goes beyond both living and dying, supplementing each with a sudden surge and a certain reprieve, deciding—*arrêtant* life *and* death, ending them in a decisive *arrêt*, the *arrêt* that puts an end to something and the *arrêt* that condemns with a sentence, a statement, a spoken word or a word that goes on speaking" (1979, 108).

42. For Derrida, the Freudian spool is a metaphor, first of Freud's, and then general, narcissism: "It is as if one were pulling this nebulous matrix with chain

fusions or fissions, with bottomless permutations and commutations, with *disseminations without return*, by only one of its strings/sons [*fils*] . . . For it is as if one wished to make it amount to one of its strings/sons, in other words to the matricial mother who would be only what she is" (1987, 341).

43. Strangely enough, this overt reference (though at the same time it is curiously circuitous: first al-Ḥarīrī, then Rückert) to one of the most fundamental tropes of Judaism—the limping Jacob, who damaged badly his hip in the struggle with one of the Elohim, the daylight-fearing Angel of Death—is overlooked by the both Jewish readers of *Beyond the Pleasure Principle*, Derrida and Bloom. Bloom merely alludes to Freud's identification with the Hebrew hero by calling him "the wrestling Sigmund," while Derrida turns this reference into a rhetorical excuse on Freud's part, saying that "this allusion to limping in a way cites the chapter itself, in its brief uselessness, summons it to appear and to testify, causing it to be remarked as a kind of atrophied member or club foot" (1987, 387). The seventh chapter of *Beyond the Pleasure Principle*, the short three-page appendix, has thus only one function of making an apology for the lack of a proper ending: instead of a beautiful finish, we get a club-footed, limping drag which apologizes for its clumsiness. But is this all that there is to it? Nothing but an excuse and apology? Or perhaps it is rather an oblique way of saying that, at least in one of the main Western traditions, this is precisely the manner in which life proceeds, and there is no sin in imitating its meandering ways?

44. I am referring here to the German original title of Samuel Weber's book *Return to Freud: Jacques Lacan's Dislocation of Psychoanalysis*, which takes up the Freudian term *Entstellung* in order to describe Lacan's interpretative strategy toward Freud.

45. Let us repeat again that Kojève's interpretation of Hegel, which deeply influenced Kojève's brilliant students—Bataille, Blanchot, and Lacan—brings a sudden change of emphasis: an unexpected rehabilitation of the master. Hegel, Kojève argues, was wrong in having dispatched the master so lightly, for the Master constitutes an immortal archetype of human existence that can fulfill itself only in the triumphant confrontation with death. It is true that in his dialectics Hegel construes an alternative model of emancipation that realizes itself through fear and work, eventually leading toward a mature self whose fears had become "worked through" and sublated. But this alternative, Kojève continues, is false, for one look at the "bourgeois ego" is enough to see that this "last man" not only did not return to himself thanks to work, but, on the contrary, became even more self-alienated. Precisely because the slave had trembled with fear in the face of death once in his life and thus betrayed his anxious will to live, he shall always remain what he is: a slave. No work can save him from this predicament. This is why History demands the return of the master, a historically repressed aristocrat of the spirit who, out of contempt for sheer life, dared to challenge death itself. The slave, if he is to leave his slavish condition, "*must* become a Warrior, that is, he must introduce death into his existence, by consciously and voluntarily risking his life, while knowing that he is mortal" (1969, 69).

46. "For in this labor which he undertakes to reconstruct *for another*," says Lacan, referring to the articulating labors of the analysand, "he rediscovers the

fundamental alienation that made him construct it *like another*, and which has always destined it to be taken from him *by another*" (ibid., 42).

47. "At every moment," says Lacan in "Aggressivity in Pyschoanalysis," "he constitutes his world by his suicide, and the psychological experience of which Freud had the audacity to formulate, however paradoxical its expression in biological terms, as the 'death instinct'" (ibid., 28).

48. In *Ethics of Psychoanalysis*, Lacan speculates on the etymology of the word "happiness" in few Indo-European languages as associated with the notion of the right timing and fortuitous event which, for him, refers to the bright side of the original, traumatic "missed encounter" of the *tuche*: "happiness" is *tuche* made fortunate, that is, still an accident, but this time without its traumatizing "too-earliness."

49. This pushing to another extreme was well spotted by one of the participants of Lacan's second seminar, Dr. Leclaire, who remarked: "I have the impression that in refusing this deliberate entification, the subject, we have a tendency, and *you* have a tendency, to carry this idolization over to another point. At that moment, it won't be the subject, it will be the other" (1991, 55).

50. Hence antithetical revision means invigoration of poetic idioms and topoi that are in danger of falling into clichés, allegories, dead letters of *ça parle*. In the *Figure of Echo*, John Hollander talks in this context about "the fiction of the leaves," which presents poetic revision as an essential trope of mortality: mortality of writers as much as mortality of words, figures, and language. "The fallen leaves, themselves full of Homeric, Virgilian, and Dantesque associations, bring together tropes of death, multitudinousness, falling and scattered generational and Sybilline leaves, and so forth. By the time the image has moved through Shelley's 'yellow, and black, and pale, and hectic red,/Pestilence stricken multitudes,' through the echoing line in Hardy's 'During Wind and Rain' ('How the sick leaves reel down in throngs!'), to Allen Tate's refrain in the 'Ode for the Confederate Dead,' the problem is almost that of a topos. Certainly, as Harold Bloom has shown [*WS*, 58–81, 375–79), the turning of the leaves in the wind in Stevens' 'Domination of Black' is an allusive and transumptive (in the senses he has given to the word) image; it has added Whitman's leaves = blades + pages . . . The 'turning' is of pages, as well as of autumnal coloring, and the Sybilline component of the trope becomes reconstituted through the presence of Whitman . . . For Stevens, the image of the leaves, revising itself in the firelight of imagination, is like 'the leaves themselves,/Turning in the wind.' Like songbirds that stand for more than the natural noises they produce, summing up over the range of nightingales and skylarks behind them (e.g., Hardy's thrush), the trope of the leaves is metaleptic, rather than merely metaphoric. Its allusiveness has been brought into the range of its subject. It is almost as if for us, now, the image 'means,' among other things: 'Even as leaves turn color and die, and the Sybil's scattered leaves are reconstituted metaphorically in all our own writings—whoever we are, and whenever we write—*even as men fall like leaves, and become mulch for new generations, even as the leaves of the book of life turn, so does the very image of fallen leaves present itself for revision*" (1981, 121–22; my emphasis).

51. This duality in approach to trauma is well reflected in Cathy Caruth's classification: "Trauma theory," says Caruth in *Unclaimed Experience*, "often divides

itself into two basic trends: the focus on trauma as the *'shattering'* of a previously whole self and the focus on the *survival function* of trauma as allowing one to get through an overwhelming experience" (1996, 131f; my emphasis). Bloom's notion of trauma-catastrophe is definitely the latter one, bound with the idea of survival.

52. Compare Lacan: "The psychoanalytic experience has rediscovered in man the imperative of the Word as the law that has formed him in its image. *It manipulates the poetic function of language to give to his desire its symbolic mediation*" (1989, 106; my emphasis).

53. Compare Charles Algernon Swinburne, "The Garden of Prosperine": "From too much love of living,/From hope and fear set free,/We thank with brief thanksgiving/Whatever gods may be/That no life lives for ever;/That dead men rise up never;/That even the weariest river/Winds somewhere safe to sea."

Chapter 4

1. This is why psychoanalysis puts on the analysand the demand finally to meet his or her destiny: "To this requirement," says Lacan in *Four Fundamental Concepts of Psychoanalysis*, "correspond those radical points in the real that I call encounters, and which enable us to conceive reality as *unterlegt, untertragen*, which with the superb ambiguity of the French language, appear to be translated by the same word—*souffrance*. Reality is in abeyance there, awaiting attention" (1979, 55–56). See also Jacques Derrida, "This Strange Institution Called Literature: An Interview with Jacques Derrida": "There is no literature without a *suspended* relation to meaning and reference. *Suspended* means *suspense*, but also *dependence*, condition, conditionality" (1992, 48).

2. In *Psyche: Inventions of the Other*, Derrida, by describing de Man's concept of deconstruction, makes an overt allusion to the Fichtean-Schlegelian *Schweben*: "An infinitely rapid circulation—such are the irony and the temporality of this text—all at once shunts the performative into the constative and vice versa. De Man has written of undecidability as an infinite and thus untenable acceleration" (1991, 206–7).

3. And the only truly interesting instances of Derrida's aporetic rhetoric are those in which he himself feels surprised by the fact that he cannot progress any further beyond the once stated antinomy: "If a mark has a structure that . . . ," he says in one of his most recent interviews, "Negotations," once again engaging in the arrival-erasure aporia of the referent, "it succeeds only in erasing itself, it succeeds only by erasing itself. Or it occurs through an erasing . . . erasing itself" (2002, 35).

4. This is precisely why, despite many misleading self-commentaries on Derrida's part, especially in the last chapter of *Aporias*, the oscillating quasi movement of the aporia has nothing to do with messianism, even as reduced as "the messianism without messianism" Derrida develops mostly in *Spectres of Marx*. "Awaiting one's death" is *not* the same as awaiting the Messiah, for, although death may indeed be "absolutely indeterminate" in its infinite mystery,

it is nonetheless "absolutely certain" (ibid., 72), which, alas, can never be said about the messianic arrival.

5. But still, even decades later, whenever the fateful question of the subject is raised, Derrida reacts with the same impatience and discomfort. In his interview with Eduardo Cadava and Jean-Luc Nancy, which eventually became a contribution to their anthology *Who Comes After the Subject?*—when asked about the impact of deconstruction on the dissolution of subjectivity, he almost angrily remarks that "if over the last twenty-five years in France the most notorious of these [discursive] strategies have in fact led to a kind of discussion around 'the question of the subject,' none of them has sought to 'liquidate' anything" (1995b, 255).

6. "A strong egoism," says Freud in "On Narcissism: An Introduction," "is a protection against falling ill, but in the last resort we must begin to love in order not to fall ill, and we are bound to fall ill if, in consequence of frustration, we are unable to love" (1989, 553). Narcissistic anxiety, therefore, is a constant negotiation between these two poles: the illness of isolation, on the one hand—and the danger of self-dissolution in the act of falling in love, on the other.

7. This unease, in itself a complex existential plot on Derrida's part, is best explained by him in *Resistances to Psychoanalysis*.

8. In "What is an Author?" Foucault famously says: "The author is ... the ideological figure by which one marks the manner in which we *fear* the proliferation of meaning" (1979, 159; my emphasis).

9. This suggestion appears already in Kierkegaard's *The Concept of Anxiety*, where anxiety, having no place in philosophical discourse, is analyzed in the language of "experimental psychology": this is also the direction taken by Harold Bloom in *The Anxiety of Influence*. Here, "experimental psychology" indicates a speculative endeavor to shift the discourse of subjectivity away from Hegel, and—in the case of the last two—explicitly closer to Freud.

10. The obvious advantage of Samuel Weber's "deconstructive reading of Freud" is that it forcefully shows how Freud's text constantly undoes its own performance; that is, how the aporetic vulnerability of the ego disavows its "animistic" dream of the total synthesis and peaceful unification of everything that is *nicht-Ich*. "The ego," says Weber, "sets itself apart not merely in *opposing* itself to what it is not, but in *dispersing* its Self in conflictual relations to other 'agencies' which it can never either fully assimilate or entirely exclude" (ibid., 25). It is, therefore, in a constant pursuit of meaning which is always bound to fail: living on agon and difference, torn between two opposite pursuits, ego cannot assimilate into its dream of total harmony the only thing it would really wish to make peaceful—*itself*.

11. Heine's God says: *Krankheit ist wohl der letzte Grund / des ganzen Schöpfungsdrangs gewesen / Erschaffend konnte ich genesen / Erschaffend wurde ich gesund.* ("Illness was the ultimate reason for my urge of creation. By creating I could get well. By creating I would get healed."). This notion of a "healing" narcissism which combines two opposite pursuits of the original narcissistic illness—pursuit toward sense-giving introjection and pursuit toward getting lost in an alien object—comes very close to the idea of narcissistic creativity as developed by D. W. Winnicott, who talked about "transitional objects,"

that is, objects which can both "hold" the psychic content and enjoy an independent existence, or, in yet other words, are neither fully "mine" nor fully "alien."

12. Graham Allen hits it in the bull's-eye when he says that "poetic meaning is equivalent to having *named something first*" (1994, 30; my emphasis).

13. Or several books, in fact, for it would not be an exaggeration to say that all of Rosenzweig as well as all of Benjamin's writings devoted to the idea of language try to deal precisely with this problem, that is, with the substitution of *davhar* for *logos* and its possible philosophical consequences. Especially Rosenzweig's obsessive motive of "the living speech" (*die lebendige Sprache*) fits well to the following description which enumerates the most salient differences between Greek and Hebrew modes of thinking. On this, see especially his *Understanding the Sick and the Healthy* to whose title our notion of the "healthier" narcissism constantly alludes.

14. Or, in original formulation of Thorleif Boman's *Hebrew Thought Compared with Greek*: "*dabhar* is dynamic both objectively and linguistically . . . The basic meaning is 'to be behind and drive forward,' hence 'to let words follow one another,' or even better 'to drive forward that which is behind'; the verb thus portrays somehow the function of speaking. *Dabhar* means not only 'word' but also 'deed' . . . *dabhar* is a power-laden word" (1970, 65–69).

15. See the definition of *arche*-trace as quasi-transcendental infrastructure by Gasché: "The arche-trace, defined as the inevitable mark of the Other born by a self-present or self-contained entity, the mark not of any constituted, particular Other, but simply the place marked for the arrival of the Other, the site of referral to an Other still to come, is an infrastructural principle of asymmetry that articulates 'nothing' but the structural or vectorial feature of being marked by an Other and of relating to an Other. 'Nothing' but a structure of pointing away from self, itself included" (1994, 12).

16. This is why I cannot agree with R. Clifton Spargo, who, in his contribution to *The Salt Companion to Harold Bloom*, "Toward an Ethics of Literary Revisionism," draws a rather misleading parallel between Bloom and Lévinas, insisting on their essentially identical attitude toward alterity. "An ethics of literary revisionism, I am proposing, must turn finally on the analogy between the belated writer's anxious apprehension of a precursor text and the *real-life* ethical scenario in which the speaking subject is already siginified by, but also becoming conscious of, the relation to the other" (2007, 88). But even if we grant, as Spargo rightly does, that Lévinas's encounter with the Other is as "signally unpleasurable" (ibid.) as it is in Bloom, it still does not justify the whole analogy. First of all, in Lévinas, the Other is a traumatizing persecutor of the ego because he disturbs the ego's traditionally conceived narcissistic state of "self-enjoyment"—whereas in Bloom, the other way around, the Other constitutes the source of a trauma because his influence threatens the self's "will-to-distinction," where narcissism is thought in a radically different way. And second, "the real-life scenario" of a dialogue with the Other can hardly be a canvas for Bloom's interpersonal poetic agon, which—and Bloom very often emphasizes this crucial distinctive feature—always takes place in the realm of writing, governed by different rules than a situation of speech.

17. Thus, in "Counter-Signatures," where Derrida speculates about the name of Ponge, which, while inscribed in the text, becomes *éponge*, a common noun for a sponge: "Whence the double relation to the name and to the loss of the name: by inscribing the name in the thing itself . . . , by inscribing the name in the thing, from one angle I lose the signature, but, from another angle, I monumentalize the name, I transform the name into a thing: like a stone, like a monument . . . *One has to lose the name in order to make it become a thing, in order to win for it in some way the value of thing, which is to say also a survival*" (1995b, 366). Then, in "Passages—from Traumatism to Promise," when he talks about another special effect of singularity, which is the date: "So the date is the mark of a singularity," he says, "of a temporal and spatial 'this here' . . . Now, I said that the structure of this mark is paradoxical and wounding because a date is at once what is inscribed so as to preserve the uniqueness of the moment but what, by the same token, loses it . . . Once it is read, whether it makes reference to the calendar or not, it is immediately repeated, and consequently, in this iterability which makes it readable, it loses the singularity that it keeps. It burns what it wants to save . . . Given that all experience is the experience of a singularity and thus is the desire to keep this singularity as such, the 'as such' of the singularity, that is, what permits one to keep it as what it is, this is what effaces it right away" (ibid., 378).

18. "But understood in these terms," Rodolphe Gasché writes critically in his comment on Derrida's notion of invention, "singularity, by refusing all translation and interpretation, becomes opaque, silent, or immediate in a nondialectical sense. It becomes quite simply thoroughly unintelligible. Such a singular would be a failure in its own terms. No longer identifiable, it could not be recognized, let alone repeated as a singular . . . Without running this essential, and hence necessary risk, by which the singular relates to the Other, it would not be a singular to begin with" (1994, 14). This brings us very close to Bloom's idea of an invention as an agonistic collision with tradition, and indeed: "For a difference to make a difference, and hence to be one in the first place," continues Gashé, "its uniqueness must be wrenched from and negotiated within a system of conventions" (ibid., 21).

19. Once again, this predicament is very well described by Weber: "It is a process of displacement," he says in *The Legend of Freud*, "that makes place for the ego by being displaced, in and as anxiety. If the ego is therefore the 'seat' of anxiety, anxiety is equally the site of the ego. And in this site, the ego is never comfortably set" (1982, 57).

20. The idiomatic understanding of subjectivity which emphasizes singularity rather than its epistemological prerogatives goes back, as we have already indicated in the second chapter of part 1, to the romantic tradition. The most persuasive shift from the idealist interpretation of a subject toward a subject as a certain slant of light, which leaves its indirect mark in an auctorial manner of seeing things, occurs in Friedrich Schlegel who, against the classicists, defended mannerism in literature and equated *das Subjektive* (the subjective) with *das Interessante* (the interested), a self-interest of the author creating his or her special perspective. The Hebraism of the romantics is another complex issue to which we can only allude here in passing, but it would seem that the notoriously romantic notion of *Ausdruck*, that is, expression, has also far more to do

with "the spirit of the Hebrew poetry," that is, with the heritage of *davhar* rather than that of *logos*. Thus, in *The Mirror and the Lamp*, M. H. Abrams interprets *der Ausdruck* in almost purely mechanical, "power-laden" terms of bringing forward the hidden content against the contrary power of pushing back, which, according to Abrams, anticipates the Freudian notion of *Verdrängung*, that is, repression. In Abrams's rendering, *Ausdruck* is not an expression of an already present subjective intention, but a pressing forward of the tectonic movements of the psyche which shakes internally to produce a word. We shall deal once again with this other, non-logocentric understanding of expression in the chapter "Fair Crossings."

Chapter 5

1. The detailed account of Bloom's various Hebrew inspirations is given by Susan A. Handelman in her very instructive book, *The Slayers of Moses: The Emergence of Rabbinic Interpretation in Modern Literary Theory*, most of all in the chapter "The Critic as Kabbalist: Harold Bloom and the Heretic Hermeneutic."

2. See Hans Blumenberg, *Arbeit am Mythos*.

3. In *The Breaking of the Vessels*, Bloom talks about his own "sense of trespass, my own guilt of becoming a Jewish Gnostic after and in spite of a Orthodox upbringing" (43).

4. The phrase "the myth of what exists" comes from Horkheimer and Adorno's *Dialectic of Enlightenment*, which is equally concerned about the threatened modern condition of the individual, and as such matches perfectly Bloom's Hebrew-Romantic intuitions as to the oppressed status of the singular poetic subject (Horkheimer 2002, xii). I modify Jephcott's translation, "the myth of that which is the case," in order to emphasize the reductive nature of the whole system of being, which, I think, is closer to the authorial intention.

5. See most of all: Franz Rosenzweig, *Star of Redemption*, the chapter "Man and His Self or Metaethics," and Walter Benjamin, "Fate and Character," in *Illuminations*, as well as "Goethe's *Elective Affinities*" where he talks about the Exodus from the generalizing forces of myth by using the example of a hubristic tragic hero, following Rosenzeig's *Star of Redemption*.

6. "It is necessary to ask oneself what a signature is," says Derrida, echoing Rosenzweig in "Ulysses Gramophone: Hear Say Yes in Joyce." "It requires a yes more 'ancient' than the question 'what is?' since the latter presupposes it; it is thus 'older' than knowledge" (1991, 590).

7. See his "Freud and Beyond" in *Ruin the Sacred Truths!*

8. "The poet *qua* poet," says Bloom, "is my obsessive concern, and the Scene of Instruction creates the poet as or in a poet" (*BV*, 46).

9. The modern waning of the fluid is also the subject of complaint in Benjamin's piece "To the Planetarium" from *One-Way Street*: "If one had to expound the doctrine of antiquity with utmost brevity while standing on one leg, as did Hillel that of the Jews, it could only be in this sentence: 'They alone shall possess the earth who live from the powers of the cosmos.' Nothing distinguishes the ancient from the modern man so much as the former's absorption

in a cosmic experience scarcely known to later periods. Its waning is marked by the flowering of astronomy at the beginning of the modern age. Kepler, Copernicus, and Tycho Brahe were certainly not driven by scientific impulses alone. All the same, the exclusive emphasis on an optical connection to the universe, to which astronomy very quickly led, contained a portent of what was to come. The ancients' intercourse with the cosmos had been different: the ecstatic trans" (1997, 92–93).

10. See *Dialectic of Enlightenment,* especially the sections on the "bad myth" in which enlightenmental thought had turned against itself; the notion of "bad myth" used by Horkheimer and Adorno corresponds well with "the myth which goes wrong" in Girard's remarks on the crisis of undifferentiation in his *Violence and the Sacred.*

11. This pessimistic diagnosis places Bloom in immediate opposition to the so-called culturalist approach with which he may be prima facie identified. The same situation which, from the culturalist perspective, is valued as unambiguously positive, that is, as the moment in which the individual, finally set free from false idols, may adequately recognize and endorse his "cultural consciousness," is perceived by Bloom as a source of new, formerly unexpected dangers and limitations. Bloom, however, chooses the more skeptical path of Nietzsche, who often alluded to the possibility that culture and history might turn to be more cruel masters than religion. Bloom, being partly a Nietzschean, approaches culturalism in a way similar to the one in which Dostoevsky's "underground man" approaches naive progressivism: there is nothing more impossible, he says, than to create culture only for the sake of culture, surrounded by nothing but culture. In *Literary Revisionism and the Burden of Modernity,* a book fully devoted to the complex modern dialectic between secularization of the religious and sacralization of the cultural, Jean-Pierre Mileur writes a propos Bloom: "Yet the archaic can only be segregated, not destroyed, for ... our conceptions of human success, the very form of our desire, remain archaic as well. Hence, in a society that eschews superstition and exalts reason, nothing is more socially acceptable that a superstitious awe of culture" (1985, 36).

12. In *The Book of J,* a Gnostic-vitalistic exegesis of this oldest of Torah writers, Bloom says: "The Blessing gives more life, awards a time without boundaries, and makes a name into a pragmatic immortality, by way of communal memory" (211).

13. Funnily enough, this diagnosis has been confirmed by Paul de Man, who, as Bloom himself asserts, used to say to him: "The problem with you, Harold, is that you don't believe in truth." And obviously, as we have already indicated in part 2, it must have been a serious problem for de Man, who, like Girard, Lacan, and the whole poststructuralist French circle, never questioned his "idolatry of truth" and was ready to dismiss any other position as simply an error.

14. See Geoffrey Hartman, "Romanticism and the Anti-Self Consciousness."

15. Bloom's typically "exodic" resistance to any kind of mythical structure as a deadening closure can be seen in many places, like, for example, in his passing allusion to Wittgenstein's critique of Freud: "The complaint of Wittgenstein against Freud—'a powerful mythology'—takes it poignance from the philosopher's sense that this power is not *quickening,* but *reducing* and even deadening, a

terrible dualism though without another metaphysics" (*MM*, 65). On this topic see also the last chapter, "Tainted Love."

16. Bloom's stage of *kenosis* as an attempt of separation has a possible equivalent in Roland Barthes, in the first of the four techniques which establish the process of *logothesis*, that is, the creation of a new style of writing, or an autonomous *écriture:* "The first technique," says Barthes in *Sade, Fourier, Loyola*, "is separation. The new language is to emerge from a material vacuum; this emptiness which precedes it allows the new language to isolate itself from other common languages—spurious and obsolete—whose noise could interfere with its voice: no contamination of signs is possible" (1971, ii; in my translation). Yet, although the Barthesian *logothesis* bears important resemblance to Bloom's *poetic revision*, the crucial difference lies in the way they both perceive the strategy of separation: for Barthes, it is a literal, revolutionary break with the languages of the past, judged as "spurious and obsolete," whereas for Bloom, it is just a cunning defense of the poetic self which *pretends* to undo the nonetheless extant burden of inheritance.

17. In *The Concept of Anxiety* Kierkegaard says: "In the realm of nature, repetition is present in its immovable necessity. In the realm of the spirit, the task is not to wrest a change from repetition or to find oneself moderately comfortable during the repetition . . . , but to transform repetition into something inward, into freedom's own task, into its highest interest, so that while everything else changes, it can actually realize repetition" (1980, 18f). Repetition, therefore, does not break with the reductive influence, but, on the contrary, takes it up and transforms it into its very opposite, that is, the freedom. Repetition, as projected by human subjectivity, mocks the natural order, where the mythical repetition rules, and thus invalidates its apparent necessities.

18. For instance, this reading of Nietzsche was championed by Michel Foucault in his seminal essay "Nietzsche, Genealogy, History."

19. Bloom's critique of disenchanting criticism follows closely the romantic mistrust in "a beneficial praxis" of demystification: he reproaches the suspicious strain for the incipient kind of closure, its stubborn, dogmatic dryness. The suspicion is always in the service of reality principle; its deconstructive hermeneutics, as Paul Ricoeur put it, "brings out the positive benefit of the ascesis required by a reductive and destructive interpretation: confrontation with bare reality, the discipline of Ananke, of necessity . . . But, in return, does not this discipline of the real, this ascesis of the necessary lack the grace of imagination, the upsurge of the possible?" (1970, 36).

20. The perfect illustration of the reductive danger incipient to *every*, however careful, critical enterprise is offered by "the agon" that has taken place between Ashbery and Bloom: the poet who became "canonized" thanks to Bloom's critical efforts and the critic who often expressed his gratitude to Ashbery for allowing him to continue his revisionist lineage past Wallace Stevens. Beneath this mutual feeling of indebtedness, however, there seems to lie a deeply agonistic grudge. Ashbery often tried to shake off Bloom's interpretation, for instance by calling him in his semiautobiographical *Flow Chart* "an old guy (who) comes up to you and tells you, reading your mind, what a / magnificent / job you've done"—while Bloom, on the other hand, occasionally scolded Ashbery for not

being faithful enough to the modernist experiment. Ashbery rebelliously pos-
tulated that "therefore a new school of criticism must be developed," meaning
precisely the kind of criticism which no longer will be a *school* at all—while
Bloom, on his part, did everything to diminish his scholarly impact on poets,
though still remaining, however reluctantly, a critic. Susan M. Schultz, who
wrote extensively about Ashbery's revenge on Bloom in "'Returning to Bloom':
John Ashbery's Critique of Harold Bloom," makes it a pretty simple case of the
"resistance to theory" on poet's part. Bloom is portrayed here as a powerful theoretical figure who represses Ashbery's poetic freedom by telling him exactly
"what a magnificent job he's done" and whose attachment to the concept of "tradition" equals T. S. Eliot. In exposing the agon between the poet and the critic,
Susan Schultz is absolutely right, yet she makes it too easy on herself by omit-
ting the fact that Bloom is one of those rare critics who is fully conscious of
what I have called here a critic's reductive aporia. And by aligning him in one
taxonomic breath with T. S. Eliot, she completely disinterprets Bloom's agonistic notion of tradition as a lineage of *betrayal* rather than recreative fidelity
(1996, 24–48).

21. As in this very instructive quote from Ashbery: "I rarely discuss my poetry.
I find it distasteful. I'd rather not know much about it myself" (Schultz 1996,
31). Or in a similar cento from Gombrowicz's *Journals:* "When I give a birth to a
book, it is a difficult and complex process . . . First, it is surrounded by darkness,
which is filled with shame. My friends are embarrassed, and they avoid me. And
I try hard not to know anything about it" (1988, 221; in my translation).

22. The nonmethodological nature of Bloom's revisionary map is usually a
target of severe criticism which complains that nothing can be done with it in
scholarly terms. Joseph Riddel, his intentions notwithstanding, is one of the
few who did not miss the point: "Bloom's first system of terms . . . becomes a
labyrinth, every repetition of the system amplifying and complicating it rather
than giving us a definitive reading and thus a 'way out'" (1976, 992–93). One
could even go so far as to see in Bloom's "skill and inventiveness of substitution,"
which evades any Procrustean bed of theory, a personalized shadow of Derrida's
différance which "commands nothing, rules over nothing, and nowhere does it
exercise any authority" (Derrida 1973, 153). Bloom's stratagem, similarly, is not
a rule or principle; it relies on highly individualized patterns which cannot be
brought under the same universally applicable scheme.

23. The promise to transform narcissistic hysteria into "common human
unhappiness" appears in Freud's private correspondence with Josef Breuer (Rieff
1965, 327).

24. Similar mistrust toward Freud's "mythological" capacity to encom-
pass, level, and reduce everything is shared by Derrida in his *Resistances to
Psychoanalysis*, an essay in which he explains why he never undertook psychoanalysis and always resisted its lure. "Can all 'resistance to analysis' always be
reduced to the interpretable status that analytic theory grants it or analyzes? Is
there another resistance?" asks Derrida defiantly (1998, 1), and then proceeds
to develop "another" notion of resistance which is strictly bound with the singularity of the self, actively *resisting the theory* in which it would vanish as the
idiosyncratic "I": "Instead," he says, "it is an idiomatic interest, I could almost

say an idiosyncratic interest, in the word 'resistance' that I would like to share with you. At stake, in sum, is that which in me could learn to say 'me' only by cultivating an idiom where . . . the word 'resistance' does not play just any role. Ever since I can remember, I have always loved this word" (ibid., 2).

25. The formative role of fantasy as a means of defiance against the power of reality has been endorsed by Bloom many times, especially in his "*Clinamen: Towards a Theory of Fantasy*" in *Agon*.

26. See our discussion on Bloom's evasion of Frye's "Myth of Concern" in the section "From Concern to Antithesis" in the first chapter of part 1.

27. "Indeed," says Schlegel in his *Speech on Mythology* in reference to the works of Cervantes and Shakespeare, the writers he most admired, "this artificially ordered confusion, this charming symmetry of contradictions, this wondrous, external exchange of enthusiasm and irony—which itself lives even in the smallest elements of the whole—already seem to me an indirect mythology in themselves" (1997, 186). The new mythology, therefore, exists for the sake of the Particular, precisely as in the system of Spinoza, whom Schlegel designates as the true precursor of the romantic movement; it exists only "for the rights of individuality (if it is what the word signifies: indivisible unity, inner lively coherence)" (ibid., 187).

28. The hint that Bloom's attempt should be read along "mythological" lines rather than as yet another work in criticism appears in Hollander, who at the same time is careful enough to notice that Bloom's "myth of creativity" is a myth precisely in the sense of opposing the prevalent critical tendency toward reduction: "*The Anxiety of Influence*," he says in the preface to *Poetics of Influence*, "is neither a contribution to the literary history of the romantic movement, like those of Meyer Abrams or W. J. Bate, nor a theory of texts and language. It provides a myth of poetic creativity at a point close to the sources of self-assertion and questioning . . . His mode of doing so is far from reductive" (1988, xvii).

29. This is why Bloom, usually rather skeptical toward contemporary philosophy, makes an exception for Nietzsche and Freud: "The art of criticism, to survive," he says, "will escape the nets of Marx and Heidegger, Foucault and Derrida, but still must accommodate itself to the prophecies of Nietzsche and Freud" (*AC*, vii). This accommodation, however, would also mean a transmutation of the way in which these prophecies are usually read: not, in fact, as *prophecies*, but merely as devices of deconstruction.

30. This phrase comes from *Pirke Aboth: The Sayings of the Fathers*, whose teachings gradually developed into Talmud. In classical Joseph Hertz's translation this passage goes as follows: "Moses received the Torah on Sinai, and handed it down to Joshua; Joshua to the elders; the elders to the prophets; and the prophets handed it down to the Men of Great Assembly. They said three things: Be deliberate in judgment; raise up many disciples; and make a fence around Torah" (1945, 1, 1).

31. As Bloom himself portrays him in "Wrestling Sigmund: Three Paradigms of Poetic Originality" in *The Breaking of the Vessels*.

32. In *Jesus and Yahweh*, Bloom draws a fascinating parallel between Browning's *Childe Roland* and the hassidic stories of Nahman of Bratslav, once again confirming his Jewish-Gnostic approach to Romantic poetry: "Reading

the Bratslaver *rebbe*, I feel frequently I am inside one of Robert Browning's dramatic monologues, say, *Childe Roland to the Dark Tower Came*. For Nahman also, the quest moves through all things deformed and broken, until unaware you come upon the place. After a lifetime training for the sight, you confront a void, from which the object of your quest has departed. Ringed by a living frame of your forerunners (Zohar, Luria, and the Ball Shem Tov among them), you confront the absence of God. However heroic your response . . . *you transcend either victory or defeat*" (*JY*, 224; my emphasis).

Chapter 6

1. On Bloom's passionate relation to Heidegger, see also John Hollander's introduction to *Poetics of Influence*.

2. Compare here a similarly vitalistic definition given by Sergio Quinzio in his *Radici ebraiche del moderno* (*Hebrew Origins of Modernity*): "Blessing is conceived here as a saving power which gives fullness of life; it can be compared to a vital force, which makes creation fertile, life long and rich in progeny; which roots man in his community, leads to success, richness, and happiness" (1990, 51; in my translation).

3. This is how Martin Buber in his commentary to Exodus reads the name YHVH, which appears in his "two sayings," or two instances of *davhar*, the powerful making itself present by the word-act: "The first says that indeed the deity is always present but in every given hour in the appearance that pleases Him, that is to say, He does not allow Himself to be limited to any form of revelation and He does not limit Himself to any of them. And the second says that He bestows His grace and mercy on whom He will, and lets no one order a criterion for Him nor Himself orders any." This unlimited freedom, however, has its consequences for the chosen ones: "But connected with this," continues Buber, "is that element called YHVH's 'demonism,' the dread of which overcomes us whenever we read about YHVH meeting Moses, His chosen and sent one, and 'seeking to kill him' (4:24). This is no survival, no 'primitive fiend' that has entered, as it were, by mistake from earlier polydemonism into this purer sphere, but it is of the essential stuff of early Biblical piety, and without it the later form cannot be understood. The deity claims the chosen one or his dearest possession, falls upon him in order to set him free afterward as a 'blood bridegroom,' as a man betrothed and set apart for Him by his blood." So far, so good, but the next few sentences sound dangerously Heideggerian: "This is the most ancient revelation of grace," concludes Buber, "the true grace is the grace of death, a gracing: man owes himself to the deity from the beginning" (1987, 52–53). Bloom himself is not totally happy with Buber's reading of the Moses episode, feeling also that it chimes too closely with Kierkegaard's *Fear and Trembling* analysis of Abraham's extreme self-dispossession, as well as with Heidegger's motif of death as being the only truly "own" possibility of man, the rest being in the hand of the powerful deity (or *Sein*). In *The Book of J* he thus comments on Buber's self-sacrificial enthusiasm: "Martin Buber, being largely free of the normative tradition, insisted in his *Moses: The Revelation and*

the Covenant that Yahweh had a motive: 'He claims the entirety of the one he has chosen'" (*BJ*, 246).

4. "That sounds more normative than I think it is," says Bloom in *The Book of J*, "but if life itself is the only good, if Yahwism is daemonic vitalism, then Shakespeare's Falstaff or Chaucer's Wife of Bath is more in J's spirit than is the prophet Jeremiah or the Jesus of the Gospels, except perhaps for the Jesus of the Gospel of Mark" (*BJ*, 302). But if this is really true of Falstaff, we shall yet have a chance to express our doubts.

5. Which is, obviously, not an orthodox reading of the story. In fact, midrashes suggest that it is precisely because of the act of rebellion against God's prohibition of magic that Moses was punished; for when he drew water from the rock, he did not do it in God's name, yet through the magical power deposited in his staff.

6. The "theomorphic" nature of Jacob is not Bloom's own invention but a hypothesis already posed by ancient Rabbis. "There is none like God," says *Genesis Rabbah*, "yet who is like God? Jeshurun, which means Israel the Patriarch. Just as it is written of God, And the Lord alone shall be exalted, so of Jacob too: and Jacob was left alone" (*Midrash Rabbah*, 710).

7. The centrality of Jacob as an emblem of belated poet in Bloom's writings— a motif which constantly recurs in our analysis—was very nicely described by Adam Lipszyc in his *Inter-People: Anthropology of Harold Bloom:* "For Bloom, Jacob is a paradigmatic figure who must constantly fight for the blessing because he was born too late—right after his brother, Esau, who is a Bloomian emblem of vital order, a lazy natural man, still not extracted from the circle of nature. Here, we encounter the same motif as in Hans Blumenberg: falling out of the natural order makes a man a deficient being and its defensive rhetoric serves as a compensation of this deficiency. Jacob's wrestling with the Angel becomes an emblem of his whole life, because due to this struggle Jacob gains a blessing and a new name (Israel), which will not be dispersed. Yet, this blessing is bought by a high price of present happiness; Jacob can never enjoy 'here and now' of the present moment, and his success—just like the success of a belated poet—is a victory only from the perspective of future generations" (2004, 122–23; in my translation).

8. That this Gnostic rebellion against divine "jealous" exclusiveness is not just a passing idiosyncrasy but the ever-present undercurrent of Jewish thought is best asserted by Franz Rosenzweig, otherwise a very "pious" Jew. In the following fragment from *The Star of Redemption*, which highly praises man's defiance, Rosenzweig proposes a model of piety that can be called an "apotropaic faithfulness" and as such closely resembles Bloom's use of the notion of the antithetical: "Specially it is defiance which emerges to the fore in the soul, that defiance which asserts the character in constant surges. It is the secret origin of the soul, it provides the soul with the strength to withstand, to stand fast. Without the storms of defiance in the self, the silence of the sea in the faithfulness of the soul would be impossible. Defiance is the arch-evil in man, bubbling up darkly; it is the subterranean root whence the juices of faithfulness rise into the soul beloved of God. *There is no bright revelation without the somber occlusion of the self, no faithfulness without defiance* (1985, 170; my emphasis). Thus faithfulness is not a

simple obedience; God may be loved, admired, feared, but he cannot be the final authority in one thing, in the deepest knowledge of *my own* being. "*I* is always a Nay become audible," continues Rosenzweig. "*I* always involves a contradiction, it is always underlined, always emphasized, always an '*I* however'" (ibid., 173).

9. . . . who, not accidentally, happen to be modern romantics. As Lionel Trilling aptly shows in his *Sincerity and Authenticity,* in the early romantic period, the intimation of vital force condensed in the "I am" becomes the very equivalent of *le sentiment de l'existence* (the sentiment of being): "A synonym for the sentiment of being is that 'strength' which, Schiller tells us, 'man brought with him from the state of savagery' and which he finds it so difficult to preserve in a highly developed culture. The sentiment of being is the sentiment of being strong. Which is not to say powerful: Rousseau, Schiller and Wordsworth are not concerned with energy directed outward upon the world in aggression and dominance, but, rather, with such energy as contrives that the centre shall hold, that the circumference of the self keep unbroken, that the person be an integer, impenetrable, perdurable, and autonomous in being if not in action . . . As the century advances the sentiment of being, of being strong, is increasingly subsumed under the conception of personal authenticity" (1980, 99).

10. Compare it once again with our discussion in part 1 on Trilling's "biological fact of life" that registers in the psyche, possibly quite "erroneously," as a vantage point which allows the psyche to negotiate with the cultural world of norms.

11. The privilege of "I am" seems, indeed, to be the true bone of contention between Gnostics and Monotheists; from the perspective of the latter, the lingering with self-sacrifice of one's "I am" amounts to unforgivable sin of pride. Simone Weil asserts her militant monotheistic faith when she says in her *Intuitions pré-chrétiennes (Pre-Christian Intuitions)*: "One has to learn that nobody in this world is a real centre for the real centre is beyond this world, and no one has the right to say 'I.' We have to renounce the illusion of power He gave to us, by allowing us to speak in the first person, for the sake of His love and truth. Only God has right to say 'I am'" (1962, 23; in my translation).

12. *Askesis* is thus best approached as the stage of indeterminacy between regeneration and entropy; as the converging point of both the greatest danger and the greatest hope. Jean-Pierre Mileur comments: "It is this fear, perhaps even conviction, that the myth of poetic entropy is stronger than that of poetic regeneration that causes Bloom to share the literary history of Walter Jackson Bate's *The Burden of the Past and the English Poet.* Paradoxically, it is through Bate's very Longinian idealizing of literary greatness that his book becomes another instance of the malaise it describes. And it is similarly instructive that Bloom's revisionism, weighed down by his melancholy, can offer us no more optimistic a model of literary history" (1985, 16–17). But is Bloom truly so close to Bate's unambiguously pessimistic diagnosis? No, he is rather stating, with his usual, "Jewish-Gnostic," tough assertiveness, the necessity of the revisionary fight to continue, despite the growing hardness of its conditions.

13. Probably the best example of *askesis* as an artistic strategy is offered by Thomas Mann in *Doctor Faustus.* For if there is any vitality to Adrian Leverkühn's genius, it lies not so much in an explosion of active energy and its unrestrained

Ja-Sagen, but, quite the contrary, in the coldest calculation possible. He is, as Bloom himself asserts, the genius of our times whose creative energy is totally absorbed by the stage of *askesis*. Thus, above all, he is a genius who cringes at the very word "genius": the old school romantic genius is the first thing he gets off the wagon, the first substantial part given away in the act of self-offering. Which, at the same time, does not make him modest at all: although Leverkühn portrays himself as a "servant" of the music he composes, his *kenosis* is, in fact, passive-aggressive, bringing down not only himself but the whole idea of art in its fake grandeur. His *askesis* is equally double-edged: by renouncing his own right to spontaneous enthusiasm, he expects his art to follow him in his coldness. The disenchanted and cynical genius, who represses the awareness of his "election," creates his music as a seemingly worthless enterprise. His works are ephemeral, fanciful, self-ridiculing, especially if their content suggests grave matters of pain and suffering—and being such little gems of self-enclosed irony they irritate Serenus Zeitblom terribly, he who would like to see his friend as a more straightforward kind of "German genius," vital and powerful in his spontaneous overflow of feeling ... and so art," comments Mann, "helps itself to *apparently unvital elements:* personal weariness and intellectual boredom, the disgust that comes with perceiving 'how it's done,' the cursed proclivity to see things in light of their own parody, the 'sense of the comic.'" Thus, if the paradigm of the German "serene" genius is Goethe, then Mann, via Leverkühn, sets himself in a stark opposition to the Weimar sage: "Thomas Mann, a great sufferer from the anxiety of influence," says Bloom in *The Anxiety of Influence*, "and one of the great theorists of that anxiety, suffered more acutely for Goethe's not having suffered at all, as Mann realized. Questing for some sign of such anxiety in Goethe, he came up with a single question from the *Westöstlicher Divan* [*West-Eastern Divan*]: 'Does a man live when others also live?' The question troubled Mann far more than it did Goethe. The talkative musical promoter in *Doctor Faustus*, Herr Saul Fitelberg, utters a central obsession of the novel when he observes to Leverkühn: 'You insist on the incomparableness of the personal case. You pay tribute to an arrogant personal uniqueness—maybe you have to do that. 'Does one live when others live?'" (*AI*, 52–53) The acute awareness of this problem— the sheer impossibility of one's life always already occupied and contaminated by others—is the key to the understanding of the stage of *askesis*.

14. And although *The Genealogy of Morals* is peppered with unkind remarks about Jewish rancor which managed to overthrow the natural hierarchy of beauty and health, it is done in a "noble" spirit, that is, with what the sublime Greeks used to call "agonistic respect" for a major enemy. In the conclusion of his essay, Nietzsche says: "The Old Testament is another story. I have the highest respect for that book. I find in it great men, a heroic landscape, and one the rarest things on earth, the naivete of a strong heart. What is more, I find a *people*" (ibid., 281).

15. This is precisely why Karl Löwith, in his *Meaning in History*, insists on an alternative translation of Psalm 12:9 which contains the word "circle"; instead of rendering it as "On every side the wicked roam" (as in JPS Hebrew-English Tanakh), he proposes "the wicked walk in a circle" in order to emphasize the futility and indignity of such movement. And comments, although already from

the Christian perspective: "The circle, in the view of the ancients the most perfect because self-contained figure, is a vicious one if the cross is the virtue of life and its meaning bound up with a purpose" (1957, 165). It is also important here that the Hebrew word for "circle"—*taba'at*—derives directly from the word *teva*, "nature."

16. Yet, even in this volume, *Ruin the Sacred Truths!* Bloom cannot really make up his mind as to the question of vitalism and offers us, practically simultaneously, two contradictory versions: the Hebrew vitalism *with* superego as the highest instance of the transgressive, expanding will and the Nietzschean vitalism *without* superego, founding itself on spontaneity of original instincts. He thus praises the Freudian revision of Yahweh as superego in "Freud and Beyond" and Falstaffian heathen vitality in "Shakespeare": "Falstaff's power," he says, "seems to me not at all a matter of class, sexuality, politics, nationalism. Power it is: sublime pathos, *potentia*, the drive for life, more life, at any and every cost. I will propose that Falstaff is neither a noble synecdoche nor a grand hyperbole, but rather a metalepsis or farfetcher, to use Puttenham's term. *To exist without a superego* is to be a solar trajectory, an ever-early brightness, which Nietzsche's Zarathustra, in his bathos, failed to be. 'Try to live as though it were morning,' Nietzsche advises. Falstaff does not need the advice" (*RST,* 82–83; my emphasis). On the other hand, Bloom, in the introduction to *Modern Critical Views: Saul Bellow,* written in about the same time (i.e., 1986), can take an openly anti-Nietzschean, very Hebraic stance and write about the closing sentences of Bellow's *Herzog:* "Herzog signs off: *Abide in light, Morgenfrüh. I will keep you posted from time to time.* This benign farewell is made not by an overdetermined bundle of territorial and sexual instincts, but by a persuasive representative of the oldest ongoing Western tradition of moral wisdom and familial compassion" (Bloom 1986, 7), meaning obviously, the Hebrew humanism. Here, "more life" has crossed the line of natural, "territorial and sexual instincts," and goes for something else, something perhaps less solar and self-evidently powerful than the Nietzschean promises of *Morgenröthe-Morgenfrüh,* but at the same time decidedly *not* self-sacrificial.

17. This salient difference has been well analyzed by Michael Walzer in *Exodus and Revolution,* where he compares the notion of bondage in Hebrew and Greek thought. Greek mentality is tragic in a sense that it sees no escape from the bondage of fate and the only liberating feeling comes with cathartic recognition of this ultimate truth. Hebrews, on the other hand, created a paradigm of liberation which leads out of the house of bondage and thus forms a basic narrative of all revolutionary upheavals: "God's promise generates a sense of possibility: the world is not all Egypt. Without that sense of possibility, oppression would be experienced as an inescapable condition, a matter of personal or collective bad luck, a stroke of fate ... Anger and hope, not resignation, are the appropriate responses to the Egyptian house of bondage." Walzer contrasts the story of Exodus with Eurypides' *Women of Troy,* which "describes a 'going out' that leads to slavery rather than to freedom": "Eurypides," he says, "makes no moral judgment; at least, he makes no judgment of the slavery into which the women are led. The feeling that he means to evoke is pity, not anger or indignation" (1987, 83–84).

18. Eric Santner calls this type of existence a "non-deadness," and although he does not seem sympathetic to it, he cannot fail to notice that the blessing of *more life* is closely connected to this deeply "unnatural" stage which is brought about by the incessant "crossing" of all boundaries set by the "natural" existence (2001, 25–46).

19. The thesis according to which this peculiar antithetical vitalism of "tender Yeses" indeed belongs to the Judaic tradition and finds an interesting confirmation in Derrida's interpretation of Walter Benjamin's "Critique of Violence" in his discussion of the concept of life: "This critique of vitalism or biologism," says Derrida in "Force of Law," "here proceeds like the awakening of a Judaic tradition. And it does so in the name of life, of the most living of life, of the value of life that is worth more than life (pure and simple, if such exist and that one could call natural and biological), but that is worth more than life because it is life itself, insofar as life prefers itself. *It is life beyond life, life against life, but always in life and for life*" (2002a, 289; my emphasis).

20. I am arguing here explicitly against the interpretation of Jean-Pierre Mileur, who follows Nietzsche in his conviction that every "Manichean" hatred of nature, Bloom's included, must produce a form of ascesis that is disgusted with life. Seduced by Bloom's ease in manipulating the above quote from Nietzsche, Mileur ascribes to Bloom a version of the ascetic ideal that, in fact, has little in common with its Nietzschean original: "Everyone suffers and dies, but by *willing his own suffering* and thus embracing death, the ascetic thinks to make these the signs of his election, the validation of his spiritual integrity" (1985, 47; my emphasis). But, as I have argued in the previous part, the very attempt to make death *mine*, to declare war on the anonymous generality of death, already indicates a radical "change in the process of willing" and turns this seemingly "willful embrace" (ibid., 48) into an antithetical struggle; nothing is further away from the naturalistic *amor fati* (love of fate) or its Heideggerian repetition in the gesture of *Gelassenheit* than this wrestling agon in which narcissistic, life-affirming tendency seeks its triumph over the all-leveling literality of death.

21. In *Life and Death in Psychoanalysis* Laplanche distinguishes very clearly between *drive* and *function*: "*function*, *need*, and *instinct* characterize generally the vital register of self-preservation in opposition to the sexual register," he says (1976, 16). "Thus the sexual object is not identical to the object of the function, but is displaced in relation to it; they are in a relation of essential *contiguity* which leads us to slide almost indifferently from one to the other, from the milk to the breast as its symbol" (ibid., 20). And further: "Sexuality in its entirety is in the slight deviation, the *clinamen* from the function. It is in the *clinamen* insofar as the latter results in an autoerotic internalization" (ibid., 22). The drive "mimics, displaces, and *denatures the instinct*" (ibid., 22; my emphasis). This is why, in the end, "The whole of sexuality, or at least the whole of infantile sexuality, *ends up by becoming perversion*" (ibid., 23; my emphasis). "Now sexuality, in its entirety, in the human infant, lies in a movement which deflects the instinct, metaphorizes its aim, displaces and internalizes its object, and concentrates its source on what is ultimately a minimal zone, the erotogenic zone" (ibid., 23).

22. I do not wish to get into the whole debate on the link between de Man's theory and his personal attempts to purge himself of life that betrayed him by

leading him into the dubious "spontaneity" of Nazi ideology, but it certainly makes an interesting instance of *askesis*. In *Death and Return of the Author,* in the prologue "The Deaths of de Man," Sean Burke gives us a succinct existential view of de Man's stage of *askesis* in its full ambivalence, that is, as a paradoxical attempt to "come to life as a biographical figure" after all: "Theoretical articulations of the void of personality find a constant analogue in de Man's voiding of his personal history," writes Burke. "Autobiography as de-facement becomes de-facement as autobiography, a cancellation of the self that is self-willed and mirrored in the life of the self-canceling subject; text and author are united under the signs of their disunion . . . In his deaths, the putting-to-death of a past self, his own biological death, and the death of the writer he announced in his writing, Paul de Man has come to life as a biographical figure with a chilling and tragic intensity" (1992, 6–7). Moreover, the case of de Man's *askesis* serves Burke for developing his general thesis about the "return (of the author) which takes place almost instantaneously with the declaration of authorial departure . . . The concept of the author," he thus declares, and Bloom would have to agree with him immediately, "is never more alive than when pronounced dead" (ibid., 7).

23. See his "Literary History and Literary Modernity" in *Blindess and Insight.*

24. This negative modification of the expressivist paradigm, which occurs in de Man, was explained very clearly by Barbara Johnson: "The sentence 'all readings are misreadings,'" she writes in "Nothing Fails like Success," "does not simply deny the notion of truth. Truth is preserved in vestigial form in the notion of error . . . the *role* of truth cannot be so simply eliminated. Even if truth is but a fantasy of the will to power, *something* still marks the point from which the imperatives of the not-self make themselves felt" (1987, 15). Thus, even if authentic expression is nothing but a fantasy of the will to power, the "not-self" of language checks this fantasy and introduces the negative truth of reality principle.

25. This is also why Bloom will say that "de Man appears to me to limit himself by the asceticism of his own concept of trope, which isolates too purifyingly the trope from the *topos* or commonplace that generates it" (*WS*, 393).

26. Or, put differently: "If a condition of poetic strength is a cunning in evading and distorting tradition, as I think it is, then what can persist and become tradition in any language must be a strength of misprision also" (*WS*, 394).

27. In the "Coda" he says: "A *topos* is not so much a commonplace or a memory place as more nearly *the place of a voice,* the place from which the voice of the dead breaks through. Hence, a *topos* is an image of voice or of speech, or the place where such an image is stored" (*WS*, 399).

28. "That there is a nonhuman aspect of knowledge," says de Man in the discussion following his reading of "The Task of the Translator," "is a perennial awareness from which we cannot escape, because language does things which are so radically out of control that they cannot be assimilated to the human at all, against which one fights constantly" (1986, 101).

29. "Between theology (system of tropes) and belief (persuasion) there comes always the aporia (figuration of doubt, uncertain notice, mental dilemma, the necessity of misreading). Theology and the system of tropes are an *ethos;* belief and persuasion are a *pathos*" (*WS*, 399).

30. On the protopsychoanalytic interpretation of the romantic expression as *Ausdruck* and its antecedents in Schelling, Keble, and Abrams see footnote 20 in chapter 4.

31. Quoted approvingly by Bloom himself in *Wallace Stevens*, pp. 395–96, this fragment comes from John Hollander's introduction to the collection of Bloom's essays *Poetics of Influence*.

Chapter 7

1. The cause of this fair gift in me is wanting / And so my patent back is swerving. / Thyself thou gav'st, thy own worth then not knowing / Or me, to whom thou gav'st, else mistaking / So thy great gift, upon misprision growing, / Comes home again, on better judgement making.

2. It is very tempting to compare this difficult moment in Bloom's narrative with Lacan's analysis of hysteria, which he defines precisely as *the anxiety of gratitude*. Bloom's poet finds himself caught in the same aporia that paralyzes the hysteric who, deeply convinced that he possesses something invaluable, defends himself against handing it over to the Other. Žižek comments: "In his unpublished seminar on anxiety (1962–63), Lacan emphasizes that hysterical anxiety consists in the hysteric's tying himself up with the essential lack in the Other which makes the Other incoherent / negated. The hysteric recognizes the lack in the Other, his impotency, incongruence, deficiency, but he does not feel *ready* to sacrifice any part of himself that would be able to fill this lacuna. This *deferral of self-offering* is reflected in the perennial complaint of the hysteric that the Other wants to gain control over his mind, manipulate and deprive him of something very precious" (2001, 31–32; my emphasis). The obvious difference here is that both Lacan and Žižek expect of the hysteric to admit finally that he has nothing precious to offer and stop defending herself against the subjection to the Other, who is defined by this very subjection—while the poet has no other choice but to maintain belief in his unique preciousness. *Tessera* can thus be seen as the first *test* of gratitude; the completion, the gesture of putting together the broken parts of the same symbol so it can be without a lack again is, by necessity, reluctant and almost negative. By behaving with such dose of hysterical ambivalence, the poet *defers his self-offering*, and thus hopes that he may still come to terms with the precursor without subjecting himself to his power.

3. Or, in Bloom's own formulation: "All that a critic, as critic, can give poets is the deadly encouragement that never ceases to remind them of how heavy their inheritance is" (*MM*, 10).

4. See the discussion on the "decisive influence" in the first chapter of part 2, "Life and Death in Deconstruction."

5. Gershom Scholem comments: "This absolute word is originally communicated in its limitless fullness, but—and this is the key point—this communication is incomprehensible!" (1995, 294). Voice uttering the name, inexhaustible in its singular fullness, totally above and beyond *logos*—this, indeed, is a proper sense of *davhar* in Bloom's interpretation.

6. On the motif of free and broken tablets see Bloom's essay in *Agon:* "Free and Broken Tablets: The Cultural Prospect of American Jewry." In the Arc of Covenant, there lie next to each other two sets of tablets: the broken original ones, which were shattered by Moses, furious with the apostasy of Israel—and the new ones, called "free," on which the Law was written for the second time (on this coexistence of tablets in the Arc see Berachot 8b). In *Es gibt Geheimnis in der Welt* (*There Is a Mystery in the World*), Gershom Scholem speculates on the metaphor of two tablets as the central figure of the relation between religiosity and secular freedom: "Two sides of this conflict," he says, "are best expressed by two phrases from the Talmud . . . which for the last two thousand years have remained alive in the Jewish tradition—'the freedom of the tablets' and 'the broken tablets,' which both lie in the Arc of the Covenant, i.e. within the same sacred sphere of Judaism" (2002, 47; in my translation). This central symbolic is already elaborated in *Pirke Aboth*, where Rabbi Joshua ben Levi says: "And the tablets were the work of God, and the writing was the writing of God, graven upon the tablets. Read not *charuth* (graven) but *cheruth* (freedom), for no man is free but he who labors in the Torah" (Hertz 1945, 6:2).

7. A brief illumination of this ambivalent, primarily repressed, semipresence appears in Bloom's essay "The Breaking of Form" from *Deconstruction and Criticism* where he, just in passing, juxtaposes Ashbery's and Benjamin's motif of an angel. "Perhaps an angel looks like everything / We have forgotten, I mean forgotten / Things that don't seem familiar when / We meet them again, lost beyond telling, / Which were ours once," says Ashbery in *Self-Portrait in a Convex Mirror*, where the double, emphasized forgetfulness stands for the repression, and the repeated missed encounters for the phenomenon of the uncanny. Bloom pairs Ashbery with Benjamin's meditation on angelhood in his little enigmatic piece called "Agesilaus Santander," being the name of Benjamin's own guarding angel (as well as his secret, true name: see our reflections on the Scene of Nomination in the second chapter of part 1): "The angel, however, resembles all from which I have had to part: persons and above all things. In the things I no longer have, he resides. He makes them transparent" (*DC*, 31). Bloom comments: "This is Benjamin's *aura* or light of the Sublime, truly visible only in the shock of its disappearance, the flight of its repression" (ibid.). Actually, even Lacan, seemingly so disenchanted, fits nicely to this angelological company: his *objet petit a*, the fragment of the real presence, always missed, never encountered, representing the fullness of life which never was, the primarily lost part never to be recovered—"has eyes" that, as Lacan often asserts, watch us from the unattainable perspective of the whole "from which we had to part." The common denominator of all these angelological speculations is the belief that angel stands for the vital missing part we had lost, forgotten—"I mean forgotten"—that is, repressed, and whose restitution only would make us whole again. Thus, the natural trope to express this nostalgia for the impossible full presence is synecdoche, a pars pro toto, which—not at all accidentally—is also a leading trope of the *tessera*.

8. Geoffrey Hartman's formulation of this difference is particularly insightful: "Derrida's semiotic turn, which does not turn from anything but is a kind of a free fall," he says, "is very different from Bloom's *clinamen* or *swerve* avoiding (as

well as voiding) an unbearable presence. The Writer in Bloom is strong because he is supermimetic—because he faces and overcomes primal influence—not because he is antimimetic" (1975, 52).

9. In "Wordsworth and the Scene of Instruction" Bloom sets himself in opposition to the optical metaphor chosen by Geoffrey Hartman: "Wordsworth, like his scholarly disciple, Hartman," he says, "prefers the after-image to the spoken-trace, but his own poem keeps forcing him to read nature and not just to hear her" (*PR*, 77).

10. The rich love-hate ambivalence of the original instruction is also a favorite theme of Jean Laplanche, Lacan's pupil, who wrote a whole book on the concept of inspirational seduction as a "romantic alternative to the form of sublimation Freud used to talk about." "In the act of inspiration," he says in the résumé put on the cover of the book, "the subject is linked to the Other (*se conjuge en autre*). Such subject is never *the* subject but always the Other: everything in him comes from the seduction, persecution, revelation" (1999). Yet, despite many similarities, the usual difference between Bloom and the Lacanians is that he nonetheless insists on the eventual possibility of *the* subject as a distinct, singular being capable of negotiation with the mighty Other.

11. See Franz Kafka, "Prometheus," *Beschreibung eines Kampfes* (*Description of a Fight*). In *Shelley's Mythmaking* Bloom comments on Kafka's parable in a way which also perfectly fits the dimming aura of a gradually burning-out agon: "All that remains of the once passionate myth at the close of this dry parable is the crag, quite inexplicable, as befits a myth which arose from the inexplicable" (*SM*, 55). The myth, and the intensity it brings, comes out of the blue and exhausts itself after a countless number of repetitions. We could also interpret this parable as a typically Jewish critic of the myth as a cyclical, ultimately entropic system, which reveals its futility as compared to Exodus, the imperative of "getting out." Such reading would be quite close to Blumenberg's interpretation of Kafka's "Prometheus" in the conclusion to *Work on Myth*.

12. This is a standard critical line, set initially by de Man, which later on was undertaken by many of Bloom's commentators. Some resolve Bloom's aporia into a more straightforward thesis, some try to keep it as a perfect instance of deconstructive "undecidability." The former group is best represented by Richard Rorty, who popularized Bloom's emblem of the strong poet in a rather simplistic, almost Darwinian manner. He took away the ambivalent romantic charm of Bloom's analysis and redefined the notion of the strong poet as "the leader of the species" whose vitality enables him to create and impose on others new vocabularies (1989, 28). For some mysterious reason, Bloom seemed to like this interpretation and endorsed it in *Agon*, where he praised Rorty for keeping up the pragmatist strain of what he himself called "The American Religion." In our present context, a more useful interpretation comes from the classical deconstructive reading of Bloom done by Joseph Riddel who, while reviewing *Kabbalah and Criticism*, the most recondite work of the Bloomian corpus, intelligently pointed to the principle of undecidability, which makes Bloom's rhetoric oscillate (once again: *Schweben*) between the registers which are traditionally associated either with the idiom of hope or with the idiom of fall. Riddel, however, does not see it as a disadvantage but merely as yet another aporia worth

his deconstructive effort, which ultimately shows that Bloom's position is curiously "self-defeating" (1976, 998). Another interesting misreading comes from Pete de Bolla, who in his *Harold Bloom: Towards the Historical Rhetorics*, claims that Bloom should go all the way and discard the trope of metalepsis as misleadingly positive; instead he should rather choose as his ultimate ratio the trope of catachresis which is more daring in its open deception toward the precursor. Inspired by Derrida (perhaps a little too much), de Bolla urges Bloom to embrace a fuller, more liberating aspect of the rhetorical *transgressio:* "We may disagree with Bloom's rhetorical analysis, preferring to see the negative moment as a catachresis, for this is what we have defined as a mistaken trope, a crossing between figure and figure . . . so that a return to the primary order cannot be made" (1988, 147). One can argue, however, that on this interpretation the whole idea of rhetorical *displacement*, which still remains *supermimetic* in reference to the primary order of influence, would be lost in favor of the Derridean dissemination.

13. Thus already in *A Map of Misreading* we may find passages which confirm the pessimistic scenario of a mere illusion: "Metalepsis or transumption thus becomes a total, final act of taking up a poetic stance in relation to anteriority particularly to the anteriority of poetic language, which means primarily the loved-and-feared poems of the precursors. Properly accomplished, this stance figuratively produces *the illusion* of having fathered one's own father" (136; my emphasis).

14. This anticlimactic confusion that hovers of the *apophrades* was very well spotted by Jean-Pierre Mileur: "The key moment, in which the ephebe becomes essential to the precursor and to the tradition," he says in *Literary Revisionism*, "remains in the realm of 'seems,' an 'effect' rather than reality. In the last, decisive moment, poetry falls short of desire, not just in the poet's career, but in Bloom's argument, which is finally unable to assert positively the reality of what we desire from poetry or for it" (1985, 8).

15. Here we use the notion of *mythopoesis* in the broadest sense possible, also including Bloom's attempts to create his own version of *Heilsgeschichte*, that is, the story of catastrophe and redemption, leading toward the poetic *tikkun*. On the unfortunate ambivalence of "mythmaking," see once again the discussion in the first chapter of part 1 ("From Concern to Antithesis") and in the first chapter of part 3 ("An Ambiguous Mythology").

16. Bloom is highly aware of this ambiguity, which he attributes to all romantics, himself included. For instance, in his review of Thomas Weiskel's *The Romantic Sublime*, he praises the author for being able to maintain the balance between the mythical "primariness" and the modern, disenchanted idiom of deidealization: "Throughout *The Romantic Sublime* Weiskel works towards a difficult kind of literary criticism, at once moral or primary and de-idealizing or antithetical. This may not be possible; certainly I, for one, have failed to achieve it" (*RST*, 120).

17. Note also how Hartman's phrasing mirrors the Hegelian description of the transformation which solves the inner contradiction of the sensuous soul: by saying that thanks to the successful Scene of Nomination, *everything shady in Jacob is removed*, he echoes Hegel's words about everything solid that is melted in

the natural soul of the Slave, so a freer, less encumbered, and more negative form of spirit can be born. Nature cannot be fought on her own grounds: rather, she has to be boldly outwitted, invalidated, and *cleared*.

18. David Fite, another commentator of Bloom, is therefore absolutely right when he says that it is a period in which Bloom's Vision gives way to Revision: that is, the romantic investment in the supranatural becomes suddenly withdrawn to allow the repressed, vengeful nature to reappear in a shockingly violent, naturalistic idiom of the interpoetic struggle. The whole subsequent tetralogy, says Fite, is a field on which this battle of idioms—Vision and Revision—takes place, never resulting in a clear victory of either side. See David Fite, *Harold Bloom: The Rhetoric of Romantic Vision*, especially the chapter "Vision's Revision."

19. The Death of Love is the moment Bloom calls "the crossing of Solipsism," which he describes as "voiding of the sense of others and otherness, and so of the possibility of any Eros save self-love" (*A*, 240), but it seems that in this stage even narcissism is "voided" of its vital, erotic component.

20. *The Course of Life*, in the translation of Michael Hamburger: "High my spirit aspired, truly, however, love/Pulled it earthward; and grief lower still bows it down./So I follow the arc of/Life and return to my starting-place." I use the German original because this translation loses the *nicht umsonst*, "not in vain," of the moment of return, which is crucial to our conclusion.

BIBLIOGRAPHY

Abrams, M. H. 1953. *The Mirror and the Lamp: Romantic Theory and the Critical Tradition.* Oxford: Oxford Univ. Press.

———. 1973. *Natural Supernaturalism: Tradition and Revolution in Romantic Literature.* New York: Norton.

———. 1991. "The Deconstructive Angel." In *Doing Things with Text: Essays in Criticism and Critical Theory.* New York: Norton.

Adorno, Theodor W. 1969. "Vernunft und Offenbarung." In *Stichworte.* Frankfurt am Main: Suhrkamp.

———. 2003. *Negative Dialectics.* Trans. E. B. Ashton. New York: Continuum Books.

———. 2006. *Minima Moralia: Reflections on a Damaged Life.* Trans. E. F. N. Jephcott. London: Verso.

Agamben, Giorgio. 2006. *Language and Death. The Place of Negativity.* Trans. Karen Pinkus and Michael Hardt. Minneapolis: Univ. of Minnesota Press.

Alcorn, Marshall W. Jr. 1994. *Narcissism and the Literary Libido: Rhetoric, Text, and Subjectivity.* New York: New York Univ. Press.

Allen, Graham. 1994. *Harold Bloom: A Poetics of Conflict.* New York: Harvester Wheatsheaf.

Allen, Graham, and Roy Sellars, eds. 2007. *The Salt Companion to Harold Bloom.* Cambridge, Eng.: Salt.

Alter, Robert. 1991. *Necessary Angels: Tradition and Modernity in Kafka, Benjamin, and Scholem.* Cambridge, Mass.: Harvard Univ. Press.

Arac, Jonathan. 1985. "Afterword: Lyric Poetry and the Bounds of New Criticism." In *Lyric Poetry: Beyond New Criticism.* Ed. Ch. Hosek and P. Parker. Ithaca, N.Y.: Cornell Univ. Press.

Arac, Jonathan, Wlad Godzich, and Wallace Martin, eds. 1983. *The Yale Critics: Deconstruction in America.* Minneapolis: Univ. of Minnesota Press.

Ashbery, John. 1991. *Flow Chart.* New York: Knopf.

Balint, Michael. 1965. "The Erotic Component of the Ego-Instincts." In *Primary Love and Psycho-Analytic Technique.* New York: Liveright.

Barthes, Roland. 1971a. "Style and Its Image." In *Literary Style: A Symposium.* Trans. and ed. Seymour Chatman. Oxford: Oxford Univ. Press.

———. 1971b. *Sade, Fourier, Loyola.* Paris: Éditions du Seuil.

Bataille, Georges. 1990. "Hegel, Death, and Sacrifice." Trans. Jonathan Strauss. Yale French Studies (On Bataille) 78. New Haven: Yale Univ. Press.

Baudelaire, Charles. 1986. "De l'essence du rire." In *Écrits esthétiques*. Paris: Union générale d'Éditions.

Beckett, Samuel. 1983. "Three Dialogues." In *Disjecta: Miscellaneous Writings and a Dramatic Fragment*. Ed. Ruby Cohn. London: John Calder.

Benjamin, Jessica. 1990. *The Bonds of Love: Psychoanalysis, Feminism, and the Problem of Domination*. London: Virago Press.

Benjamin, Walter. 1978. "On Language as Such and on the Language of Man." Trans. Edmund Jephcott. In *Reflections: Essays, Aphorisms, Autobiographical Writings*. New York: Schocken Books.

———. 1983. *Das Passagen-Werk*. Frankfurt am Main: Suhrkamp.

———. 1996. "Goethe's *Elective Affinities*." Trans. Stanley Corngold. In *Selected Writings: Volume 1: 1913–1926*. Ed. Marcus Bullock and Michael W. Jennings. Cambridge, Mass.: Belknap Press.

———. 1997. *One-Way Street and Other Writings*. Trans. Edmund Jephcott and Kingsley Shorter. London: Verso.

Bielik-Robson, Agata. 2000. "Bad Timing: The Subject as a Work of Time." *Angelaki: Journal of Theoretical Humanities* 5 (3): 71–91.

———. 2002. "Freedom and Dependence. A Psychoanalytical Contribution to the Problem of Determination." *Angelaki: Journal of Theoretical Humanities* 7 (3): 45–62.

———. 2007. "Promises and Excuses: Derrida and the Aporia of Narcissism." *Journal of the British Society for Phenomenology* 38 (2): 181–201.

Blanchot, Maurice. 1948. *L'arrêt de mort*. Paris: Gallimard.

———. 1962. "L'indestructible, être Juif." *La Nouvelle Revue Française* 112 (April).

———. 1972. *La part du feu*. Paris: Gallimard.

———. 1981. *De Kafka à Kafka*. Paris: Gallimard.

———. 1982. *The Space of Literature*. Trans. Ann Smock. Lincoln: Univ. of Nebraska Press.

———. 1991. "Who?" In *Who Comes After the Subject?* Ed. Eduardo Cadava, Jean-Luc Nancy, and Peter Connor. London: Routledge.

———. 1992. *The Step Not Beyond*. Trans. Lycette Nelson. Albany: State Univ. of New York Press.

———. 1993. *The Infinite Conversation*. Trans. S. Hanson. Minneapolis: Univ. of Minnesota Press.

———. 1995. "Literature and the Right to Death." In *The Work of Fire*. Trans. Charlotte Mandell. Stanford: Stanford Univ. Press.

Bloom, Harold. 1981. "Auras: The Sublime Crossing and the Death of Love." *Oxford Literary Review* 4 (3).

———. 1986. Introd. to *Saul Bellow: Modern Critical Views*. Ed. Harold Bloom. New York: Chelsea House.

Blumenberg, Hans. 1979. *Arbeit am Mythos*. Frankfurt: Suhrkamp.

———. 1981. *Wirklichkeiten in denen wir leben: Aufsätze und eine Rede*. Stuttgart: Reclam.

Bohrer, Karl Heinz. 1989. *Die Kritik der Romantik. Der Verdacht der Philosophie gegen die literarische Moderne*. Frankfurt am Main: Suhrkamp.

Boman, Thorleif. 1970. *Hebrew Thought Compared with Greek*. New York: Norton.

Booth, Wayne C. 1974. *A Rhetoric of Irony*. Chicago: Univ. of Chicago Press.

Borch-Jacobsen, Mikkel. 1988. *The Freudian Subject*. Trans. Catherine Porter. Stanford: Stanford Univ. Press.

Brisman, Leslie. 2007. "Bloom upon Her Mountain: Unclouding the Heights of Modern Biblical Criticism." In Allen and Sellars 2007.

Brown, Norman O. 1977. *Life Against Death. The Psychoanalytical Meaning of History*. Middletown, Conn.: Wesleyan Univ. Press.

Browning, Robert. 1994. *The Works of Robert Browning*. Hertfordshire, UK: Wordsworth Editions.

Bruss, Elizabeth W. 1982. *Beautiful Theories. The Spectacle of Discourse in Contemporary Criticism*. Baltimore: Johns Hopkins Univ. Press.

Brzozowski, Stanisław. 1910. *Legenda Młodej Polski: Studya o strukturze duszy kulturalnej*. Lwów: Księgarnia Polska Bernarda Połonieckiego.

———. 1912. *Głosy wsród nocy: Studya nad przesileniem romantycznem kultury europejskiej*. Lwów: Księgarnia Polska Bernarda Połonieckiego.

Buber, Martin. 1987. "'Holy Event' (Exodus 19–27)." In *Exodus: Critical Modern Interpretations*. Ed. Harold Bloom. New York: Chelsea House.

Bürger, Peter. 2000. *Ursprung des postmodernen Denkens*. Göttingen: Velbrück Wissenschaft.

Burke, Kenneth. 1957. *The Philosophy of Literary Form: Studies in Symbolic Action*. New York: Vintage Books.

———. 1962. *A Grammar of Motives: A Rhetoric of Motives*. Cleveland: Meridian Books.

Burke, Seán. 1992. *The Death and Return of the Author: Criticism and Subjectivity in Barthes, Foucault and Derrida*. Edinburgh, UK: Edinburgh Univ. Press.

Caruth, Cathy. 1983. "Speculative Returns: Bloom's Recent Work." *Modern Language Notes* 98 (5).

———. 1996. *Unclaimed Experience: Trauma, Narrative, and History*. Baltimore: Johns Hopkins Univ. Press.

Cavell, Stanley. 1990. *Conditions Handsome and Unhandsome: The Constitution of Emersonian Perfectionism*. Chicago: Univ. of Chicago Press.

Cohen, Tom, Barbara Cohen, J. Hillis Miller, and Andrzej Warminski, eds. 2001. *Material Events: Paul de Man and the Afterlife of Theory*. Minneapolis: Univ. of Minnesota Press.

Con Davis, Robert, and Ronald Schleifer, eds. 1985. *Rhetoric and Form: Deconstruction at Yale*. Norman: Univ. of Oklahoma Press.

Critchley, Simon, and Peter Dews, eds. 1996. *Deconstructive Subjectivities*. Albany: State Univ. of New York Press.

Culler, Jonathan. 1982. *On Deconstruction: Theory and Criticism After Structuralism*. Ithaca, N.Y.: Cornell Univ. Press.

de Bolla, Peter. 1988. *Harold Bloom: Towards the Historical Rhetorics*. London: Routledge.

de Certeau, Michel. 1984. *The Practice of Everyday Life*. Trans. Steven F. Rendall. Berkeley: Univ. of California Press.

Deleuze, Gilles. 1994. *Difference and Repetition.* Trans. Paul Patton. London: Athlone Press.

de Man, Paul. 1953. "Montaigne et la transcendence." *Critique* 9.

———. 1971. *Blindness and Insight: Essays in the Rhetoric of Contemporary Criticism.* Minneapolis: Univ. of Minnesota Press.

———. 1979a. *Allegories of Reading: Figural Language in Rousseau, Nietzsche, Rilke and Proust.* New Haven: Yale Univ. Press.

———. 1979b. "Shelley Disfigured." In *Deconstruction and Criticism.* Ed. Harold Bloom. New York: Continuum.

———. 1984. *Rhetoric of Romanticism.* New York: Columbia Univ. Press.

———. 1986. *The Resistance to Theory.* Minneapolis: Univ. of Minnesota Press.

———. 1993. *Romanticism and Contemporary Criticism: The Gauss Seminar and Other Papers.* Ed. E. S. Burt, Kevin Newmark, and Andrew Warminski. Baltimore: Johns Hopkins Univ. Press.

———. 1996. *Aesthetic Ideology.* Ed. Andrzej Warminski. Minneapolis: Univ. of Minnesota Press.

Derrida, Jacques. 1967. *L'écriture et la différence.* Paris: Éditions du Seuil.

———. 1972. "Structure, Sign and Play in the Discourse of the Human Sciences." In *The Structuralist Controversy: The Languages of Criticism and the Sciences of Man.* Ed. Richard Macksey and Eugenio Donato. Baltimore: Johns Hopkins Univ. Press.

———. 1973. *Speech and Phenomena and Other Essays on Husserl's Theory of Signs.* Trans. David B. Allison. Evanston: Northwestern Univ. Press.

———. 1975. "The Purveyor of Truth." Yale French Studies 52. New Haven: Yale Univ. Press.

———. 1976. *Of Grammatology.* Trans. Gayatri Chakravorty Spivak. Baltimore: Johns Hopkins Univ. Press.

———. 1978a. "Coming into One's Own." Trans. James Hulbert. In *Psychoanalysis and the Question of the Text.* Ed. Geoffrey H. Hartman. Baltimore: Johns Hopkins Univ. Press.

———. 1978b. *Writing and Difference.* Trans. Alan Bass. Chicago: Univ. of Chicago Press.

———. 1979. "Living On: Borderlines." In *Deconstruction and Criticism.* Ed. Harold Bloom. New York: Continuum.

———. 1981a. *Disseminations.* Trans. Barbara Johnson. Chicago: Univ. of Chicago Press.

———. 1981b. *Glas.* Paris: Denoël/Gonthier.

———. 1982. *The Margins of Philosophy.* Trans. Alan Bass. New York: Harvester Wheatsheaf.

———. 1985. "Deconstruction in America. An Interview with Jacques Derrida." *Critical Exchange* 17 (Winter).

———. 1986. *Memoires: For Paul de Man.* The Wellek Library Lectures at the University of California, Irvine. Trans. Cecile Lindsay, Jonathan Culler, and Eduardo Cadava. New York: Columbia Univ. Press.

———. 1987. *The Postcard: From Socrates to Freud and Beyond.* Trans. Alan Bass. Chicago: Univ. of Chicago Press.

———. 1988. "Like the Sound of the Sea Deep Within a Shell: Paul de Man's War." *Critical Inquiry* 14 (Spring).

———. 1989a. "Psyche: Inventions of the Other." Trans. C. Porter. In *Reading de Man Reading*. Ed. L. Waters and W. Godzich. Minneapolis: Univ. of Minnesota Press.

———. 1989b. *Of Spirit: Heidegger and the Question*. Trans. Geoffrey Bennington and Rachel Bowlby. Chicago: Univ. of Chicago Press.

———. 1991. *A Derrida Reader: Between the Blinds*. Ed. Peggy Kamuf. New York: Harvester Wheatsheaf.

———. 1992a. *Acts of Literature*. Ed. Derek Attridge. New York: Routledge.

———. 1992b. *Derrida: A Critical Reader*. Ed. David Wood. Oxford: Blackwell.

———. 1994a. *Given Time: I. Counterfeit Money*. Trans. Peggy Kamuf. Chicago: Univ. of Chicago Press.

———. 1994b. *Specters of Marx: The State of the Debt, the Work of Mourning, and the New International*. Trans. Peggy Kamuf. London: Routledge.

———. 1994c. *Aporias*. Trans. Thomas Dutoit. Stanford: Stanford Univ. Press.

———. 1995a. *On the Name*. Ed. Thomas Dutoit. Trans. David Wood ("Passions: 'An Oblique Offering'") and John P. Leavey (*Sauf le nom*). Stanford: Stanford Univ. Press.

———. 1995b. *Points . . . Interviews, 1974–1994*. Ed. Elisabeth Weber. Trans. Peggy Kamuf et al. Stanford: Stanford Univ. Press.

———. 1995c. *The Gift of Death*. Trans. David Willis. Chicago: Univ. Chicago Press.

———. 1996. *The Archive Fever: A Freudian Impression*. Trans. Eric Prenovitz. Chicago: Univ. of Chicago Press.

———. 1998. *Resistances to Psychoanalysis*. Trans. Peggy Kamuf, Pascale-Abbe Brault, and Michael Naas. Stanford: Stanford Univ. Press.

———. 1999. "On the Gift: A Discussion Between Jacques Derrida and Jean-Luc Marion, Moderated by Richard Kearney." In *God, the Gift, and Postmodernism*. Ed. John D. Caputo and Michael J. Scanlon. Bloomington: Indiana Univ. Press.

———. 2002. "Negotiations." In *Negotiations: Interventions and Interviews 1971–2001*. Ed. and trans. Elizabeth Rottenberg. Stanford: Stanford Univ. Press.

———. 2002a. *Acts of Religion*. Ed. and trans. Gil Anidjar. New York: Routledge.

Derrida, Jacques, and Marie Francoise Plissart. 1999. *The Right of Inspection*. New York: Monacelli Press.

Dews, Peter. 1987. *Logics of Disintegration: Post-Structuralist Thought and the Claims of Critical Theory*. London: Verso.

Donoghue, Denis. 1981. *Ferocious Alphabets*. Boston: Little Brown.

Eliot, Thomas Sterns. 1934. "Tradition and the Individual Talent." In *The Sacred Wood: Essays on Poetry and Criticism*. London: Methuen.

Emerson, Ralph Waldo. 1990. *Ralph Waldo Emerson: The Oxford Authors*. Ed. Richard Poirier. Oxford: Oxford Univ. Press.

Felperin, Howard. 1985. *Beyond Deconstruction: The Uses and Abuses of Literary Theory*. Oxford: Clarendon Press.

Fichte, Johann Gottlieb. 1844. *Erste Einleitung in die Wissenschaftslehre*. In *Werke*. Ed. I. H. Fichte. Leipzig: Mayer & Müller.

————. 1994. *Introductions to Wissenschaftslehre and Other Writings (1797–1800).* Ed. and trans. Daniel Breazeale. Indianapolis: Hackett.

Finkelstein, Norman. 1992. *The Ritual of New Creation. Jewish Tradition and Contemporary Literature.* Albany: State Univ. of New York Press.

Fite, David. 1985. *Harold Bloom: The Rhetoric of Romantic Vision.* Amherst: Univ. of Massachusetts Press.

Foucault, Michel. 1970. *The Order of Things: An Archaeology of the Human Sciences.* London: Routledge.

————. 1979. "What Is an Author?" In *Textual Strategies: Perspectives in Post-Struturalist Criticism.* Ed. José V. Harrari. Ithaca, N.Y.: Cornell Univ. Press.

————. 1991. "Nietzsche, Genealogy, History." In *The Foucault Reader.* Ed. P. Rabinow. London: Penguin Books.

Frank, Manfred. 1996. "Identity and Subjectivity." In *Deconstructive Subjectivities.* Ed. Simon Critchley and Peter Dews. Albany: State Univ. of New York Press.

Freedman, Harry, and Maurice Simon, eds. 1961. *Midrash Rabbah,* vol. 1. London: Socino Press.

Freud, Anna. 1996. *The Ego and the Mechanisms of Defense.* Madison, Conn.: International Universities Press.

Freud, Sigmund. 1933. *New Introductory Lectures on Psychoanalysis.* Trans. W. J. H. Sprott. London: Hogarth Press.

————. 1950. "Family Romances." In *Collected Papers,* vol. 5. Ed. and trans. James Strachey. London: Hogarth Press.

————. 1953–74. *The Standard Edition of the Complete Psychological Works of Sigmund Freud.* 24 vols. Trans. James Strachey. London: Hogarth Press.

————. "Project for a Scientific Psychology." In Freud, *Standard Edition,* vol. 1.

————. *Interpretation of Dreams.* In Freud, *Standard Edition,* vol. 5

————. *The Psychopathology of Everyday Life.* In Freud, *Standard Edition,* vol. 6.

————. 1959. *Inhibitions, Symptoms and Anxiety.* Trans. Alix Strachey. New York: Norton.

————. 1962. *Three Essays on the Theory of Sexuality.* Trans. James Strachey. New York: Basic Books.

————. 1984. *On Metapsychology: The Theory of Psychoanalysis.* Trans. J. Strachey. The Penguin Freud Library, vol. 11. London: Penguin Books.

————. 1989. "On Narcissism: An Introduction." In *The Freud Reader.* Ed. Peter Gay. New York: Norton.

Frye, Northrop. 1969. *Fearful Symmetry: A Study of William Blake.* Princeton, N.J.: Princeton Univ. Press.

————. 1972. "The Archetypes of Literature." In *Twentieth Century Literary Criticism: A Reader.* Ed. David Lodge. London: Longman.

————. 1982. *The Great Code.* New York: Harcourt, Brace and World.

Gasché, Rodolphe. 1994. *Inventions of Difference: On Jacques Derrida.* Cambridge, Mass.: Harvard Univ. Press.

————. 1998. *The Wild Card of Reading: On Paul de Man.* Cambridge, Mass.: Harvard Univ. Press.

Gilbert, Sandra M., and Susan Gubar. 1979. *Madwoman in the Attic: The Woman Writer and the Nineteenth Century Literary Imagination.* New Haven: Yale Univ. Press.

Girard, René. 1961. *Mensonge romantique et vérite romanesque*. Paris: Editions Bernard Grasset.

———. 1965. *Deceit, Desire, and the Novel: Self and Other in Literary Structure*. Trans. Yvonne Frevvero. Baltimore: Johns Hopkins Univ. Press.

———. 2005. *Violence and the Sacred*. Trans. Patrick Gregory. New York: Continuum.

Gombrowicz, Witold. 1988. *Dzienniki 1961–1966 (Journals 1961–1966)*. Cracow: Wydawnictwo Literackie.

Haase, Ullrich, and William Large. 2001. *Maurice Blanchot*. New York: Routledge.

Hamacher, Werner. 1996. *Premises. Philosophy of Literature from Kant to Celan*. Trans. Peter Fenves. Stanford: Stanford Univ. Press.

Hamacher, Werner, Neil Hertz, and Tom Keenan, eds. 1989. *Responses: On Paul de Man's Wartime Journalism*. Lincoln: Univ. of Nebraska Press.

Handelman, Susan A. 1982. *The Slayers of Moses: The Emergence of Rabbinic Interpretation in Modern Literary Theory*. Albany: State Univ. of New York Press.

Harpham, Geoffrey Galt. 1987. *The Ascetic Imperative in Culture and Criticism*. Chicago: Univ. of Chicago Press.

Hartman, Geoffrey H. 1965. "Wordsworth, Inscriptions, Nature Poetry." In *From Sensibility to Romanticism: Essays Presented to Frederick A. Pottle*. Ed. Frederick W. Hilles and Harold Bloom. Oxford: Oxford Univ. Press.

———. 1966. *The Unmediated Vision: An Interpretation of Wordsworth, Hopkins, Rilke, And Valéry*. New York: Harcourt, Brace and World.

———. 1971. *Wordsworth's Poetry 1787–1814*. New Haven: Yale Univ. Press.

———. 1975. *The Fate of Reading and Other Essays*. Chicago: Univ. of Chicago Press.

———. 1980. *Criticism in the Wilderness: The Study of Literature Today*. New Haven: Yale Univ. Press.

———. 1981. *Saving the Text: Literature, Derrida, Philosophy*. Baltimore: Johns Hopkins Univ. Press.

———. 1986. "The Struggle for the Text." In *Midrash and Literature*. Ed. Geoffrey H. Hartman and Sanford Budick. New Haven: Yale Univ. Press.

———. 1987. "Touching Compulsion." In *The Unremarkable Wordsworth*. London: Methuen Press.

———. 1993. "Romanticism and the Anti-Self Consciousness." In *Romanticism*. Ed. Cynthia Chase. New York: Longman.

Hegel, Georg Wilhelm Friedrich. 1905. *Enzyclopädie der philosophischen Wissenschaften im Grundrisse*. Ed. Georg Lasson. Leipzig: Verlag der Dürr'schen Buchhandlung.

———. 1932. *Jenenser Realphilosophie I: Die Vorlesungen von 1803–1804*. Ed. J. Hoffmeister. Leipzig: Felix Meiner.

———. 1959. *Encyclopedia of Philosophy*. Trans. Gustav Emil Mueller. New York: Philosophical Library.

———. 1976. *Ästhetik*, vol. 1. Berlin und Weimar: Aufbau-Verlag.

———. 1977. *Phenomenology of Spirit*. Trans. A. V. Miller. Oxford: Clarendon Press.

Heidegger, Martin. 1959. *Gelassenheit.* Pfullingen: Verlag Günther Neske.

———. 1962. *Being and Time.* Trans. John Macquarrie and Edward Robinson. Oxford: Blackwell.

Hertz, Joseph, trans. 1945. *Pirke Aboth: The Sayings of the Fathers.* London: Behrman House.

Holland, Michael, ed. 1995. *The Blanchot Reader.* Oxford: Blackwell.

Hollander, John. 1981. *The Figure of Echo: A Mode of Allusion in Milton and After.* Berkeley: Univ. of California Press.

———. 1988. Introduction to *The Poetics of Influence: New and Selected Criticism,* by Harold Bloom. Ed. John Hollander. New Haven: Henry R. Schwab.

Horkheimer, Max, and Theodor W. Adorno. 2002. *Dialectic of Enlightenment: Philosophical Fragments.* Trans. Edmund Jephcott. Ed. G. Schmid Noerr. Stanford: Stanford Univ. Press.

Hughes, Robert. 1993. *Culture of Complaint: The Fraying of America.* Oxford: Oxford Univ. Press.

Idel, Moshe. 2007. "Enoch and Elijah: Some Remarks on Apotheosis, Theophany and Jewish Mysticism." In Allen and Sellars 2007.

Jacobs, Carol. 1993. *Telling Time: Lévi-Strauss, Ford, Lessing, Benjamin, de Man, Wordsworth, Rilke.* Baltimore: Johns Hopkins Univ. Press.

Jauss, Hans Robert. 1982. *Toward an Aesthetic of Reception.* Trans. Timothy Bahti. Minneapolis: Univ. of Minnesota Press.

Johnson, Barbara. 1978. "The Frame of Reference: Poe, Lacan, Derrida." In *Psychoanalysis and the Question of the Text.* Ed. Geoffrey H. Hartman. Baltimore: Johns Hopkins Univ. Press.

———. 1985. "Gender Theory and the Yale School." In *Rhetoric and Form: Deconstruction at Yale.* Ed. Robert Con Davis and Ronald Schleifer. Norman: Univ. of Oklahoma Press.

———. 1987. *A World of Difference.* Baltimore: Johns Hopkins Univ. Press.

Johnson, M. L., and J. E. Grant, eds. 1979. *Blake's Poetry and Designs.* New York: Norton.

Jonas, Hans. 2001. *The Gnostic Religion.* Boston: Beacon Press.

Jones, Ernst. 1961. *The Life and Work of Sigmund Freud,* vol. 3. Ed. Lionel Trilling and Steven Marcus. New York: Basic Books.

Kafka, Franz. 1948–49. *The Diaries, 1910–1923.* Trans. Joseph Kresh and Martin Greenberg. Ed. Max Brod. New York: Schocken.

———. 2000. *Die Aphorismen: Bertachrungen über Sünde, Leid, Hoffnung und den wahren Weg.* In *Gesammelte Werke.* Frankfurt am Main: Europabuch.

———. 2008. "Prometheus." In *Beschreibung eines Kampfes und andere Schriften aus dem Nachlaß.* Frankfurt am Main: Fischer Taschenbuch.

Kermode, Frank. 1957. *Romantic Image.* London: Routledge and Kegan Paul.

Kierkegaard, Søren. 1965. *The Concept of Irony: With Constant Reference to Socrates.* Trans. M. Lee. Bloomington: Indiana Univ. Press.

———. 1980. *The Concept of Anxiety: A Simple Psychologically Orienting Deliberation on the Dogmatic Issue of Hereditary Sin.* Ed. and trans. Reidar Thomte. Princeton, N.J.: Princeton Univ. Press.

———. 1983. *Fear and Trembling* and *Repetition*. In *Kierkegaard's Writings*, vol. 6. Ed. and trans. Howard V. Hong and Edna H. Hong. Princeton, N.J.: Princeton Univ. Press.

———. 1985. *Philosophical Fragments*. Ed. and trans. Howard V. Hong and Edna H. Hong. Princeton, N.J.: Princeton Univ. Press.

———. 1992. *Concluding Unscientific Postscript to "Philosophical Fragments."* Trans. Howard V. Hong and Edna H. Hong. Princeton, N.J.: Princeton Univ. Press.

Klein, Melanie. 1950. *Contributions to Psycho-Analysis*. London: Hogarth Press.

———. 1952. *Developments in Psycho-Analysis*. London: Hogarth Press.

Kojève, Alexandre. 1969. *Introduction to the Reading of Hegel: Lectures on the "Phenomenology of Spirit" Assembled by Raymond Queneau*. Trans. James H. Nichols Jr. Ed. Allan Bloom. New York: Basic Books.

Kristeva, Julia. 1987a. *Tales of Love*. Trans. L. S. Rodiez. New York: Columbia Univ. Press.

———. 1987b. *Soleil noir: Dépression et mélancolie*. Paris: Éditions Gallimard.

Lacan, Jacques. 1979. *The Four Fundamental Concepts of Psycho-analysis*. Ed. Jacques-Alain Miller. Trans. Alan Sheridan. London: Penguin Books.

———. 1989. *Écrits: A Selection*. Trans. Alan Sheridan. London: Routledge.

———. 1991. *The Ego in Freud's Theory and in Technique of Psychoanalysis: The Seminar of Jacques Lacan 1954–1955, Book 2*. Ed. Jacques Alain-Miller. Trans. Sylvana Tomaselli. New York: Norton.

———. 1992. *The Ethics of Psychoanalysis: The Seminar of Jacques Lacan 1959–1960, Book 7*. Ed. Jacques-Alain Miller. Trans. Dennis Porter. London: Routledge.

———. 2004. *Le séminaire, livre X. L'angoisse*. Ed. Jacques-Alain Miller. Paris: Éditions du Seuil.

Lagache, Daniel. 1960. "Situation de l'agressivité," *Bulletin de Psychologie* 184 (Nov.).

Laplanche, Jean. 1976. *Life and Death in Psychoanalysis*. Trans. Jeffrey Melham. Baltimore: Johns Hopkins Univ. Press.

———. 1999. *Entre séduction et inspiration: L'homme*. Paris: Quadrige / Presses Universitaires de France.

Laplanche, Jean, and J.-B. Pontalis. 1988. *The Language of Psychoanalysis*. Trans. D. Nicholson-Smith. London: Karnac Books.

Layton, Bentley. 1987. *The Gnostic Scriptures: A New Translation with Annotations and Introductions (The Anchor Bible Reference Library)*. New York: Doubleday.

Lear, Jonathan. 1998. *Love and Its Place in Nature: A Philosophical Interpretation of Freudian Psychoanalysis*. New Haven: Yale Univ. Press.

———. 2000. *Happiness, Death, and the Remainder of Life*. Cambridge, Mass.: Harvard Univ. Press.

Lentricchia, Frank. 1980. *After the New Criticism*. Chicago: Univ. of Chicago Press.

Lévinas, Emmanuel. 1986. "The Trace of the Other." Trans. Alphonso Lingis. In *Deconstruction in Context: Literature and Philosophy*. Ed. Mark C. Taylor. Chicago: Univ. of Chicago Press.

———. 1991. "La mort et le temps." *L'Herne* 60.

———. 1996. "The Regard of the Poet." In *Proper Names*. Trans. Michael B. Smith. London: Athlone Press.

Lindsay, David. 1977. *A Voyage to Arcturus*. Boston: Gregg Press.

Lingis, Alphonso. 1989. *Deathbound Subjectivity*. Bloomington: Indiana Univ. Press.

Lipszyc, Adam. 2005. *Międzyludzie: Koncepcja antropologiczna w pismach Harolda Blooma*. Cracow: Universitas.

Löwith, Karl. 1957. *Meaning in History: The Theological Implications of the Philosophy of History*. Chicago: Univ. of Chicago Press.

Lyotard, Francois. 1977. "Jewish Oedipus." Trans. Susan Hanson. *Genre* 10 (3).

———. 1989. "The Sublime and the Avangarde." Trans. Lisa Liebmann. In *The Lyotard Reader*. Ed. Andrew Benjamin. Oxford: Blackwell.

MacCannell, Juliet Flower. 1985. "Portrait: de Man." In *Rhetoric and Form: Deconstruction at Yale*. Ed. Robert Con Davis and Ronald Schleifer. Norman: Univ. of Oklahoma Press.

Mack, Michael. 2003. *German Idealism and the Jew: The Inner Anti-Semitism of Philosophy and German Jewish Responses*. Chicago: Univ. of Chicago Press.

Mann, Thomas. 1997. *Doctor Faustus*. Trans. John E. Woods. New York: Knopf.

Marcuse, Herbert. 1966. *Eros and Civilization: A Philosophical Inquiry into Freud*. Boston: Beacon Press.

Marquard, Odo. 1987. *Transzendentaler Idealismus, romantische Naturphilosophie, Psychoanalyse*. Köln: Verlag für Philosophie J Dinter.

McQuillan, Martin. 2007. "Is Deconstruction Really a Jewish Science? Bloom, Freud and Derrida." In Allen and Sellars 2007.

Merleau-Ponty, Maurice. 1964. *L'Oeil et l'ésprit*. Paris: Gallimard.

———. 1968. *The Visible and the Invisible*. Ed. Claude Lefort. Trans. Alphonso Lingis. Evanston: Northwestern Univ. Press.

Mileur, Jean-Pierre. 1985. *Literary Revisionism and the Burden of Modernity*. Berkeley: Univ. of California Press.

Mizumura, Minae. 1985. "Renunciation." Yale French Studies 69. New Haven: Yale Univ. Press.

Moynihan, Robert. 1986. *A Recent Imagining: Inteviews with Harold Bloom, Geoffrey Hartman, J. Hillis Miller, and Paul de Man*. Hamden, Conn.: Archon.

Nehamas, Alexander. 2000. *The Art of Living: Socratic Reflections from Plato to Foucault*. Berkeley: Univ. of California Press.

Nietzsche, Friedrich. 1917. *Thus Spake Zarathustra*. Trans. Thomas Common. New York: Modern Library.

———. 1956. *The Genealogy of Morals: The Birth of Tragedy*. Trans. Francis Golffing. New York: Doubleday Anchor Books.

———. 1968. *The Will to Power*. Trans. Walter Kaufmann and R. I. Hollingdale. New York: Vintage.

———. 1997. "On the Uses and Disadvantages of History for Life." In *Untimely Meditations*. Ed. D. Breazeale. Trans. R. J. Hollingdale. Cambridge: Cambridge Univ. Press.

Norris, Christopher. 1982. *Deconstruction: Theory and Practice*. London: Methuen Press.

———. 1988. *Deconstruction and the Interests of Theory*. London: Pinter.

Novalis. 1946. *Fragmente des Jahres 1798*. In *Gesammelte Werke*. Ed. Carl Seelig. Zurich: Bühl-Verlag.

O'Hara, Dan. 1982. "The Review of Harold Bloom's *The Breaking of the Vessels*." *Journal of Aesthetics & Art Criticism* 41.

Ozick, Cynthia. 1983. *Art and Ardor: Essays*. New York: Knopf.

Perloff, Marjorie. 1978. "Review of Harold Bloom's *Wallace Stevens: The Poems of Our Climate*." *American Literature* 50 (1).

———. 1992. "Modernist Studies." In *Redrawing the Boundaries: The Transformation of English and American Literary Studies*. Ed. Stephen Greenblatt and Giles Gunn. New York: MLA.

Poulet, Georges. 1972. "The Self and the Other in Critical Consciousness." *Diacritics* 2 (Spring).

Prang, Helmut. 1972. *Die romantische Ironie*. Darmstadt: Wissenschaftliche Buchgesellschaft.

Przybyszewski, Stanisław. 1892. *Zur Psychologie des Individuums*. Berlin: Fontane.

Quinzio, Sergio. 1990. *Radici ebraiche del moderno*. Milan: Adelphi Edizioni.

Ricoeur, Paul. 1970. *Freud and Philosophy: An Essay on Interpretation*. Trans. D. Savage. New Haven: Yale Univ. Press.

Riddel, Joseph. 1976. "Review of Harold Bloom's *Kabbalah and Criticism* and *Poetry and Repression*." *Georgia Review* 30 (Summer).

Rieff, Philip. 1965. *Freud: The Mind of the Moralist*. New York: Methuen Press.

Rorty, Richard. 1982. "Philosophy as a Kind of Writing." In *Consequences of Pragmatism*. Minneapolis: Univ. of Minnesota Press.

———. 1989. *Contingency, Irony, and Solidarity*. Cambridge: Cambridge Univ. Press.

———. 1998. *Achieving Our Country. Leftist Thought in Twentieth Century America*. Cambridge, Mass.: Harvard Univ. Press.

Rosenzweig, Franz. 1985. *The Star of Redemption*. Trans. William W. Hallo. Notre Dame: Univ. of Notre Dame Press.

———. 1999. *Understanding the Sick and the Healthy: A View of World, Man, and God*. Trans. Nahum Glatzer. Cambridge, Mass.: Harvard Univ. Press.

Salusinszky, Imre. 1987. *Criticism and Society*. New York: Methuen Press.

Santner, Eric. 2001. *On the Psychotheology of Everyday Life: Reflections on Rosenzweig and Freud*. Chicago: Univ. of Chicago Press.

Schiller, Friedrich. 1906. *Gedichte und Erzählungen*. In *Werke*, vol. 3. Ed. Albert Koester. Leipzig: Insel.

———. 1962. "Über das Pathetische." In *Schillers Werke: Philosophische Schriften*, vol. 20. Ed. Benno von Wiese. Weimar: Hermann Bohlhaus Nachfolger.

———. 1966. *Naive and Sentimental Poetry and On the Sublime: Two Essays*. Trans. Julius A. Elias. New York: Frederick Ungar.

Schlegel, Friedrich. 1882. *Lyceum-Fragmente*. In *Prosaische Jugendschriften*. Ed. J. Minor. Vienna: Konegen.

———. 1967. *Kritische Friedrich-Schlegel-Ausgabe*, vol. 2. Ed. Ernst Behler. Munich: Verlag Ferdinand Schöning.

———. 1969. *Athenäum Fragmente: Eine Zeitschrift von A. W. Schlegel und F. Schlegel*. Ed. C. Grützmacher. Jena: Eugen Diederichs Verlag.

————. 1971. *"Lucinde" and the Fragments.* Trans. P. Firchow. Minneapolis: Univ. of Minnesota Press.

————. 1997. "Speech on Mythology." In *Theory as Practice: A Critical Anthology of Early German Romantic Writings.* Ed. Jochen Schulte-Sasse, Haynes Horne, Elizabeth Mittman, and Lisa C. Roetzel. Minneapolis: Univ. of Minnesota Press.

Scholem, Gershom. 1972. "Walter Benjamin und sein Engel." In *Zur Aktualität Walter Benjamins.* Ed. Siegfried Unseld. Frankfurt am Main: Suhrkamp.

————. 1973. "Zehn unhistorische Sätze über Kabbala." In *Judaica 3.* Frankfurt am Main: Suhrkamp.

————. 1976. "Martin Buber's Conception of Judaism." In *On Jews and Judaism in Crisis: Selected Essays.* Ed. Werner J. Dannhauser. New York: Schocken.

————. 1995. *The Messianic Idea in Judaism: And Other Essays on Jewish Spirituality.* New York: Schocken.

————. 2000. "Über Klage und Klagelied." In *Tagebücher nebst Aufsätzen und Entwürfen bis 1923: Zweiter Halbband 1917–1923.* Frankfurt am Main: Jüdischer Verlag im Suhrkamp Verlag.

————. 2002. *Es gibt Geheimnis in der Welt.* Frankfurt am Main: Suhrkamp.

Schopenhauer, Arthur. 1958. *The World as Will and Representation.* Trans. E. F. J. Payne. New York: Dover.

Schultz, Susan M. 1996. "'Returning to Bloom': John Ashbery's Critique of Harold Bloom." *Contemporary Literature* 27 (1).

Segal, Hanna. 1991. *Dream, Fantasy, and Art.* London: Travistock/Routledge.

Shelley, Percy Bysshe. 1891. *A Defense of Poetry.* Ed. Albert S. Cook. Boston: Ginn.

Smith, Gary, and Andre Lefevre, trans. 1989. *The Correspondence of Walter Benjamin and Gershom Scholem 1932–1940.* New York: Schocken Books.

Solger, K. W. F. 1815. *Erwin. Vier Gespräche über das Schöne und die Kunst.* Berlin: Realschulbuchhandlung.

Spargo, R. Clifton. 2007. "Toward an Ethics of Literary Revisionism." In Allen and Sellars 2007.

Spielrein, Sabina. 1987. "Die Destruktion als Ursache des Werdens." In *Sämtliche Schriften.* Freiburg: Kore.

Spinoza, Benedict de. 1951. *Ethics.* In *The Chief Works of Benedict de Spinoza,* vol. 2. Trans. R. H. M. Elwes. New York: Dover.

Stevens, Wallace. 1951. *The Necessary Angel: Essays on the Reality and the Imagination.* New York: Vintage Books.

Taylor, Charles. 1989. *Sources of the Self: The Making of the Modern Identity.* Cambridge, Eng.: Cambridge Univ. Press.

Trilling, Lionel. 1957. "Freud and Literature." In *Liberal Imagination: Essays on Literature and Society.* New York: Doubleday Anchor Books.

————. 1965. *Beyond Culture: Essays on Literature and Learning.* New York: Harcourt Brace.

————. 1979. *The Opposing Self: Nine Essays in Criticism.* New York: Harcourt Brace.

————. 1980. *Sincerity and Authenticity.* New York: Harcourt Brace.

Turner, Victor. 1969. *The Ritual Process: Structure and Anti-Structure.* London: Routledge.

——. 1974. "Some Variations on the Theme of Liminality." In *Dramas, Fields, and Metaphors.* Ithaca, N.Y.: Cornell Univ. Press.

Vattimo, Gianni. 1988. *The End of Modernity: Nihilism and Hermeneutics in Postmodern Culture.* Trans. J. R. Snyder. London: Polity Press.

——. 1993. *The Adventure of Difference: Philosophy After Nietzsche and Heidegger.* Trans. Cyprian Blamires. Oxford: Polity Press.

Walzer, Michael. 1987. "Exodus and Revolution." In *Exodus: Modern Critical Interpretations.* Ed. Harold Bloom. New York: Chelsea House.

Weber, Samuel. 1982. *The Legend of Freud.* Minneapolis: Univ. of Minnesota Press.

——. 1991. *Return to Freud: Jacques Lacan's Dislocation of Psychoanalysis.* Trans. Michael Levine. Cambridge, Eng.: Cambridge Univ. Press.

Weil, Simone. 1962. *Intuitions pré-chrétiennes.* Paris: La Colombe, Éditions du Vieux Colombier.

Weiskel, Thomas. 1976. *The Romantic Sublime: Studies in the Structure and Psychology of Transcendence.* Baltimore: Johns Hopkins Univ. Press.

West, Cornel. 1989. *The American Evasion of Philosophy: A Genealogy of Pragmatism.* Madison: Univ. of Wisconsin Press.

Wilde, Oscar. 1902. *The Decay of Lying: An Observation.* New York: Sunflower.

——. 1997. *The Critic as Artist.* Kobenhavn: Green Integer.

Winnicott, Donald Woods. 1971. *Playing and Reality.* London: Routledge.

——. 1986. *Home Is Where We Start From: Essays by a Psychoanalyst.* London: Penguin Books.

Wood, David. 2002. *Thinking After Heidegger.* London: Polity Press.

Wordsworth, William. 1994. *The Works of William Wordsworth.* Hertfordshire, UK: Wordsworth Editions.

Yeats, William Butler. 1994. *The Works of W. B. Yeats.* Hertfordshire, UK: Wordsworth Editions.

——. 1998. *Mythologies.* New York: Touchstone (Simon and Schuster).

Yerushalmi, Yosef Hayim. 1996. *Zakhor: Jewish History and Jewish Memory.* Seattle: Univ. of Washington Press.

Žižek, Slavoj. 1997. *The Plague of Fantasies.* London: Verso.

——. 2000. *The Fragile Absolute, or Why Is Christian Legacy Still Worth Fighting For?* London: Verso.

——. 2001. *Die gnadenlose Liebe.* Trans. N. G. Schneider. Frankfurt am Main: Suhrkamp.

INDEX

Abrams, Meyer H., 13, 22, 41, 68, 304, 362n28; as Bloom's teacher, 27, 34
works: *Doing Things with Texts*, 343n5; *The Mirror and the Lamp*, 358n20; *Natural Supernaturalism*, 35, 36; *Prelude*, 324n3
Adorno, Theodor W., 65, 81, 99, 235, 251, 314, 316, 320n5; quoted, 16, 91
works: *Dialectic of Enlightenment*, 101, 358n4; *Negative Dialectics*, 78, 86
Agamben, Giorgio, *Language and Death*, 178, 345n11, 345n14
al-Harīrī of Basra, 352n43; *Maqāmāt*, 349n30
Allen, Graham, 6, 319n1, 356n12
works: *Harold Bloom: The Poetics of Conflict*, 322n20, 334n3; *The Salt Companion to Harold Bloom*, 320n5, 323n27, 334n4, 356n16
Alter, Robert, *Necessary Angels*, 59–60
American-Jewish-Gnostic amalgam, 25. *See also* Gnosticism
American pragmatist tradition, 24, 25, 26
"Angelic Schools," 23, 27, 79
Angel of Death. *See* Jacob as hero
"angels of death," 27
antithetical stance, 10, 27, 40–42, 47, 49–51; antithetical man, 34, 37; "antithetical completion," 12; antithetical vitalism (*see* vitalism); opposing self, 52
aporia, 104, 192–93, 285–86

Arac, Jonathan, 79; *The Yale Critics* (ed.), 336n16
Archimedean point, 92, 93
Arendt, Hannah, *Between Past and Future*, 349n32
Ariadne's thread, 92, 93
Aristotle, 238
Arndt, Walter, 141
Arnold, Matthew, 13, 27
Ashbery, John, 9, 25, 259, 283, 361n21
works: *Flow Chart*, 360–61n20; *Self-Portrait in a Convex Mirror*, 22, 371n7

Balint, Michael, 315
Balzac, Honoré, 327n216
Barthes, Roland, 23, 253, 319n1, 360n16
Bataille, Georges, 125, 131, 337n25, 345n11, 352n45
Bate, Walter Jackson, 362n28; *The Burden of the Past and the English Poet*, 365n12
Baudelaire, Charles, 197; "The Painter of Modern Life," 329n27
beautiful soul (*belle âme*), 190, 194–96, 198–99, 201, 210, 220, 224
Beckett, Samuel, 256; "Three Dialogs," 232
Being, concept of, 26, 97, 139, 143, 147; forgetfulness of, 153, 190; and Non-Being, 176; truth of, 97, 147
Bellow, Saul, 367n16

Agata Bielik-Robson is a professor of Jewish studies at the University of Nottingham in the United Kingdom and a professor of Post-Secular Philosophy at the Institute of Philosophy and Sociology of the Polish Academy of Sciences in Warsaw.